The SONORAN DESERT

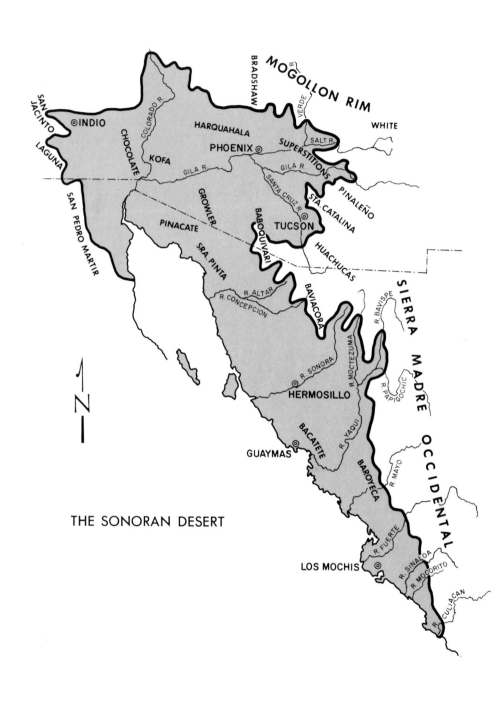

THE SONORAN DESERT

The
SONORAN DESERT

Its Geography,
Economy,
and People

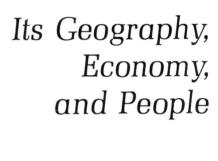

ROGER DUNBIER

THE UNIVERSITY OF ARIZONA PRESS
Tucson, Arizona

About the Author . . .

ROGER DUNBIER, whose special areas of interest include
arid and urban land utilization and the economics of
underdevelopment, has drawn upon extensive personal
research and travel in Northwest Mexico and Arizona in
preparing this volume. A man of diverse vocations and
avocations, he holds the Doctor of Philosophy degree
from Oxford University as well as the B.A. in geography,
the latter earned while holding a Marshall Scholarship.
He is a *summa cum laude* graduate of the University of
Nebraska at Omaha with a B.A. in economics and history,
served on the faculty of that institution for three
years, and has traveled in more than twenty-five countries.
More recently, he has lived in Phoenix, Arizona, where he
has developed numerous computer programs centered mainly
about the storage and retrieval of geographical information
including the production of maps directly by computer.

First printing 1968
Second printing 1970

THE UNIVERSITY OF ARIZONA PRESS

I. S. B. N. -0-8165-0082-7
L. C. No. 66-18528

Contents

Maps and Charts

Preface

Although possessing a common physical heritage, the Sonoran Desert has taken on highly contrasting forms in its American and Mexican portions. This work does not, therefore, attempt a regional study in the usual sense of the term, but is rather an examination of disparate economic development, much influenced by contrasting technological achievements as well as the accidents of history. Although the significance of geographic regionalism is implicit throughout this study, no attempt is made to show any overriding unity at work, geographical or otherwise, welding together a "desert region." Instead the desert acts as a stage for social drama in which drought and extreme heat provide the essential backcloth. The scarcity of water and man's inability to grow crops without irrigation have not, indeed, changed with time, and only constant reference to this immutable factor can give meaning to the evolution of human activities within the desert.

Facing the Gulf of California, a little-traveled backwater, and surrounded by mountain barriers, the Sonoran Desert is isolated from both the core areas of the United States and Mexico. Disconnected mountains and continuous basins form from one end of the desert to the other a uniformity seldom to be seen over such a wide area of complexly faulted and deeply eroded rock. Time and again the same sequence of rugged mountain, smooth mountain pediment, and gradually sloping valley is to be seen between the Salton Basin of California to the north and the valleys of Sinaloa on the south.

A rainfall seldom exceeding 12 inches is deficient for normal agricultural purposes. High summer temperatures, mild winters, and cloudless skies provide an environment which has proscribed, as well as fostered, certain activities. Perhaps the most important of these is the complete absence of direct reliance upon rainfall for the cultivation of crops and forage. For this reason streamflow and underground water supplies assume overriding importance.

Each individual stream capable of supplying more than a few hundred acres of irrigated land is treated individually. Both the average total amount of water and the average runoff over the entire watershed is noted for each stream. The availability of groundwater is thoroughly discussed.

The evolution of desert society is traced from its aboriginal beginnings through a series of significant alterations. European civilization continued to develop new resources as it introduced one innovation after another.

The earliest Spanish incursions almost obliterated the native society on the southern margin of the desert. The colonial advance faltered, however, when resistance stiffened among the tribes inhabiting the coastal desert of northern Sinaloa and southern Sonora. New institutions had to be substituted for the *encomienda* which had proved so successful in the more humid south. The mission in particular became the principal instrument of Spanish colonial settlement in the desert. Both religious and secular methods of colonization are examined as they were adapted to an arid environment.

The advance of the frontier is traced from valley to valley northwards across the desert until the Spaniard finally retreated in the face of Apache resistance. The effects of disease, the introduction of domestic animals, mining, and numerous other factors are treated as they helped to mold the distribution and density of population along the desert frontier. A "Mexican" population was formed in these valleys as populous tribes, such as the Opata, lost their identity and disappeared completely. Populations declined at first rapidly only to grow once again slowly as the isolated frontier oases widened their economic base. The introduction of wheat gave these people a winter crop to balance corn, the aboriginal staple. Wheat, cattle, and horses usually preceded the actual frontier of settlement giving the trans-frontier tribes an opportunity to strengthen their own economies and resist absorption.

Spanish, and much later American, exploration of the desert is related to the development of primitive roads and, eventually, railways. Early gold and silver mining is shown to be replaced by low-grade copper mining as railways and modern inventions created ore from what was once considered waste rock.

What remains of a true native economy is described as an isolated and shrinking relic. Occupying ancestral lands and finding subsistence in much the same economic activities, American Indians have progressively abandoned many crafts and agricultural techniques. Large-scale irrigated agriculture has encroached on their land and their primitive irrigation systems are deprived of floodwater as upstream dams have diverted streamflow.

The Mexican economy is undergoing a period of dynamic expansion resulting in a complete re-orientation of population toward the coast, an area shunned by earlier settlement. Major river-development schemes have created there an entirely new economy based on mechanized agriculture and a year-round system of cultivation. Market conditions not only in Mexico but abroad are introduced in order to understand more fully the particular problems of each crop. The Mexican livestock industry is besieged by many difficulties and these are examined in some detail. Industry and commerce in the rapidly growing towns and cities which line the West Coast highway depend pre-eminently upon local agriculture. The isolated valleys of eastern Sonora provide yet another stage of economic development somewhere between that of the aboriginal enclaves and the modern economy of the coast. Subsistence agriculture and cattle ranching provide a livelihood for a population which has changed little since colonial times. Poor roads traverse only with great difficulty the rugged mountains enclosing these narrow valleys, and, until this isolation is lessened, the gap between the rapidly developing coast and the stagnant back country will continue to widen.

North of the border an economy which was until very recently based primarily on irrigated agriculture, livestock, mining, and tourism has recently undergone a surprising industrial revolution. At about the same time that Mexico began to develop large-scale irrigation a number of wartime industries were attracted to Phoenix and Tucson. These have now been placed on a permanent basis and provide a livelihood for thousands of immigrants, making Arizona one of the most rapidly growing states in the Union. Unlike the pioneer industries such as cotton growing and copper mining, the new industries rely not on tangible local resources but upon a number of intangibles. The value placed on climate and other amenities contradicts the long-accepted maxims of industrial location.

The invasion of Mexico by American capital, the border town, and distribution of Colorado River water, among other factors, are examined, with the particular problems of an arid environment in mind.

Finally, the conflict for land and water both in Mexico and the United States is associated with the various forms of desert land tenure. Beginning with pre-Columbian tribal forms and including the *encomienda, hacienda, ejido,* and Indian reservation, they are examined within a local context. Contemporary racial distributions are seen to be little more than a legacy of earlier occupation of the land. Within the irrigated areas, population densities are certainly not low and competition for land and water among Indian, Mexican, and Anglo-Americans is strong indeed. The underlying forces of urbanization are contrasted north and south of the border and a significant difference is found between the two.

This work contains a number of tables which outline for the first time the overall pattern of rainfall, temperature, streamflow, irrigated acreage, and crop acreage for the entire desert. Only when this data is clearly set out may one make any generalizations concerning the contrasting levels of development north and south of the border. All in all the Sonoran Desert is found to be a remarkable "laboratory" in which the distribution of the above factors may be related to a number of social intangibles so that the latter may be seen more clearly.

Due to the disparate statistical sources both north and south of the border complicated by two Federal systems and two systems of weights and measurements, the overall integration of data was made difficult. This very often took the form of not being able to exactly match in point of time statistical information from Mexico and the United States as well as between various jurisdictions, particularly in Mexico. Because of this it has been necessary to freeze in time certain data contained in this work despite the fact that information was available for a more recent year. Most tabular information breaks off about the year 1960 since more recent data is not available at least for some area usually within the Mexican sector. This decision to forego in certain instances absolute currency in favor of balance in time between the two nations is, in fact, basic to the geographical thesis upon which this entire work is founded.

I should like to express my thanks to all those who have given me so much help in the writing of this book. Most works of this kind are based on the exchange of ideas, advice, and encouragement. In this one the exchange has been very much in my favor. I owe a particularly large debt of gratitude to various persons and institutions on both sides of the Atlantic as well as on both sides of the border.

First among the many is C. F. W. R. Gullick, Senior Tutor of St. Edmund Hall who sustained me with generous counsel throughout my years at Oxford. He introduced me to the formal study of geography and the systematic differentiation of national resources. To this gentleman I find it difficult to state my thanks adequately. I should like to express my gratitude to Professor E. W. Gilbert in the School of Geography, Oxford. As my advisor, his patience was inexhaustible. For Dr. Robert Beckinsale, a tutor and examiner, I feel genuine affection, and owe a great deal indeed to his precision of mind which in fact was impossible to emulate. He did, however, in the dénouement of the examination schools look favorably upon my work. I owe a great deal also to Professor Herbert Fraenkel of Nuffield College, Oxford, who gave me my earliest understanding of the economics of underdevelopment.

To the staffs of the Bodlean and Rhodes House Libraries in the University of Oxford I should like to express my gratitude. I would like to acknowledge the helpfulness and courtesy of the library staffs at the University of London and the Royal Geographical Society, London. In addition, I am grateful to the staffs of the Bancroft Library at the University of California, Berkeley, the Huntington Library, Pasadena, and the University of Arizona Library, Tucson. In Mexico I received valuable assistance from many members of the Mexican government, in particular Recursos Hidráulicos. To the numerous officials in the state governments of Arizona, California, Baja California, Sinaloa, and Sonora, I would like to offer my thanks. In particular to those who spoke only Spanish, I regret that my knowledge of their language did not match their letter-perfect patience. To Kit Scheifele, my editorial companion in this work, I bear witness to the fact that superior knowledge and patience are combined in one person. The numerous maps are the work of Wes Jernigan, whose extra effort is plainly visible throughout.

ROGER DUNBIER

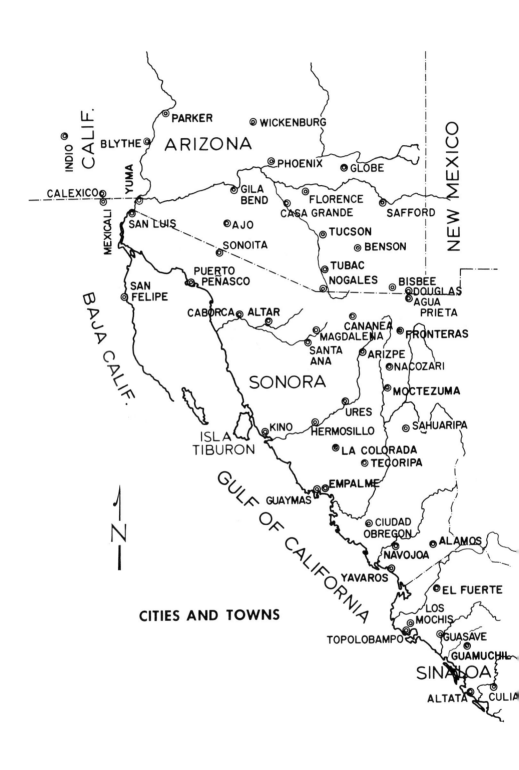

CITIES AND TOWNS

CHAPTER ONE

The Desert and Desert Landforms

Across northern Mexico and the southwestern United States where rainfall is deficient there are many areas to which the name "desert" has been applied. Unfortunately, there is seldom any agreement over the extent, or even the individual names, of these deserts. Since the border between the two countries crosses some of the most arid of these, an additional handicap is placed upon the geographer who attempts to delineate the boundaries of any coherent region deserving the name desert.

Extremely arid conditions are to be found in a number of not-clearly-defined areas radiating from the Lower Colorado Valley. Desert and steppe conditions prevail in Baja California and the state of Sonora, in southeastern California, Nevada, and other areas of the Great Basin, in Arizona, and across the Continental Divide into New Mexico and Chihuahua. The hot desert heart of this wider region has come to be called the Sonoran Desert after the Mexican state and the earlier province of New Spain. Included within it are districts to which the name "desert" has also been applied, such as the Arizona Upland, Colorado, Yuma, and Altar deserts among others. Sometimes other areas are included as integral parts of the Sonoran Desert, such as the peninsular desert areas of Baja California and the Mohave Desert of California.

A number of criteria could be used which would either limit the area of the Sonoran Desert to the extremely arid core region at the head of the Gulf of California, or extend its boundaries to include the barely contiguous marginal deserts and transitional semiarid grasslands. The margin of the desert does in fact shift seasonally and annually so that

[1]

"during a series of dry years the Sonoran Desert expands, joining with the deserts of Nevada, Chihuahua, and the Salt Lake. In wet periods the Sonoran Desert contracts markedly, leaving many small desert enclaves surrounded by newly created steppe lands."[1]

Drawing a boundary based on climate is difficult because of widely-spaced meteorological stations, the short duration of records, and the capricious rainfall of the region.[2] In addition, stations are located near settlements which often occupy sites most favorable to pastoral and other human activities. Few records have been kept in thousands of square miles of unoccupied desert. Nevertheless, low mean annual rainfall combined with high temperatures is the basis for a number of climatological classifications which have found some use in depicting the extent of major subtropical deserts. R. L. Ives has applied the best known of these systems to the Sonoran Region, demonstrating more than anything else their incongruous diversity.[3] It became apparent quite early that climate alone was an inadequate measure of a desert's boundaries and could be used as no more than a guide to further enquiry.

A desert boundary drawn on botanical criteria offers perhaps a sounder alternative. The often-observed fact that natural vegetation closely mirrors any climatic regime gives the careful observer an opportunity to witness an organic reaction to climate before outlining the more complex relationship between man and an arid environment. To adopt a botanical delineation indirectly but forcefully points to the principal role of a rainless climate in the formation of a desert while allowing other considerations some leeway.

MacDougal, Harshberger, Livingston, Shreve, Dice, and others have noted the effects of climate on vegetation within the region and have outlined a desert biotic province, giving it the name "Sonoran."[4] Though there is seldom identity in detail, there is greater agreement than among climatologists. The name "Sonoran" was in fact used first by botanists, only later being adopted by other students of the desert and more

---

[1]   R. L. Ives, "Climate of the Sonoran Desert," *Annals of the Association of American Geographers,* Vol. 39 (1949), p. 152.

[2]   *Ibid.*

[3]   *Ibid.,* pp. 149-52.

[4]   D. T. MacDougal, *Botanical Features of North American Deserts,* Publication No. 99, Carnegie Inst., (1908); J. W. Harshberger, "Phylogeographic Survey of North America," *Vegetation der Erde,* Vol. 8 (1911); B. E. Livingston and F. Shreve, *The Distribution of the Vegetation in the United States as Related to the Climatic Conditions* (1922); L. R. Dice, "The Sonoran Biotic Province," *Ecology,* Vol. 20 (1939), pp. 118-29; F. Shreve, *Vegetation of the Sonoran Desert,* Publication No. 591, Carnegie Inst., (1951).

Shallow blows and drifts over the desert near Altar, Sonora. Sparse vegetation and steep volcanic mountains characterize this desert landscape. Land similar to this under irrigation nearby produces abundant crops.

A portion of the Algodones Sand Hills west of Yuma, Arizona. The lack of vegetation is atypical of the Sonoran Desert.

— ESTHER HENDERSON

recently by the general public.[5] At the present time few Americans could, with any certainty, point to the Sonoran Desert on a map of North America, let alone have any idea of its boundaries!

The boundaries of the desert as they appear throughout this work are primarily those of Shreve (1951), based upon biotic criteria. To the west the equally hot and dry deserts of Baja California and the Mohave are excluded since they have distinctly different flora and are coherent geographical entities possessing names in many ways better known than the Sonoran Desert itself. Thus, the Sonoran Desert to the west of the Colorado River includes only the deltaic Lower Colorado Desert and Salton Basin.

To the north and east, desert vegetation climbs the mountain face of central Arizona and the Mexican Sierra Madre but gradually gives way to steppe under semiarid conditions.[6] This transitional zone, mapped carefully by Shreve, is approximately the northern and eastern boundary of the desert. To the south, I have extended the desert boundary drawn by Shreve (which falls north of the Río Mayo) to include the Río Mayo as well as the downstream Fuerte, Sinaloa, Mocorito, and Culiacán valleys. This was done in order to include within the desert an arid (though perhaps not desert) littoral which continues as far south as the Río Culiacán, and which requires irrigation in no way dissimilar to that practiced in the desert core.

The desert is thus indirectly a climatic province with only its extreme upland and southern margins receiving more than 12 inches of rainfall annually. Primarily, however, the Sonoran Desert is a distinct biotic province recognized by all students of its natural vegetation. It is thereby also an agricultural province, whose cultural landscape has been shaped since prehistoric times by the inexorable search for water. In general outline it is a roughly wedge-shaped area of approximately 120,000 square miles (roughly the area of Italy) occupying the coastal plain and low-elevation basins to the north and northeast of the Gulf of California. It is separated from the Pacific Coast by the Coastal and Peninsular ranges of Southern and Baja California. To the east a rugged mountainous barrier interposes itself between the low-elevation desert and the economic core areas of Mexico and the United States. The Sierra Madre Occidental of Mexico is a formidable hindrance to communication with both the Mesa Central and the northern states of Durango

---

[5] It is interesting to note that the first vegetational map of North America clearly naming and delimiting the Sonoran Desert — that of Harshberger in 1911 — was published in the same year that the first major dam — Roosevelt — within the desert was dedicated.

[6] Shreve, *Vegetation of the Sonoran Desert.*

and Chihuahua. The extension of this chain of mountains into Arizona (variously referred to as the Mexican, Central Arizona, or Mogollon Highlands) is a less significant barrier to contact with the Great Plains and Mississippi Valley but nevertheless has existed as a control on communications to the north and east. Only on the northwest toward the Mohave and on the southeast along the narrowing Costa de Sinaloa does the Sonoran Desert open freely upon surrounding regions although desert conditions and continuing isolation control contact with the outside world.

Lying on both sides of an international boundary, which perhaps more than any other in the world divides contrasting cultures and levels of economic development, the Sonoran Desert is a strikingly homogeneous natural region of considerable size. Similarities rather than contrasts are visible in the natural landscape from the Coachella Valley of California to the rivers of Sinaloa.

BASIN AND RANGE

Characteristic of the Sonoran Desert from one end to the other are the isolated block-faulted mountains and intervening outwash plains. From roughly northwest to southeast the rugged disconnected mountains line the desert so that they are never out of sight, seldom forming less than an uninterrupted and encircling mountainous border to the viewer no matter where he stands in the desert. Move where one will across the face of the desert, the mountains are always there in the background between the arid plain and the sky.

This alternation of plain and mountain has been aptly defined physiographically as the Basin and Range Province. In more exact terms it is characterized by roughly parallel and discontinuous mountain ranges, separated by continuous basins. The width of the basins or troughs is almost everywhere greater than the intervening isolated mountains. On the western margin of the desert the basins generally occupy well over half of the total surface (Kirk Bryan estimates 80 percent) and are at low elevations ranging from below sea level to 2,000 feet.[7] On the eastern borders of the desert the basins are not narrower but comprise a smaller proportion of the total area. The eastern desert basins lie at a higher elevation, usually between 2,000 and 4,000 feet.

The mountain ranges, which follow a very marked trend from

---

[7] Kirk Bryan, *The Papago Country, Arizona: A Geographic, Geologic, and Hydrologic Reconnaissance with a Guide to Desert Watering Places.* U. S. Geological Survey Water Supply Paper 499 (1925), p. 101.

roughly north-northwest to south-southeast, are of lower elevation in the desert of the Lower Colorado where they rise between 1,000 and 3,000 feet above the valley fill. Among the higher and more massive of these western ranges are the Chuckwalla, Kofa, Harquahala, and Sierra Pinacate ranges, all of which have a maximum elevation of between 4,300 and 4,900 feet. More typical are the Gila, Sierra Pinta, and Growler ranges whose maximum elevations are around 3,000 feet.

On the eastern margin of the desert, extremely massive mountains rise much higher from valleys of higher elevation. These include the Santa Catalinas northeast of Tucson, the Santa Ritas southeast of Tucson, the Chiricahuas in southeasternmost Arizona, and the Pinaleños (commonly called the Graham Mountains) whose Mt. Graham, with an elevation of 10,713 feet, is the highest point in southern Arizona.

The eastern basin ranges average eight to fifteen miles in width, whereas the western ranges are seldom more than four miles across. There is nevertheless a repetitious simplicity in the overall pattern which is most striking. This repetition, taken in conjunction with a relatively homogeneous climate, allows the regional geographer an opportunity to make generalizations over a wide area which would elsewhere be unwarranted and subject to considerable skepticism.

The following description of a "typical basin range" mountain is as graphically accurate as any:

> The range is one of many more or less parallel ranges. Lengths of fifty to seventy miles are common; there are more smaller than larger ones. Within its length, whatever it be, there is no great and sudden variation in height and breadth, though the crest may be very jagged; the range is not deeply notched and segmented; the bulk is fairly continuous, a general straightness is more noteworthy than the opposite. In many cases the straightness of the foot is more marked than that of the range itself and is quite independent of a complex structure of strong and weak rocks. The generalized slope from base to summit is not excessive, but the appearance of steepness is enhanced by the fact that the slope does not flatten out near the base. The abrupt meeting of valley floor and mountain side, and the uniform slopes of the latter, are among the striking features of the Province.[8]

It should be added that the desert ranges are quite symmetrical. The individual summits are not only of approximately equal height but are laterally equidistant from their valley margins.[9]

A detailed knowledge of the stratigraphical geology of the Sonoran

8   Nevin M. Fenneman, *Physiography of Western United States* (New York, 1931), p. 330.
9   L. Waibel, "Die Inselbergerlandschaft von Arizona und Sonora," *Zeitschrift der Gesellschaft fur Erdkunde zu Berlin,* sonderband zur 1928, p. 87.

The basin and range physiography so characteristic of the Sonoran Desert stands out clearly in this picture taken from still another of the ranges in the seemingly endless alternation of plain and mountain. This picture was taken from the slopes of the Santa Catalina Mountains. The city of Tucson can be seen in the distance.

Desert is not of primary importance to an understanding of this region's social geography. The early geological history of the Sonoran Desert Region of the Basin and Range Province is obscured through subsequent diastrophic violence which has resulted in the extreme fragmentation of block faulting. The isolated desert mountain ranges containing few recognizable fossils yield little information concerning early geologic events. In addition, the arid cycle of erosion is far advanced in these mountains, leaving a preponderance of wide and uniform mountain pediments and alluvial plains. It is essential to note that the present stage of geomorphological development little reflects the familiar contrast between hard and soft rocks of advanced age which have undergone long periods of subaerial denudation *in situ*.

PHYSIOGRAPHY

The all-important features of the desert landscape are the products of relatively recent and violent orogenic forces, which have articulated in rough outline the desert basins and ranges with little regard to the lithological sequence of geologic time. Erosion has, of course, moved more quickly against some rocks than others, creating the contemporary landscape of isolated rugged mountains, smooth carved rock-pediments, and depositional plains. Nevertheless, neither the original lithogenic nor recent erosional processes give the key to the physiography of this large region. Instead it is the complex and unfortunately little understood intervening orogenic forces which acted with particular violence in this Pacific Province. The down-faulted Gulf of California and the Salton Basin to the west, the epeirogenically uplifted volcanic rocks of the Sierra Madre to the east, as well as the striated faults which line the desert were all roughhewn through relatively recent diastrophism.

Within the Sonoran Desert the processes of erosion and sedimentation are fairly well understood. The recent physiographic evolution of desert landscapes has been more closely controlled by the prevailing arid conditions than through any tectonic action. The greatly eroded mountain forms are the result of long-continued subaerial denudation; and the alluvium-filled valleys, of subsequent deposition.[10]

Beginning with the desert mountain range, it has been observed that the angle of slope is controlled by the physical properties of the rocks, since chemical action is of small importance under such desiccating conditions.[11] Instead, violent expansion and contraction due to rapid

---

[10]   Waibel, pp. 87-90.

[11]   *Ibid.*

Of the thousands of streams draining the desert mountain ranges few flow with such permanency as Sabino Creek in the Santa Catalinas northeast of Tucson. At this elevation erosion is taking place. Five miles downstream deposition is the rule.

changes in desert temperatures are the greatest cause of fracture and comminution. Rocks with widely spaced joints that resist breaking up into small blocks form mountains whose slopes are steep.[12] For example, ranges whose slopes exceed 45 degrees from the horizontal are developed on granite, granite gneiss, massive lava, and intrusive fine-grained porphyritic rocks. These steep slopes are stable under the existing arid conditions of erosion. The steeply sloping mountains composed of these rocks grow smaller in size but maintain the same angle of slope until they are totally reduced.[13]

More often, when the slopes of the desert mountains are inclined between 20 and 45 degrees, the rock may be the same as the above, but is more finely jointed as well as finely grained.[14] Bedded lavas disintegrate very rapidly, forming a talus of rock waste that gradually mantles the entire mountain slope. Very thick and massive lava flows form cliffs which retard the recession of the mountain slope and increase its average steepness.

Mountain slopes at angles less than 20 degrees are seldom encountered in the Sonoran Desert since most mountains are composed of relatively resistant rocks which erode into the steep slopes described above.[15]

Even in the driest subregions of the desert, stream erosion is an effective agent shaping the mountain ranges — cutting at a faster rate than that of slope recession. The typical desert mountain with its crenelated summit and its projecting spurs has been produced both by the cutting of canyons and the recession of slopes. The existence of attenuated spurs and other major irregularities is due more to differentiated erosion of streams than to the general recession of slopes.[16] As the residual mountain mass is reduced to island-like hills, slope recession continues, retaining the slope characteristic of its constituent rock until no more than a mountain pediment remains.

The "mountain pediment," as its name implies, is a broad platform of solid rock which surrounds and forms the base of desert mountains. Often covered with a thin mantle of alluvium which is usually from two to five feet in thickness, these pediments are an inconspicuous but impor-

---

[12]   Kirk Bryan, *Erosion and Sedimentation in the Papago Country, Arizona,* U. S. Geological Survey Bulletin No. 730 (1922), pp. 42-43. Hereafter cited as *Erosion and Sedimentation.*

[13]   *Ibid.,* p. 43.

[14]   Eldred P. Wilson, "New Mountains in the Yuma Desert, Arizona," *Geographical Review,* Vol. 21 (1931), p. 224.

[15]   Bryan, *Erosion and Sedimentation,* p. 46.

[16]   Bryan, *The Papago Country,* p. 86.

tant part of the physiographic landscape of the Sonoran Desert. It has been estimated that in the Arizona and Sonora portions of the desert they occupy two-fifths of the total area while mountains occupy only one-fifth.[17]

Erosion of the mountain pediment is carried on by streams which, even though they carry considerable waste to the foot of the mountains, are still able to shift their courses, corrading laterally, planing the rock surface to a pediment. This, in conjunction with the recession of the mountain slope, broadens the bedrock platform at the expense of the mountain itself.[18] The pediment takes the form of a remarkably level plain inclined upward toward the foot of the mountain.[19]

A lowered base level of ephemeral streams flowing from the mountain canyons will cause these streams to dissect the mountain pediment. As this erosion is extended back toward the mountain the pediment becomes more completely eroded by arroyos and their minor lateral affluents, which carve the pediment into "a maze of small hills . . . whose original surface is preserved only in the tops of hills or inter-stream areas."[20]

The origin of the desert basins is intimately tied to that of the mountain ranges. Even if these valleys are primarily erosional depressions, they are at the present time being filled with detritus carried down from the mountain slopes, and for this reason alone, should never be considered apart from their mountainous margins.

Apart from those exogenous streams which occupy desert valleys and — under present conditions at least — occasionally reach the sea, the physiographic processes now in operation in the basins are largely those of transportation and deposition. Erosion, which is the dominant process on the mountain slopes and pediments, is inoperative in the enclosed valleys except where the rock-walled canyons of the pediment spill their water out onto the margins of the valley alluvium, forming arroyos. As a proportion of the total valley, these areas of erosion are quite small.

Where a desert valley is occupied by a larger stream, usually one that originates in areas of higher rainfall, the process of erosion may once again assert itself. These larger streams are able, at least through part of their courses, to remove more material from the valley than they deposit there. Man, however, through his construction of large dams,

---

[17] W. J. McGee, "Sheetflood Erosion," *Bulletin of the Geological Society of America,* Vol. 8 (1897), p. 91. He estimates that the remaining two-fifths is occupied by detritus or valley fill.

[18] Fenneman, pp. 346-47, 371.

[19] Waibel, pp. 83-84.

[20] Bryan, *The Papago Country,* p. 99.

has eliminated the possibility of a net balance in favor of erosion throughout an entire drainage basin. With exits to the coastal plain blocked, many of the desert basins which once carried silt-laden exogenous streams are now being filled with that same material. Erosion taking place in the upstream valley is more than balanced by reservoir siltation.

The alluvial plain of the desert valley may appear to be quite flat, but in fact rises steadily and with increasing steepness from its axial trough toward the marginal mountains, reaching 6 or even 9 degrees at the foot of the mountains.[21] The upper slopes often take the form of alluvial fans which may be no more than a thin mantle of alluvium over the eroded pediment. These fans are most distinct where ephemeral streams leave the mountains, but lose their identity toward the center of the valley as they coalesce, producing a single broad slope. Where the alluvial fans are distinct, and erosional forms occasionally visible, the term "upper bajada" is used.[22] After the fans have disappeared, forming a uniformly gentle and sloping plain of aggradation, the term "lower bajada" is substituted. The lower bajada seldom rises more than one degree from the floodplain or desert playa forming the bottom of the basin. The floodplain is located where a slope originating at the foot of one range meets the slope from another range, and is marked by a "wash" which is the axial streamway for the desert basin.

The arroyo, which has its beginnings in a desert mountain, may be continued on the upper bajada, but shallows, becomes reticulate, and disappears on the lower bajada as scouring is impossible. Runoff will then travel in what has been described as a "sheetflood," filling incipient channels as it creates them.[23] Sheetfloods are caused by water heavily charged with material flowing over an even plain whose gradient is too little to keep the load suspended. The lighter material will, of course, be carried farther. The result is a gradation of valley fill from the coarse-grained upper bajada to the finely sifted lower bajada. The playa, should one exist, contains the finest material of all.

• The existence of a playa depends not only on the absence of an outlet to another drainage system but on the ability of runoff within the basin occasionally to reach the basin's center. In a region where evap-

---

21   Fenneman, p. 340.

22   The terms "bajada," "bolson," and "playa" are of Spanish origin and are in common use by the inhabitants of Mexico's Northwest. In accordance with a practice first instituted by C. H. Tolman, *Journal of Geology*, Vol. 18 (1909), students of the Sonoran Desert have used these terms to describe more exactly the physiography and soils of the outwash plain.

23   See McGee, "Sheetflood Erosion," *Bulletin of the Geological Society of America,* Vol. 8.

The rich alluvial plains of the larger desert streams provide opportunities for settlement. In the smaller communities these are very similar in appearance both north and south of the border. The village of Carmen in the Santa Cruz Valley of Arizona could from its appearance in this photo be located two hundred miles to the southeast in the foothills of the Sierra Madre.

oration is high and soils porous, the development of playas is limited. Except in the case of the Salton Sea, no permanent lakes result. (The development of this "man-made" body of water is described in a later section.) When the water does reach the terminal basin, it is often charged with salts and thick with mud. It usually covers an extremely flat area which may extend for miles, not reaching a depth greater than one foot. A playa lake may fill with a single shower; usually, however, a number of downpours during the rainy season results in the creation of this ephemeral body of water which disappears through evaporation during the rest of the year.

In some playas the quantity of salts left by the evaporating water is so great that the entire "flat" is encrusted to a depth of several inches. The appearance is that of freshly fallen snow. The regional names given to these areas are "alkali flat" or the Spanish *salina*. Usually a playa's surface is composed of hard dry mud with a *café au lait* color.

The true playa and other conditions of internal drainage described above occupy a relatively small proportion of the contemporary desert. It is not clear whether these conditions were formerly more common throughout the region, and that the present continuous drainage pattern evolved through the filling of basins with eroded material until the lines of drainage would pass from a formerly independent basin to a lower basin. In time this enlarged drainage basin might fill so that its floodwaters would reach the Gulf. The possibility of headwater erosion effecting the capture of streamways from a higher basin must also be considered as an agent capable of unifying a complex drainage system such as the Gila's.

When two basins are united through these processes, the new base level of erosion established in the upper valley is that of the lower basin, despite the irregular flow of water between the two. (In such an arid region the unified drainage pattern has been looked upon as a curiosity.)[24] The entrenchment of the upper basin's streams follows, resulting in the creation of terraces. At first these are well marked, but continued lateral entrenchment reduces the terraces to a series of discontinuous bluffs that parallel a relatively wide and level floodplain established at the new base level. The Gila, Santa Cruz, Sonora, and Altar valleys, among others, are lined by terraces which are sometimes continuous and other times poorly defined, thus displaying varying stages of development.

---

[24]   Bryan, *Erosion and Sedimentation*, p. 66.

CHAPTER TWO

Climate

The climate of the Sonoran Desert is marked by extreme heat and low rainfall. Lying too far south to receive much rain from the mid-latitude westerlies and too far north to partake of any more than a short period of intermittent rain from tropical sources, the Sonoran Desert resembles a number of other subtropical west coast littorals. Mountain ranges circle much of the desert, stealing moisture that might otherwise be available to the dry lowland plains. Months of cloudless skies permit the sun to bake relentlessly down upon a scorched earth. Temperatures rise sharply each morning as the sun moves overhead and fall more slowly every evening. Darkness and the cool night are only a prelude to another day just like the last. Finally the rains come. The diurnal monotony is broken for a short time. Temperatures fall slightly. Clouds fill the sky but soon the sun reappears and the desert is reborn.

A number of factors contribute to the dryness of the Sonoran Desert climate. They may be summarized as follows: (1) a location at the eastern margin of the North Pacific High where normal subsidence contributes to the stability of atmospheric conditions; (2) additional subsidence along a coastline where surface air is controlled by a cold ocean current; (3) the relative weakness of any internal pressure system; (4) distance from the polar and tropical zones of convergence; (5) the heating of incoming air; (6) an intermontane location; and (7) intense local sunshine and evaporation.

RAINFALL

Rainfall throughout all but a small portion of the eastern desert margin is less than 15 inches annually, with the western half of the desert receiving less than 8 inches. This limited rainfall is divided into

[15]

A summer storm in the desert begins in the early afternoon as intense heat creates convection currents which begin the buildup of cloud in an air mass moving northwest from the Gulf of Mexico. Later, the rising air and subsequent condensation bring about local thundershowers as the great majority of the desert remains in brilliant sunlight. Later yet, the rains become more general but still the desert is in large measure dry. Much of the time this entire sequence takes place after sunset with the daylight hours subject to dust and sandstorms. Equally common is the "frustrated" thunderstorm in which there is much cloud, wind, dust and blowing sand, but no rain. These frustrated storms may continue for several days prior to eventual rain.

— CHUCK ABBOTT

— ESTHER HENDERSON

— BILL SEARS

two well defined rainy seasons. Winter rainfall begins usually in November and continues, with many interruptions, into March. These rains are of the "Mediterranean" type, being the same as those which provide the strong winter maximum in California. They occur during the period when the Pacific subtropical high has moved farthest south, allowing the passage of low pressure areas across the southern margin of the continental land mass.[1] The storms cover large areas with the heavier rains occurring sometimes over the entire desert.

The northwestern desert, exposed as it is to the more frequent passage of mid-latitude cyclonic disturbances, receives a higher percentage of its annual rainfall during the winter rainy season.[2] This proportion decreases to the southeast, which borders on the southern limit of winter cyclonic rains. Southeastern Arizona and all but the extreme northwestern part of Sonora lie in an area where the cyclonic energy of winter storms has diminished considerably.[3] Generally, higher elevations do tend to increase winter rainfall so that the Central Highlands region of Arizona, standing across the most frequently traversed path of these depressions, receives the highest winter rainfall totals, and forms the northeastern boundary of the desert.[4]

Summer rainfall, the bulk of which falls in July, August, and September, has a contrasting tropical origin. The North Atlantic subtropical anticyclone strengthens in June and penetrates westward across Texas and northern Mexico. This anticyclonic circulation is not apparent at the surface but is conspicuous at higher altitudes.[5] A westward circulation of air around the southern margin of the high brings moist tropical air into the region from the Gulf of Mexico in late June. It replaces a westerly flow from the stable eastern end of the North Pacific anticyclone which dominates the desert during the early part of the month.[6] The abrupt beginning of thunderstorm activity, first in the south and then progres-

---

1   L. R. Jurwitz, "Arizona's Two Season Rainfall Pattern," *Weatherwise,* Vol. 6 (1953), p. 96.

2   *Ibid.,* pp. 96-98.

3   W. V. Turnage and T. D. Mallery, *An Analysis of Rainfall in the Sonoran Desert and Adjacent Territory,* Carnegie Publication No. 529 (Washington, D.C., 1941), p. 4.

4   C. K. Cooperrider and G. G. Sykes, *The Relationship of Streamflow to Precipitation on the Salt River Watershed above Roosevelt Dam,* Univ. of Arizona Tech. Bull. No. 76 (1938), pp. 2-7.

5   T. R. Reed, "The North American High Level Anti-Cyclone," *Monthly Weather Review,* Vol. 61 (1933), pp. 321-23.

6   A. Bryson and W. Lowry, "Synoptic Climatology of the Arizona Summer Precipitation Singularity," *Bulletin of the American Meteorological Society,* Vol. 36 (1955), pp. 329-39.

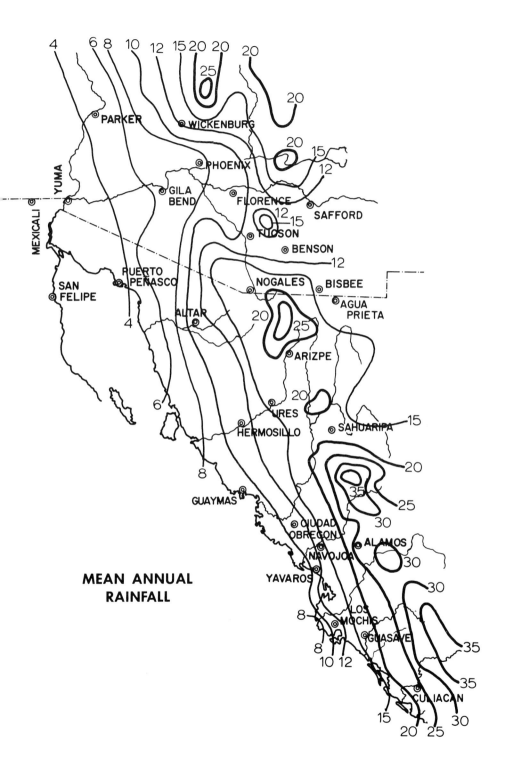

MEAN ANNUAL
RAINFALL

sively farther north, hails the arrival of Gulf tropical air. The Pacific anticyclonic flow is forced to the north by the humid southeasterly current from the Gulf of Mexico.[7]

The summer showers are brief, occurring over the entire region for several days, followed by several days of dry weather. They are scattered, with each storm seldom affecting more than a few square miles.[8] Rainfall totals for any small desert region are areally erratic. Individual showers are separated from one another by wide areas of dry ground. The individual observer is often convinced through an observational illusion that "it rained everywhere but here."[9] Almost all summer showers take place between noon and midnight, the amount of precipitation increasing toward sunset. Heavy showers often fall in midafternoon from massive cumulus clouds which were nonexistent at dawn. The thunderstorms are of short duration but are very intense, particularly at the beginning of a storm.[10] This "cloudburst" which may last only a few minutes gives rise to flash- or sheetfloods, accelerated gullying, and damage to crops, roads, and other works. Many storms conclude with several hours of gentle rain.[11]

Summer and Winter Rainfall, Selected Sonoran Desert Stations

Station	Lat.	Summer Rainfall inches	Winter Rainfall inches	Summer as % of Winter
Parker	34.09	2.0	3.2	63
Gila Bend	32.56	2.6	3.4	76
Ajo	32.24	4.6	4.1	112
Altar	30.40	7.3	2.7	270
Hermosillo	29.15	8.1	1.4	578
Navojoa	27.04	13.0	2.9	448
Guamuchil	25.28	18.3	2.9	630
Culiacán (outside desert)	24.50	21.4	3.5	606

The summer or "monsoon" rainfall increases toward the south so that everywhere south of Tucson the summer rainfall exceeds that of the winter.[12] To the southeast of a sinuous line drawn from the Gulf

---

[7] R. A. Bryson, *The Annual March of Precipitation in Arizona, New Mexico, and Northwestern Mexico,* Univ. of Arizona Inst. of Atmospheric Physics Tech. Report No. 6 (1957).

[8] R. R. Humphrey, "A Detailed Study of Desert Rainfall," *Ecology,* Vol. 14 (1933), p. 33.

[9] J. E. McDonald, "It Rained Everywhere But Here! The Thunderstorm Encirclement Illusion," *Weatherwise,* Vol. 12 (1959), pp. 158-60.

[10] Turnage and Mallery, p. 3.

[11] *Ibid.,* pp. 3-6.

[12] *Ibid.,* p. 8.

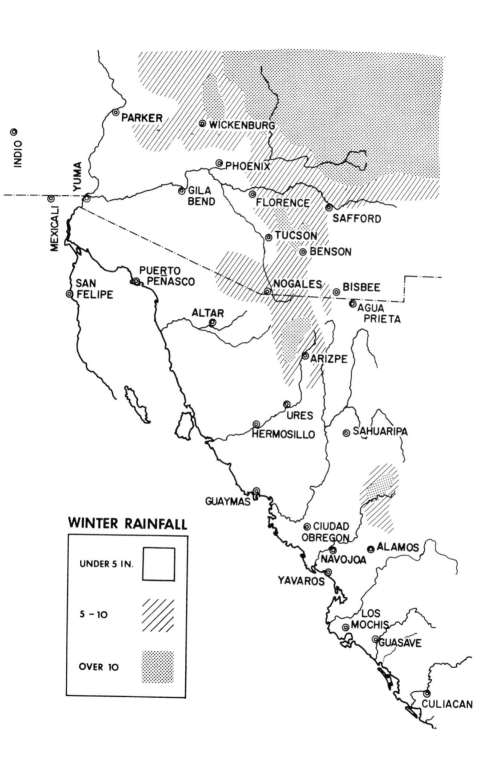

INDIO ⊙

PARKER ⊚   ⊚ WICKENBURG

YUMA

MEXICALI ⊚   ⊚ PHOENIX

⊚ GILA BEND   ⊚ FLORENCE   ⊚ SAFFORD

⊚ TUCSON

⊚ BENSON

SAN FELIPE ⊚   PUERTO PEÑASCO ⊚   NOGALES ⊚   BISBEE ⊚

⊚ ALTAR   ⊚ AGUA PRIETA

⊚ ARIZPE

URES ⊚

⊚ HERMOSILLO   ⊚ SAHUARIPA

GUAYMAS ⊚

⊚ CIUDAD OBREGON   ⊚ ALAMOS

⊚ NAVOJOA

YAVAROS ⊚

LOS MOCHIS ⊚   ⊚ GUASAVE

⊚ CULIACAN

WINTER RAINFALL

UNDER 5 IN.	
5 – 10	
OVER 10	

west of Altar to the border near Douglas, the summer rainfall is usually twice that of the winter months, but the "mediterranean pattern is not completely lacking."[13] There is, however, a greater absolute increase in summer rainfall south of the line of seasonal parity than there is in winter rainfall to the north. The result is that summer rainfall totals for the desert as a whole exceed those of the winter.

It should be noted that winter and summer alike the western desert regions receive less rainfall than the elevated eastern margins.[14] In the winter this is attributable to low elevations and the existence of a rain shadow to the lee of the California mountain ranges. In the summer, easterly and southeasterly maritime air loses nearly all its moisture in crossing the eastern upland margin of the desert, leaving very little available to the western desert. Furthermore, it is warmed by descent, increasing its stability and lessening any possibility of convection.[15]

The relatively steady increase in rainfall along a line from Death Valley in the north to Mazatlán (outside the region) to the south (see above), is certainly not a function of latitude alone. Orographic factors, such as the less perceptible rain shadow to the south of the San Pedro Martir and other northern mountains, allow the passage of more westerly and southwesterly storms into the southern desert than do the more formidable barriers to the north. In addition, the summer storms which originate in an eastern or southeastern air mass and are "triggered" by the Sierra Madres carry over into the narrowing coastal plain so that southern lowland stations register higher summer rainfall totals than would otherwise be the case. If latitude were the only consideration it could be noted that along almost any given line of longitude rainfall decreases rather than increases from north to south.

The rainfall records for Sonoran stations show that rainfall variability tends to be great when the amount of rain per month is small, and small when the total rainfall is great. Likewise, variability in the driest western deserts is greater than in the upland deserts to the east. Rainfall variability for the desert as a whole is extremely high.[16]

It is not unusual for a station in the Lower Colorado Desert to receive in a short period most of its annual rainfall or even more than the annual figure. Yuma, for example, has an average annual rainfall of 3.48

13   R. L. Ives, "Climate of the Sonoran Desert," *Annals of the Association of American Geographers*, Vol. 39 (1949), p. 160.

14   Christine R. Green, *Arizona Statewide Rainfall*, University of Arizona Institute of Atmospheric Physics, Tech. Report No. 7 (1959), p. 3.

15   *Ibid.*

16   Ives, "Climate of the Sonoran Desert," *Annals of the Association of American Geographers*, Vol. 39, pp. 168-69.

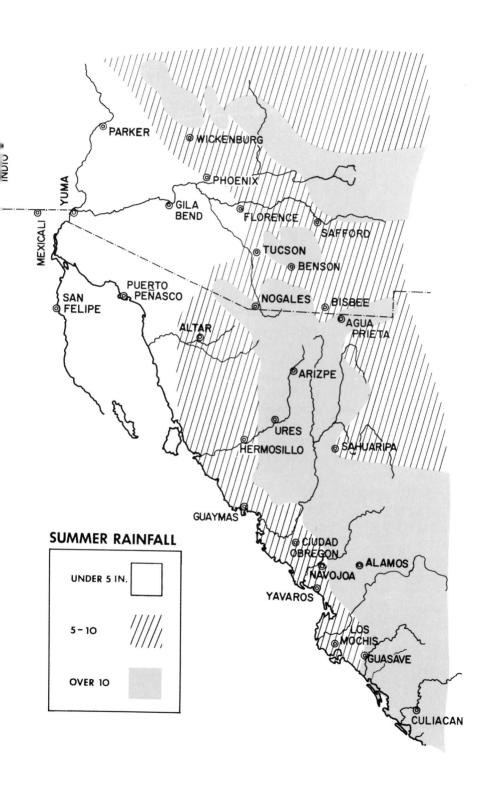

SUMMER RAINFALL

UNDER 5 IN.

5 - 10

OVER 10

PARKER
WICKENBURG
PHOENIX
GILA BEND
FLORENCE
SAFFORD
TUCSON
BENSON
YUMA
MEXICALI
INDIO
SAN FELIPE
PUERTO PEÑASCO
NOGALES
BISBEE
AGUA PRIETA
ALTAR
ARIZPE
URES
HERMOSILLO
SAHUARIPA
GUAYMAS
CIUDAD OBREGON
ALAMOS
NAVOJOA
YAVAROS
LOS MOCHIS
GUASAVE
CULIACAN

inches but received 4.01 in 24 hours on August 15-16, 1909.[17] Most Sonoran Desert stations have had at least one month (usually July) and sometimes several months in which rainfall has exceeded the lowest annual totals.[18]

It should also be noted that average annual rainfall figures do not convey the actual drought which often besets the desert. Years may pass at a given station under a desiccating sun with little more than 3 or 4 inches of rain. Yet a 35-year average may show rainfall in excess of 10 inches for the same station. Averages mean little.

Despite this, the popular conception of rainfall intensity in a desert storm exceeding that of a humid region is utterly false. Whereas many stations in the Mississippi Valley have received more than 10 inches of rainfall in a 24-hour period, the record for most desert stations seldom exceeds 4 inches.

Daily Extremes of Rainfall at Four Typical Desert Stations[19]

Station	Record No. of Years	Inches	Date
Gila Bend	50	2.61	Aug. 1951
Phoenix	57	4.98	July 1911
Safford	55	3.04	Sept. 1944
Tucson	49	2.94	Aug. 1940

The above are typical of Sonoran Desert stations where records have been kept over a significant period of time.

A rain of exceptional intensity in Tucson in September, 1944, had the following maximum for five periods:

Rainfall Intensity Record, Tucson[20]

	2 min.	15 min.	1 hr.	6 hrs.	12 hrs.
Depth in inches	.50	1.05	1.59	2.56	2.59
Intensity per hr. in inches	15.00	4.20	1.59	.43	.22

It is quite apparent that rainfall of extreme intensity may continue for a few minutes or hours but rain seldom falls steadily in periods of six hours or longer with any great intensity.

Snow is extremely important to the Sonoran Desert because it provides much of the runoff upon which irrigation depends. However,

---

17   Climatic Summary of the United States, Sec. 26, p. 7, quoted in Jassim M. Khalaf, *The Water Resources of the Lower Colorado River Basin*, Univ. of Chicago Research Paper No. 22, 1951.

18   F. Shreve, "Rainfall Run-off and soil Moisture under Desert Conditions," *Annals of the Association of American Geographers*, Vol. 24 (1934), p. 134.

19   H. V. Smith, *The Climate of Arizona*, University of Arizona Experiment Station Bulletin No. 279 (Tucson, 1956).

20   *Ibid.*, p. 72.

MONTHLY RAINFALL

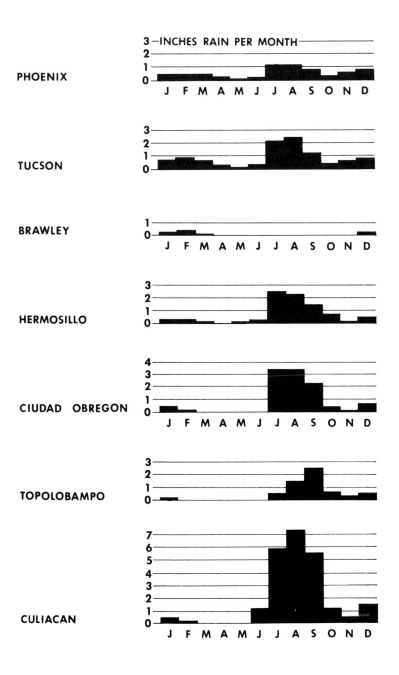

PHOENIX

3 —INCHES RAIN PER MONTH
2
1
0
J F M A M J J A S O N D

TUCSON

3
2
1
0

BRAWLEY

1
0
J F M A M J J A S O N D

HERMOSILLO

3
2
1
0

CIUDAD OBREGON

4
3
2
1
0
J F M A M J J A S O N D

TOPOLOBAMPO

3
2
1
0

CULIACAN

7
6
5
4
3
2
1
0
J F M A M J J A S O N D

this snowfall is almost entirely outside the desert but within the water-sheds of the exotic streams that eventually flow into desert reservoirs. Few Sonoran Desert stations get more than a trace of snow and then only occasionally. Phoenix received some snow — usually a trace — in only thirteen years out of a total of fifty-eight years recorded.[21] In Sonora and Sinaloa most coastal stations have never had any snow.

TEMPERATURES

Unlike rainfall, temperatures in the Sonoran Desert are consistent, varying little from year to year. The temperature cycle is relatively simple and quite predictable. The summer months are hot with temperatures regularly exceeding 100 degrees F. In Tucson (2,500 ft. elev.) there is a fifty-fifty chance of temperatures reaching 108 degrees F. every June and July. In Yuma (110 ft. elev.) temperatures have exceeded 100 degrees F. in at least four months (June, July, August, and September) of every year since 1870. At this station the month of July has never failed since 1920 to produce at least one day in which the temperature exceeded 110 degrees F. At nearby San Luis, Sonora, what may be the world's record high temperature was set on August 11, 1933, when the thermometer registered 136.4 degrees F. in the shade.[22]

Low relative humidities keep sensible temperatures at an almost tolerable level. Outdoor work is regularly carried on at midday during the summer months at the hottest desert stations. Discomfort is, however, high, notwithstanding the protestations of local boosters to the contrary.

Winter temperatures are cool to mild, with the northern stations as well as those located at higher elevations being subject to freezing weather on a number of occasions during a winter season which lasts usually three to four months. At lower elevations and on the extreme southern margin of the desert, frosts are uncommon and winter temperatures may rise to 80 or 90 degrees F. Yuma has exceeded 90 degrees F. in every month of the year except December when the highest recorded temperature is 83 degrees F. In the two coldest winter months (December and January), temperatures in Yuma may be expected to reach 78 degrees F. at least once. At the other extreme, one can expect in Yuma to see the thermometer register a low of 29

---

[21] *Ibid.,* p. 82.
[22] N. McWhirter, *The Guinness Book of Records* (1961 edition), p. 43. A reading of 140 degrees F. at Delta, Sonora, is not now accepted.

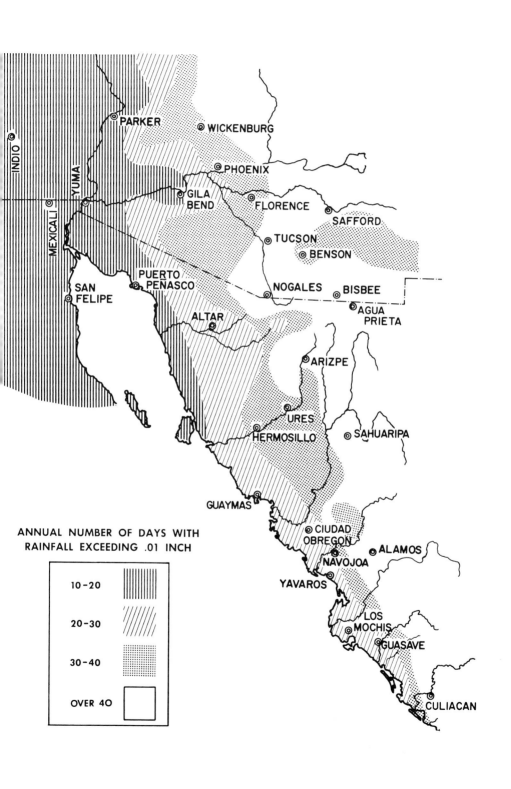

ANNUAL NUMBER OF DAYS WITH
RAINFALL EXCEEDING .01 INCH

10-20	
20-30	
30-40	
OVER 40	

degrees F. at least once in every year while the record low is 19 degrees F.[23]

In the extreme south, as desert is gradually replaced by a tropical semiarid climate, winter temperatures are higher and frost very uncommon. Temperatures are generally 10 degrees higher in January on the coastal plain south of the Río Yaqui than they are at stations in the Lower Colorado Valley. The Yaqui is something of a climatic boundary, in that south of this river killing frosts seldom occur. This has definite effect upon the kinds of crops grown either to the north or south of this river.

Growing seasons nevertheless vary greatly from year to year at any station. The average duration of frostfree periods has been established statistically. It varies from a minimum of about 220 days on the northern and upland margin of the desert to a number of stations in the south which have to date never recorded frost.

Throughout the desert, elevation is a significant control on the annual number of frostfree days. The length of the growing season is reduced by about 30 days for each 1000-foot increase in elevation. Whereas Phoenix (elev. 1,114 ft.) has a mean of 304 frostfree days, Tucson (elev. 2,500 ft) has only 250.[24] There is throughout all the major irrigated basins of the Sonoran Desert a growing season sufficiently long to plant and harvest two crops.

Diurnal temperature ranges throughout the desert are great at any season, being slightly wider in the early summer than in the winter. Clear skies contribute to the violent temperature fluctuations that take place during each twenty-four-hour period. Brawley, California, registers a mean diurnal variation of 32.2 degrees F. in January and 36.5 degrees F. in June.[25] Ground-level temperature ranges are much wider than those registered on the standard meteorological shelters located about five feet above the ground. These variations have exceeded 100 degrees during a single twenty-four-hour period.[26]

WINDS AND OTHER PHENOMENA

The surface winds of the Sonoran Desert are controlled 'in general by the interaction of the North Pacific High and the "Sonoran" Low.

[23] H. V. Smith, p. 19.

[24] *Ibid.,* p. 50.

[25] *Ibid.,* p. 46.

[26] Ives, "Climate of the Sonoran Desert," *Annals of the Association of American Geographers,* Vol. 39, p. 171. In the Yuma desert during the summer "the sun daily heats the exposed rock surfaces to 150° or more while the night cools them to 75°." Eldred Wilson, "New Mountains in the Yuma Desert, Arizona," *Geographical Review,* Vol. 21, p. 224.

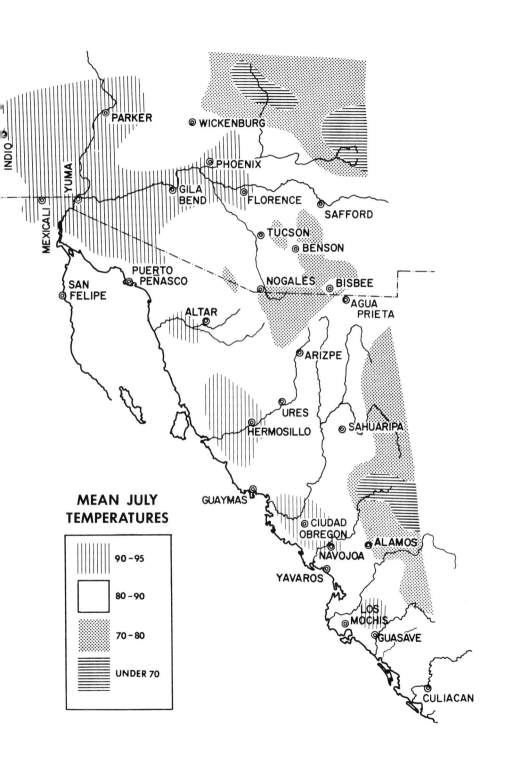

MEAN JULY
TEMPERATURES

‖‖‖	90–95
☐	80–90
▦	70–80
≡	UNDER 70

INDIO

PARKER   WICKENBURG

YUMA   PHOENIX

MEXICALI   GILA BEND   FLORENCE   SAFFORD

TUCSON

BENSON

SAN FELIPE   PUERTO PEÑASCO   NOGALES   BISBEE

AGUA PRIETA

ALTAR

ARIZPE

URES

HERMOSILLO   SAHUARIPA

GUAYMAS

CIUDAD OBREGON   ALAMOS

NAVOJOA

YAVAROS

LOS MOCHIS

GUASAVE

CULIACAN

The Pacific High pressure system shifts with the seasons from about 40 degrees N. to 24 degrees N. latitude while the latter system is a more or less permanent phenomenon which centers usually a little to the southeast of the Colorado River Delta. The effects of the Sonoran Low are most clearly observable in the winter months when circulation around this center closely follows textbook theory. Winds in central Arizona and Sonora are out of the south and southeast, while in the western desert winds are from the opposite direction. On the other hand, equinoctial and summer conditions are marked by uncertainty. The Sonoran Low breaks up into a number of centers in the spring and then expands so that it occasionally joins with another low-pressure area which centers over the deserts of Chihuahua. During these periods "surface winds are not those indicated by simple theories . . . but consist of the resultant of the gradient winds and the local air drainages."[27] The westward circulation of air at high elevations, which announces the arrival of the summer rains, does not immediately interrupt the surface flow of air which remains from the south or southwest. During this turbulent period wind direction remains very uncertain despite the deepening and widening Sonoran Low.[28]

With the progression of the summer season, convection currents bring about stronger local controls on air circulation. The overall regional pattern is blurred by the rising and subsiding currents which form cells over each enclosed basin. After sunrise a wind begins to blow outward in all directions from the center of the desert.

The peripheral mountains engender conditions resulting in the concentration of convection currents over their flanks and summits. These eminences are often marked by banner clouds. Shortly after sunset the opposite conditions prevail with a desiccating hot wind blowing down the bajadas toward the basin's center.[29] This adiabatically heated air continues throughout the early evening only to be replaced by a quite cold wind from the same direction before dawn.

It is well known that higher elevations encourage greater rainfall and this appears to be an important factor in the distribution of rainfall in the desert.[30] The higher desert plains to the east receive more rain

---

[27]   Ives, "Climate of the Sonoran Desert," *Annals of the Association of American Geographers,* Vol. 39, p. 175.

[28]   *Ibid.,* pp. 172-75.

[29]   *Ibid.,* p. 177.

[30]   A. J. Henry, "Rainfall in Relation to Altitude," *Monthly Weather Review,* Vol. 47 (1919), pp. 33-41.

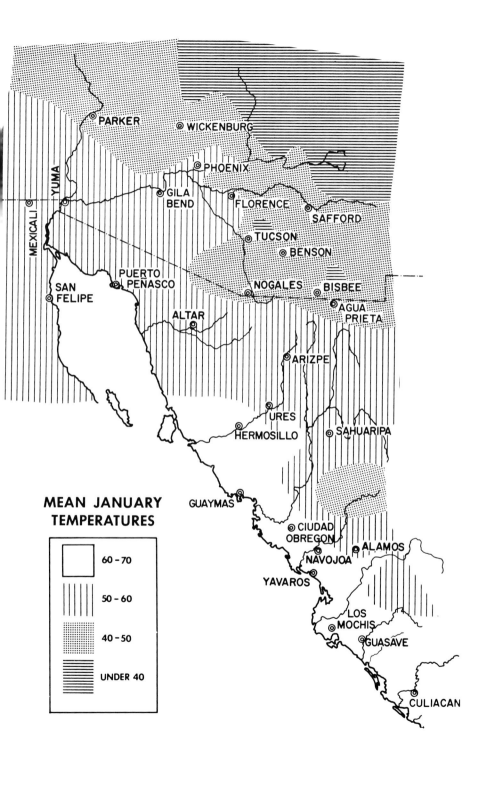

MEAN JANUARY
TEMPERATURES

	60 - 70
	50 - 60
	40 - 50
	UNDER 40

PARKER

WICKENBURG

YUMA

PHOENIX

MEXICALI

GILA
BEND

FLORENCE

SAFFORD

TUCSON

BENSON

PUERTO
PEÑASCO

SAN
FELIPE

NOGALES

BISBEE

AGUA
PRIETA

ALTAR

ARIZPE

URES

HERMOSILLO

SAHUARIPA

GUAYMAS

CIUDAD
OBREGON

ALAMOS

NAVOJOA

YAVAROS

LOS
MOCHIS

GUASAVE

CULIACAN

during all seasons than the western Lower Colorado and Coastal Desert. On the other hand, the effect which individual mountain ranges have upon precipitation is less clearly understood. Studies carried on within the Sonoran Desert have demonstrated that elevation alone may have little influence on rainfall totals.[31] An isolated mountain range such as the Tucson Mountains has little effect, if any, upon rainfall in its vicinity during the winter months. High and massive mountains such as the Santa Catalinas (9,185 feet) just north of Tucson have a marked influence upon rainfall totals throughout these months. During the summer rainy season intermediate-size mountains seem to encourage a rainfall total which slightly exceeds that recorded in nearby valleys. All in all, it might be observed that elevation has less effect upon increased rainfall over a narrow isolated desert range than it does over a massive barrier of no greater elevation.[32]

The relative humidity of the desert throughout the year is low, reaching its lowest point usually in the heat of early June before the summer rains. Most Sonoran Desert stations average about 30 percent annual relative humidity (at noon) with higher figures achieved both in winter and summer.

Fog associated with west coast littorals is usually absent from the Sonoran Desert due to the intervening Gulf and California Peninsula. Coastal fog known locally as *lloranos* causes considerable discomfort in the often inadequate housing of Sonora and Sinaloa.[33]

Dust is much less of a problem in the desert than it is in the semi-arid plains. The surface of the soil being composed of coarse material, there is little blowing dust except for a few days each year, usually prior to a summer rainstorm or during a winter cyclonic disturbance. Blowing sand is a major factor in the shaping of desert land forms but a minor irritant climatically.

Much of the Sonoran Desert is covered with cloud less than 15 percent of the time. Annual sunshine totals are as high as anywhere in the United States or Mexico.

---

[31]   G. Sykes, "Rainfall Investigations in Arizona and Sonora by means of Long Period Rain Gauges," *Geographical Review,* Vol. 21 (1931), p. 229; Turnage and Mallery, p. 12.

[32]   Turnage and Mallery, pp. 12-14.

[33]   Ives, "Climate of the Sonoran Desert," *Annals of the Association of American Geographers,* Vol. 39, p. 177.

CHAPTER THREE

Soils

The first ten feet of the earth's surface is the creator and in part the creation of its vegetation. If the surface is composed of solid rock or drifting sand it will probably be unable to support a plant cover and will not usually be termed soil. Only a very small percentage of the earth's surface falls into this desolate category. Some areas of the Sonoran Desert are devoid of soil by this definition. Within these regions where plants are unable to take root the "soil" (if one may use that term) is deprived of its vital, organic constituent. In the study of the natural environment soil and vegetation cannot be separated nor can they be examined without constant reference to the climatic conditions under which both are in constant formation. It is also impossible, particularly in a desert milieu, to separate soil from the material out of which it was formed and upon which it lies. Climate, soil, subsoil, and vegetation must be considered as interacting agents if a true picture is to be obtained. The truth of this may be seen in Shreve's observation that there is little relation between annual rainfall totals and the amount of moisture in the soil. An individual rain of under 15 inches has usually little effect on soil moisture, and rainfall over 75 inches a diminishing effectiveness due to runoff.[1]

In an area as large and physically diversified as that of the Sonoran Desert there is bound to be a large range of soils. There are, however, a number of factors at work greatly limiting the variety of soil types within the region and promoting a certain degree of similarity between soils developed under like conditions over large areas manifesting a wide range of parent materials. In determining the character of the soil, desert climate and landforms take precedence over differences in parent material. Throughout the desert, extreme arid conditions, heat, and

---

[1] Shreve, "Rainfall Run-off and Soil Moisture under Desert Conditions," *Annals of the Association of American Geographers,* Vol. 24 (1934), pp. 134-36.

wind, working upon the isolated blockfaulted mountains and the slopes of the larger ranges, have repeatedly produced similar landforms, soils, and vegetation "over and over again in hundreds of valleys and intermont plains. There are hills or mountain slopes with rock in place and pockets of soil, there are pediments, upper bajadas with shallow coarse soil, lower bajadas or plains with deeper soil of uniform but rather coarse texture and flood plains or playas with deep fine soil. The physiographic features of the basin determine the physical character and distribution of the soils."[2] There are greater differences in soils between the upper slopes of a desert mountain and its adjacent intermont plain than between the soil of that plain and that of another, similarly located two hundred or more miles distant.

The repetitive occurrence of like soils in similar situations over a wide expanse of desert is due to the textural differences of soils which develop in a vertical sequence from mountain top to floodplain. There is in addition a similar sequential variation in the quantity of soil moisture available to plants. Taken together, texture and moisture content are of unequalled importance in establishing a significant basis for soil differentiation within the desert. Of considerable importance is the depth of soil and the nature of its surface. These more often than not vary in the same vertical sequence from mountain to plain and along with soil texture determine the amount of moisture retained by the soil.

In the following outline of desert soil types any emphasis placed on desert landforms is not an attempt to discount the role of climate in soil formation. The important features of the region's climate not only differentiate the character of the desert's soils from that of neighboring areas but are responsible in large measure for the development of the familiar mountain, bajada, and playa forms upon which the characteristic desert soils have developed.

It must be remembered that climate indirectly affects desert soil through the limitations placed on plants. An incomplete plant cover leaves the soil exposed and results in high rates of erosion and deposition both by wind and water. Restricted plant growth results in the low humus content of desert types. Sonoran soils therefore have in general a sandy dry texture and are light colored due in part to this lack of humus.[3]

The texture of the upland soils is generally coarse and that of the low-lying soils, fine. All soils are generally shallow, with a low humus

---

2   Shreve, *Vegetation of the Sonoran Desert*, p. 29; Bryan, *The Papago Country*, p. 66, makes much the same observation.

3   Khalaf, pp. 51-53.

Over large areas of the Sonoran Desert, a sandy soil supports no perennial plants other than the creosote bush (Larrea) and the bur sage (Franseria). This soil is fine, with a low humus content — due in large part to restricted native plant growth. Even such unpropitious plains as these, given enough water, will bring forth abundant crops.

content. Most desert soils lack a well-defined profile. Moisture is low and water tables are often lacking. Harmful salts are left out of solution when there is insufficient soil moisture to dissolve them. When on occasion there is sufficient moisture these dissolved salts are brought to the surface and precipitated out by rapid evaporation. Soils with high alkali contents are formed in the same manner and are common. A hardpan or caliche formation is thus characteristic of many Sonoran soils.[4]

FLOODPLAINS OR DESERT PLAYAS

The material from which these silty soils originate has been transported either from surrounding territories by rivers, such as the Colorado,[5] which rise outside the desert or are endogenous in character, being the end product of the erosion of nearby mountain ranges and "uplands." These alluvial soils are the finest and most uniform to be found within the desert. They occur throughout the region but are concentrated where one might expect them on the deltaic plains of the larger rivers and in the lower portions of the areas of inland drainage.[6] In the upland areas of Arizona and Sonora these soils are restricted either to the narrow floodplains or are absent altogether. The Imperial, Colorado, Gila, Magdalena, Sonora, and Yaqui valleys are in large part composed of these fine alluvial soils, as is most of the coastal plain from the Yaqui River southwards. These uniformly fine and very level soils are of recent deposition and are usually uneroded and unterraced.

Any consideration of the fertility of these low-lying soils rests upon the reciprocal relation between air content and water content. Because of their location along river margins and flooring desert bolsons, this type of desert may suffer more than others from poor soil aeration encouraged by fine texture and concomitant poor drainage.[7] Immediately after heavy rains floodwaters may accumulate on these plains and saturate the soil which in turn may remain waterlogged for a period of days even under the most intense sunshine. The saturated soil is unable to drain itself underground and its fine texture encourages the upward movement of water, which during the period of flooding had soaked

[4]   H. A. Hoffmeister, "Alkali Problem of Western United States," *Economic Geography,* Vol. 23 (1947), pp. 1-9.

[5]   G. Sykes, *The Colorado Delta,* American Geographical Society Special Pub. No. 19 (New York, 1937), pp. 127-44.

[6]   *Ibid.,* pp. 155-75.

[7]   J. G. Holmes, "Soil Survey of the Yuma Area, Arizona, California," *Field Operations,* Bureau of Soils (1902), pp. 777-91.

to a lower level. This kind of long-period saturation of the soil will kill most desert plants. As a result of this an extremely open stand of plants grows on these excessively watered floodplains and playas.[8]

Related to-this is the solution and subsequent deposition of soluble salts contained in the alluvial soils. The evaporation of the floodwaters may leave behind a white crust which creaks when you walk over it, and in concentration, spells death to all but the hardiest desert plants.[9]

Along the perennial streams such as the Colorado River, where soils are constantly waterlogged and salts are readily dissolved and removed, the fine alluvial soils are capable of supporting a non-arid palustrine vegetation.[10]

LOWER BAJADAS

The soils of this particular portion of the desert outwash plain are sometimes known as mesa soils but should not be confused with the residual soils of true mesas.[11]

The lower bajada with its even, gradual slope, is located above the alluvial valley bottoms. Over large areas of the Lower Colorado Valley, northern and central Sonora, as well as along the rivers flowing into the Gulf south of the Yaqui, this type of landform dominates most of the desert area. The soils of the lower bajada are transported as are the lower-lying soils of the floodplain, but the bajada soils have a higher proportion of locally derived material in their composition. What is important is the ability of the coarser soils of the bajada to collect and retain the scarce rainfall, conserving it, and making it available gradually,[12] whereas the fine soils of the floodplain may be subject to alternate periods of extreme drought and inundation with the results noted above.[13]

The mixed colluvial-alluvial soils of the lower outwash plains (lower bajadas) are generally composed of sand and gravel with a superficial covering of larger fragments which may give the soil a stony appearance

---

[8] Burton Livingston, *Relation of Desert Plants to Soil Moisture and to Evaporation,* Carnegie Inst. Pub. No. 50 (1906).

[9] Hoffmeister, "Alkali Problem of Western United States," *Economic Geography,* Vol. 23, pp. 4-5.

[10] Sykes, *The Colorado Delta,* p. 161 and photos following p. 158.

[11] "Outwash plain" or "lower bajada" will be used instead of "mesa" with regard to soils.

[12] Shreve, "Rainfall Run-off and Soil Moisture under Desert Conditions," *Annals of the Association of American Geographers,* Vol. 24, p. 153.

[13] Khalaf, p. 54.

it does not merit. These stones are the residue after desert sheetfloods and wind have removed the lighter material. In extreme cases this may result in a "desert pavement." Normally, however, the surface of the flat or slightly hummocky lower bajada is gravelly or stony and is the result of intermittent floodwaters and the constant wind.

The "typically balanced" association of creosote bush (*Larrea divaricata*) and burro bush (*Franseria dumosa*) is the signature of the lower bajada-type soil. A change in this dominant association usually signifies an underlying change in soil. The sandy soils of the lower bajada may gradually vary toward the silty clays more typical of the flood plains. At the other extreme they may vary toward the gravelly soils of the upper bajada. In either case the landform remains typical of the lower bajada with its associated rainfall and drainage. Finally, the soils of the lower bajada may be overridden by shallow blowsand, or in the very arid districts, be replaced by sand dunes. The soils of the lower bajadas are much more diversified than the seemingly endless miles of creosote bush suggest.[14]

UPPER BAJADAS AND MOUNTAIN PEDIMENTS

These two landforms with their characteristic soils dominate the uplands of the desert in the east to almost the same extent as the lower bajadas and their associated soils dominate the lowland plains to the west. Almost all the larger mountains, even those in the areas of least rainfall, have provided sufficient material for the formation of sharply eroded pediment and steep uniform outwash plains or upper bajadas. The soils of these formations, regardless of slope, are invariably coarse in texture, being composed of sandy gravel, and gravel with a considerable admixture of larger material. This fact, in combination with the higher rainfall of the more elevated bajadas and mountain pediments, makes these areas "better suited to the retention and penetration of moisture" than any of the lower-lying soil types.[15]

On the uniformly sloping upper bajadas where a "balance has been struck between erosion and deposition" the soils are more maturely developed than all but some mountain types. These soils maintain some of the most striking vegetation of the desert.[16]

There is much in common between all upper bajada and pediment

---

[14]   John B. Marks, "Vegetation and Soil Relations in the Lower Colorado Desert," *Ecology*, Vol. 31 (1950), pp. 186-89.

[15]   Shreve, *Vegetation of the Sonoran Desert*, p. 53.

[16]   Marks, "Vegetation and Soil Relations in the Lower Colorado Desert," *Ecology*, Vol. 31, p. 179.

An upper bajada. This photo taken near Tucson, Arizona, shows clearly an alluvial fan descending from the foot of the distant mountain. In the foreground an arroyo has cut its way into the coarse upper-valley fill. The saguaro and little leaf palo verde dominate the landscape.

soils but it should be kept in mind that whereas the soils of the lower outwash plains are almost always a mixture of material from numerous sources, the soils of the upper bajadas and pediments are derived from a single mountain range.

MOUNTAINS

Volcanic Mountains and Lava Fields

The extrusive rock formations of the Sonoran Desert vary greatly, from the older volcanic mountains of andesite, rhyolite, and basaltic conglomerate, to the recent basalt lava flows or malpais. The distinction between the "older" volcanics and the recent is generally made on the basis of the stage of physiographic development of their surfaces rather than on the basis of their geological sequence. Many of the "older" volcanics are probably of the same age as the basalt lava flows. In addition, the "older" volcanics are more highly dissected with very narrow ridges showing deep erosion and the surface is either bare rock in place or an accumulation of coarse angular stones with pockets of deeply eroded and poorly developed soils. Thus the "older" volcanics generally have "immature" soils. However, if provided with sufficient moisture, these warm soils situated in the protected valleys of desert mountain ranges provide an excellent habitat for the development of lush "desert garden" vegetation.[17] The poorly developed soil may be compensated for on these slopes by better moisture conditions and root anchorage.

The most mature volcanic soils are developed on the large expanses of former lava flows known as either volcanic mesas or lava beds (malpais). The former is an "older" formation but nevertheless, as its name denotes, much of its surface is level or nearly so. These types of volcanic formations cover large areas, particularly in the Lower Colorado Valley (southwestern Arizona and northwestern Sonora), and in the Foothills of Sonora (south of Moctezuma). Their soils comprise the largest areas of reasonably level residual soils found within the desert.

Once these generalizations are made there is little in common between the type of material that mantles these expanses of lava. The lava fields of the Lower Colorado region have surfaces which range from jagged fields of fantastic rock and slag formations nearly devoid of anything which could be termed soil to areas of fairly deep soil covered locally by heaps of volcanic rubble.[18]

---

17   Livingston, p. 23.
18   Bryan, *The Papago Country,* p. 70.

The mountain pediment here heavily mantled with desert vegetation is an inconspicuous part of the landscape. A remarkably level surface, the pediment ends abruptly at the foot of the mountain.

The alternation of plain and mountain defined as the Basin and Range Province is clearly seen in this photograph. Beyond the eye of the camera, the same repetition takes place to the islands of the Gulf of California.

The lava fields of the Foothills show the effect of more active weathering which is the result of the higher rainfall of that region. Once again rock is very much in evidence, the surface appearing to be the worst kind of "bad land." A closer examination, however, reveals that the rockiest sections of the malpais are usually underlain by deep black loam. Large areas are, at the same time, free of surface rocks.

It is difficult to generalize regarding the amount of water available to plants in the dark soils of the lava fields. On the western lava flows where rainfall is less than 4 inches, the volcanic soils give every indication of having a better water supply than the adjacent bajada soils.[19] However, on the volcanic mesas of eastern Sonora where the rainfall measures between 10 and 16 inches, the level dark volcanic soils appear to be drier than either the bajada or crystalline residual soils. There seems to be very little runoff but the high temperature of the soil encourages evaporation while soil depth allows the water table to fall to a level which prevents utilization.

Granitic Mountains and Hills

Soils developed on this type of terrain are widespread throughout the desert, being totally absent only in the deltaic regions south of the Yaqui River and near the mouth of the Colorado. These soils most typically occur on the small isolated block-faulted mountains of the eastern desert.

The soil of these mountain ranges has developed largely *in situ,* the product of the weathering of granite, gneiss, or schist, which disintegrate more rapidly than eruptives. The weathering of granite desert mountains often produces immediately a fine gravel and sand from exposed rock surfaces without intervening stages of rubble. This gravel and sand is swept away by rainwater so that the parent material is continuously exposed to agents which promote the most rapid granular disintegration. Throughout the mountain ranges composed of crystalline rock there has been sufficient subaerial disintegration to provide a soil although it may occur only as pockets on the steep mountain slopes, where outcrops of rock dominate the landscape. Soil formation does, however, proceed apace beneath the surface and in the interior of the granite boulder piles where the sun never reaches and where diurnal temperature variations are small.

The soil of the granitic mountain slopes is usually composed of a coarse sand, gravel, and rock at the surface, where the lighter particles

---

[19] *Ibid.,* p. 71.

The Superstition Mountains loom in the background. A lonely saguaro holds its arms aloft. On the ground, smaller plants fail to cover the surface. Despite the number of trees and tree-like cacti, nowhere within the desert away from the streamways are plants able to establish ground cover for any length of time.

have been removed by wind and rainwater. Immediately below the surface the more mature product of soil formation is a sandy loam or
loams. The soil of the arroyo bottom is composed of the materials
washed from the mountains. It varies from deep, well-watered sandy
loams to sand-choked arroyos, coarse talus slopes, and boulder heaps.

— CHUCK ABBOTT

*Although far less numerous than many desert species, the giant
saguaro, because of its size and unusual appearance, dominates large
areas of the Sonoran Desert landscape. The largest cactus north of
the international border, the saguaro's fruit was an important item
in the subsistence of many of the Sonoran Desert's aboriginal peoples.*

CHAPTER FOUR

Vegetation

The single outstanding characteristic which distinguishes the Sonoran Desert from that of the other major deserts of North America is the size, diversity, and wide distribution of trees and tree-like cacti which have earned for the region the seemingly contradictory designation of "arborescent desert." With certain reservations (which will be discussed in detail) this term does not fall far from the mark. Giant cacti and small xerophytic trees dominate the landscape over immense tracts seldom equalled in any other desert. However, one should not confuse "arborescent" with any conception of a tree-covered or "forested" countryside gained outside the desert. Even in the most favored areas of dense desert vegetation, barren soil and rock are always exposed, the plants seldom being able to form a closed cover.

The plants that have been able to perpetuate themselves in this marginal environment are specially adapted to gather and conserve moisture, to withstand great heat and wide diurnal temperature variation, and to be able to overcome the danger of wind-blown particles and shifting sand. The success as well as magnitude of these plant adaptions may be witnessed in the surprising dimensions and unique appearance of the vegetation of most Sonoran Desert landscapes. The infinitely changing size and composition of desert plant associations mirrors this ability of vegetative forms to exist and prosper under adverse soil and climatic conditions.

A solitary walk in the desert should never fail to impress the thoughtful observer of the numberless subtle machinations of living things pitted against compelling forces of inanimate nature. The balance achieved is to be seen in the variety and spread of vegetation, and at the same instant, in the incomplete grip plants have on the parched desert soil. This has led even the keenest students of desert plant life to overemphasize the conflict between vegetation and environment (such as climate and soil) to the neglect of a more realistic assessment of the concurrent competition between individuals or species.

The inability of the vegetation to form a closed cover, and the previously mentioned structural adaptions to climate which reduce maximum performance, are only two of at least four limitations placed by the desert environment on the full development of plant life. In addition, plants are unable to "attain a considerable size" and maintain vegetational activity throughout the year. The better able any species is in overcoming these handicaps the more easily it will gain dominance over its competitors.

The remarkable adaptions so apparent in structure and physiological processes made by plants to withstand great heat are equally advantageous in allowing individual plants and species to take precedence over competitors. This is true even when "each creosote bush, mesquite, palo verde, iron wood, each clump of galleta grass is a perfect botanical specimen growing in its own invisible tub, standing above and quite untrammelled by its neighbors."[1]

Although not obviously apparent, crowding is a real problem in a desert plant community where resources are desperately scarce. "Invisible tubs" are just what one might suspect — nonexistent!

LOWER COLORADO VALLEY DESERT

The desert reaches which border the lower course of the Colorado River and the extreme northern end of the Gulf of California are distinguished by their sparse and monotonous vegetation. These barren deserts have many local names but are grouped together by botanists into a single vegetational subdivision.[2] This is done in spite of the fact that this is the largest subdivision with the greatest variety of landforms and soil types. However, well over four-fifths of the total area is low-elevation desert composed of low-gradient or nearly level plains of gravelly outwash or sand.

Upon the extensive intermontane plains the vegetation is usually limited to low and very open stands of creosote bush (*Larrea divaricata*) or mixed stands of creosote bush and burro bush (*Franseria dumosa*).

---

[1] W. T. Hornaday, *Camp Fires on Desert and Lava* (New York, 1908), p. 41.

[2] Shreve, *Vegetation of the Sonoran Desert,* pp. 40-41.

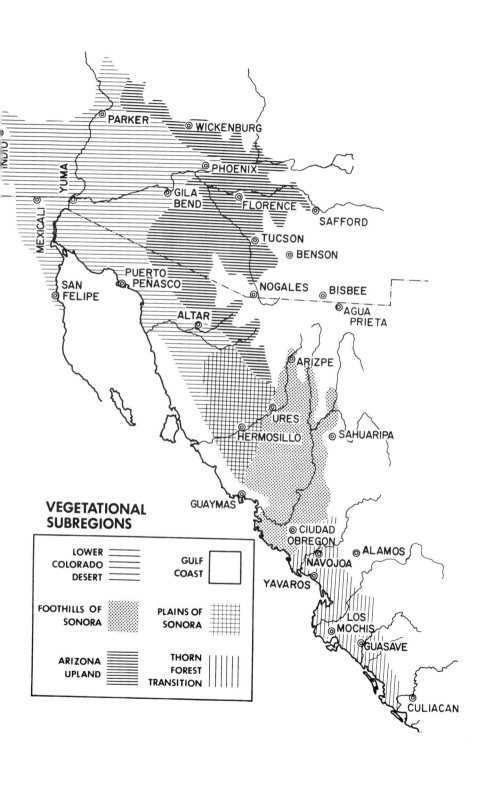

VEGETATIONAL SUBREGIONS

LOWER COLORADO DESERT

GULF COAST

FOOTHILLS OF SONORA

PLAINS OF SONORA

ARIZONA UPLAND

THORN FOREST TRANSITION

PARKER
WICKENBURG
YUMA
PHOENIX
MEXICALI
GILA BEND
FLORENCE
SAFFORD
TUCSON
BENSON
PUERTO PEÑASCO
SAN FELIPE
NOGALES
BISBEE
ALTAR
AGUA PRIETA
ARIZPE
URES
HERMOSILLO
SAHUARIPA
GUAYMAS
CIUDAD OBREGON
ALAMOS
NAVOJOA
YAVAROS
LOS MOCHIS
GUASAVE
CULIACAN

The two species make up perhaps 95 percent of the plant population of these plains and give the entire region its distinctive stamp.[3]

The creosote bush is, in Jaeger's words,

> the most widespread and common of all our desert shrubs and is certainly typical of the entire Sonoran Desert. It is believed to have originated in the deserts of South America. Often it covers extensive areas, in pure stands. It is remarkable for its ability to withstand protracted periods of extreme drought, and for its subsequent rapid comeback after only slight penetration of the soil by rain. Its glutinous, strong scented foliage gives a characteristic color to much of the desert landscape. When wet the leaves fill the air with a pleasant, memory-provoking odor; no other scent is more reminiscent of the desert.[4]

The burro bush, sometimes known as the bur sage, is, next to the creosote bush, the most widespread species of the Sonoran Desert. Its low moisture requirements allow it to share in the occupation of the huge desert reaches where the rainfall does not exceed 4 or 5 inches. Its hardiness and drought resistance allow it to form a low stand over the most unfavorable desert soils and to meet increased competition, growing denser and taller where moisture conditions permit. Nevertheless, on the arid intermontane plains and bajadas that make up the major portion of the Lower Colorado Valley Desert the stands of *Larrea* or *Larrea-Franseria* are open, uniform, and free of infrequent associates.[5] Pure stands of these plants almost always indicate extremely low rainfall as well as fine and compact soils.

An increased size of the dominants may mark the margins of small streamways. This mirrors the improved moisture conditions along the edges of these intermittent desert streams. An introduction of new species including small trees is to be expected along the larger desert arroyos where there is considerable sub-irrigation. Not only the size of the drainageways but also their distribution is significant to the vegetation – a dendritic pattern results in a very uneven spread of large species along the banks of dry streams, which contrasts greatly with the sparse vegetation of the plain.

Where the drainage is reticulate the plants of higher water requirements do not form continuous borders along the streamways but are spread more uniformly over what appears to be a plains or bajada

---

3   *Ibid.*, p. 41.

4   E. C. Jaeger, *The North American Deserts* (Stanford, Calif., 1957), p. 74.

5   Dice, "The Sonoran Biotic Province," *Ecology*, Vol. 20, p. 121, holds that the *Larrea-Franseria* association is the vegetation climax in the western (Lower Colorado) desert.

— CHARLES H. LOWE

On the arid intermontane plains and bajadas of the Lower Colorado Valley, pure stands of creosote (above), burro bush (below) or combinations of these two mirror the extreme aridity and unfavorable soils of the region. In the lower picture, the dark clumps on the horizon are western honey mesquite — an indication of an ephemeral desert stream.

— CHARLES H. LOWE

community. On closer examination, however, one finds that their location and size are dependent on the location and size of the less conspicuous reticulate drainageways, and one may be surprised to find that the rainfall is the same as it is in a nearby district which supports a low and open stand of creosote bush.

The trees which are commonly found along the larger streamways are the mesquite *(Prosopis juliflora)*, blue palo verde *(Cercidium floridum)*, ironwood *(Olneya tesota)*, and the beautiful smoke tree *(Dalea spinosa)*. The latter is almost wholly confined to the bottoms of sandy washes where water is most easily obtainable.[6] Nature has almost completely dispensed with the smoke tree's leaves, and encouraged the growth of masses of thorns which take their place as food synthesizers. Along the smaller streamways these trees may occur only as shrubs or may be entirely absent.

Away from the streamways of these arid western deserts Shreve has noted that "on ascending a bajada a gradual change in the vegetation is observable, the stands of plants become thicker, the stature greater, the number of trees and large cacti increases, and new species make their appearance."[7]

These improvements in the vegetation indicate greater subterranean moisture as well as better root anchorage in the coarser soils, ascending a typical desert bajada. The almost pure stands of *Larrea-Franseria* begin to be occasionally interspersed with new species. Ironwood and palo verde *(Cercidium floridum, C. microphyllum)* are present though the smoke tree is absent. Mesquite and the giant saguaro *(Cereus giganteus)* begin to occupy the uplands, particularly east of the Colorado River.[8]

Ocotillo and catclaw *(Acacia greggii)* are frequently found on the better-drained upper bajadas on either side of the river. Cacti may also become a prominent part of the desert scene. As the optimum soil moisture conditions for these species are reached, the creosote and burro bush remain present but go unnoticed in the more spectacular desert vegetation.

Less than one-fifth of the Lower Colorado Valley Desert is occupied by sandy plains and dunes which provide some of the least favored environments for plant growth. The dunes which border the Colorado River and the Gulf of California are in part moving too fast to become

---

[6]   G. Glendinning, "Desert Contrasts Illustrated by the Coachella Valley," *Geographical Review,* Vol. 39 (1949), p. 226.

[7]   Shreve, *Vegetation of the Sonoran Desert,* p. 53.

[8]   *Cereus* never descends along the streamways of the lower bajadas and is only found in a few isolated stands to the west of the Colorado River near Parker.

— CHUCK ABBOTT

These palm trees in Palm Canyon of the Kofa Mountains, southwestern Arizona, are the only palms native to the state. Sheltered mountain canyons provide the habitat for a number of isolated palm-tree groves both in the United States and Mexico. Here massive andesite forms almost vertical mountain walls.

stabilized by plants. When stabilization occurs it is due largely to the coarse bunch grass known as big galleta (*Hilaria rigida*). Moving dunes may also support a large shrubby wild buckwheat (*Eriogonum deserticola*) which on occasion attains a height of five feet on this unstable footing. Creosote bush or burro bush may take root and tenuously survive in the dunes, as will a few other species of especially adapted plants, but for the most part the more rapidly moving dunes are devoid of plants.

In the regions west and southwest of Ajo, lava flows — which include the great Pinacate lava fields, and the large lava fields near Sentinel — account for a large proportion of the desert's surface. The vegetation of these areas varies. At the base of volcanic hills it is usually denser than it is on the higher slopes. Where there are thick beds of lava and deep soil the better water supply encourages an increased growth of plants. Over large areas there is virtually no soil and consequently very few plants.

The more weathered volcanic hills and mountains of the lower Colorado Valley usually have a very poor soil and lie within the desert's driest reaches, both of which discourage plant growth. The only important additions to vegetation made by these low mountains to the dominant *Larrea-Franseria* association of the plains are brittle bush (*Encelia farinosa*) and the ocotillo (*Fouquieria splendens*).

In general, granitic mountains have a heavier plant cover than those composed of volcanic material. Cacti may be very abundant on slopes of southern aspect. Palo verde, ironwood, ocotillo, saguaro, and the brittle bush are often numerous on the slopes of granitic mountains.[9] The torote or elephant tree (*Bursera microphylla*) with its leafy bark and frequently leafless stem is a conspicuous member of this desert plant community.

ARIZONA UPLAND DESERT

In contrast to the Lower Colorado Desert to the west, the Arizona Upland Desert can most easily be characterized by an increased rainfall and a more rugged relief. These factors help to explain the wealth and diversity of vegetation which give this desert region its unique stamp.

Taking relief first, it has been estimated that well over half of the total surface area is composed of mountains, rolling mountain pediments, and even sloping upper bajadas. The coarser soils which have developed on these landforms best support the distinctive larger forms such as the

---

[9]   Bryan, *The Papago Country*, pp. 42-44.

In the Arizona Upland Desert, more rugged relief and increased rainfall support the distinctive larger forms, such as the palo verde and the saguaro. Teddy bear cholla, ocotillo, and brittle bush are important species in a palo verde-saguaro community. Together with innumerable varieties of cacti, these trees and shrubs form a truly arborescent desert over wide expanses.

massive saguaro cactus and the omnipresent palo verde. Large trees and tree-like cacti are able to take root in any porous and well-drained soil. Consequently, the vegetation may vary little from the fine soils of the upper bajadas to the stony tops of the small ragged mountains that dominate the landscape.

However, on the poorly drained clay and clay-loam soils of the lower bajada and salt-impregnated soils of the desert playas, a vegetation similar to that of the western deserts ekes out an existence. Greater variation in landforms, aspect, soil, and drainage within the Arizona Upland results in a varied plant cover which is unequalled in the Lower Colorado Desert where there is a dearth of upland soil types.

Of at least equal importance to plant growth is the increased rainfall which is, of course, in part due to the general higher elevations and more massive mountain ranges that intercept the rain-bearing air masses which pass unimpeded over the low-lying plains, deltas, and miniature mountains to the west and southwest. Only at the lower ends of the valleys of the Bill Williams, Gila, Sonoita, and Magdalena rivers does the annual rainfall total approach the 8-inch figure that is seldom exceeded in the Lower Colorado Desert. It is in these valleys that the vegetation "more closely approaches that of the Colorado Valley Desert."[10] Except in the extreme south, the rainfall has a decided biseasonal winter-summer maximum that encourages the growth of a large assortment of grasses and small annuals of every description.

Desert vegetation can be expected up to about 3,000 feet elevation on the mountain ranges to the north and east which rise above desert conditions. Twelve to 15 inches annual rainfall generally coincides with this elevation and gives an approximate boundary between true desert and semiarid vegetation.

Within the Arizona Upland the large shrubs and trees combine with an amazing display of cacti to form a truly arborescent desert over wide expanses. Whereas in the Lower Colorado Desert only the most favored situations along the well-watered arroyos and sheltered mountain slopes[11] support a scattered growth of palo verde, ironwood, and ocotillo, the upland deserts of southern Arizona and northern Sonora are densely mantled by large members of these species and many others as well.

As in the west, the ground-hugging creosote bush is dominant over

---

[10]   Shreve, *Vegetation of the Sonoran Desert*, p. 42.

[11]   D. T. MacDougal, "North American Deserts," *The Geographical Journal*, Vol. 39 (1912), p. 116, refers to the mountains of the Lower Colorado Desert as being "biological islands."

Prickly pear and mesquite (left and center foreground), desert hackberry (behind prickly pear), foothill and blue palo verde, brittle bush, catclaw, and saguaro grow on this bajada. There are marked differences between the vegetation of the bajada and that of the mountainside depicted in the preceding picture.

large reaches of low-elevation desert with very fine soil, or on arid sandy outwashes. It has, however, a much larger number of associates and is seldom found in pure stands but mixed with burro bush, the related Fremont bur sage (*Franseria deltoidea*), and others. In this environment the areas between individuals are usually bare or nearly so.[12]

On the rocky slopes and coarse soils of the desert mountains and upper bajadas where there is sufficient sub-irrigation there grows the little leaf or foothill palo verde (*Cercidium microphyllum*) sometimes called the "tree of the desert" because of its density and wide range. Early in May it bursts into flower, giving the entire desert a light yellow cast. Its lowland relation, the blue palo verde (*Cercidium floridum*) gives an even more violent yellow hue to the arroyos and canyons.[13]

The upper bajadas and mountain slopes also support a variety of large desert shrubs and small trees. The velvet mesquite (*Prosopis juliflora*) is widespread, being stunted and shrub-like when its far-reaching roots are unable to find water. Where there is abundant subterranean water these trees attain a considerable size, often exceeding 30 feet in height, and grow in dense stands.[14] This, however, generally occurs only in the bottomlands. The mesquite has suffered grievous harm from man's depredations resulting from the many uses that the excellent wood may be put to, and the recent lowering of the water table. The dense mesquite forests of a century ago are only a memory.

Ocotillo is a common constituent of the aborescent desert where its flaming red flowers punctuate the pastels of a desert spring. On occasion the spidery stems of this plant attain a height in excess of 20 feet and form surprisingly pure stands.

The Fremont thornbush (*Lycium andersonii*) and the thorny crucillo (*Condalia spathulata*) are two of the many head-high species that fill the gaps between the larger forms. Ironwood is present in the upland desert but occurs less frequently than in the western deserts.

Far less numerous than all the above species is the giant saguaro which nevertheless, because of its height and surprising appearance, dominates its lilliputian neighbors. The saguaro is one of nature's most highly developed answers to an arid environment. The prodigious water storage capacity, tough green skin, and sharp spines, were developed to meet the special conditions imposed by the hot, arid climate in a manner unequalled by many desert plants. After soaking rains the roots may draw up more than a ton of water, which is absorbed in the sponge-

---

[12]   *Ibid.*, p. 117.

[13]   Shreve, "Establishment and Behavior of the Palo Verde," *Plant World,* Vol. 14 (1911).

[14]   Bryan, *The Papago Country,* pp. 41-42.

Variety in an arborescent desert is exemplified by these photos, both taken in the Arizona sector of the Sonoran Desert. The picture above, photographed near Tucson, is dominated by palo verde trees in bloom. Below, tree-tall yucca equally dominate a scene in Mohave County north of Parker.

like pulp of the stem. The accordion pleats of the stem swell, only to contract during long periods of drought. Its flowers are white, and its fruit red and very edible. This is the largest cactus found north of the international border — exceeding 50 feet on occasion.[15]

Among the most common cacti are the staghorn cactus (*Opuntia versicolor*) whose slender branches reach 12 feet in height. The cactus is well named, its slender branches resembling the antlers of a deer. Entirely different in appearance is the prickly pear (*Opuntia engelmannii*) whose flat spaniel-ear stems seldom exceed 6 feet in height, and clump together forming impenetrable thickets sometimes 30 feet across.

Of the common desert cacti, among the most interesting, as well as potentially uncomfortable, are the cholla (various *Opuntia*). These beautiful cacti grow to a height of eight feet and have joints covered with dense, needle-sharp spines hanging in chain-like clusters.[16]

Less frequently encountered is the barrel or biznaga cactus (*Ferocactus wislizeni*) which is stoutly columnar in shape and may reach 6 feet in height. The organ pipe cactus (*Cereus thurberi*) whose lithe stems sometimes attain a height of 20 feet, may be found on the warm southwestern slopes in the uplands extending south from Ajo into Sonora.[17] Also found on the rocky southern slopes is the far-from-cuddly teddy bear cholla (*Opuntia bigelovii*) whose densely interlaced spines are to be avoided with extreme care.[18] The various chollas, which propagate by budding, form particularly dense "colonies" when they have been disturbed by cattle or wild life.

There are many other factors that may take precedence locally over elevation and rainfall in determining the composition of the vegetation in marginal districts with elevations ranging between 2,000 and 3,500 feet, and rainfall between 10 and 20 inches. Along the mountainward edge of the Arizona Upland Desert these areas were more often than not supporting a mixed vegetation of desert shrub, cacti, and grasses. Because of heavy grazing, many of the grasses have been thinned out or entirely eliminated. Cacti and desert shrubs such as the creosote bush and mesquite have invaded this transitional zone, and due to their ability to compete with the grasses for moisture, have further depleted the grasses.[19] This has changed the aspect of these semiarid lands from

[15]   D. T. MacDougal, "The Saguaro or Tree Cactus," *Journal of the New York Botanical Garden,* Vol. 6 (1905), pp. 129-33.

[16]   Lyman D. Benson, *The Cacti of Arizona* (Tucson, 1950), pp. 15-16.

[17]   Referred to as the *pitahaya* in Mexico.

[18]   Benson, p. 14.

[19]   R. R. Humphrey, *The Desert Grassland,* Ariz. Exper. Sta. Bull. No. 299 (1958), pp. 31-37.

A photo taken east of Tucson pictures the Arizona Upland Desert at its luxuriant climax. Standing before the Santa Catalina Mountains are the saguaro. In the foreground are the staghorn and jumping cholla as well as the barrel or bisnaga cactus.

one of grassland and scattered desert shrubs to one of typical desert shrub with only a scattered stand of grass, usually the least palatable varieties, such as big galleta (*Hilaria rigida*). The net result has been an extension of desert vegetation outward into regions with higher elevations and rainfall. Wherever the original grass was most heavily grazed this change has been the greatest.

An interesting phenomenon of common occurrence along these desert margins alters locally any simple correlations to be drawn between elevation, rainfall, and vegetational types. Steep south-facing slopes overlooking bajadas with marginal xeric woodland vegetation may themselves be clothed with desert vegetation. This generally indicates a marked nocturnal temperature inversion, altering the expected sequence of desert plants on mountain slopes and in adjacent valleys. This is one of the factors that results in making the desert mountain one of the most favored of the Arizona Upland habitats.[20]

In the central part of the Upland Desert between the Salt River and the Altar River the soils of the intermontane plains are typically those of the upper bajadas, being coarse in texture and derived from the rocks of the adjacent mountains. This results in a more varied desert vegetation where larger forms are important members of the plant community. Likewise, south of Santa Ana the lower bajadas differ from those farther north in the greater number of mesquite and palo verde interspersed with the prevailing *Larrea*.

The intermittently flowing desert streamways of this region provide an especially favorable environment for the growth of large trees such as blue palo verde, ironwood, and mesquite, which form a sharp contrast with the low and very open stands of creosote bush nearby.

GULF COAST DESERT

Extending in a narrow strip along the central gulf coast of the state of Sonora from the sand-choked deltaic plain of the Río Magdalena southwards to the wide alluvial delta of the Río Yaqui, with its dense stands of carrizo, is the driest of all the vegetational subdivisions, the Gulf Coast Desert.

As defined by Shreve it seldom exceeds twenty miles in width before increasing rainfall to the east brings about a gradual change to vegetation more typical of the Plains of Sonora. The rainfall is between 2 and 9 inches and is of summer regime, restricting the growth of many winter

---

[20]   Shreve, *Vegetation of the Sonoran Desert*, p. 68.

ephemerals common to the Colorado Desert. However, both winter and summer rainfall is sporadic, and several seasons in succession may pass without any measurable quantity. This places a severe restriction on the number and size of perennials represented. Many of the plains have deep fertile soils, and plant growth is limited only by the scant water supply. The banks of washes have more favorable edaphic conditions and carry the densest vegetation, forming a sharp contrast with that of the surroundings.

Desert ironwood, blue palo verde, ocotillo, and the deep-rooted honey-bean mesquite (*Prosopis juliflora*) are dominant, taking the place of the *Larrea-Franseria* association on the sandy plains and dunes to the north.

The most striking single species is the *cirio* (*Idria columnaris*) whose gaunt profile may be seen in limited numbers just south of Puerto Libertad. This is the only occurrence of *cirio* outside of Baja California. The giant *cardón* (*Pachycereus pringlei*), largest of all desert cacti, is represented locally on this coast, being more common to the peninsula. Individual specimens may attain a height of 50 feet or more. *Cirio* and *cardón* are the two most distinctive species, and link this region botanically with the deserts of Baja California. Most common of the smaller cacti represented are the cholla. The very arid and rugged offshore island of Tiburón has much the same vegetation as the mainland.

South of the Estrecho de Infierno which separates Tiburón from the mainland, are isolated hills that give way to the low featureless *llanos* (plains) of the deltas of the Ríos Bacovachi and Sonora. On the looser mixed soil of the hills and where soil-water conditions of the plains are adequate, a magnificent vegetation occurs. The dominant species are desert ironwood, copal (*Bursera microphylla*), blue palo verde, and creosote bush. The entire landscape is punctuated by the gigantic *cardón*.

PLAINS OF SONORA

On the long, gently-sloping bajadas reaching down from the jagged desert mountain ranges to the parched arroyos and playas of Central Sonora, is a desert region known as the Plains of Sonora. Wedged between the flat deltaic coastal desert and the rugged uplands to the east, this desert is related to, yet distinct from, the neighboring deserts to the north.

Mountains, though conspicuous on the horizon at all times, are small and relatively few. Elevations are almost entirely under 2,500 feet and range down to less than 500 feet.

The plains are made up of gently sloping outwashes from the

— CHUCK ABBOTT

Three close relatives dominate the desert between the border and the thorn forest transition far to the south. The senita *and organ pipe cactus (left) find an attractive environment along the border near the oasis of Sonoita. These large succulents reach their northern limit in the Organ Pipe Cactus National Monument. To the south of the border they achieve larger size. The photo below shows the giant* cardón *growing on the coastal plain within sight of Empalme. As large as oaks, some of these tree cacti provide roosting places for buzzards.*

— ORME LEWIS, JR.

mountain pediments and compose by far the largest area of the desert. The surface of the upper bajadas is a coarse, gravelly outwash that becomes progressively finer toward the center of the intermontane plain. There are no recent lava flows and true desert playas are insignificant except perhaps on the borders of the Coast Desert.

Rainfall ranges from 7 to 12 inches annually and is of summer incidence, sporadic, and often lacking entirely for many seasons in succession. Vegetation must be as drought resistant as that of the Lower Colorado Valley, while at the same time able to withstand greater desiccating heat during the long periods of drought. The diminished winter rainfall is particularly limiting to winter ephemerals.

There are, however, compensating factors. Frosts are fewer and less severe, summer rainfall is higher, and temperatures are slightly less than those of the Lower Colorado deserts. The onset of the summer rains which the Mexican *peon* "knows" will begin on St. John's Day, the twenty-fourth of June, brings about a most wondrous change not equalled in the north. Within a few short days the distant mountains change color from grey-brown and purple-brown to light green.

The physiographic, climatic, and vegetation features mentioned above constitute the criteria for creating a separate desert subdivision for these arid plains.[21] This desert is the southern termination of the very arid type of basin-range desert that extends far to the north outside the Sonoran Desert. Here are also found the first botanical features which characterize the semiarid littoral stretching far to the south.

Throughout the region the vegetation is very open, allowing magnificent vistas. The trees are small and interspersed with irregular stands of columnar cacti. Among the latter the organ pipe (*Lemaireocereus thurberi*) and the *senita* or old man cactus (*Lophocereus shottii*), so called because of the long bristles at the upper end of the older stems, are conspicuous.

Palo verde, honey-bean mesquite, and ironwood are the dominant trees. They reach their maximum size and abundance within the plains subdivision. The resinous-stemmed shrub *incienso* or brittle bush (*Encelia farinosa*), which is confined to rocky slopes farther north, is ubiquitous and attains a large size.

The creosote bush seldom occurs in pure stands and the burro bush not at all. Also conspicuous by its absence or reduced numbers is the saguaro which is replaced in the south by the giant *Pachycereus pecten-aboriginum*. Colonies of *Opuntia* are relatively infrequent, but dense. A spotty grass cover develops in favored situations. In general

---

[21]   Shreve, *Vegetation of the Sonoran Desert,* p. 72.

The Gulf Coast Desert near Puerto Libertad. In rocky situations like this, the vegetation of this region reaches its maximum development, often rivaling in its variety the Arizona Upland Desert. In the foreground, ocotillo, brittle bush, Jatropha, *white bursage, jojoba, and a young* cardón *are to be seen, while the background is dominated by boojum trees. These weird trees grow only within ten miles of here and in Baja California.*

the important, easily recognizable features of the desert — low stature, open spacing, and diversity of life forms — are still prevalent but are beginning to wane. The gradual enrichment of the plant communities by arborescent introductions from the thorn forest brings about a strong contrast between the north and south.

North of Carbo the vegetation is much the same as that of the deserts to the north. Colonies of creosote bush are interspersed in very open "forests" of palo verde, ironwood, mesquite, and ocotillo on the gravelly-to-deep clay loam soils of the plains.

On the volcanic hills, palo verde and ironwood are dominant in association with organ pipe cactus, saguaro, and *crucillo* (*Condalia spathulata*) among many others in dense stands. The limestone hills, on the other hand, are relatively barren of large trees, lacking both the palo verde and ironwood.

Between Carbo and Hermosillo the amount and annual distribution of rainfall is much the same as it is to the north, while the soils are generally finer, there being a larger proportion of low-lying plains. After the summer rains, grasses cover much of these plains, forming low-lying summer pastures. Shrubbery and small trees increase in density but not in stature, while one sees but few of the familiar cacti of the Arizona deserts.

South of Hermosillo the amount of summer rain increases gradually and the terrain is more broken. Both of these features are more marked to the east than they are on the arid plain of San Juan Bautista along the coast. This accounts for a heavier vegetation to the southeast where the flora is enriched by thorn-forest species and is the recipient of the improved moisture and soil conditions. Creosote bush is less often seen to the southeast of Hermosillo; its place is taken by several important trees. First among these is the *jito* (*Forchammeria watsoni*), a hardy, densely-leafed tree with light and spongy wood. The white-barked tree morning glory or *palo santo* (*Ipomea arborescens*) is completely leafless during the dry season and breaks into majestic flower after the first summer rains.

The aptly-named palo blanco *(Acacia willardiana)* extends its virtually leafless white branches from rocky hillsides where it grows in association with cactus colonies. In this area more than any other the advent of the first summer rains completely changes the delicate greys and buffs of the dry season to a mosaic of violent yellows, greens, and reds.

FOOTHILLS OF SONORA

The low but rugged mountains, lava flows, and narrow valleys of the middle courses of the Sonora, Matape, and Yaqui main streams and tributaries of the rivers are designated by Shreve as a vegetational subdivision "distinctly desert in character," having a plant cover which is "heavier and more continuous than . . . the other sub-divisions of the Sonoran Desert."[22] This rich desert flora ultimately owes its existence to a rainfall which is greater than any of the other desert regions. It ranges in amount from 10 inches in the Bacatete near Guaymas to over 20 inches locally southwest of Sahuaripa.

At the north of the region in the Arizpe, Ures, and Moctezuma districts, the rainfall has a decided summer incidence, which increases toward the south with the area immediately to the north of the Yaqui delta receiving in three summer months about 75 percent of its annual total.[23] Since the rainfall over the year is much the same in the north as it is in the south, the winter half-year droughts are more severe in the Southern Foothills region, thus imposing a limitation on vegetation.

In comparing the vegetation of the subdivision as a whole with the very similar Arizona Upland Desert, Shreve comments that in spite of the heavy summer rainfall the area is subjected to long periods of drought, and these are "accentuated in their effects on the vegetation by the fact that the warm season is longer in the Foothills (i.e. the south) and that the drought periods are accompanied by slightly higher temperatures."[24]

At the northern limit of the Foothills, desert vegetation is confined to the narrow valley floors and the warm south slopes above them. However, descending the long pediments it becomes apparent that on the rocky slopes the stands of trees and shrubs are heavier than on all but the most propitious situations in the deserts to the north. The deeply incised and precipitous cuestas[25] as well as the coarse outwashes are heavily clothed with sizeable trees and shrubs. The densest stands are along the margin of the arroyos. Mesquite, various acacias, and organ pipe cacti are common. Here flourishes the interesting tree-like *jatropha* (*Jatropha cordata*) with its yellowish shedding bark and rubbery branches. This is found in association with the delicate green-stemmed Sonoran palo verde (*Cercidium sonorae*). The entire landscape is punctuated by the skyrocket-like tall ocotillo (*Fouquieria macdougalii*).

---

[22] *Ibid.*, p. 78.

[23] México, Secretaría de Recursos Hidráulicos, *Datos de la Región Noroeste,* Boletín No. 10 (México, D.F., 1952), pp. 108-22. Hereafter cited as *Datos de la Región Noroeste.*

[24] Shreve, *Vegetation of the Sonoran Desert,* p. 44. Climatic records indicate for example that April temperatures in the Yaqui Valley are 5 or 6 degrees warmer than for stations in the Gila Valley.

[25] In English "cuesta" has come to mean escarpment, in Spanish it has a looser significance, i.e., a steep slope.

Ironwood and various bursera are important members of these desert "forests." Here in the most favorable situations the guaycan tree (*Guaiacum coulteri*), a large shrub with crooked branches, fragrant blue or violet flowers, and durable wood, also occurs. These species are very much sought after for their wood, which burns with a hot flame, and consequently the stands are depleted near settlements. The very large flowering tree cactus (*Pachycereus pecten-aboriginum*) is widely scattered among the new trees of the southern range which are now becoming more common.

Desert palms, which may grow to a height of 60 feet, are first encountered in the southern foothills north of the Yaqui delta and south of Tecoripa where so many southern plants reach their northern limits.[26] Where the valleys widen out and emerge from the foothills, dense thorn forests line the streams and better-watered margins, but terminate sharply at a distance from the streamways where the drier valley soils are clothed by desert vegetation. Sometimes this desert vegetation takes on the appearance of islands where plants grow in close proximity only to be separated by barren ground.

THORN FOREST TRANSITION

Proceeding south along the coast of the Gulf of California from the mouth of the Colorado River to the mouth of the Culiacán River, there is a gradual change from sandy desert with a very low and open plant cover to an arborescent desert and finally to an open thorn forest as the rainfall increases from 3 inches or less to 15 inches or more annually. Botanists have often drawn lines somewhere between the Yaqui and Mayo rivers to denote the transition between the arborescent desert and the sub-humid forests to the south.[27]

Should the trip again be made from the Colorado to the Culiacán River, not along the coast, but instead on a line fifty miles inland, the change is much more rapid, the vegetation becoming a "thick jungle" before reaching Navojoa.[28] This is the direct result of a rainfall distribution that increases toward the south but at a more rapid rate inland than on the coast. The gradual change from mid-latitude desert to low latitude semiarid conditions (dry forest) is greatly influenced by the orographic features of the western Sierra Madre. On the outer coastal

---

[26] Shreve, *Vegetation of the Sonoran Desert*, p. 97.

[27] Jaeger, pp. 56-69; H. S. Gentry, *Rio Mayo Plants*, Carnegie Institute Pub. No. 527 (Washington, D.C., 1942); and Dice, "The Sonoran Biotic Province," *Ecology*, Vol. 20, p. 122.

[28] Jaeger, p. 59.

— E. TAD NICHOLS

The desert in Mexico displays a much more tropical appearance. The picture above was taken east of Rayón on the road to Ures in the state of Sonora. It is a natural oasis. Two hundred miles to the south, the desert gives way to the thorn forest seen in the photo below taken outside the true desert. The transition is extremely gradual to the south, but much more precipitous to the east.

— DAVID A. HENDERSON

plain south of the Yaqui the change from desert vegetation to thorn forest is gradual in a direction that parallels the coast. Inland the zone of transition is narrow.

Despite this, the landscape of the coastal plain is no longer that of the seemingly endless, low and open arboreal desert to the north. Areas covered by large trees, *mottes* of dense shrubbery, carrizo (*Arundo donax,* a bamboo-like cane), and mangrove swamps occupy a much larger proportion of this transitional subdivision where desert, thorn forest, and littoral vegetation come together. If one were to consider natural vegetation alone, there would be little reason for including much of the coastal plain south of the Yaqui delta within a desert classification. However, rainfall is deficient for the maximum growth of cultivated plants, and much the same agricultural methods must be utilized on the Lower Río Culiacán with 15 inches annual rainfall as have been adopted in the Imperial Valley with less than one-fourth that amount.[29]

South of the Río Mayo there is a general increase in the height and density of plants. This is particularly noticeable along the perennial streams that flow toward the Gulf of California in ever-widening valleys of subirrigated, rich, alluvial soils. On these well-watered river margins mesquite may reach a height of 40 feet or more. The other important trees such as espino (*Acacia cymbispina*), palo verde, *jito,* and ironwood, attain a considerable size not matched outside these valley habitats. Even more striking is the rank growth of secondary plants. The valley floor is covered with a tangle of thorny plants whose barbed members take firm hold of the trespasser's clothing. Nearly every plant in this forest is armed with spines, some of which are mildly poisonous. Many familiar species of cacti are present, and form impenetrable clumps. After the summer rains the trees are decorated not only with deep green leaves and clusters of flowers, but are draped with sinuous vines and creepers. The floor of the thorn forest becomes one immense thicket which can only be traversed with the greatest difficulty and considerable pain.

The same could be said of the banks of the smaller streams and arroyos, but here the deficient groundwater supply restricts these thorny jungles to narrow bands or occasional small *bosques.*[30] In general, the valleys of the rivers south to the Río Culiacán contain dense thorn forests which fit fairly well the above description.

On the gently rolling inter-riverine tracts between the valleys, the

---

29   Shreve, *Vegetation of the Sonoran Desert,* pp. 85-88.
30   A wood or forest.

vegetation is more open but on the average quite different from the arborescent deserts to the north. Along the coast the rainfall does not usually exceed 12 to 15 inches, and the porous, gravelly soils encourage the deep penetration of the rainfall that is not immediately lost to runoff. The soil is consequently too dry to support a rich, carpet-like vegetation, but provides conditions suitable for the growth of trees whose roots are more capable of tapping the deeper supplies of water. These trees are not as high as those of the valleys but are usually the same species. The vegetation is of a stature which merits the term "thorn forest" and not "arborescent desert."

As the river valleys widen out, they finally meet to form a distinctly lower outer coastal plain. These seaward margins have fine soils and receive the least rainfall of this southernmost subdivision. The vegetation is often characterized by very open areas of low shrub divided by alkali flats, intermittent lakes, tidal flats, and lagoons. Old river channels are choked with dense stands of carrizo. Occasionally this low-lying coastal plain is interrupted where the upland mesa soils reach the Gulf. Along the coast there is usually a sandy beach, but this is interrupted by salt lagoons which support a dense growth of cane.

Thus one can see an amazing diversity of desert vegetation which under aboriginal conditions supported with varying success an indigenous population. With the introduction of Old World crops and animals, great changes took place but reliance upon the natural vegetation of this arborescent desert continued. Winter wheat in particular lessened the dependence of desert agriculturists upon gathering as a means of subsistence. Better communications allowed formerly isolated communities to rely upon imports of food stuffs rather than the aboriginal reliance upon the root and seed of native plants.

On the other hand, the introduction of domesticated animals, principally cattle, caused an increased dependence upon Sonoran vegetation. As in the Old World, most animals were left entirely to forage for themselves and rangy Andalusian cattle were admirably suited to this means of subsistence in an arid region. As centuries passed, cattle ranching was extended into areas that formerly supported only a sparse aboriginal population but it is interesting indeed that the extremely hot and arid desert reaches of the Lower Colorado Desert supported vegetation which was suited in the long run neither for an earth-bound aborigine nor for the mounted Spanish, Indian, Mexican, and Anglo-American cowboys that followed. The influence of natural vegetation upon the various forms of economic enterprise continues to this day both as a challenge and a fulfillment.

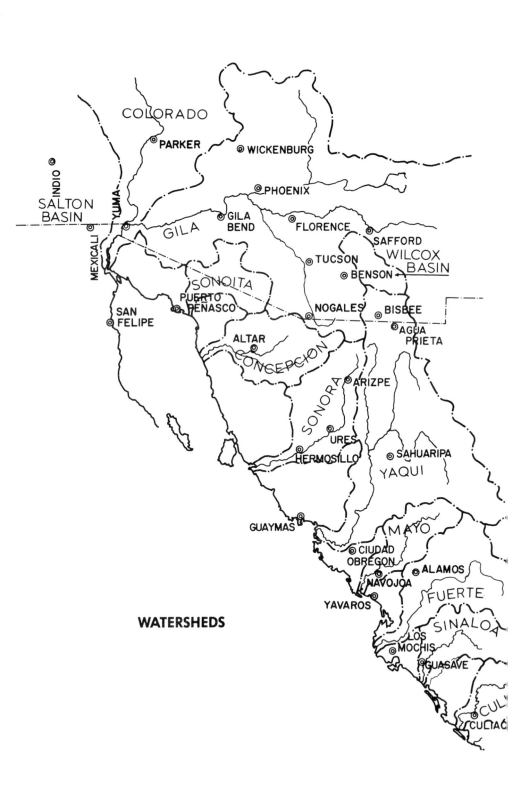

WATERSHEDS

CHAPTER FIVE

Water

All permanent streams of the Sonoran Desert originate outside the desert itself. Under natural conditions these streams disgorged their waters into the Gulf of California, but lost volume mainly through evaporation in their passage of the desert. Under present conditions these rivers do not flow with regularity into the Gulf. Their downstream volumes are not indicative of their former size because diversions now cut off the flow of some rivers entirely over long periods. The desert's permanent streams which under natural conditions flowed throughout the year into the Gulf of California are, in order of size, the Colorado, Fuerte, Culiacán, Yaqui, Sinaloa, and Mayo.[1] The Salt and Gila tributaries of the Colorado were also formerly permanent.

All other major streams which originate on the desert margins are intermittent. These streams flow for only part of the year. The period of flow is fairly definite in its time. The streamways begin to carry water after the first seasonal rains and dry up shortly after they cease. The Santa Cruz, San Pedro, Sonoita, Altar, Magdalena, and Sonora rivers are, among others, intermittent in their regime.

Many of the larger intermittent streams are also interrupted, and

---

[1] Size is measured in total annual streamflow at the hydrometric station recording the largest total prior to any depletion through diversion. Reports of U. S. hydrometric stations are contained in U. S. Bureau of Reclamation, *Reclamation Project Data* (Washington, D.C., 1961), hereafter cited as *Reclamation Project Data,* and in *Compilation of Records of Surface Waters of the United States through September, 1950: Part 9, Colorado River Basin,* U. S. Geol. Survey, Water Supply Paper 1313 (Washington, D.C., 1954) — hereafter cited as *Compilation of Surface Waters, 1950, Part 9.* Reports of Mexican hydrometric station are contained in *Datos de la Región Noroeste.*

as a result have a permanent flow over short stretches during the entire year. Aboriginal people settled along these most favored reaches where water was perennially available. The Santa Cruz above Tucson, the Sonoita near the oasis of the same name, the Altar above Oquitoa, and the Moctezuma above Moctezuma are some of the streamways which carry water throughout the entire year almost every year, but are at the same time dry over much of their length.

The most common type of stream which originates in the desert is ephemeral in nature. Ephemeral streams flow only during or after a rain and as an immediate result of the rain. The largest of them rise on the steep slopes of desert mountain ranges or on the higher alluvial plains. They form continuous drainage channels for distances which may exceed 50 miles. Although they carry water for only short periods of time they are important for they enable livestock to spread out into territory where they are normally unable to graze. As the streamways dry up the stock is moved back into areas of more certain water supply.[2]

The conditions of aggradation which prevail throughout most of the desert valleys allow the water of the ephemeral stream to spread widely over the alluvial plains at the foot of the more steeply sloping bajadas. This in turn allows the primitive agriculturist to utilize the waters of the spreading "sheetflood" by installing a minimum of dams and channels. Deeply incised ephemeral streams are avoided by small-scale irrigators who seek aggrading streamways as a source of runoff.

It may be seen that water which flows both over and under the surface of the Sonoran Desert does in large part originate outside the desert itself. Water, whatever its origin, flows in part to the sea and in part to internal drainage basins where much of it is dissipated into the atmosphere. Hydrologic conditions must be examined with this in mind.

The following hydrographic provinces will be treated in order: (1) Areas of internal drainage; (2) the watersheds of streams that originate within the Sonoran Desert which now or in the past disgorged water into the Gulf of California;[3] and (3) the watersheds of streams

---

[2]   R. R. Humphrey, *Arizona Range Resources,* University of Arizona Agricultural Experiment Station, (1957).

[3]   The valleys of the Sonoran Desert, unlike the Great Basin to the north, drain toward the sea and not toward a large number of independent drainage basins, each with its central playa. The term "basin" is used throughout this work to describe the longitudinal valleys which are divided from each other by desert ranges even if one basin slopes into another, and that into another, so that through a circuitous course water may reach the sea. That much of the desert, from western Arizona to central Sonora, fails to send water to the sea is due to its desiccating climate rather than the existence of independent, centripetal drainage systems.

which originate outside the desert. This third category is further divided into (a) the Upper Basin of the Colorado River; (b) the Central Arizona Highlands north of the Gila River; (c) the Sierra Madre south of the Yaqui; and (d) the Uplands between the Gila and the Yaqui.

AREAS OF INTERNAL DRAINAGE

The only large areas within the desert or its margins exhibiting internal drainage to a central playa are the Salton Sink of southeastern California and the Willcox Basin of southeastern Arizona.[4]

The Salton Sink, which is largely below sea level, is the center of a 10,000-square-mile depression that encompasses the area between the Coast Ranges and the Chocolate Mountains.[5] The latter divides the watershed of the Salton Sink from that of the Colorado River to the east. In the past, this river has drained sometimes into the Salton Sink, at other times — shifting across its delta to the left — disgorging once more into the Gulf. The delta of this river forms a dam across the northern end of the Gulf of California, separating the below-sea-level Salton Depression from the Gulf itself. This deltaic dam rises about 40 feet above the level of the sea. Throughout the areas draining toward the Salton Sea there is, in effect, zero "runoff." This inland sea would not exist without external increments of Colorado River water. Evaporation within the basin so greatly exceeds rainfall that there is no parallel between the Salton Sea and the Great Salt Lake, a representative "balanced" inland sea. Average evaporation is 30 times precipitation in the Salton Basin.[6] It is estimated that if the entire flow of the Colorado River was turned into the Salton Depression, evaporation would stop the rise of the Salton Sea before it could overflow the 40-foot deltaic dam between it and the Gulf. Should the inland lake reach this elevation it would have an area of about 2,200 square miles.

Much smaller in size is the Willcox Basin. Should this region be filled to overflowing, its waters would join the Río Bavispe, an affluent

---

[4] The Willcox Basin and the other upland valleys and mountains of southern Arizona and northern Sonora are not strictly within the climatic or vegetational boundaries of the Sonoran Desert. Nevertheless, their location between the lower elevation deserts and their intimate hydrologic, geologic, transportational, and economic relation with the desert itself will necessitate their repeated inclusion in this work.

[5] Gordon Glendinning, "Desert Contrasts Illustrated by the Coachella Valley," *Geographical Review*, Vol. 39, p. 221.

[6] D. T. MacDougal, "North American Deserts," *The Geographical Journal*, Vol. 39 (1912), p. 110; also "A Decade of the Salton Sea," *Geographical Review*, Vol. 3 (1917), p. 457.

Obviously the playa of the Willcox Basin in southeastern Arizona provides little in the way of pasture for the pictured cow. Throughout the desert, "pastures" such as these support a livestock industry of considerable importance.

of the Río Yaqui. Under present pluvial conditions this is impossible and the Willcox Basin which only intermittently contains water in its playa is definitely an area of internal drainage despite the fact that this basin is often incorrectly shown as part of the Yaqui watershed.

DESERT STREAMS

An account of surface runoff within the Sonoran Desert itself must of necessity be short. The true desert produces little runoff. With rainfall seldom more than 10 inches, and annual evaporation exceeding 10 feet at some stations such as Bartlett Dam, there is little surplus available.[7] It has been observed how water will rush down the smaller desert mountains and bajadas after a sudden shower, but seldom do these scattered streams come together in what could, by the greatest stretch of the imagination, be called a river. A "flood" on one of the streams that originates in the desert usually signifies, in local parlance, that there is some water flowing over the usually dry streamway, an amount of water which elsewhere might be termed a brook or creek.

*   *   *

Within the Sonoran Desert proper under present conditions only one stream, the Bill Williams River, carries any significant quantity of water into the mainstream Colorado. This ephemeral river has an average runoff of only 0.3 inches for its entire watershed (a volume of water 0.30 inches deep over the entire watershed). Most of this is attributable to its headwaters in the Santa Maria Mountains where rainfall exceeds 20 inches annually. The streamflow of the Bill Williams River is extremely erratic and subject to flash floods. During the decade 1931–1940, the annual streamflow varied from 11,800 acre-feet to 307,000 acre-feet.[8]

The Bill Williams, and all other streams flowing directly into the Colorado River from below Hoover Dam, augment that stream by less than an estimated 75,000 acre-feet annually.[9]

Just south of the border the interrupted Río Sonoita runs intermittently beyond the little oasis of the same name. The Sonoita collects water from a series of basins but has never been known to send its floods to the Gulf despite the existence of a gently sloping deltaic plain which at one time undoubtedly carried its water to the sea.[10] This stream

---

[7] H. V. Smith, p. 93.

[8] *Compilation of Surface Waters, 1950, Part 9*, p. 256.

[9] *Ibid.*, pp. 252-62.

[10] R. L. Ives, "The Sonoyta Oasis," *Journal of Geography*, Vol. 49 (1950), p. 2.

comes as close to being a strictly endogenous desert river as any found within the Sonoran. Near the oasis there is almost always water in the river, which is entirely utilized in irrigation except for the occasional flood flowing into the sands between Sonoita and the Gulf.[11]

The Río Concepción formed at the confluence of the Altar and the Magdalena rivers is, in itself, a desert stream while its two major headwater streams drain the region of higher rainfall south of Nogales. The Río Altar yields 0.4 inches over its basin measured at a point quite close to its source.[12] Further downstream the water of the Altar and the Magdalena is either utilized or dissipated before it reaches the Gulf. The Río Concepción is intermittent below Pitiquito and only occasionally does its water reach the coast across the desiccating plains that interpose themselves between this town and the Gulf of California.

South of the Río Concepción delta there are desert streamways to which the name "río" has been attached. These streams pass through such deserted country that little is known about them. Such names as Bacovachi and San Ignacio sometimes appear, and sometimes don't, on maps of the area. They are no more than arroyos whose waters seldom, if ever, flow into the Gulf of California. There are no hydrometric stations on these washes. The same may be said for the Río Matape which rises in the basin and range country near the town of the same name. It has an intermittent flow that provides surface water for a number of communities near its headwaters.

STREAMS THAT ORIGINATE OUTSIDE THE DESERT

The Colorado River

The Upper Basin of the Colorado, although large in area, is semi-arid except in its mountainous eastern margin. Lying in the rain shadow of the Sierra Nevada and dominated by high pressure throughout much of the year, only the highest elevations receive more than 20 inches of rainfall. Most of this is dissipated as the streams from the mountains fan out in broad, braided channels, where the water percolates into the soil or is evaporated. These intermittent streams carry very little runoff in relation to the size of their watersheds. Overall, the Upper Basin yields under natural conditions (at Lee's Ferry, Arizona) no more than

---

[11] *Ibid.,* pp. 1-2.

[12] Santa Teresa Station near Atil. *Datos de la Región Noroeste,* p. 15. This and all the following figures depicting average annual runoff over the entire basins of streams within Mexico are abstracted from data contained in this publication.

The barrier canyons of the middle Colorado River provide a container for the water the Sonoran Desert needs so desperately. The photo above graphically depicts the arid nature of Black Canyon, which holds Lake Mead. For thirty years this reservoir has provided the water-, silt-, and flood-control needed to cultivate the fields of the lower Colorado Valley (below).

3 inches of water over its entire basin,[13] and, under present conditions, it will be shown that less than one inch of this is utilizable. Even under natural conditions the potential water supply of this river is often highly overestimated. The Colorado ranks no higher than twenty-third in annual streamflow among those rivers hydrometrically measured in the United States.[14]

The Colorado River has one of the most irregular streamflows of major North American rivers. With 67 percent of the annual runoff occurring during the period April to July inclusive, the Colorado, in spite of its very large drainage basin, has an extremely marked seasonal runoff.[15] This irregularity of flow is also seen in the nonperiodic variation which takes place in runoff from year to year. The virgin flow (a term used by hydraulic engineers to denote the quantity of streamflow prior to man-made alteration) of the Colorado measured at Lee's Ferry, Arizona, has been as high as 25,255,000 acre-feet in 1909 and as low as 5,501,000 acre-feet in the drought year of 1934.[16] There is a tendency for the years of high streamflow or the years of low streamflow to be grouped. The mean annual flow of this river calculated at 16,270,-000 acre-feet has little significance during any single year.[17] The eccentric rainfall totals registered across the largely arid and semiarid reaches of the Upper Basin watershed are responsible for the violently fluctuating streamflow of the Colorado at the point where it enters the hot desert valley of its Lower Basin.

The total estimated amount of water that would enter the Lower Colorado Basin under natural conditions is diminished by irrigation and other uses in the Upper Basin. The increasing number of acres under irrigation in the Upper Basin, when taken in conjunction with the erratic streamflow of the Colorado, succeed during prolonged dry periods in curtailing drastically the amount of water available to the downstream Colorado. Under all conditions, year after year, millions of acre-feet of potential runoff are utilized in the Upper Basin. In addition, the Colo-

---

[13] The Upper Basin has an area of 102,000 square miles, or approximately 65 million acres, and delivers less than one-quarter of its total rainfall to the Lower Basin in the form of runoff.

[14] Khalaf, p. 65.

[15] U. S. Bureau of Reclamation, *The Colorado River: A Comprehensive Report on the Development of Water Resources of the Colorado River* (Washington, D.C. 1946), p. 161. Hereafter cited as *The Colorado River: A Comprehensive Report.*

[16] *Ibid.,* p. 281.

[17] *Ibid.* Estimates vary on this. California water supply studies support a figure of 15,200,000. All figures are suspect due to the pressure of the Colorado Conflict. Khalaf, pp. 184-85, gives a table of conflicting claims and elsewhere analyzes the actual amount of water available to the Lower Colorado Valley.

rado River Compact has placed an upward legal limit on the total amount of water that the Sonoran Desert may receive in any single year from the Upper Basin through the main channel of the Colorado. Even the reservoirs, so necessary to the regulated distribution downstream of the Colorado's water, remove thousands of acre-feet by exposing huge surfaces to evaporation.[18] As early as 1945 there were eighty reservoirs in the Upper Colorado River Basin having capacities of 100 acre-feet or more. At the time of writing, there are many more than this number of individual reservoirs completed or projected, some of them immense, as well as numerous smaller reservoirs and tanks that add to the man-made evaporation totals.

An interesting facet of man's tampering with nature is the considerable quantity of water lost to the Upper Basin through diversions to neighboring basins. In 1959 more than 523,000 acre-feet of water was lost to the South Platte, Arkansas, Rio Grande, Bonneville, and other watersheds. In Colorado, twenty-two trans-mountain diversions took 412,000 acre-feet of water, while in Utah seven diversions carried 111,000 acre-feet of water into other watersheds. There was also one small diversion in Wyoming.[19]

The construction of Hoover Dam has created in Lake Mead another huge water surface exposed to evaporation. An estimated 650,000 acre-feet of water are lost through evaporation each year from this reservoir alone. The losses from reservoirs between Lake Mead and the international boundary approximate an additional 300,000 acre-feet.[20] All told this is enough water to irrigate approximately 200,000 acres.

Additional water is lost to the desert province through "unusable spill" from Lower Basin reservoirs, evaporation from the surface of the river itself, seepage to adjacent valley lands from which it is subsequently evaporated, water entrapped in sloughs and former river channels during floods and later evaporated, possible seepage to underlying strata, water diverted out of the natural watershed to the metropolitan districts of Los Angeles and San Diego, and unavoidable release into the Gulf of California.[21]

---

[18] *The Colorado River: A Comprehensive Report*, p. 280.

[19] *Surface Water Supply of the United States, 1959, Part 9: Colorado River Basin*, U. S. Geol. Survey, Water Supply Paper 1633 (Washington, D.C., 1961), pp. 314-15 — hereafter cited as *Surface Water Supply, 1959, Part 9;* and "The Colorado," *Ten Rivers in America's Future*, U. S. President's Water Resources Policy Commission (Washington, D.C., 1950), Vol. 2, pp. 444-46 — hereafter cited as *Ten Rivers.*

[20] *Ten Rivers*, II, 439.

[21] *The Colorado River: A Comprehensive Report*, p. 282.

The importance of all this lies in the fact that the total amount of water available to the Sonoran Desert from the Colorado River for "beneficial consumptive use" at the present time has been estimated at only 5,850,000 acre-feet.[22] This is presently diminished by dam filling and the legal protection furnished to upstream irrigation. It may be diminished yet further during any period of extended drought. Nevertheless, the Upper Colorado Basin is the largest single source of surface water used within the Sonoran Desert.

Streams of the Central Arizona Highlands North of the Gila River

In Arizona, Sonora, and Sinaloa along the northern and eastern margin of the desert, precipitation ranges from 10 to 35 inches in the north and from 10 to 55 inches in the south. Although the upper figure occurs only in scattered upland and windward locations, the entire province is an area of perennial water supply and the source of streamflow to the desert itself. Rapid runoff decreases the amount of water lost by evaporation. In addition a very real limit is placed by topography on the utilization of water *in situ*. The broad alluvial plains and mesas of the Upper Colorado River Basin which encourage irrigated farming are not present, and a high percentage of the available quantity of water within this rugged catchment province flows out onto the lowlands immediately to the southwest.

Since this mountainous district receives the highest amounts of rainfall it contributes the largest amount of surface water to the Arizona desert below. This runoff is not uniform, however, and varies widely owing to differences in terrain which directly influence rainfall and temperature.[23]

The Salt River gathers runoff from the more precipitous windward slopes of the Arizona Highlands, and provides a major source of surface water supply for the deserts of central Arizona. The average runoff for the entire Salt River watershed above Roosevelt Dam is 2.8 inches, or an average of 649,670 acre-feet per year. However, this is extremely irregular. During any given year the runoff from the 5,830 square-mile watershed of the Salt River above Roosevelt Dam may be as much as 2,650,000 acre-feet, or as little as 162,000 acre-feet.[24] The seasonal flow is equally irregular, having a marked late winter maximum.

---

22   C. E. Corker, "The Issues in Arizona vs. California: California's View," in *Resources Development: Frontiers for Research,* Franklin S. Pollak, ed. Western Resources Conference, 1959 (Boulder, Colo., 1960), pp. 108-109.
23   Khalaf, pp. 124-28.
24   *Reclamation Project Data,* p. 665.

The midstream Salt River pours water into a series of storage dams above the Phoenix agricultural region. Below the city of Phoenix the Salt is dry, having had all its water distributed — mainly for agricultural purposes.

The streamflow of the Verde River is similar to the Salt, discharging an average of 351,000 acre-feet into the Salt River at their confluence. This flow is only slightly less irregular than that of the Salt, having a maximum runoff of 1,107,000 acre-feet per year and a minimum of 185,000 acre-feet. The catchment basin of the Verde does not contain the higher elevations which are responsible for the higher rainfall and runoff totals registered in the Upper Salt River Valley. This, combined with the fact that the Verde River has a larger watershed than that of the Salt, results in the low 1.4-inch average runoff for the entire Verde River Basin.[25]

The course of the Upper Gila River marks the southern limit of this zone. Its left-bank tributaries, such as the San Pedro River and San Simon Creek, yield a runoff of less than half an inch annually to the Gila, and should not be considered along with the right-bank tributaries discharging much larger quantities of water from the Central Arizona Highlands. Like the Salt and the Verde the streamflow of the Upper Gila is extremely irregular, ranging from over 4.5 million acre-feet to practically no measurable flow.[26] Here along the upland margin of the desert, overgrazing and the destruction of woodland have damaged productive and manageable watersheds. Small perennial upland streams have become rampaging torrents for a few hours or days and dry washes during the remainder of the year. It has been demonstrated conclusively that the arrival of cattle in large numbers was followed by the cutting and trenching of streams, the dissection of bottomlands, and the exaggeration of erratic streamflow. Perennial and intermittent streams have been altered by the white man's economic activities so that today any streamflow at all is termed a "flood."[27]

Taken together, the basin of the Upper Gila and all its tributaries contribute an average of only 0.6 inches annual runoff to the San Carlos Reservoir behind Coolidge Dam. The large, relatively arid southern

---

[25] The drainage area of the Verde River above Bartlett Dam is 6,160 square miles. The total annual runoff for the Verde River Basin is measured at Bartlett Dam. The Verde River Basin in its entirety is considerably larger than this.

[26] *Summary of Records of Surface Waters at Stations on Tributaries in Lower Colorado River Basin, 1888-1938,* U. S. Geological Survey, Water Supply Paper 1049 (Washington, D.C., 1947), pp. 230-38. Hereafter cited as *Summary of Records, 1888-1938.*

[27] James R. Hastings, "Vegetation Changes and Arroyo Cutting in Southeastern Arizona During the Past Century," *Journal of the Arizona Academy of Science,* Vol. 1, No. 2 (1959), pp. 60-67.

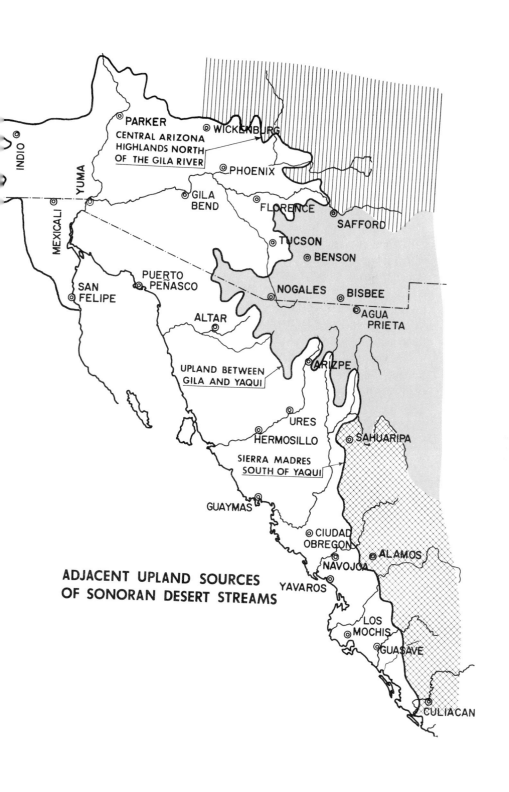

INDIO

PARKER

WICKENBURG

CENTRAL ARIZONA
HIGHLANDS NORTH
OF THE GILA RIVER

YUMA

PHOENIX

GILA
BEND

FLORENCE

SAFFORD

MEXICALI

TUCSON

BENSON

PUERTO
PEÑASCO

NOGALES

BISBEE

SAN
FELIPE

AGUA
PRIETA

ALTAR

UPLAND BETWEEN
GILA AND YAQUI

ARIZPE

URES

HERMOSILLO

SAHUARIPA

SIERRA MADRES
SOUTH OF YAQUI

GUAYMAS

CIUDAD
OBREGON

ALAMOS

NAVOJOA

ADJACENT UPLAND SOURCES
OF SONORAN DESERT STREAMS

YAVAROS

LOS
MOCHIS

GUASAVE

CULIACAN

half of the basin, with its deep sandy subsoil, diminishes the runoff from the Gila's left bank tributaries.[28]

Just below Phoenix, Arizona, the Salt River, which has received the waters of the Verde, combines with the Upper Gila to form the Lower Gila River. The character of this river is so markedly dissimilar to that of its upstream affluents that it is seldom considered as a single stream. The works constructed on its upper tributaries have been responsible in large measure for this bipartite division of the Gila.

Under natural conditions the Lower Gila received the floodwaters of the Verde, Salt, San Pedro, and other rivers which caused it to flow with great seasonal irregularity; nevertheless, it was a permanent stream which flowed in a deep and narrow channel, being navigable by flatboat, at least during some seasons, from the Pima villages to the Colorado.[29] Although little water entered the channel below the Pima villages due to the low rainfall of the western desert, the Gila continued to flow throughout the year to its junction with the Colorado, but with steadily decreasing volume.[30]

Today the Gila River is dry in western Arizona (near its confluence with the Colorado) for long periods. No flow is recorded at downstream stations throughout entire years.[31] "The channel is sandy waste with many winding and braided subsidiaries constantly shifting in position with no low water flow except in favored places."[32]

During historical times the channel has widened and become more shallow through aggradation. Within the last eighty years man has completely altered the regime of the Lower Gila. Flood-control and irrigation projects along its principal headwater tributaries have deprived the downstream Gila of an estimated 1,270,000 acre-feet of discharge which formerly flowed into the Colorado.[33] Today this large sand-choked wash occasionally carries violent runoff from downstream arroyos and water from the very largest floods on the Salt and Verde rivers. The Gila, which at one time disgorged water into that river throughout

---

[28] *Compilation of Surface Waters, 1950, Part 9,* contains the mean annual runoff for the Gila River and its major tributaries in numerous tables.

[29] The Pima Villages were located approximately at the confluence of the Salt and Gila rivers. Edward F. Castetter and Willis H. Bell, *Pima and Papago Indian Agriculture* (Albuquerque, N.M., 1942), p. 13.

[30] *Ibid.,* p. 14.

[31] "Since 1941 not a single drop of its water has reached the Colorado River." Khalaf, p. 32.

[32] Usually underground drainage from nearby land under irrigation. Castetter and Bell, p. 14.

[33] *The Colorado River: A Comprehensive Report,* p. 284.

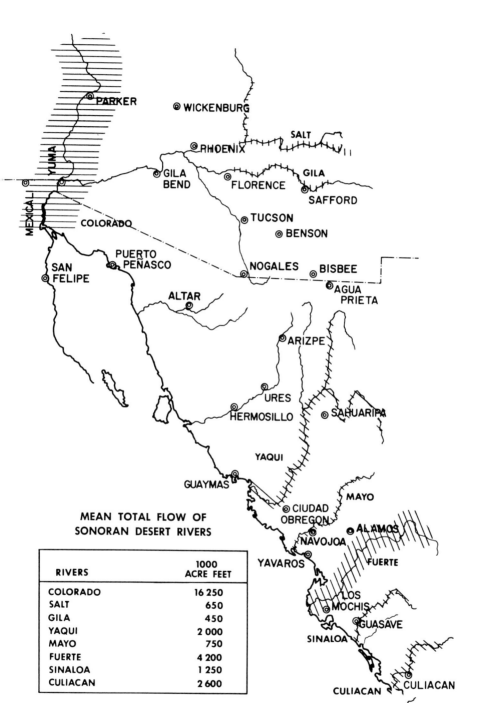

MEAN TOTAL FLOW OF
SONORAN DESERT RIVERS

RIVERS	1000 ACRE FEET
COLORADO	16 250
SALT	650
GILA	450
YAQUI	2 000
MAYO	750
FUERTE	4 200
SINALOA	1 250
CULIACAN	2 600

most of the year, is now no more than the desiccated victim of upstream progress. Even torrential floods on the upstream tributaries would have great difficulty in reaching the Colorado over all the man-made barriers placed across these rivers.[34]

Streams of the Sierra Madre South of the Yaqui

Far to the southeast the Sierra Madre Occidental rises from the coastal desert in rugged confusion to meet the plains of Chihuahua and Durango. It has a much larger areal extent and is the source of even greater average annual runoff per mile than the Mogollon country of Arizona, but its effect on rainfall and runoff is similar and should be considered before the intervening semiarid uplands.

There is a particularly marked increase in rainfall south of the Upper Yaqui River along the boundary between Chihuahua and Sonora. The streams cascading down these slopes that form the precipitous barrancas pass over narrow floodplains where they exist at all. Very little water is able to find its way into the thin alluvial mantle which only intermittently shields the impermeable rock of the Sierra. Thin vegetation fails to hold either water or soil.

Five major rivers flow from this southern highland zone out onto the western desert. These rivers carry a heavy runoff. The largest river, in average annual volume of streamflow, is the Fuerte, followed in order of size by the Culiacán, Yaqui, Sinaloa, and Mayo. Each of these rivers is utilized principally for irrigation on the coastal plain. Their individual regimes are marked by maximum streamflow between the months of July and October. Winter cyclones give an occasional second maximum, usually in January or February.

The Río Fuerte, although it drains a watershed one half the area of the Yaqui, has a streamflow almost as large as the next two of the five rivers combined. The reason for this is found in its mountainous catchment basin where rainfall is seldom less than 20 inches annually. This basin yields 4.9 inches of runoff over its entire area.

A much larger runoff totaling 7.5 inches throughout an average year is found in the basin of the Río Culiacán.[35] However, the Culiacán's watershed is less than seven thousand square miles, which results in the lower total volume of water available for utilization on the plain.

---

[34]   C. P. Ross, *The Lower Gila Region, Arizona: A Geographic, Geologic and Hydrologic Reconnaissance with a Guide to Desert Watering Places*, U. S. Geological Survey, Water Resource Paper 498 (Washington, D.C., 1923). This work contains a complete description of the Lower Gila.

[35]   One of its tributaries, the Tamazula, measured at Picachos yields 11.30 inches over its entire basin.

STREAMFLOW
MONTHLY PERCENTAGE OF TOTAL FOR
SIX MAJOR RIVERS

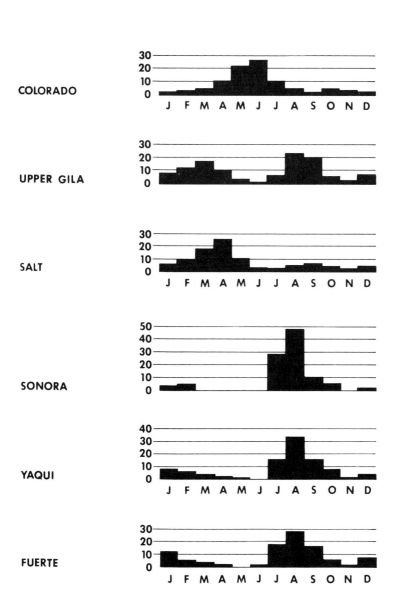

Having a regime quite similar to the Culiacán is the Río Sinaloa which has a runoff on its main stream equalling seven inches over its entire catchment area. Both the Culiacán and the Sinaloa drain the barranca country with its heavy rainfall and impermeable soils.

Between these two rivers is the minuscule Río Mocorito which, though not being one of the five major streams mentioned above, merits comment. Its headwaters have been captured by the tributaries of its larger neighbors both to the north and south, leaving the Mocorito with only a limited area of rolling upland and depriving it of access to the true Sierra with its greater runoff. For this reason the runoff is equal to only 2.5 inches over its entire watershed.

The Río Mayo's streamflow is typical of the rivers originating in the Sierra Madre. With a pronounced late summer maximum runoff, it is nevertheless subject to nonperiodic winter flooding. Its headwaters, reaching into the barrancas of western Chihuahua, were captured by the Río Papigochic, a tributary of the Río Yaqui. Being deprived of a larger, more highly productive watershed, its average runoff amounts to 3.2 inches, exceeding only the Yaqui among these five.

The Río Yaqui resembles the Gila River in reverse, having left-bank tributaries producing large average yields from relatively small drainage basins, while the much larger, but more arid, right-bank watersheds produce little runoff on an areal basis. The Río Papigochic draining the southern portion of the Yaqui's watershed yields an average of 3 inches over its upper basin while the Bavispe takes only 0.9 inches from the broken high plains north of the Yaqui's main stream.

Streams of the Uplands between the Gila and Yaqui Rivers

The Gila and Yaqui form, in effect, the boundaries for a third and middle zone of the Eastern Highlands. This hydrographic region is semiarid, being outside the Sonoran Desert, but is an important contributor of runoff to the desert itself. The middle zone contrasts markedly with the surrounding watersheds of central Arizona and the Sierra Madre both in topography as well as climate. Whereas rainfall in the Mogollon Highlands and the Sierra Madres rarely is less than 20 inches in an average year, the highlands between the Gila and Yaqui rivers seldom receive that quantity. Except in a triangular area between Nogales, Nacozari, and Ures, as well as in isolated mountains, such as the Santa Catalinas, average rainfall is without exception under 20 inches.

This low rainfall results in average runoff figures which universally are less than one inch over the basins which are included within this middle zone. The Willcox Basin is the only area within the Eastern Highlands which has internal drainage, but there are numerous regions

— CHARLES H. LOWE

In eastern Arizona, Aravaipa Creek is lined by broadleaf trees. Behind them in the surrounding Arizona Upland Desert is the typical palo verde-saguaro climax. The large shade trees are limited entirely to areas of perennial subsoil moisture along Aravaipa Creek.

The Río Bavispe near Huasavas, Sonora. This picture taken in April shows a broad stream swollen with runoff from the winter rains. Streams such as this shrink through the following months until the rains of late June and July once again fill an almost-dry streambed.

— MARGARET COHN

that over several years do not produce any surface runoff to downstream channels.

It has been noted that the San Pedro River and San Simon Creek discharge less than half an inch annually into the Gila. The Santa Cruz River is an intermittent stream only very rarely yielding any water to the Gila in spite of its relatively large watershed.[36] Streamflow on this river, as on the other major waterways within the zone, occurs as flash floods following thunderstorms. As floodwaters flow downstream from the mountainous areas, which receive the highest rainfall, the volume of the flood decreases rapidly.[37] Factors contributing to this depletion are infiltration, evaporation, channel storage, and bank stream runoff.

In Mexico, along the northern tributaries of the Yaqui, much the same conditions prevail. In addition to the Río Bavispe, the Río Moctezuma has an intermittent flow discharging less than an average half inch of water into the Yaqui from its entire basin.

The regime of the Río Sonora is characteristic of those rivers draining the middle zone. Its headwaters reach into the above-mentioned triangular area where rainfall exceeds 20 inches per year. However, the Río Sonora, in its middle course, passes through more arid terrain, and by the time the river reaches El Oregano, well within the desert, the loss through such factors as evaporation and percolation is so great that the streamflow amounts to a mere 0.3 inch average over the Sonora River basin. Under natural conditions this stream only occasionally reaches the Gulf of California.

FLOODS

Throughout the marginal Eastern Highlands heavy rainfalls which result in floods have a profound effect on the total amount of water available for irrigation and other uses. Because porous soils and evaporation extract such a toll of water available for ultimate utilization from shallow, slow-moving, dry-season streams, fast-flowing flood torrents contribute disproportionately to dam filling.

The major floods originating in the Central Highlands of Arizona are caused by cyclonic disturbances moving eastward from the Pacific Ocean, usually in winter or early spring. These winter rains are the most

---

36 Bryan, *The Papago Country*, p. 119. D. T. MacDougal, "North American Deserts," *The Geographical Journal*, Vol. 39 (1912), p. 114, comments that flow from the Santa Cruz has reached the Gila only a few times in the memory of living men.

37 McGee, "Sheetflood Erosion," *Bulletin of the Geological Society of America*, Vol. 8, p. 100.

important contributors to runoff because they are widespread and soaking, providing both rain and snow to the Highlands.[38] In contrast, the summer rains are local, covering only a small proportion of any drainage basin, and are subject to higher rates of evaporation.

Of the annual runoff in the Salt River watershed, 68 percent occurs between January and May. The minimum flow occurs in June and early July immediately before the summer rains commence. Thus, dam filling must take place during the winter months.[39]

Large floods have occurred along the Salt River. In February, 1891, a flood cresting at 300,000 cubic feet per second inundated its lower valley. In November, 1905, the Verde River crested with a flow of 96,000 cubic feet per second at its union with the Salt. Occasionally other floods in the Mogollon country occur which would, under natural conditions, inundate much of Phoenix and its satellite cities.

Major flooding has been limited by the construction of dams across the threatening streams, principally the Verde and Salt. However, extremely heavy rainfall in short spans of time has caused water to pour into these rivers in large quantities below the storage dams. The Cave Creek flood control dam, on the tributary of the same name, was built only after floods actually swept through the State Capitol Building in Phoenix, causing extensive damage and long-overdue action by the legislators.[40]

Under the presently controlled conditions, mainstream flooding on the Salt happens only once in ten years or so, and normally there is little damage inasmuch as floodwater is usually confined to the channel of the river. A real threat faces Phoenix if weather conditions happened to bring heavy late winter rains over the upper Salt River watershed at a time when the storage reservoirs are filled to capacity. Water would flow over the dams in tremendous quantities inundating Phoenix and the lower Salt River Valley. (In the winter of 1965-66 and again in December of 1967, exactly this happened, causing extensive damage, although much larger floods than the ones that occurred are within the realm of possibility). The threat of local flooding has been increased by the denudation of native vegetation and more particularly by the construction of roads, housing projects, and airfields, which have obstructed natural drainageways causing water to concentrate in those few which

[38] Jurwitz, "Arizona's Two Season Rainfall Pattern," *Weatherwise,* Vol. 6, pp. 96-99.

[39] Cooperrider and Sykes, pp. 1-10.

[40] Hal R. Moore, "The Salt River Project," *Arizona Highways,* Vol. 37, No. 4, p. 6.

remain. In the larger metropolitan areas loss of life by drowning is reported regularly.

During recent years the rapid expansion of the economy has brought many newcomers to Arizona, many of whom believe that the sandy washes never run with water. Even worse, many don't recognize an arroyo when they see one. Apartments, housing tracts, and trailer parks are inhabited by people who have not the slightest idea that the black clouds hanging over Squaw Peak just north of Phoenix in the summer are capable of washing their homes in low-lying areas off their foundations and into the Salt River.

Within the middle zone of the Eastern Highlands and in the desert below, flood conditions occur less frequently, floods are usually less violent, and — because of a smaller population — cause less damage. Between the Gila and Yaqui rivers the generally lower rainfall is more quickly absorbed by larger intermontane alluvial plains. The overall effect is that even flood torrents resulting from unusually heavy rains lead only an ephemeral existence along the sandy streamways.[41] Under these conditions dam filling becomes an impossibility, and engineers have despaired of building dams. Aside from the dams on the Gila and Yaqui which exist principally to impound water originating in either the Central Highlands of Arizona or the Sierra Madre, only two dams, both in Sonora, have been constructed to hold back water originating within the middle zone of the Highlands. Except on the San Pedro where there has been advance planning for a dam, there is little excuse for their construction south of the mainstream Gila.

The Río Sonora, with a basin 2,000 square miles larger than the Salt, has had a flood crest of 148,000 cubic feet per second,[42] only about one-half the current registered by the greatest recorded flood on the Salt River. Another contrast between rivers north and south of the Gila is the summer maximum flow of the southern rivers. Approximately 90 percent of the average annual runoff of the Río Sonora occurs between July and October,[43] and is due to the summer rains which reverse the seasonal maximum of the Central Arizona Highlands. The result is that flooding along the streamways of northern Sonora takes place usually in the four months beginning in July, and producing, in nine years out of ten, 98 percent of the Río Sonora's total runoff. It is, however, in

---

[41]   Whereas a flood on the Salt River has resulted in a flow of 300,000 c.f.s. from a 6,220-square-mile drainage basin, the Río Bavispe has disgorged no more than 74,000 c.f.s. from a drainage basin of 7,259 square miles.

[42]   This figure is an estimate which may be as much as four times too large. *Datos de la Región Noroeste*, p. 456.

[43]   *Ibid.*, pp. 105-106.

this tenth year that an unusually heavy winter rain may produce a surprising flood tide that might exceed within a few days the total flow of the summer months.[44] Dam filling must nevertheless rely usually upon the more dependable summer runoff.

The regime of the Río Bavispe shows a more balanced seasonal runoff with only a slight summer maximum. This summer runoff is usually incapable of filling La Angostura Dam, largely because of increased evaporation over the Bavispe's large drainage basin. Here in eastern Sonora it is the same occasional cyclonic disturbance bringing heavy rainfall during the winter months which will cause water to flow over the top of La Angostura Dam. In most years the more reliable summer runoff must provide water for downstream utilization.

Along the Río Bavispe, the Sonora, the Salt, and for that matter all the streams which originate in the Eastern Highlands, the months of lowest runoff are May and June. This is one of the few hydrographic constants which remain true throughout the eastern watersheds from north to south.

To the south of the mainstream Yaqui, along the rivers that originate in the higher, more mountainous Sierra Madre, the summer maximum runoff increases quite regularly to flood stage. On the Fuerte, a river whose regime is typical of these southern streams, seldom a summer passes which does not produce a flood with a maximum flow of 400,000 cubic feet per second.[45] It is here more than in the valleys of Sonora that rainfall in the mountains quickly reaches the rivers that flow out on the arid coast. Under natural conditions, this coastal plain is inundated over hundreds of square miles. Although these floods usually occur in midsummer, an occasional, violent cyclonic storm brings about terrifying midwinter floods. The worst of these ever measured hydrometrically took place in January of 1949 when all the rivers south of the Río Sonora, in Sonora and throughout Sinaloa, overflowed their banks.[46] The Río Fuerte flowed with a maximum tide of 370,000 cubic feet per second. The much smaller Río Mayo, whose watershed was deluged with as much as a yard of water in 20 days, crested with a torrent equalling 190,000 cubic feet per second.[47]

This was the greatest flood ever recorded on the Mayo, as well as on the Papigochic. It is a little-realized fact that the greatest floods

---

[44] During five days in January and ten days in February of 1949 runoff on the Río Sonora surpassed the total runoff recorded for the July-October period of the same year. *Ibid.*, p. 105.

[45] *Ibid.*, p. 380.

[46] *Ibid.*, pp. 275-83.

[47] *Ibid.*, pp. 450-54.

The destructive power of floods in normally dry streamways is graphically illustrated in these pictures taken in December following unusually heavy precipitation. *Left above*, the swollen Santa Cruz River has completely cut away U. S. Highway 89 between Tucson and Nogales. Further south *(left below)*, near Imuris, Sonora, the tracks of the mainline railroad have been washed out by a suddenly rushing wash. The normally dry Salt River in flood east of Phoenix *(right above)* spreads out over the floodplain, and, further west *(right center)*, near Litchfield Park, a wash closes a main thoroughfare to all traffic. The perils of attempting such a crossing are amply demonstrated by a buried station wagon which has been washed a good distance downstream.

— TUCSON DAILY CITIZEN

— TUCSON DAILY CITIZEN

— HERB AND DOROTHY MC LAUGHLIN

— ARIZONA REPUBLIC

occurring on these streams which originate in the Sierra Madre and flow out onto the southern Sonoran Desert are quite capable of taking place in the winter during what is generally thought to be the "dry season." All of the rivers and their tributaries from the Yaqui south — to and including the Culiacán — which have had their greatest floods recorded over the years at thirty-five separate stations, show that twenty-two of the highest floods have occurred between November and March, leaving only thirteen all-time record floods taking place during the "rainy season."[48] However, the average annual high-water mark is reached — as it is on all the rivers south of the mainstream Gila — during the four months between July and October.[49]

GROUNDWATER

The distribution of underground sources of water is extremely irregular throughout the Sonoran Desert and its upland margins. Low and unequal rainfall which sinks into the ground either directly or after running for a distance in a stream is the ultimate source of underground supplies of water. Most rainfall which wets the upper levels of the soil evaporates immediately.[50] A large share of that remaining is lost through transpiration from plants; each desert plant helps to reduce the supply of water available to ultimate underground storage.[51] Thus rainfall, the existence of streams, the distribution of natural vegetation, and other factors affect the original distribution of water available to desert aquifers. What little water remains to percolate underground is stored unevenly in the alluvial basins which spread across the desert.

The Basin and Range lowlands provide storage space up to many thousands of feet in thickness across the alluvial plains, but the basin ranges and rock pediments which often occupy one-half or more of the total area of the desert are like the marginal highlands, unable to hold any significant quantity of water. Among the hard rocks, only the volcanics have been found to hold large recoverable supplies of water.

Even the deeply filled and saturated alluvium holds uneven amounts

---

48   *Ibid.*, pp. 420-24.

49   *Ibid.*, pp. 385-87. In 23 of 28 recent years on the Río Culiacán the largest daily maximum flow took place during one of these four months, August having the highest flood on 11, and September on 10 separate occasions. Of the five years with winter maximum floods, three occurred during December, while twice these floods took place in January.

50   Shreve, "Rainfall Run-off and Soil Moisture under Desert Conditions," *Annals of the Association of American Geographers,* Vol. 24, pp. 145-49.

51   Khalaf, p. 79.

of groundwater. Valley fill varies from region to region with regard to porosity. In addition, molecular attraction and other adhesive forces cause the retention of water underground which varies from one aquifer to another.

In general, however, where deep alluvium overlies the impermeable rock floor constituting the bottom of the basin, groundwater may possibly be found in great quantities throughout a saturated zone approaching the surface. Under natural conditions some basins were filled through the centuries to overflowing and groundwater returned to the surface at the lowest elevations after passing very slowly through pore spaces in sand and gravel.[52]

Before the present century the underground water of the Sonoran Desert was in what is termed a dynamic hydrologic balance over large areas. Since that time man, by diverting surface and groundwater from the system, has upset this balance by drawing heavily from underground reserves. Presently, throughout most of the desert, outflow greatly exceeds inflow as man continues to "mine" excessive amounts of water from storage. Today the amount of water annually seeping into the water table, from streams originating in the Highlands, and from desert rainfall, is many times less than that pumped by man.

It must be remembered that the great body of water saturating the alluvium up to the water table was only gradually accumulated over the ages. During some of this time there quite possibly existed humid conditions. Any annual increase in the level of the water table which may result from heavy rains is probably much less than one percent of the total water in underground storage. Conversely, the present depletion of these underground reserves continuing year after year, through periods of drought and relatively heavy rain, depresses the water table to such an extent that natural inflow would fail under present climatic conditions to re-elevate the water table to its former level even if all withdrawals were terminated. For the present at least, groundwater must be looked upon as a body of ore, to be mined until depletion. For this reason alone the distribution of aquifers is of considerable economic importance.

At the present time throughout the Sonoran Desert local groundwater conditions fall into the following categories: (1) Areas where mountains or thin alluvial covering of rock pediments do not allow for underground storage of water. These regions may be fairly well ascertained by reference to a relief map. The desert ranges and their immediate margins yield little or no water. (2) Areas where thick

---

[52] *Ibid.*, p. 75.

alluvium exists but rainfall and surface water are so little that ground-water has not accumulated, at least at economic depths. Much of the Salton Sink, Papaguería, and the coastal deserts of Sonora fall into this group. (3) Areas where thick beds of saturated alluvium exist near the surface at economic depths. The valleys of the Upper Gila and Santa Cruz, the Costa de Hermosillo, and numerous other regions are in this favorable position. (4) Areas where the above conditions formerly existed but heavy pumping has resulted in the rapid decline of water tables that will lead to the ultimate depletion of underground water supplies, the growing salinity of groundwater, or excessive cost in extraction. Large districts in the Salt River, Casa Grande, and Lower Gila valleys are already in this category.

CHAPTER SIX

Social Evolution

In the year of the first Spanish incursion, the Sonoran Desert was inhabited by a large number of scattered tribes. There is good reason to believe that the desert had been continuously occupied for several thousand years prior to the first Spanish entrada. The importance of this lies in the fact that an outwardly inhospitable milieu had for centuries provided a considerable aboriginal population with a livelihood. Indeed, the Hohokam Indians of central and southern Arizona had, by A.D. 800, developed a sophisticated system of controlled irrigation through a series of small diversion dams and canals, thus making possible an agricultural base which supported a large, quite concentrated population. These people, however, had scattered by the time the Spaniards arrived and the canals had largely fallen into disuse.

Even so, the native population of the Sonoran Desert, prior to the introduction of cattle, horses, small grains, tree crops, wheeled vehicles, and firearms, was able to wrest a subsistence from native desert plants and animals while at the same time cultivating a variety of domestic plants. With no method of systematically controlling major streamflow, the aborigines' agriculture was limited to very small plots and subject to the erratic runoff of small washes or distributaries. Either flood or drought constantly plagued the agriculturalist. The deep isolation of desert valleys helped militate against any trade of food between surplus and deficit areas. With regard to food products, each tribe existed most of the time as if it were alone on an arid planet. Too often this isolation was interrupted only by intertribal warfare, although this may not have been a major limitation on the size of population. Undoubtedly it was starvation and disease which provided a grim control on population. From the least civilized nonagricultural people to the most civilized irrigators, mere subsistence was a year-round occupation. Populations perennially pressed hard against the economic base provided by the desert. Activities other than farming, gathering, and hunting were few indeed. The manufacture of pottery, baskets, and farm implements was tied to subsistence agriculture. Other preparations were made for the hunt. At any time all remaining activities had to be dropped in order to obtain food.

THE ABORIGINAL POPULATION

Estimates of the native population at the time of the Spanish entrada range as high as 400,000. Excluding the Tahue (largely outside the Sonoran Desert to the south) and the upland barranca tribes (Fuerte and Mayo rivers), perhaps as many as 300,000 Indians lived in the Sonoran Desert during the early sixteenth century, although an estimate of 200,000 would probably not be far from wrong. This would amount to an average of about two inhabitants per square mile.[1] The great majority of these were concentrated in a few southern river valleys. The Cahita-speaking tribes of the downstream Yaqui, Mayo, Fuerte, Sinaloa, and Ocoroni rivers comprised perhaps 35 percent of the total desert population. Densities in these regions were, by Sonoran Desert standards, considerable, exceeding ten inhabitants per square mile. On the upstream affluents of the Yaqui and Sonora rivers the numerous Opata and Pima Bajo, along with the smaller Jova tribe, constituted a relatively dense occupation of the land. All told, these tribes, located in what is today central and southern Sonora and northern Sinaloa, comprised 60 to 70 percent of the desert's aboriginal population. To the northwest of the Opata lived the Pima Alto, who were largely concentrated in riverine settlements such as those of the Altar, Santa Cruz, and Gila. At that time, these tribes, all of which spoke Uto-Aztecan languages, had seemingly attained the most successful accommodation with their arid environment.

---

1 For extended discussions of the prehistoric populations, see Carl O. Sauer and Donald Brand. *Prehistoric Settlements of Sonora* (Berkeley, 1931), and *Aztatlan: Prehistoric Frontier on the Pacific Coast* (Ibero-Americana: 1, Berkeley, 1931); Sauer's *The Distribution of Aboriginal Tribes and Languages in Northwestern Mexico* (Ibero-Americana: 5, Berkeley, 1934), hereafter cited as *The Distribution of Aboriginal Tribes*, and *The Aboriginal Population of Northwestern Mexico* (Ibero-Americana: 10, Berkeley, 1935); R. L. Beals, *The Comparative Ethnology of Northern Mexico Before 1750* (Ibero-Americana: 2, Berkeley, 1932), and *The Aboriginal Culture of the Cahita Indians* (Ibero-Americana: 19, Berkeley, 1943); A. L. Kroeber, *Uto Aztecan Languages of Mexico* (Ibero-Americana: 8, Berkeley, 1934), and *Cultural and Natural Areas of Native North America* (Berkeley, 1939).

The Economic Bases of the Aboriginal Population
(after Sauer)[2]

I.	Intensive Agriculture with Irrigation	Tahue
II.	Agriculture with Irrigation	Chinipa
		Opata
		Pima Bajo, Ures
		Pima Bajo, Nebome
		Pima Alto, Soba
		Pima Alto, Gila
		Pima Alto, Sobaipuri
III.	Agriculture (inundation)	Cahita
		Jova
		Comanito and Mocorito
		Barranca tribes
		(except Chinipa)
		Other Pima Bajo
IV.	Agriculture (inundation) and Seminomadic Activities	Papago
		Yuma, Cocopa, Chemehueve
V.	Largely Nomadic with some Agriculture	Apache
VI.	Non-Agricultural Fishing and Gathering	Seri
		Guasave

Farther to the north and west lived other tribes usually much smaller in size which spoke languages not belonging to this great linguistic group. The Seri, Yuma, and Cocopa (Yuman), the Chemehueve (Shoshonean), and the Apache (Athabascan) were nomadic or seminomadic in their way of life. Agriculture of any kind played a much smaller part although in every case except the Seri some crops were planted. Gathering and hunting of course occupied a much greater place in their economies. All of these northern and western tribes were seemingly incapable of creating dense settlements in what is largely a less favorable environment. Nevertheless, numerous riverine areas capable of supporting relatively dense populations were not exploited. Thus, cultural differences between the more sedentary tribes and their neighbors to the north and west explain in large measure the widely varying population densities between what eventually became the Mexican and American deserts.

---

2   Sauer, *The Aboriginal Population of Northern Mexico,* pp. 18-35.

THE PAPAGO EXAMPLE

Ranging culturally and geographically across this frontier were the aboriginal Papago. Speaking a Pima Alto dialect (Uto Aztecan), but occupying a particularly desolate terrain, the Papago were in most ways a cultural and economic midway point between the most advanced and least advanced inhabitants of the desert, and for this reason exemplify in many respects aboriginal life in the Sonoran Desert. The following is a description of the economy of a single people, but much of what is outlined applies to other tribes ranging from the barrancas of Sinaloa to the canyons of the Colorado.

The difficulties encountered in an abbreviated analysis of this kind are amply demonstrated by investigations of the aboriginal Papago who did not practice what is normally defined as irrigation. The Papago, because of their extremely limited access to water, were seminomadic, planting and caring for their fields in the rainy season, while wandering about in search of wild products and water during the dry season.[3] In the desert reaches inhabited by the Papago, permanent sources of water in association with tillable land are rare. This situation necessitated a compromise between a sedentary life and a migratory existence which expressed itself in seasonal movement.[4]

This migration was usually between two types of settlements. Those known as the "Wells" were situated at permanent sources of water in the mountains or foothills, and were occupied during the winter months. The other type of village, designated as the "Fields," was in the open desert basin adjacent to the cultivated areas and as much as twenty to thirty miles from the winter settlements. The Papago's seminomadic life was not directed primarily by the needs of hunting or agriculture but was enforced by the necessity to obtain drinking water. Even with the semiannual migration, sources of water were so widely scattered that the women spent more time fetching water than gathering food.

The "Wells" settlements were located as near as possible to the infrequent springs such as those found at about 3,000 feet in the western canyons and foothills of the Baboquivari Mountains. These winter villages of the Papago were usually bordered by a few acres of cultivated land.[5] Here water continued to be elusive and long journeys were neces-

---

3   Castetter and Bell, p. 40.

4   *Ibid.*, pp. 41-42.

5   The largest of these, Fresnel, in 1915 had 35 acres planted to beans, melons, corn, etc. This settlement differed from the 13 remaining wells settlements in that it was partially occupied throughout the year. *Ibid.*, pp. 160-64.

Two Papago scenes photographed in 1894. Above, a Papago family at Quero-babi, Sonora, at their more permanent winter dwelling. Below, a summer brush village at Vamori. (William Dinwiddie, Bureau of American Ethnology, courtesy University of Arizona Library, Special Collections)

sary when wells or springs dried up. When this happened, water was to be had only by grubbing in the sandy streambed of the arroyos, where it was usually encountered in small quantities along a plane of contact between sand and bedrock.[6]

Families did not move down to the "Fields" settlements until the summer rains had begun. To arrive before some water had collected in the man-made "mudtanks" meant hardship. The "fields" were located in the desert valleys where the washes fanned out and the water disappeared into the sandy soil. Here at the arroyo "mouth,"[7] the majority of the Papago families engaged in what has been termed "flash-flood farming" or sometimes "arroyo flood farming." This type of agriculture was characterized by the planting of crops at the base of the alluvial fans which lie at the foot of each arroyo.

The native farmers planted their crop usually six or seven days after the first summer rains had caused a sheetflood to spread out from the mouth of the disgorging streamway. If further runoff was available, the fields might be irrigated a number of times, but the initial irrigation often had to suffice. Dikes and canals were not utilized in flash-flood farming.

At other points floodwaters (runoff) were led from the smaller streamways by low earthen dikes protected in front by brush which was in turn supported by stakes. These dikes were constructed either to hold water or as diversion dams. Under both circumstances, the dike was constructed either directly across a streamway or to one side. If the structure was placed directly across the ephemeral streamway, it had to hold all the water carried by the stream when in flood, or a spillway would have to be provided. In order to avoid this difficult task, the Papago took advantage of the aggrading streamway's tendency to spread out in numerous diverging channels. One or more of these lateral distributaries would be slightly deepened so that a controlled quantity of water could flow through this ditch and eventually into a small reservoir. During large floods no ditch was necessary, for the overflow would spread across the gentle alluvial fan following these distributaries.[8] Once contained by the earthen dike, water was conveyed to the field by short ditches. These fields could expect water no more than three or four times after the capricious summer rains. Low retaining walls, seldom more than a

6   J. W. Hoover, "The Indian Country of Southern Arizona," *Geographical Review*, Vol. 19 (1929), pp. 50-51.

7   The Papago termed the arroyo mouth *akchin* and at least six villages inhabited by these people in southern Arizona or northern Sonora were named Akchin or some modification of it. Bryan, *The Papago Country*, pp. 168-69.

8   Bryan, *The Papago Country*, pp. 144-47. This work contains detailed diagrams illustrating primitive irrigation works utilized in Papaguería.

foot in height, surrounded fields in which water was allowed to stand and seep into the soil.[9]

In September and October the Papago harvested their crops, dried what was not immediately used, and stored it in baskets which could be transported easily. When all the mudtanks dried up, the villagers moved back to the permanent springs or shallow wells in the mountains.

Since cultivated plants seldom provided these people with a subsistence diet, natural vegetation was always exploited to the utmost. "In years when the rainy season was late they lived entirely on wild foods, without planting at all."[10] In contrast, wild products were not neglected in years when rainfall conditions provided an abundant harvest of cultivated crops.

A number of small and medium-size plants were gathered and used as greens. The buds and joints of the unlikely-looking cholla and prickly pear, plants which grow plentifully in Papaguería, constituted a staple crop. Mescal was gathered in the uplands along the present international boundary and was consumed by all Papagos. The shoots of the night-blooming cereus were eaten as greens. The pulp of the barrel cactus — which contains a considerable quantity of water and thus was doubly useful — was also consumed. Roots, tubers, and bulbs were dug and consumed in large quantities by the aboriginal Papago. The sand root, which appears on the floodplains after the rains, was a staple crop.

A great variety of wild fruits, berries, and nuts were gathered. The most important wild fruit crop was that of the giant saguaro cactus which ripens before the onset of the summer rainy season. Special camps were set up on the slopes where this cactus grows.[11] In July and August another migration was made by some of the Papago to the high grass-lands south of Papaguería to harvest acorns. The organ pipe cactus, which finds its northern range within the reservation, also yielded fruit. A number of other fruits were gathered by the Papago, but mainly from the semiarid upland margins of the desert.[12]

---

[9] Castetter and Bell, p. 125. When dikes, ditches, and bolsas were employed the term "arroyo flood irrigation" has been used to describe it. George F. Carter, *Plant Geography and Culture History in the American Southwest* (Viking Fund Publications in Anthropology No. 5, New York, 1945), p. 114.

[10] Edward F. Castetter and Ruth M. Underhill, "The Ethnobiology of the Papago Indians," *Ethnobiological Studies in the American Southwest,* Vol. 4 No. 3 (1935), pp. 15-17. In addition, a large number of other small greens were utilized, including lamsquarter (*Chenopodium murale*), pigweed (*Amaranthus palmeri*), and saltbush (*Atriplex wrightii*). The stalks and leaves were consumed during the summer months. *Ibid., p.* 14.

[11] W. H. Bell and Edward F. Castetter, "The Aboriginal Utilization of the Tall Cacti in the American Southwest," *Ethnobiological Studies in the American Southwest,* Vol. 5, No. 1 (1937).

[12] Castetter and Underhill, "The Ethnobiology of the Papago Indians," *Ethnobiological Studies in the American Southwest,* Vol. 4, No. 3, p. 18.

Mesquite beans, which ripen in August near the summer villages, where an important wild crop. A number of other seed crops were regularly harvested from desert trees and shrubs, among them the palo verde and the ironwood.[13]

Lacking domesticated animals, the Papago depended on wildlife for their meat. Deer, antelope, mountain sheep, and peccary provided, at one time, plentiful large game.[14] Small animals, which are abundant in the Sonoran Desert, comprised an important part of the aboriginal diet. Rabbits, packrats, quail, reptiles, and even worms were eaten with relish.[15]

The Papago and all other aboriginal people, as Sauer stated, existed in "a sort of Malthusian balance with the land."[16] This simple and easily understood balance was destroyed with the coming of the Spaniard.

THE SPANISH ENTRADA

The Spanish settlement of the Sonoran Desert actually began in 1521 when Cortez, through his capture of Mexico City, gave Spain a new base of operations for further conquest. By 1522 Cortez had established a settlement at Zacatula on the Pacific in the Province of Michoacán.[17] Between that year and 1529 the port of Zacatula was the major northern base of operations for maritime exploration of the Pacific Coast from Panama to the vicinity of San Blas.[18]

The belief was widely held at this time that North America was a part of Asia, more particularly that Mexico was a southeastward projection of this continent. To be sure, nobody had any idea of the vastness of its size, but North America was, for a long time, not regarded as unusually large. Opinion was general among the Spaniards that it would prove to be not much wider than it was at the place where they had crossed it in New Spain and that a comparatively short voyage to the north would take them to Asia.[19]

---

[13] *Ibid.,* p. 24.

[14] *Ibid.,* pp. 41-42.

[15] *Ibid.,* pp. 42-43.

[16] Sauer and Brand, *Aztatlan,* p. 51.

[17] C. E. Chapman, *A History of California: The Spanish Period* (New York, 1923), pp. 44-49.

[18] H. H. Bancroft, *The History of the North Mexican States and Texas* (2 vols.; San Francisco, 1884-89), I, 19-25.

[19] Chapman, *A History of California,* pp. 45-46. He points out that Magellan's long voyage across the Pacific had earlier demonstrated that Asia was far away, but men only "gradually began to realize" that North America was like South America, a hitherto-unknown continent of great width. The long-prevalent idea of a narrow land mass persisted among the English and Dutch colonists of the Atlantic Seaboard as late as the 17th century. "Witness their string-like grants 'from sea to sea.'"

A most persistent belief was the existence of a strait which would lead them to fabulous India. The Spaniards looked for it at Panama where the land narrows, but the strait eluded them. Since it was not in the south it had to be in the north. The first overland expedition to explore the northwest coast of New Spain, which put the Sonoran Desert on the expanding map, was headed by Nuño de Guzmán, who set out from Mexico City in 1529. Leading an army of five hundred Spaniards and perhaps ten thousand native allies, Guzmán passed through Jalisco, crossed the Sierra del Tepic, and descended to the coastal plain. Guzmán's advance was marked everywhere by complete devastation, with few Indian pueblos escaping the torch. Even the most peaceful Indians were provoked to hostility "that there might be an excuse for plunder and destruction and carnage, and especially for taking slaves."[20]

Crossing the Río Tololotlán into unexplored territory, Guzmán carried the carnage into Sinaloa which he claimed in the name of the King of Spain. The southern Sinaloa districts, known as Chametla Quezala and Piastla, containing a hospitable native population, were enslaved. The Guzmán retinue was, however, lured further north by stories of incredibly rich provinces yet to be found, stories inspired more than likely by the Indians to encourage the invaders' earliest possible departure.

In 1531, Guzmán founded, in the province of Culiacán, near the confluence of the Río Tamazula and Humaya, the settlement of Colombo, which was probably a little above the present city of Culiacán.[21] It was used as a base of exploration, both inland and along the coast further to the northwest. One of Guzmán's lieutenants was sent to explore the coast, and succeeded, with little difficulty, in reaching the Río Petatlán, so called from the *petates* or palm-leaf mats which were used in the construction of native dwellings. The Río Petatlán is today called the Río Sinaloa. Its banks were reported to hold no large towns. The country between Culiacán and the Río Sinaloa contained a more sparse vegetation and a "rude people."[22] The Sonoran Desert had been discovered.

During these explorations Guzmán had enslaved the people of Culiacán while forcing many of the surviving Aztecs and Michoacán Indians, who had accompanied him, to remain in the north much against their will. These people were divided among some of Guzmán's soldiers who were also left behind, becoming the human base for the extension

---

[20] Bancroft, *History of the North Mexican States and Texas,* I, 29.

[21] *Ibid.,* p. 35. The Indian settlement which was given the name Colombo was apparently one of the largest pueblos in the Ciguatan (Culiacán) Province.

[22] Sauer, in *The Distribution of Aboriginal Tribes* and in *The Road to Cibola* (Berkeley, 1932), identifies these "rude people" with the Cahíta.

of the *encomienda* system which, from the beginning, had more interest in men than land. The grant of a native village or two along with the land carried with it the right to collect tribute and exact services such as labor in the fields. Encomiendas were often created with little difficulty as the Spaniards were able to take the place of native overlords with a minimum disturbance to existing practices. The first *mestizo* children were born in Sinaloa before Nuño de Guzmán returned to Jalisco with the remainder of his invading army in 1531. In Sinaloa, "survivors were driven out in gangs and sold as slaves. . . ."[23]

Thus, only ten years after the conquest of Mexico City, the southern margin of the Sonoran Desert had been explored and occupied by Spaniards. Of much greater significance was the very early creation in the semiarid Northwest of a "Mexican" population. This process was accelerated throughout the rest of the century. It was irreversible. Rebellion was disastrous to the native population, only hastening the eventual destruction of tribal identity. If the indigene ran away or was killed, the encomendero replaced him with others caught in the settlements still outside the encomiendas, or with Indians brought from Jalisco, Michoacán, or Mexico. Weak tribes were absorbed by the stronger ones, and many "faded out in the process of Mexicanixation."[24] Some Negro slaves were introduced, further confusing the racial pattern.[25]

By the 1560's, the introduction of mining in the sierra behind Mazatlán further hastened this process of assimilation. Mortality rates were extremely high in conjunction with mining, and "recruiters" were forced to expand their activities. The result was the very rapid and usually complete destruction of the many tribes which inhabited the sierra and its foothills.[26] Mining attracted more outsiders — especially Mexicans and Spaniards — into the region than any other activity. "Native customs and race gave ground rapidly and quietly, without events that would attract attention in the contemporary chronicles. This is the simple explanation of the apparent paradox that some of the least accessible sections of the Sierra Madre are barren of aboriginal survivals. The old mining districts have the most purely Hispanic culture of the entire Mexican Northwest."[27]

---

[23] Sauer, *The Road to Cibola*, p. 7.

[24] Sauer, *The Distribution of Aboriginal Tribes*, p. 1.

[25] Sol Tax, *Heritage of Conquest: The Ethnology of Middle America* (Glencoe, Ill., 1952).

[26] Sauer, *The Distribution of Aboriginal Tribes,* describes the destruction in some detail.

[27] *Ibid.,* p. 15.

What was happening in the sierra was taking place to a lesser degree on the coastal plain. Tribes lost their identity, and the children of those who survived were usually *mezclada* (mixed) in language and culture, if not in blood. So thorough was the destruction of the cultural integrity of southern Sinaloan tribes and so complete was their absorption into a "Mexican" society, that the best histories of northwestern New Spain have little more to say about this region.[28] Thus at the end of the first period of Spanish adventure on the Pacific Coast there existed two distinct realms divided somewhere near the region where tropical thorn forest is replaced by desert vegetation. The Sinaloa River, which was an aboriginal dividing line separating the more advanced and tractable Tahue and other southern tribes from a less densely settled and ruder people to the north of that river, was perpetuated as a boundary after the Spanish entrada.[29]

This division, which existed in nature as a climatic and vegetational boundary, and as an indigenous tribal limit, gained significance during the last decades of the sixteenth century as the rapid destruction of pre-Columbian society took place to the south of the Río Sinaloa. Here the encomienda was the institution which so quickly took hold in order to convert, discipline, and exploit the native population. From the first *repartamientos* granted to Guzmán's soldiers, Spanish encomenderos successfully divided the southern Sinaloan Indians as well as their land among themselves. Only on the Fuerte and Ocoroni frontier did the encomiendas fail completely due, primarily, to complete rebellion among the Cahita tribes of these rivers.[30] To the north the Cahita, Pima, Opata, and other tribes maintained their complete independence for many decades.

SPANISH EXPLORATION OF THE DESERT

The first white man to traverse much of the Sonoran Desert was Alvar Núñez Cabeza de Vaca.[31] He reached Culiacán in 1536 after a curious odyssey which began in 1528, with the ill-fated Narvaez expe-

[28] "The Southern Provinces from Chametla to Culiacán, a narrow strip along the coast, came as near to having no recorded history as is possible in a country where some civilized men lived, and where each year may be supposed to have had its complement of days." *Ibid.,* p. 17.

[29] Sauer and Brand, *Aztatlan,* p. 49.

[30] Sauer, *The Distribution of Aboriginal Tribes,* p. 25.

[31] The actual route of Cabeza de Vaca is a subject of continuous investigation and conjecture. See Sauer, *Road to Cibola,* and Cleve Hallenbeck, *Alvar Núñez Cabeza de Vaca: The Journey and Route of the First European to Cross the Continent of North America* (Glendale, Calif., 1940).

dition and ended with his rescue by encomendero slave-hunters on the Río Sinaloa.[32] Núñez, more commonly known as Cabeza de Vaca, had heard in his eight-year journey from the Gulf of Mexico that there was indeed a great kingdom to the north called Quivira, and that it was this nation which contained the fabled Seven Cities of Cibola. "This story gave an extraordinary stimulus to Spanish exploration, especially since it corresponded so exactly with what Spaniards had long expected to find in the north."[33] In order to substantiate these recurring rumors, Fray Marcos de Niza, a Franciscan friar, and Estevan, a Negro who had made the journey with Cabeza de Vaca, were sent north from Culiacán in 1539. They crossed the desert, probably northward via the Yaqui and Sonora River valleys perhaps to the vicinity of the Zuñi pueblos of New Mexico where Fray Marcos thought he saw Cibola from a distance.[34]

Meanwhile, a sea expedition was equipped under Francisco de Ulloa to seek the fabled wealth of the north. Ulloa set sail from Acapulco in 1539, following the coast of the mainland to the mouth of the Colorado River, proving Baja California to be a peninsula. The Ulloa expedition found nothing which contributed to the confirmation of the existence of the Cibolan cities. Instead, it brought back stories of an arid desolation which would deter effective occupation of the northern margins of the Gulf.[35]

In 1539, Francisco Vásquez de Coronado, the newly appointed governor of Nueva Galicia,[36] received the optimistic reports of Fray Marcos. To verify these, Coronado moved overland along the coast to Culiacán while dispatching a maritime expedition under Hernando de Alarcón from San Blas to accompany and supply him. Alarcón sailed northwest along the coast of the mainland. Reaching the mouth of the Colorado, he sailed upstream where he may have reached the mouth of the Gila.[37] Meanwhile, Coronado himself crossed the short rivers which

---

[32] Bancroft, *History of the North American States and Texas,* I, 62-69.

[33] Chapman, *A History of California,* pp. 52-53.

[34] Estevan, who actually reached the pueblos, was killed.

[35] Sykes, *The Colorado Delta,* pp. 7-8.

[36] This is a name for the territories north of Jalisco and west of the Sierra Madre chosen to replace the name España Mayor given it by Guzmán. Coronado, as well as his predecessors, Oñate and Pérez de la Torre, were kept busy suppressing revolts by the miserable natives of southern Sinaloa and Tepic who had been "reduced" to slavery by Guzmán. The more humane policies of Guzmán's successors did little to alter the irreversible forces at work destroying the tribal integrity of the coastal and mountain tribes from the Sinaloa River south. Bancroft, *History of the North Mexican States and Texas,* I, p. 7.

[37] Chapman, in his *History of California,* p. 148, claims that he did not. The exact locations reached by this early explorer have been subject to considerable argument.

flow into the Gulf. In order to provision his huge retinue, some 5,000 sheep and 150 cattle were driven north with the expedition.[38] This impeded progress considerably and caused many animals to be abandoned in what came to be known as Sinaloa. This was in fact the beginning of the desert cattle industry. Twenty years later Francisco de Ibarra found "thousands of their descendants running wild in this territory."[39]

Arriving at what was called the Río de la Señora,[40] Coronado established a presidio called Corazones after the name given to it by Cabeza de Vaca. This is believed to have been near the present town of Ures. Exploration was carried on downstream among the Seri Indians as the greater part of the expedition moved up the "Senora" River and on into what is now the United States. They crossed the Gila River and left the Sonoran Desert for the Pueblo Indian country of New Mexico, and eventually the plains of Kansas.[41] A lieutenant of Coronado, Melchor Díaz, who remained at Corazones, led another expedition across the desert to the west, exploring the Gulf Coast and marching, with great hardship, to the Colorado River. He crossed that river and became the first white man to enter California overland, probably somewhere below the present international boundary.[42] Failing to find the Alarcón expedition, Díaz returned to Corazones.[43]

Thus by 1541, Ulloa, Alarcón, and Díaz had all investigated the lower Colorado River, establishing the fact that California was a peninsula separated from New Spain by a terrible desert and not by any body of water larger than the Colorado River.

At this time great overland expeditions to the Northwest ceased and aside from an occasional individual wandering, the Sonoran Desert was for nearly two centuries avoided. The knowledge gained by these early explorers was forgotten and during these centuries, California was represented on maps as being an island.[44] It remained for the intrepid

---

[38] John Wesley Powell, "Report of the Director," Bureau of American Ethnology, *Annual Report* XIV, part I (Washington, D.C., 1892-93), p. lvi.

[39] J. J. Wagoner, *History of the Cattle Industry in Southern Arizona, 1540-1940,* University of Arizona Social Science Bull. 20 (Tucson, 1952), p. 8.

[40] The name "Sonora" is thought to be derived from "Señora" which referred to the Virgin.

[41] The *relación* of the Coronado expedition by Pedro de Castañeda gives a firsthand account of the fruitless search for the rich cities of Cibola. Castañeda's *Narrative* is contained in Frederick W. Hodge's *Spanish Explorers in the Southern United States, 1528–1543* (New York, 1907).

[42] Sykes, *The Colorado Delta,* p. 9.

[43] H. E. Bolton, *Coronado: Knight of Pueblos and Plains* (New York, 1949), and Sauer, *The Road to Cibola,* pp. 32-37.

[44] Sykes, *The Colorado Delta,* pp. 9-10 and "The Isles of California," *Bulletin of the American Geographic Society,* Vol. 47 (1915), pp. 745-61.

Father Eusebio Kino in 1700 to reestablish in the European mind the peninsularity of California.

The negative effects of the exploration of the arid land at the head of the Gulf of California were in part overshadowed by a number of salutary benefits. If California was to remain *terra incognita,* at least the higher civilization and fertile fields of New Mexico were discovered and soon colonized. A route which became the West Coast Camino Real was opened as far north as the Santa Cruz Valley near Tucson. Over this route the relatively docile Pima and Opata were brought into the circle of history, forming in part the base of a Sonoran population. Spanish colonial society on the West Coast was forced by the desert and its uncivilized aboriginal inhabitants to consolidate its gains in the valleys of Sinaloa and Sonora through which the Camino Real passed. Finally, the explorations either ending or beginning in the Sonoran Desert determined the continental dimensions of North America.

The eastern north-south valleys of the Sonora and Yaqui systems became one of the important northward lines of advance to New Mexico. Among those who followed this route was the Oñate expedition which conquered that province in 1598.[45] Leaving the valleys of Sonora, this party crossed the Continental Divide to the northeast, through the sparsely occupied territory of the Apaches. It was vainly hoped that missions could be established among these people once the desert valleys inhabited by the Opata and other intervening tribes were settled.

It should not be forgotten that apart from these occasional expeditions, the Río Sinaloa remained for many years the northern boundary of effective Spanish occupance — an occupance which in fact was little more than a thin veil. López de Velasco, writing between 1571 and 1574, said there were approximately fifteen hundred Spaniards in all of Nueva Vizcaya, a large frontier province which contained, at that time, most of the population of northwestern New Spain on both flanks of the Sierra Madre Occidental. Guadalajara was its largest town with 150 Spaniards.[46] Aside from the mining districts, the only Spanish settlement at that time in what later became Sinaloa was Culiacán with about thirty Spaniards. There had been other short-lived settlements in the past and there was already a significant population of mixed blood. One of these earlier settlements was made by Francisco de Ibarra in 1564. He

---

[45]   This adventure finally carried Oñate westward from New Mexico to the Colorado River. This occurred in 1604 when Oñate traveled west along the Bill Williams River to the Colorado and then downstream to its mouth, after which he returned to New Mexico. H. E. Bolton, *Spanish Exploration in the Southwest: 1542–1706* (New York, 1916), pp. 440-61.

[46]   Chapman, pp. 155-56.

founded the town of San Juan Bautista de Carapoa on the banks of the Fuerte River. This presidio was soon destroyed by the Suaqui Indians.[47]

In 1583, Pedro de Montoya founded another town on the Fuerte, calling it San Felipe y Santiago de Carapoa, but it was destroyed in a short time along with its founder. In 1585, Hernando Bazán re-founded the settlement which had been twice destroyed, but this time he located it on the banks of the Río Sinaloa, some fifty miles south, calling it once more San Felipe y Santiago. By 1589, this frontier post had no more than five Spanish settlers, the majority having deserted to the relative serenity of Culiacán.[48]

This little presidio, which came to be called San Felipe de Sinaloa, and finally Sinaloa, on the Río Sinaloa, was reinforced in 1596. At that time it was garrisoned by twenty-five men, a relatively large number for the Sonoran frontier.

Coeval with these developments, the Franciscans and Dominicans had been making conversions "so that the region south of the Río Sinaloa had become Christian, nominally at least, by the end of the sixteenth century, and after some futile revolts, was definitely reduced to the Spanish crown. So, despite the scant white population of Nueva Galicia [Sinaloa], that part of it lying south of [the Río] Sinaloa was fast losing the characteristics of a frontier province."[49] Father Zapata's report of 1678 concluded that the districts south of the Rio Sinaloa had been thoroughly reduced. The province (Nueva Galicia) had been Christianized, and possessed a white population of six hundred. There were many more of mixed blood; at San Felipe de Sinaloa alone, there were 1,200 *gente de razón*.[50] Moreover, Indians from the Central Plateau were still being resettled in this area. During the late sixteenth and early seventeenth centuries, Aztec speech became established as far north as the Río Sinaloa. The mines which "stripped the surrounding area of natives as well as timber"[51] were largely responsible for this continuing influx. The aboriginal conditions were so quickly blurred by the ravages of these early mining camps and the encomienda system, that many observers were led to believe that these tractable sedentary Indians of

[47] J. L. Mecham, *Francisco de Ibarra and Nueva Vizcaya* (Durham, N.C., 1927).

[48] At that time this was called San Miguel de Culiacán. Peter M. Dunne, *Pioneer Black Robes on the West Coast* (Berkeley, 1940), pp. 21-23.

[49] Chapman, p. 156.

[50] This is a term signifying "civilized people" which included whites, mestizos, and Negroes — all but the Indian population. *Ibid.*

[51] Sauer, *The Distribution of Aboriginal Tribes*, p. 1.

Aztecan speech had resided here from the time of the legendary southward Aztec perigrination to the Central Plateau. Nahua place names were
given as proof of this fact.[52] The truth, however, lay in the nearly complete displacement of the original inhabitants by natives from the south
who, in turn, were losing their tribal identity through continuing contact
with the Spaniard, the mingling of tribal stocks, and breakdown of
tribal consciousness.

---

[52]   The errors made by Orozco y Berra, *Geografía de las Lenguas* (México,
1860), and by Cyrus Thomas and John R. Swanton, *Indian Languages of Mexico
and Central America* (Bureau of American Ethnology Bull. 44, Washington, D.C.
1911), are pointed out in Sauer, *The Distribution of Aboriginal Tribes,* pp. 3-14.

CHAPTER SEVEN

The Mission Period

Conditions at the beginning of the seventeenth century were ripe for an advance across the four rivers held by the uncivilized and powerful Cahita tribes. The second year of that century witnessed the arrival on the frontier of Diego Martínez de Hurdaide, Captain General and Governor of the Province of Sinaloa.[1] Five years earlier the presidio at San Felipe de Sinaloa had been reinforced, and ten years earlier the first Jesuits had entered the province.

Hurdaide realized, however, that with a force of no more than twenty-five soldiers the occupation and settlement of the arid coastal plain and broken sierra to the north must depend on something other than military force or the faltering encomienda system. The decision that he and his fellow frontiersmen made with the support of the authorities in Mexico City and Madrid set the pattern for the pacification, occupation, and settlement of the entire Pacific coast to the borders of Oregon. The mission was to become the vehicle of Spanish conquest. To this end Hurdaide and the Jesuit fathers and those who replaced them gave their undivided attention for over two hundred years. The missions, presidios, and pueblos which these men established were the seeds from which so many of the great cities of Western America grew — Hermosillo, Tucson, San Diego, Los Angeles, San Jose, San Francisco. Sinaloa was to become the base from which succeeding generations might advance into the wilderness of Sonora, and eventually from Sonora into Pimería Alta and California.

THE MISSIONS OF SINALOA

Prior to the advent of the missions, the Cahita inhabitants of the coastal Sinaloa plain practiced agriculture. A wide variety of crops was

---

[1] H. P. Johnson, "Diego Martinez de Hurdaide," unpublished Ph.D. thesis, University of California (1935).

[117]

grown, usually under irrigation (the Guasave tribe being an exception, as far as irrigation was concerned). Corn, beans, squash, pumpkins, melons, as well as the agave and prickly pear cactus were carefully cultivated.[2] Lacking draft animals and beasts of burden, they had to work hard to extract from their dry soil a mere subsistence. They were "robust and well formed,"[3] capable in later years of supplying the mines and ranches of Sonora with their best workers.

They were, of course, tied to the land as are all people who practice even a primitive form of irrigation. The Cahita lived in rather large villages, sometimes with populations numbering in the thousands.[4] They were extremely jealous of their tribal lands, seldom wandering far from them,[5] and for over fifty years protecting them from encroachment of Spanish settlement.

The encomienda on the West Coast broke down as an effective means of exploitation after it had advanced successfully to the southern margin of the Sonoran Desert. This is undoubtedly due in part to the encomenderos' inability to realize any profit from such marginal lands.[6] Ferocity, recalcitrance, and sabotage, not the nomadic tendencies of the native people, destroyed the encomienda on these Sinaloan rivers. The Jesuit missionaries succeeded because they were willing to deal with these uncivilized people in a land which promised little economic return.[7]

Thus began the second, and for the Sonoran Desert, the most significant period in the evolution of frontier settlement in the Pacific Northwest of New Spain. It has been shown that the work of the Jesuit missions was far from being the first religious influence on the West Coast. Secular priests had for some time been active under the *Patronato Real*[8] among the Indians. Subject to the secular authority of the Spanish King, they accompanied troops in the earliest entradas as well as the later explorations and subjugation of native populations. There were,

---

2   *Ibid.,* p. 27.

3   Clark Wissler, *The American Indians* (New York, 1922), p. 26.

4   These aboriginal villages are described as being larger than the average desert ranchería. Peter M. Dunne, *Andrés Pérez de Ribas: Pioneer Black Robe of the West Coast, Administrator, Historian* (New York, 1951), pp. 32-33.

5   Dunne, *Pioneer Black Robes on the West Coast* (Berkeley, 1940), p. 97.

6   L. R. Jones, "Notes on the Geographical Factors which Controlled the Spanish Advance into Northern Mexico and Southern California," *The Scottish Geographical Magazine,* Vol. 39 (1923), p. 163.

7   W. E. Shiels, *Gonzalo de Tapia* (New York, 1934).

8   "Royal Patronage": a system under which the Church in New Spain was administered from Madrid by Spanish officials and not from Rome. The state had the final decision in the appointment of missionaries and their advance into new territory. Dunne, *Pioneer Black Robes on the West Coast,* p. 63.

however, no missions in the conquered lands between the provinces of Chametla and Culiacán. Mission history in Sinaloa and Sonora began with the Jesuits.

The first Jesuit frontier missions were established on the middle Río Sinaloa and its right-bank tributary, the Río Ocoroni, by two lonely priests.[9] This was the very region in which the encomiendas of Ibarra had failed most miserably, and the natives had reverted to their former condition. A mission was established at Cubiri on the Sinaloa just below San Felipe de Sinaloa, and at the pueblo which today carries the name of the right-bank affluent: Ocoroni. At the same time, consolidation of earlier religious gains was taking place to the south on the Río Mocorito. A start was made on the lower Sinaloa among the Guasave tribe, a mission being established on the banks of the Sinaloa at the pueblo which took the name Guasave from the indigenous population. Inevitable setbacks occurred, including outbreaks of disease which decimated many missions;[10] priests were martyred, and their charges fled to the sierra, but progress was achieved. Even before the reinforcement of the presidio at San Felipe de Sinaloa, there were enumerated over 4,500 Christians on the Sinaloa and Ocoroni living in sixteen pueblos which were regularly visited by the Jesuit fathers.[11] There were also a few conversions on the Río Fuerte. Additional priests were sent to the Sinaloa missions, and in the year 1595, Captain Hurdaide took command of the northwestern frontier. This was the signal for an advance to the Río Fuerte.

The first mission was established on the Fuerte in 1605, at Ahome among the most receptive of the tribes that occupied the valley. Hurdaide opened up the country by repeated military campaigns so that the warlike Suaquis, Sinaloas, and Tehuecos were led to ask for missions among their people.[12] In a short period of time all three of these Cahita tribes had missions among them. A total of eight missions were strung out along the Fuerte from the Ahome Mission upstream, including those of San Miguel, Mochicahue, Charay, Sivirijoa, Tehueco, Toro, and Vaca.[13]

---

[9]   *Ibid.*

[10]   S. F. Cook, *The Extent and Significance of Disease Among the Indians of Baja California, 1697-1773* (Ibero-Americana: 12, Berkeley, 1937). Although dealing with the peninsula, this is the best documented study of the ravages of disease which destroyed the missions of Baja California.

[11]   In the *anuas* for the year 1595 there were listed thirteen pueblos with 2,312 Christians on the Río Sinaloa; its tributary the Río Ocorino had three pueblos with 1,270 Christians; the Río Mocorito had five pueblos with 1,588 Christians; and there were 600 Christians on the Río Fuerte. Dunne, *Pioneer Black Robes on the West Coast*, pp. 44-45.

[12]   Dunne, *Andrés Pérez de Ribas*, pp. 12-14.

[13]   Dunne, *Pioneer Black Robes on the West Coast*, p. 78.

During these early years of the seventeenth century, the destruction of tribal organization and cohesiveness was carried forward in the Sinaloa and Fuerte valleys almost as effectively as it was to the south during the worst years of the encomiendas. The missionaries brought to these two valleys Aztec and Tarascan Christians to instruct the neophytes.[1] Dispersed coastal Indians were herded into the river missions, often with little regard to tribal boundaries. Thousands of aborigines living deep in the Sierra Madre were enticed into the coastal missions. Hurdaide was able, in only one of the many well-documented occasions

> to persuade fifteen hundred [Comanito Indians] to settle in lower and more accessible country . . . the Captain lent them pack animals for the transportation of their goods and provisions, and he made over to them in this lower country certain fields for sowing which had belonged to Christian groups. He asked these to help the newcomers in the sowing of their crops and the building of their houses. Thus there sprang up a *pueblo* (Cahuemeto) of fifteen hundred people.[15]

In this way a mountain people were transplanted and "Mexicanized." This fusion was carried forward through many other diverse occasions. Tribal gods were dishonored, tribal conflicts settled, and tribal land tenure was replaced by mission lands and individual plots. Even martyrdom resulted in the retributive destruction of tribalism as well as the tribes themselves.[16]

Success on the Sinaloa and Fuerte rivers betokened further success on the Mayo and Yaqui. The Yaqui Indians, however, presented a number of problems to the missionaries. They were a numerous tribe which the Jesuit Father Ribas estimated to have thirty thousand members[17] living along the last forty miles of their river. No other northwestern tribe was so densely concentrated in a relatively small area. In addition, they had the reputation since the first entrada (by Diego de Guzmán in 1533,

---

[14]   Dunne, *Andrés Pérez de Ribas,* p. 27.

[15]   Dunne, *Pioneer Black Robes on the West Coast,* p. 98.

[16]   An example of such destruction following martyrdom was recorded in this first mission period when two mountain peoples "paid a terrible price for rebellion; eight hundred of the Varohios and Guazapares were destroyed, and of both tribes only eighty families remained. Most of these were soon after reconciled by Father Francisco Torices, and, together with the Chinipas, went to live lower down on the Fuerte River in the territory of the Sinaloas. Here was easy contact with the fathers and trade with many other nations of the West Coast. Eighty families soon lost their identity (or perhaps starved) as did the much larger number of loyal mountain Chinipas who were similarly transported, as well as the coastal Sinaloas who received them. None of these tribes exist today; their descendants speak only Spanish and have no tribal awareness. *Ibid.,* p. 214.

[17]   Dunne, *Andrés Pérez de Ribas* (1951), p. 32.

for being brave and fierce in battle.[18] Missions on the Mayo and Yaqui rivers would have to await the pacification of this tribe. This was accomplished — temporarily at least — through force of arms between 1604 and 1610. Hurdaide's victories brought peace to these Sonoran valleys, allowing the first mission to be established on the Río Mayo in 1614.

By 1620 the records show that thirty thousand Mayos had been baptized. The Mayo Valley was divided into three *partidos* or mission districts with missions at Etchojoa, Navojoa, and Camoa. Acceptance of the mission system was complete within six years. Thus the first major conquest of the west-coast missions which would eventually extend beyond San Francisco Bay was effected among the Cahita of the Río Mayo, Sonora.

The first mission among the Yaqui was established in 1617 by two Jesuits working alone. By 1623 nearly thirty thousand Yaquis had been baptized and were congregated in eight towns where mission churches had been built.

The mission, as it was to develop, fell under the *Patronato*. Not a mission could be founded, or a missionary go to the frontier, without the assent of the royal authorities. The mission was, in the eyes of the Spanish government, little more than effective support given to the meager number of troops in keeping the Indians of a particular region under control, and indirectly contributing to the security of the royal domain. The first Jesuit missions along the Río Sinaloa, through their pacification of the local Indian population, supported the military in their conflict with the trans-frontier barbarian.[19] The missions, however, went much further than this, assisting in actual conquest. The missions planted on the Fuerte, Mayo, and Yaqui rivers existed as isolated spores which germinated the ultimate conquest of these regions.

The individual mission site was thus chosen with frontier military factors in mind. On the west coast of New Spain, the Sierra Madre and Gulf of California limited the possibilities of expansion to the narrow coastal plain as well as the foothills and *cuencas* of the western Sierra. This has been called the "West Coast Corridor."[20] Strategy was at first no more than the successive occupation and settlement of the valleys

---

[18] This reputation is still untarnished as the Yaquis were the last North American tribe to wage open warfare against the whites, finally laying down arms in 1928.

[19] H. E. Bolton, "The West Coast Corridor," *American Philosophical Society Proceedings,* Vol. 91 (1947), pp. 426-29.

[20] H. E. Bolton, *The Evolution of Society in Sinaloa and Sonora, Mexico,* (Berkeley, 1939).

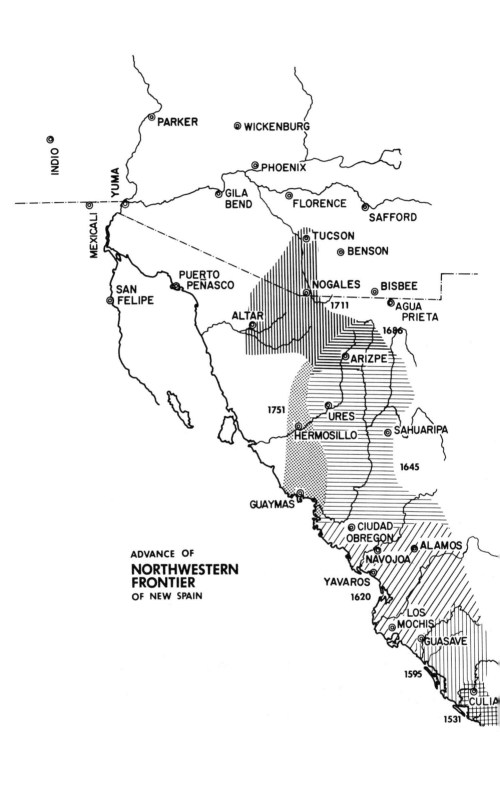

INDIO

PARKER

WICKENBURG

MEXICALI

YUMA

PHOENIX

GILA
BEND

FLORENCE

SAFFORD

TUCSON

BENSON

SAN
FELIPE

PUERTO
PEÑASCO

NOGALES

BISBEE

1711

AGUA
PRIETA

ALTAR

1686

ARIZPE

1751

URES

SAHUARIPA

HERMOSILLO

1645

GUAYMAS

ADVANCE OF
**NORTHWESTERN
FRONTIER**
OF NEW SPAIN

CIUDAD
OBREGON

ALAMOS

NAVOJOA

YAVAROS

1620

LOS
MOCHIS

GUASAVE

1595

CULIA

1531

which descended from the Sierra. "River by river, valley by valley, the Spaniards, during the first quarter of the seventeenth century, advanced up the coastal region: the Sinaloa, Fuerte, Mayo, Yaqui. . . ."[21]

The time of foundation, the tribe among whom the mission was to be planted, and the general location of the mission were decisions which were made by secular edict. Nevertheless, the mission was itself an isolated and nearly self-sufficient economic unit. For this reason, the exact site of the mission was chosen by the individual priest with the economic possibilities of the vicinity in mind. The mission site was of course determined by the existence of an aboriginal population; usually one of the larger existing rancherías was selected. However, the success of the mission necessitated the concentration of as many neophytes as possible in close proximity to the mission buildings.[22] If a tribal majority could be physically contained by mission walls, the chances of rebellion were substantially lessened. This goal was seldom attained but was always kept in mind. The mission lands then had to be able to feed more than the local aboriginal population. This meant that the first mission church was almost always situated among the most fertile and best-watered fields. Neighboring rancherías were often deserted through conscription.

The establishment of missions greatly altered the distribution of population from the Río Sinaloa northward. The mission settlements became the major centers of population while the missions themselves controlled much of the best irrigated land within the mission communities. Since the amount of land under cultivation in the desert was absolutely limited, under primitive methods, by the amount of water available, this competition was great. During the first years when no white population existed near the mission communities, there was of course no interracial conflict. Sooner or later, however, a white population developed which wanted the mission lands and the Indian labor upon them.[23] This day was usually forestalled by the fact that the earliest white settlers were little interested in agriculture, and congregated in the upland mining districts. This, and the continuing bellicose nature of many tribes, as well as certain animosity between the religious and secular colonial interests, kept the mission lands intact.[24]

---

21   Sauer, *The Distribution of Aboriginal Tribes,* p. 19.

22   Dunne, *Pioneer Black Robes on the West Coast,* pp. 32-33.

23   If there were mines nearby, Indian labor was valued much more highly than the irrigated land.

24   H. E. Bolton, "The Mission as a Frontier Institution in the Spanish-American Colonies," *American Historical Review,* Vol. 23 (1917), pp. 42-61.

The greater size of mission settlements necessitated larger and improved works of all kinds. Irrigation by canal was upgraded where it existed, and introduced where it did not. The very size of the mission settlements worked in favor of a controlled irrigation system using water from the larger streams. The organization of labor needed to accomplish this, however, would have often been impossible to achieve under aboriginal conditions.

A great variety of crops was introduced to supplement those already grown. Often European crops would precede the establishment of missions. Wheat was usually grown by the tribes who lived beyond the mission frontier, being seldom introduced by the missionaries themselves.[25] So valuable were the agricultural innovations and crop introductions of the missionaries that an aboriginal population which had always existed close to the starvation level was strongly attracted to the missions.

Livestock allowed the Indian to utilize more fully an important resource — desert vegetation. The herds of mission cattle provided a new food base. As noted before, herds of wild cattle, descendants of those brought there by the Coronado expedition, seemed to thrive on the forage provided by the southern desert. Many of these were undoubtedly assimilated by the increasing mission herds.[26] Horses and mules extended communications, and through the use of the plow the sowing of crops could be expanded. The Jesuit fathers introduced sheep "so that wool besides cotton was had for clothing or for barter."[27] Each advance in the prosperity of the mission Indians acted as a magnet upon the trans-frontier tribes who continually sent emissaries to the missionaries requesting the establishment of additional missions among their people.[28]

All did not, however, go well. The early missionaries contributed unwittingly to the continued destruction of the native race. While the mission system replaced the most reprehensible features of the encomiendas, it probably encouraged the pernicious spread of disease.

European epidemics undoubtedly preceded the white man into this area. Prior to the establishment of missions, however, the natives north of the Río Sinaloa who usually lived in scattered rancherías or

---

[25] H. E. Bolton, *An Outpost of Empire* (Vol. 1 of *Anza's California Expeditions,* Berkeley, 1930, 5 vols.) and most other authorities comment at one time or another on this interesting fact.

[26] Wagoner, pp. 7-10.

[27] Dunne, *Andrés Pérez de Ribas,* p. 71.

[28] Dunne, *Pioneer Black Robes on the West Coast,* pp. 80, 89-93.

small pueblos were able to escape the worst ravages of the introduced diseases. "With the best of intention the missionaries, by 'reducing' the Indians to compact *pueblos* and gathering them together regularly for worship, instruction and joint labor, exposed them to contagion by European diseases."[29] The protective isolation of scattered aboriginal settlement gave way quickly to the spread of one European disease after another. "Famine normally followed on pestilence presumably because the natives caught in the epidemic failed to plant their crops and consumed their supply of seed grain. Whenever a mission became so diminished in population that there was room for its remnants in another village, the missionaries depopulated the site and transferred the remnants."[30] The abandoned settlement was usually given over to a white grantee. Encroachment by Spaniards on Indian lands continued to narrow the native base of subsistence, eliminating the possibilities of recuperation.[31]

In 1684 an event took place which further destroyed the serenity of mission life, particularly among the Mayo. One of Mexico's richest discoveries of silver was made at Alamos in the Sierra Madre foothills thirty miles above Navojoa. Additional Spaniards were attracted, some of whom eventually took up mission lands deserted by Indians who, with the Spaniards, had gravitated to Alamos. The Yaqui were less affected since they occupied more remote lands. Yaqui mission prosperity continued until the first major revolt in 1740 despite the fact that encroachment increased with the prosperity of the silver mines. Yaqui farms from 1680 on provided a surplus of grain for the mines as well as for the new missions, both in Baja California and Sonora.[32]

The site and plan of the mission church itself merits comment. It usually was on a rise above the floodplain, should one exist. The first churches were scarcely more than *jacales*[33] like those found throughout the desert today used as houses for the poorer people. These crude structures were supported by tree trunks which formed the framework for more slender branches. The roof was laid over with straw and covered with mud. On at least one side of this structure there was usually located a porch-like ramada which was made much like the dwelling

---

[29]   Sauer, *Aboriginal Population of Northwestern Mexico*, p. 12.

[30]   *Ibid.*, p. 13.

[31]   Cook, *The Extent and Significance of Disease Among the Indians of Baja California, 1697–1773.*

[32]   Edward H. Spicer, *Cycles of Conquest: The Impact of Spain, Mexico, and the United States on the Indians of the Southwest, 1533–1960* (Tucson, 1962), p. 51.

[33]   Dunne, *Andrés Pérez de Ribas,* pp. 43-46.

itself minus the walls. These buildings served both as church and residence for the first missionaries.

The first recognizable churches in the region were built of massive adobe by a Jesuit missionary to the Guasave tribe in the years after 1598. Although these first imposing structures were destroyed by a great flood in 1604, they were forerunners of a rich mission architecture, examples of which were ultimately scattered across the Sonoran Desert. Throughout the desert to this day many small oasis communities look with great pride at what is still their largest building, the mission church.

THE MISSIONS OF SONORA

Before the Jesuit fathers consolidated their gains among the Yaqui, a start was made with the Indians of Sonora. This province, as it was first defined, included the Yaqui Valley north of its delta, as well as the valley of the Río Sonora. Its boundaries were later expanded to include the valleys of the Magdalena system and the north-flowing tributaries of the Río Gila. The present-day state of Sonora includes the lower courses of the Río Yaqui and Río Mayo which, in early days, were included as part of Sinaloa and later as the province of Ostimuri. The name Sonora has always applied, however, to the land occupied by the Pima and Opata Indians. Immediately north of the last Yaqui village at Cocorit, the Yaqui River makes its last bend westward to the sea. North of this bend the Yaqui, its affluents, the Río Matape, the Río Sonora and its tributaries, all flow from north to south between the rugged but disconnected ranges, which make central Sonora one "vast washboard."[34] More than any other single factor this coarse mountainous grain, with its marked north-south trend, effected the peaceful conquest and settlement of Sonora.

The land of the Lower Pima and Opata, enclosed as it was within these north-south ranges, was further isolated by the extremely arid deserts to the west, as well as by the even more broken ranges of the Sierra Madre to the east and southeast. Once having achieved some success among the deltaic Yaqui, the missionary fathers perceived that the middle reaches of that river opened funnel-like upon a series of valleys containing a number of alluvial basins where the sedentary Pima and Opata already practiced irrigated agriculture. Whereas the coastal plain of Ostimuri had encouraged, through ease of communication, recurring general insurrection among the neophytes, these valleys afforded much-needed isolation to the projected missions.

---

[34] H. E. Bolton, *Rim of Christendom: A Biography of Eusebio Francisco Kino, Pacific Coast Pioneer* (New York, 1936), p. 244.

In his history of the mission frontier in Sonora, Father Bannon notes that there is a marked difference between Sonora and the region to the south:

> In Sinaloa, the main watercourses follow a west to southwest direction and thus lay directly across the path of the advancing frontier. In Sinaloa the forward progress was slow because of the necessity of occupying each river valley from the Sierra to the Gulf before passing on. In Sonora . . . the advance could be made up the rivers rather than along them. This made for a series of salients and also a more rapid expansion. It was safe to push far up one river valley, without having to worry too much about the friendliness or hostility of the sedentary Indians on either side. Thus the Sonora frontier seems to have moved forward with a surprising rapidity as compared with that of Sinaloa.[35]

These valleys of Sonora also provided an agricultural base which compared favorably with the coast to the south. What has been attributed to higher fertility, must, in the light of twentieth-century developments on the Coast, be considered as the result of more successful agricultural techniques practiced by the Sonoran tribes. Sauer clearly differentiates between the Opata and Pima Bajo on one hand, and the coastal Cahita on the other, putting forward the aboriginal practice of irrigation by the former and its absence among the latter.[36] Whether or not this was the case, it stands to reason that the smaller and more confined streams which intermittently flow through the valleys of Sonora are more amenable to controlled irrigation. The torrential rivers of the coastal plain even to this day wash away the works constructed to carry water to the fields. This alone would be sufficient to make inland Sonora a veritable Eden despite the fact that the crops planted were the same as those cultivated on the coast, and similarly, there was a heavy reliance upon gathering.

Of even greater significance than the productivity of the land was the realization that the Indians of Sonora were culturally more advanced than their neighbors.[37] As the Pueblo Indians of New Mexico had attracted early Spanish settlement, so the Opata in particular were to act as a magnet for Spanish settlers. In time the assimilated Opata became the springboard for further advance into Pimería Alta, and eventually

---

[35] J. F. Bannon, *The Mission Frontier in Sonora, 1620–1687,* (New York, 1955), pp. 10, 12.

[36] Sauer, *The Aboriginal Population of Northwestern Mexico,* map in front cover. An early letter from the Opata frontier states that they "do not know hunger for they have water with which to irrigate their fields." Bannon, p. 28.

[37] Bannon, p. 14, discusses at some length the cultural achievements of these folk, summarizing that they "responded well to the efforts of the padres." In Sonora their achievements approached more closely those of their fellow Jesuits in the better known and more widely publicized Reductions of Paraguay.

California. It seems quite probable that the Spaniards who had used this effective technique with the Tlascalans, Aztecs, Tarascans, Tehuecos, and others had this in mind when they first moved into the Sonoran valleys.

The larger rancherías and small pueblos[38] of the Pima Bajo and Opata, strung out as they were only along the narrow valleys, were easily absorbed by the mission *reducciones*. A compartmentalized geography also inhibited the rapid spread of European infections, there being an apparent decline in mortality through epidemic disease once the mission frontier advanced into Sonora.[39]

The Nebomes, some of whom had accompanied Cabeza de Vaca southward from the Middle Yaqui, were the first Pima Bajo tribe visited by the Jesuit missionaries — only two or three years after the first missions were established among the Yaqui.[40]

With the establishment of order among the Nebomes it was possible to extend the mission frontier into the upstream Yaqui and Middle Sonora areas occupied by the Opata nation.[41] The first permanent mission among these people was established in 1628 at Sahuaripa, the chief pueblo of the Sisibotaris.[42] A year or so later Jesuit missionaries moved among the Aivino Opata on the Upper Matape and the Batuco Opata at the mouth of what came to be called the Río Moctezuma. Still later an entrada was made among the Opata on the Río Sonora and among the Ures Pima Bajo who lived near the present town of Ures.[43]

In 1644, the Jesuit padres made an entrada into the valley of the Moctezuma, ministering to the Opusuras and Cumupas, two Opata bands. The Indians were gathered into two large mission pueblos which had been formed at two locations where the valley widened out, providing sufficient irrigable land for the enlarged pueblos. To the east, the Guazabas Opata on the Río Bavispe were brought into the fold a year later. And so it was throughout Opataría; perhaps more than any other indigenous people, the Opata were within less than twenty-five years irrevocably and completely "reduced."[44] They "almost immediately intermingled and intermarried with Spanish settlers and adopted Spanish

---

38   The Opata, like the Cahita, lived in large rancherías scattered along desert waterways. These usually contained more buildings and people than the Pima rancherías, but most observers avoid the term "pueblo," reserving it for the definitely larger settlements in New Mexico and northern Arizona. E. H. Spicer, "European Expansion and the Enclavement of Southwestern Indians," *Arizona and the West*, Vol. 1, No. 2 (1959), p. 141.

39   Sauer, *The Aboriginal Population of Northwestern Mexico*, p. 11.

40   Bannon, pp. 22-38.

41   J. B. Johnson, *The Opata: An Inland Tribe of Sonora*, University of New Mexico Publications in Anthropology, No. 6 (Albuquerque, 1929).

42   *Ibid.*, p. 45.

43   *Ibid.*, pp. 65-68.

44   Spicer, *Cycles of Conquest*, p. 96.

ways."[45] This process was hastened by the mines which were quickly developed in the metalliferous sierras of this frontier province.[46] Once again mining had brought the Spaniards and led to the more rapid destruction of native culture and tribal identity. "The story of Sonora is one of continued encroachment of Spaniard on Indian lands and of absorption of local Indians into Spanish haciendas and mines, opposed stoutly but vainly by the Jesuits."[47] In contrast, it is difficult to say whether the Yaqui, who had come under Spanish domination at an earlier time but remain to this day largely unassimilated, demonstrated a greater intransigence, or that their independence was insured by the unattractive nature of the coastal plain which lacked the gold and silver always coveted by the far-wandering Spaniard.

Thus by the year 1645, Jesuit missions or *visitas* stood astride all the major streams of old Sonora. The missions at Cucurpe and Opodepe on the Río San Miguel formed the northwestern frontier of Christendom. On the isolated north-flowing headwater of the Río Bavispe the missions at Bavispe and Bacerac held a tenuous grasp on the frontier of Apachería. The next three years saw the establishment of missions on the headwaters of the Río Sonora at Arizpe, Chinipa, and Bacoachi. With this, however, was ended the great period of expansion northward. For forty years the former limits of Opataría were the northwestern frontiers of New Spain.[48] North of the rapidly disintegrating Opatas were the more primitive Pima Altos and the most warlike Apaches. The former, though less advanced than the Opatas or Pima Bajos, were a sedentary agricultural people very similar to many of the tribes which had been previously missionized. The Apaches, on the other hand, were always seminomadic with some bands relying on cultivated crops while most gathered wild products such as acorns, mescal, sahuaro fruit, and mesquite beans.[49] Though bellicose, the pre-Conquest Apache covered a narrow range in his difficult search for food.[50] But the acquisition of the horse from the Spanish widened the Apaches' range and at the same time enabled them to raid easily the Spaniard's vast herds of cattle.[51]

The last years of the seventeenth century saw increasing difficulty

---

[45]   Spicer, "European Expansion and the Enclavement of Southwestern Indians," *Arizona and the West,* Vol. 1, No. 2, p. 145.

[46]   Bannon, pp. 136-39.

[47]   Sauer, *The Aboriginal Population of Northwestern Mexico,* p. 28.

[48]   G. B. Eckhart, "A Guide to the History of the Missions of Sonora," *Arizona and the West,* Vol. 2, No. 2 (1960), pp. 169-70.

[49]   Kroeber, *Cultural and Natural Areas of Native North America,* pp. 36 ff.

[50]   The Western Apache groups, which concern us here, lived beyond the certain range of the buffalo herds which were the main source of food for the Eastern Apache.

[51]   Bolton, *Rim of Christendom,* p. 245.

Two views of the mission at Caborca. The first, taken prior to its recent restoration, shows the effects of both age and gunfire. The second is that of the front after its restoration. This far-western mission is one of the most magnificent architectural relics of the desert.

— BILL SEARS

along the Apache frontier. Occasional raids on the most isolated missions and ranches were followed by distressingly frequent and rapacious forays deep into the heart of Sonora.[52]

The problems of the Sonora *reducciones* did not end with the Apache. The western border was menaced during this period by the least advanced of all the desert tribes, the Seri. Numbering only an estimated 5,000 at most, the Seri harassed the far western missions and ranches. Occasionally, as in 1660, punitive expeditions were mounted by the Spaniards to "kill off as many as possible" and deport their women and children. At other times attempts were forcibly made to settle Seri bands adjacent to already established missions, such as Cucurpe among the Opata, or Belen among the Yaqui.[53] At all times the Seris constituted a threat to the western border, taking soldiers away from the more dangerous Apache frontier. Even the Yaqui, though at this time a Christian nation, were not to be left unattended. Sonora was an exposed salient whose Spanish and civilized Indian inhabitants were connected only tenuously with Mexico. The Jesuit frontier to the west of the Sierra Madre had far outrun that on the eastern slope. Revolt among the mountain Tepehuanes, Tarahumares, and others exposed the entire right flank of the West Coast missions to danger. In order to quell these disturbances, further advance to the north would have to be postponed.

PIMERIA ALTA

In the period 1645–1685, the civilian frontier was advancing behind the temporarily stalled Jesuits. The missions planted on the Río Sonora, Río Yaqui, and their affluents had opened up another mineralized area. Although there were no important bonanzas, a number of discoveries brought miners into Opataría. In 1685, a new *visitador*[54] reported mining operations in the Cedros Valley, the Mulatos Valley near San Miguel, and near Tecoripa. On the extreme northern frontier in the Valle de Bacanuche, there was intense mining activity. In the vicinity of Chinipa and further northeast, mining had not begun. This area, the scene of a number of later mining booms, was still mission country. The Nacozari region was already studded with mines, as were the Sierras to the south near Opusura and Tepachi.[55]

In the last years of the seventeenth century, the above-mentioned

---

[52] *Ibid.,* pp. 243-46.

[53] Sauer, *The Aboriginal Population of Northwestern Mexico,* pp. 25-26.

[54] This was General Don Gabriel de Isturiz, *visitador* of the provinces of Sinaloa, San Ildefonso de Ostimuri, and Sonora, all on the western slope of Nueva Vizcaya. Bannon, p. 136.

[55] *Ibid.,* pp. 136-39.

silver discoveries at Los Frailes near Alamos were to inspire renewed interest in the northwestern frontier.[56] At about the same time there arrived in Sonora the Jesuit priest, who, more than any other single man, advanced the Spanish flag into the desert wilderness of Pimería Alta — Father Eusebio Francisco Kino. Beginning in 1687 Father Kino undertook to convert the Pima tribes on the northwestern frontier of Sonora to Christianity.[57] Being less primitive than their mainly non-agricultural neighbors, the Pima were, in effect, the only likely field for missionary endeavor on the borders of Sonora.

The Upper Pima occupied the headwaters of the Río San Miguel and Río Sonora whose southern courses had, for over forty years, been within the civilized pale. They were more numerous on the western and northern streams which descend the Sierra Huachuca. The above-mentioned San Miguel and Sonora, along with the westward-flowing Ríos Magdalena and Altar, as well as the northward-flowing Santa Cruz and San Pedro rivers, form a whorl of streams descending from the sierra astride which the present-day boundary divides Mexico from the United States.

The Upper Pima were divided into a number of tribes, all of which practiced some form of irrigation — from well-constructed ditches to the "arroyo flood farming" employed by the Papago.

The Himuris or Pima Proper occupied the headwaters of the major south-, north-, and west-flowing streams, largely on the semi-arid margin of the Sonoran Desert. The valleys of the downstream Magdalena and Altar were the home of the Soba Pima who ranged to the Gulf Coast. The region near Caborca below the junction of these two streams was their chief center. From Tubac north along the Santa Cruz, and from the same latitude on the San Pedro, the Pima Proper were replaced by the Sobaipuris, another Pima-speaking tribe. The Gila Pimas were settled along the Gila from Casa Grande westward nearly to the bend of that river. In the eighteenth century the San Pedro Sobaipuris were destroyed or driven from that river by the Apaches. Finally, to the west of the Santa Cruz were the Papagos, whose economy relied less on agriculture and more on gathering than their Pima brethren.

The first mission among the Upper Pima was established by Father Kino in 1687 at Cosari on the upstream San Miguel. He called this mission Dolores.[58] Within the year he crossed over to the west-flowing

---

[56]   F. R. Almada, *Diccionario de Historia, Geografía y Biografía Sonorenses* (Chihuahua, 1952), p. 12.

[57]   Eusebio Francisco Kino, *Kino's Historical Memoir of Pimería Alta,* H. E. Bolton, trans. (Berkeley, 1948).

[58]   Eckhart, "A Guide to the History of the Missions of Sonora," *Arizona and the West,* Vol. 2, No. 2, p. 170.

San Xavier del Bac Mission on the San Xavier Papago Reservation near Tucson. One of the three missions established along the Santa Cruz River in Arizona by the Jesuit Father Eusebio Kino, it was founded in 1700 at the old Papago village of Bac. It is still in use today although the building pictured here was built by the Franciscans late in the same century. The fields around the mission have probably been cultivated on and off since prehistoric times.

Río Magdalena, laying the groundwork for missions at Imuris and distant Caborca. By 1690, missions were strung along the upstream Río Magdalena and its rightbank tributary, the Río Altar. In 1691, Kino traveled north along the Santa Cruz River proselytizing, making notes for future reference, and gathering the natives together in *ranchos* and *visitas*. Like his predecessors in Sinaloa and Opataría, Father Kino introduced stock-raising among the Indians who were taught the principles of animal husbandry. It is not generally thought that cattle, either wild or domesticated, preceded Kino into the Pimería Alta.[59]

Until the year 1711, when he died, Father Kino explored, pacified, and established mission settlements among his beloved Pimas. He reached the Colorado River, which he crossed, establishing in his letters the peninsular character of California, but not the nature of the intervening country.[60] As he pressed north and west, he distributed wheat and sent herds of cattle and horses into a desert which he felt certain could support them. His missions were extended to the distant oasis of Sonoita, and he looked forward to the day that missions would be planted along the Gila to the Colorado. He put down rebellion and organized resistance against the Apache, whose raids on the San Pedro and Santa Cruz valleys increased with the greater prosperity of the Pima missions. Kino struggled against civilian encroachment on mission lands until his death.[61]

The missions of Pimería Alta declined after the death of Father Kino. From 1725, efforts were made to reinvigorate the mission economies. In 1730, additional Jesuit priests were sent to this frontier. Six years later the famous Planchas de Plata silver strike was made in the district of Arizonac in Pimería Alta just south of the international boundary.[62] This resulted in an influx of Spanish miners who were, aside from the Jesuits, Pimería Alta's first white population. The high-grade ore in these mines, however, was soon worked out, and the miners straggled back to the south.[63] This was the farthest advance of the

---

[59]   Wagoner, pp. 10-17.

[60]   Father Kino was probably Arizona's first "booster," never mentioning the extreme heat and arid conditions of Pimería Alta.

[61]   Aside from Bolton's translation of Kino's *Memoir,* there are a number of authoritative works on the life and works of Father Kino. Bolton's own *Rim of Christendom* stands at the head of the list. A contemporary account is Juan Mateo Manje's *Luz de Tierra Incógnita, 1693–1721,* trans. by H. J. Karns (Tucson, 1954).

[62]   Arizonac was the Hispanicized form of the Papago words for "small" (ali) and "place of the spring" (shonak). The name of the state of Arizona takes its name through further modification. Byrd H. Granger (ed.), *Will C. Barnes' Arizona Place Names,* rev. ed. Tucson, 1960), p. xv. Arizonac was a *visita* for Saric mission and was located one mile south of the boundary and about eight miles west of Old Sasabe.

[63]   G. P. Hammond, "Pimeria Alta After Kino's Time," *New Mexico Historical Review,* Vol. 4 (1929), pp. 220-25.

mining frontier in northwestern New Spain. It was during the excitement of this strike that the discovery of the mines at Ajo was made by Spanish prospectors. Thus, the existence of the first great Sonoran copper mining district was made known, although distance, drought, and economic conditions precluded, for over a century, its eventual development.

This last period of the Sonoran Jesuit frontier missions, which ended in 1767, with the expulsion of the Jesuits from New Spain, was a study in frustration. The frontier did not move ahead, but instead a number of isolated ranchos and pueblos were abandoned to the Apache, particularly in the San Pedro and Bavispe valleys. In Pimería Alta the followers of Kino were unable to establish missions among the great majority of the Papago,[64] the mission at Sonoita being abandoned in 1751. The Gila Pimas remained outside the mission frontier despite their desire to be included. The Seris remained a nuisance on the left flank, and the Apaches were growing stronger on the right. Pimería Alta, as well as Sonora itself, continued to comprise an exposed salient. The absence of any major mining discoveries meant that there was little to stimulate immigration, and white population grew only slowly. Native agricultural techniques declined in the missions, an exception being the rapidly disappearing Opatas and sturdy Yaquis. These two tribal groups continued to produce the agricultural surplus which the frontier needed.[65]

THE DESERT PUEBLO

The foundation and settlement of towns in the arid lands of northwestern New Spain were based upon the laws and practices of the mother

---

[64]   R. K. Wyllys, "Padre Luis Velarde's 'Relacion of Pimeria Alta,' 1716," *New Mexico Historical Review,* Vol. 6 (1951), pp. 111-57.

[65]   The account of the development of Sonora and Pimería Alta after the death of Father Kino has received belated attention with the publication of a number of anonymous *relaciones* during the last 20 years. Among these are the "Estado y Descripción de la Provincia de Sonora, 1730," *Boletín del Archivo General de la Nación* (1945), and *Rudo Ensayo, by an Unknown Jesuit Padre, 1763* (Tucson, 1951). Sedelmayr's *"Relación* of 1744–1751," *Jacobo Sedelmayr: Missionary, Frontiersman, Explorer in Arizona and Sonora,* trans. and annotated by P. M. Dunne (Tucson, 1955), is another interesting account of this period. The interpretation of these relaciones and others including Father Velarde's, are to be found in S. Mosk, *Economic Problems in Sonora in the late Eighteenth Century* (Glendale, Calif., 1939); Russell C. Ewing, "The Pima Uprising of 1751: A Study of Spanish-Indian Relations on the Frontier of New Spain," *in Greater America: Essays in Honor of Herbert Eugene Bolton* (Berkeley, 1945), pp. 259–94; Ursula Schaefer, "Pimeria Alta, 1711–1767," unpublished Ph.D. thesis, University of California (Berkeley, 1944); Theodore Treutlein, "The Economic Regime of the Jesuit Missions in Eighteenth Century Sonora," *Pacific Historical Review,* Vol. 8 (1939), pp. 289–300; and R. L. Ives, "The Sonoran Census of 1730," *Records of the American Catholic Historical Society of Philadelphia,* Vol. 59, No. 4 (1948).

country as they were continually being modified in the American colonies. The morphological development of these settlements clearly bears the Iberian stamp. Spain itself was a Roman colony and many of its famous cities were founded as colonial towns which, to this day, carry the mark of Imperial Roman town planning. The public square and centuriated pattern of city blocks and lots are the most plainly visible testimonials to the Roman origins of many Spanish towns.[66] On several occasions after the decline of Roman Spain, the peninsula was recolonized. The most recent was the medieval Christian advance across Spain, ending with the fall of Granada. Not only were colonial towns once again being formed on a frontier of conquest in Spain, but the Catholic Church was an active agent of colonization foreshadowing the events which were to take place in the New World. In addition, much of Spain is semiarid, and irrigation had long been practiced. The *acequia* (irrigation ditch) was an integral part of the Spanish cultural landscape, the *huertas*[67] and pueblos being sited adjacent to this indispensable conduit. As the frontiers of New Spain were thrust farther and farther into the Sonoran Desert, the more valuable were the Iberian lessons in the urban colonization of arid lands.

The grid pattern which characterizes the town plans of New Spain had its origin in the Roman plan of many Spanish towns, or perhaps more directly in the Spaniards' knowledge of Roman instructions to their colonizers.[68] The codified instructions of Phillip II in 1573 regarding the establishment of towns on a grid pattern bear a striking similarity to those of the Roman planner Vitruvius.[69] No other European nation could have been as well-equipped through experience to establish towns in the arid expanses of North America.

Colonial settlement was governed by laws enacted under Charles V and Phillip II that attempted to impose as explicitly uniform regulations as possible on the founding of towns.[70] A *pueblo* grant was usually four square leagues of land laid out systematically in the form of a square or an oblong.[71] The first point to be chosen was the town square

---

[66]   Dan Stanislawski, "Early Spanish Town Planning in the New World," *The Geographical Review,* Vol. 37 (1947), pp. 101-105.

[67]   The irrigated fields of Spain are referred to as *huertas,* and in Mexico the term *riego* is often used.

[68]   Stanislawski, "Early Spanish Town Planning in the New World," *The Geographical Review,* Vol. 37, pp. 101-105.

[69]   Stanislawski gives the Spaniard "who had never known of such a [grid] pattern" little credit for any observational ability. *Ibid.,* p. 97.

[70]   Blackmar, p. 161.

[71]   The four-square-league grant had replaced an earlier grant of one square league which was law prior to the general advance into the arid north of New Spain. "An evident response to the aridity of the climate." G. M. McBride, *The Land Systems of Mexico* (New York, 1923), p. 108.

or rectangular plaza. The settlement was then laid out in the form of a grid centered on the plaza while the church and major public buildings were located facing this square. After the location of the public buildings the land which comprised the remainder of the town's blocks was granted to the founders in the form of *solares* (town lots). The solares were large, having an area which would hold the sprawling buildings and ramadas which usually surrounded a large patio.[72] Usually no more than two to four solares could be fitted into a town block.

As settlement progressed and pueblos were founded in the Sonoran Desert, these ideal plans were seldom followed — for a number of reasons. The physical conditions militated against the perfect functioning of a system which was both agricultural in purpose and regular in plan. Many of the first settlements were mining camps where the systematic distribution of farmland meant nothing. In addition, some of these mining camps were on a steep slope or in a narrow canyon where the grid plan, with its central plaza and square blocks, could not be delineated. Nacozari is an example of this physical limitation resulting in an irregular town plan. Agricultural settlements were also subject to the same limits imposed by topography. In the valleys of Old Sonora, there was seldom an irrigable area four square leagues in extent. The narrow valleys placed lateral limits on the expansion of irrigation, and pueblo lands were laid out paralleling the streamways. There was almost always enough room, however, for the town to be built following the grid pattern with its centrally-located plaza, church, and public buildings.

A more effective agent working against a perfectly functioning plan was the prior existence of missions which had appropriated much of the limited land available to irrigation. The missionaries did, however, plan the mission settlements in accord with the accepted practices, but fought diligently against the division of the mission lands among the Spanish colonizers.

Agricultural settlements founded during the colonial period which were completely independent of prior mission rights to the land were rare. A region whose arable land was already densely settled by a sedentary indigenous population left little room for the establishment of entirely new towns. Only as missions were abandoned did land usually become available for outside settlement, and by this time the mission stamp was on the countryside.

Presidios were another nucleus for the later foundation of agricultural settlements. Pitic (Hermosillo), established as a post on the Seri frontier, took shape as a presidio whose central grid-like streets

---

[72] Spanish law provided that each settler should receive a building lot thirty *varas* square (about 83 feet), but this varied considerably.

Fronteras differs from the other three in that it was originally a military presidio. Today it gives the appearance of a fort, although the original is in ruins.

Four settlements in isolated eastern Sonora. Each of these towns was founded in the seventeenth century under instructions from the Spanish crown.

San Miguel Horcasitas, another mission settlement, was the old capital of Sonora. De Anza departed from here with his group of settlers who crossed the western desert to found San Francisco in 1775–76. This photo taken in 1957 might have been taken two centuries before.

[138]

— E. TAD NICHOLS

The Plaza at Los Angeles, Sonora. The old church is at the opposite end of this two-block-long plaza. The façade in this shot is the front of an old mill which burned about 1940.

Moctezuma is sited on a terrace above the river of the same name. A former mission among the now-extinct Opata tribe, its adobe walls enclose spacious patios. Single-story buildings made from the same material closely line streets that are regularly laid out on a grid plan.

and plazas bear the unmistakable mark of colonial planning slightly modified by the desert mountains which constrict the even spread of streets. Tubac and Fronteras, both of which were located like Pitic in areas of agricultural possibilites, exhibit in their yet embryonic form the planning manifestos of the colonial period.

Most Sonoran agricultural settlements which had their origins during the colonial period display a composite settlement pattern where a civilian pueblo was superimposed on a mission or presidio pattern. The result, as may be seen in such towns as Ures, Huepac, Bocoachic, Moctezuma and Cumpas, is a quite regular grid pattern whose deviations are due to topography more than any other factor.

APACHERIA

The advance of the Spanish mission frontier north along the West Coast Corridor stalled and finally retreated before the Apaches, who occupied the high plains, mountains, and basins to the north and northeast of the Sonoran Desert.[73] The numerous Apache tribes or bands have been separated by scholars into two main divisions. Only the western division directly concerned the Sonoran frontier but the Apache, through their grip on the high plains of Chihuahua, New Mexico, and Texas affected all three of the corridors leading north from Mexico. By shifting their attack from one sector to another over a wide front they were able to bring unbearable pressures against any of the three corridors.

The horse transformed the Apache from plodding hunters, gatherers, and farmers into a nation of mounted soldiers. In the words of Herbert Eugene Bolton:

> When first heard of, the Apaches, though warlike, covered a narrow range and were devoted somewhat to agriculture. But the Spaniards brought horses to the frontier, the Apaches acquired them, and their range widened. The Spaniards had also vast herds of cattle which the Apaches came to prize as food. In other words, the Spaniards raised stock and at the same time gave the Apaches the means of stealing it. As the 17th century waned, the raids became longer and longer, until by Kino's day the Apaches not only ravaged border missions and outlying ranches, but penetrated the very heart of Sonora, supplementing theft with fire and murder.[74]

It is interesting to note that the Spanish conquest of Mexico effected one of its greatest cultural metamorphoses beyond the frontier of New

---

[73] The history of this contact up to the year 1700 is dealt with in Jack D. Forbes, *Apache, Navaho and Spaniard* (Norman, Okla., 1960).

[74] Bolton, *Rim of Christendom*, p. 244.

Spain,[75] and that it resulted in the Apache's almost complete abandonment of farming and other sedentary enterprise.

Centuries of abrasive contact with Spanish imperialism led the Apache to "neglect his former peaceful avocations in order to specialize in the art of border warfare, first in self defence" and later as an "alternate means of making his livelihood."[76] His former natural and cultural resources were mainly discarded. The Spaniards and their Indian allies became, in effect, his primary resources. Along the Sonoran frontier, the Apache and his horse were able to live on the high chaparral and grassy plains, occasionally descending with quiet devastation upon an irrigated oasis and returning to Apachería unchallenged, driving herds of cattle and horses before him. The high plains of Apachería were the best defense these horsemen had. Wide and grassy, they gave the Apache invisibility and his pony food. Most importantly, these plains did not provide the Spaniard with agricultural possibilities. This precluded establishment of the virtually self-sufficient native pueblos which were the economic base of the Spanish military success among the sedentary people of the West Coast. The Sonoran Desert had provided a more benign milieu for colonial expansion, despite the much larger native population, than did the high plains. The margin of the desert proved to be the frontier of effective Spanish occupation on the northeastern border of the West Coast Corridor. Opatería, unfortunately, became a rampart against the Apache rather than a steppingstone toward them. "Thus at the moment when the Sonoran frontier, on its right flank, seemed about to achieve its logical goal, union of the Western Slope with New Mexico, its progress was halted; and its energies turned to the less spectacular task of defending itself."[77]

Toynbee advances the argument that in his relationship with the Apache the Spaniard "duly repeated the classical mistake . . . which on other frontiers between a civilization and barbarians had eventually given the barbarians the victory; and it is not inconceivable that history might have followed the same course in North America as in the Old World."[78] The Spaniard's mistake was to give provocation to the Apache "by starting an aggressive advance into their country, to be deterred upon reaching the edge of an apparently forbidding tract of terrain from proceeding with their occupation in the teeth of this local obstacle

---

[75] Hammond, "Pimeria Alta after Kino's Time," *New Mexico Historical Review*, Vol. 4, p. 220.

[76] Arnold Toynbee, *A Study of History*, Vol. 8, Appendix 36 (London, 1954).

[77] Bannon, *The Mission Frontier in Sonora, 1620–1687*, p. 140.

[78] Toynbee, VIII, p. 634.

until their advance had brought them to a natural frontier with no potential trans-frontier barbarians beyond it."[79] The "forbidding terrain" spoken of is the semiarid high plains. The Spaniard, by failing to come quickly to grips with this environment and its inhabitants, gave the Apache time to adopt one of the Spaniard's chief weapons, the horse, which eventually he used with greater skill than his civilized opponent.

This argument is convincing if one overlooks the fact that the high semiarid plains of Apachería are not significantly different from the semiarid central plateau of Mexico where the Spaniard met with success, or for that matter, from the Spanish Meseta. Even the desert itself is not terribly dissimilar climatically from the plains of La Mancha. The "forbidding terrain" of Apachería must have reminded many a Spaniard of his native Castile.

There is nothing in the land itself which made this semiarid expanse forbidding. Only as its inhabitants failed to accept quickly and peacefully the first Spanish missionaries and soldiers as almost every Sonoran Desert tribe had,[80] did the land become "forbidding." Only as time proved that wild or stolen horses thrived and multiplied on the short grass of Apachería were the Spaniards forced to reassess this terrain. Instead of being used as the foundation of a northern colonial society, the Apache rose to challenge on horseback the pyramidal structure which Spain had built on an indigenous base throughout the territory to the south. As Walter Prescott Webb concluded, "One would judge that with experience the task of conquest and occupation would grow lighter, but on the contrary, it became heavier and eventually impossible."[81] A moving, aggressive frontier of assimilation was replaced on the upland margin of the desert by a defensive limes — a line of presidios which would in time approximate the international boundary when another nation brought an end to Apachería.

The sedentary tribes of the trans-frontier desert were also undergoing a period of transformation during the Apache ascendency although permanent Spanish or Mexican settlement of the Sonoran Desert did not advance to the north of the middle Santa Cruz, or to the west of the Altar-Magdalena valleys, in the century and a half following Father Kino's death.[82] The introduction of winter wheat among the native people beyond the frontier during this period allowed them to augment

---

[79]   *Ibid.,* pp. 635-36.

[80]   Spicer, "European Expansion and the Enclavement of Southwestern Indians," *Arizona and the West,* Vol. 1, No. 2.

[81]   Webb, *The Great Plains* (New York, 1931), p. 98.

[82]   Hammond, "Pimería Alta after Kino's Time," *New Mexico Historical Review,* Vol. 4, pp. 220-22.

beneficially their summer corn harvest. This allowed some groups, such as the Gila Pima, to abandon in large measure their hunting and gathering activities.

The growing strength of mounted Apache bands in the Sonoran Desert pressed hard against the more sedentary desert tribes. The Apache threat was met by the Gila Pimas through a concentration of their people in larger settlements which provided suitable defense against these marauders. The Pima villages contracted from their spread of fifty-five miles along the Gila to about twelve. A number of villages came to rely on a common canal system which necessitated the regular allocation of water. Wheat provided the increased productivity needed to insure a greater amount of food from the smaller cultivated area. However, the Pimas of the Gila River never developed an agricultural system which achieved "environmental control." A drought in 1854 forced them to rely once more on the mesquite bean for survival.[83]

Among the Papago, the introduction of wheat at an early date had less significance than it did among the Pima. A scarcity of water in the deserts of Papaguería precluded the irrigation of large fields of wheat, and nomadic activities continued.[84]

The addition of livestock gave these seminomadic people an economic alternative which transformed the desert environment. A horse was particularly useful, making the semiannual treks from valley to mountain and back less arduous. The Papago attached to the horse a value even greater than its usefulness. Ownership of horses became a source of prestige. Horses and cattle were individually owned, in contrast to land, which was considered the property of the tribe, and was allocated to individuals by the elders. Thus the concept of individual ownership was furthered by the introduction of livestock. In addition, horses allowed the Papago to quit the western desert during extended drought, and ride down into the irrigated valleys to the east. There he worked on the Pima and Mexican farms and ranches for pay. The mobility afforded by the horse brought the Papago for the first time into contact with the wage market economy of New Spain.[85]

Indirectly, the advent of the horse evoked another change in Papaguería. The mounted Apache moved far to the west, forcing the Sobaipuri from the San Pedro Valley.[86] Their raids extended to the

---

[83] Robert A. Hackenberg, "Economic Alternatives for Native People in Arid Lands," *Arid Lands Colloquia,* Vol. 1 (Tucson, 1961), pp. 46-51.

[84] Castetter and Bell, pp. 51-53.

[85] *Ibid.,* p. 51.

[86] Alice Joseph, Rosamund Spicer, and Jane Chesky, *The Desert People: A Study of the Papago Indians* (Chicago, 1949), pp. 18-19.

western part of the present Papago Reservation. The frequent incursions of mounted Apache warriors had many effects. The Papago, who had lived in rather small villages, began to abandon these settlements in order to congregate in large defense villages. They started to rely more on winter crops and livestock whose diversity could prevent starvation after Apache raids. In time, the mounted and seminomadic Papago did, in fact, protect themselves rather well against the Apache. One result was that as the Apache decimated the mission settlements along the irrigated valleys to the east and southeast, the Papago occupied land formerly belonging to the Pimas of the Santa Cruz and Altar valleys. The Papago, originally far less numerous than these riverine Pimas, survived the Apache Wars to a much greater degree than the latter. Settling in the valleys, they adopted the sedentary economic activities of mission life. Meanwhile, those who remained in Papaguería gradually managed to improve their lot, despite the Apache, finally drifting back to many of the village sites occupied in Kino's day.[87]

---

[87]   Castetter and Bell, p. 9.

CHAPTER EIGHT

Westward Crossings, Discovery and Development

The need for Spain to establish an overland route to Alta California was amply demonstrated in the first years of settlement. In the Portolá expedition in 1769, it took one vessel 54 days to reach San Diego from San Blas and another ship, 110 days.[1] The voyage from San Blas north was extremely difficult due to the prevailing northwesterly winds.[2]

During these same years the intrepid Franciscan Father Garcés, whose mission was at San Xavier del Bac, south of Tucson, was exploring alone along the Lower Colorado.[3] Crossing the river he wandered as far as the present site of Mexicali where he observed that an overland crossing to the Pacific Coast of California would be possible over this route. He related this information to Juan Bautista de Anza, a Sonoran by birth who had also desired to open a route to California. An expedition headed by Anza was readied after great delay. Leaving the valleys of old Sonora in late 1773, he planned to organize the final crossing of the Lower Colorado Desert at San Xavier and then to proceed north and west along the Santa Cruz and Gila to the Yuma crossing. An Apache raiding party, however, carried away many of their horses, necessitating a return to the Altar Valley where they hoped to requisition replacements.[4] Having arrived there, Anza decided to travel directly

---

1   Bolton, *An Outpost of Empire*, p. 40.

2   L. Rodwell Jones, "Notes on the Geographical Factors Which Controlled the Spanish Advance into Northern Mexico and Southern California," *The Scottish Geographical Magazine,* Vol. 39, pp. 169-70.

3   Elliott Coues, *On the Trail of a Spanish Pioneer: The Diary and Itinerary of Francisco Garcés in his Travels through Sonora, Arizona and California.* (2 vols.; New York, 1900).

4   Bolton, *An Outpost of Empire*, pp. 68-77.

northwest over Kino's old trail to Sonoita Oasis and from there over what later was called the Camino del Diablo to Yuma.[5] After a difficult crossing, they reached the Colorado River. Fording it, they set out across the even more desolate plains and playas of the Colorado Desert west of Yuma. After many dry camps and much suffering the little expedition reached the mission of San Gabriel, having left the desert south of the San Jacinto Mountains.[6]

Returning to Sonora and Mexico via the Gila Valley, Anza organized a second expedition, recruiting his pioneers from the old pueblos of Sinaloa and Sonora. Forsaking the route west to Sonoita, Anza and his immigrant train followed the Gila River and reached California in the same year as the U. S. Declaration of Independence and the founding of San Francisco. Thus Father Garcés and Captain Anza opened two of the most important routes west across the Sonoran Desert and were the first to reach coastal California overland. The Anza expedition introduced the first cattle into Alta California. These heat-and-thirst-hardened animals soon multiplied, becoming the primary economic base of that province.[7]

Fifty years later the first Anglo-Americans to visit the northern desert opened another route to the Pima villages and the Lower Gila. Sylvester and James Ohio Pattie, father and son, fur trappers and explorers, obtained permission from the Governor of Nuevo Mexico to trap along the Gila River.[8] Leaving Socorro in December, 1824, they spent five months in the Gila Valley and then returned to the Rio Grande after considerable deprivation. Three years later the Patties traversed the same route from the headwaters of the Gila to its mouth and then over much of the same route across the Lower Colorado Desert that Anza had pioneered.[9] This in fact marked the first complete crossing of the northern desert from east to west, coming almost three hundred years after its first south-north crossing.[10]

The Gila River route pioneered by Fathers Kino and Garcés, Captain Anza and the Patties, was first made known to the American public during the Mexican War when Colonel Stephen Watts Kearny led a

---

[5]   G. Sykes, "The Camino del Diablo with Notes on a Journey in 1925," *Geographical Review,* Vol. 17 (1927), pp. 70-72. Sykes describes this route with particular emphasis on the extreme desiccating heat and the effects thereof.

[6]   Bolton, *An Outpost of Empire,* pp. 118-72.

[7]   Wagoner, pp. 20-21.

[8]   James Ohio Pattie, *Pattie's Personal Narrative.* . . . (Cleveland, 1905). Vol. 18 of *Early Western Travels,* ed. by R. G. Thwaites.

[9]   *Ibid.,* pp. 13-15.

[10]   E. W. Gilbert, *The Exploration of Western America, 1800–1850* (Cambridge, 1933), pp. 166-67.

small army over the Patties' route down the Gila to Yuma Crossing and California. At the same time Philip St. George Cooke pioneered another trail called Cooke's Wagon Road. Leaving the Rio Grande Valley thirty miles above Doña Ana, Cooke's expedition proceeded west across the high plains of Mesilla to Guadalupe Pass (near the point common to Mexico, Arizona, and New Mexico). Joining the San Pedro Valley southwest of the present Bisbee, the party followed that river north for approximately fifty miles, crossing over to the Santa Cruz Valley at Tucson and then across the waterless plain to the Pima villages.[11]

The routes west across the desert explored by Garcés and Anza, Pattie, Kearny, and Cooke were first traveled by significant numbers in the years following the discovery of gold at Sutter's Mill, California, in 1848. As early as the latter part of that year thousands of Sonorans set out from Altar and Tucson for the goldfields. Traveling either over the Camino del Diablo or via the Pima villages, they traversed the parched Lower Colorado Desert en route to Yuma and California. Poorly equipped, they suffered untold hardships. The bones of many of their number were already bleached white by the time the first Anglo-American entered the same desert a year later.

The Gila River route across North America carried fewer argonauts in 1849 than either the Platte Valley route or the sea and sea-land routes via Cape Horn or Central America.[12] Nevertheless, a number of newspapers advised their readers to use this means of crossing the continent to the diggings in California. An estimated 9,000 Forty-niners followed their advice.[13] Some of these crossed the Sierra from Parral to Ures and then traversed the desert west to Altar and Yuma over the Camino del Diablo. Others chose to avoid this barren waste by traveling north to Tucson and the Pima villages.[14]

Larger numbers, however, looked to Santa Fe and El Paso as points of embarkation across the desert. From there they followed the route pioneered by Cooke to Tucson or by Pattie and Frémont to the Pima villages.[15] Still others left Janos in Chihuahua for the west through Guadalupe Pass and then along Cooke's Road to Tucson. Another more dangerous alternative was from Santa Fe west to the Zuñi Pueblos and

---

[11] The "Pima Villages" were those Gila Pima rancherías located along the Gila above its confluence with the Salt.

[12] R. P. Bieber, "The South-western Trails to California in 1849," *Mississippi Valley Historical Review,* Vol. 12 (1925), p. 343.

[13] *Ibid.,* p. 375.

[14] *Ibid.,* p. 351.

[15] *Ibid.,* p. 372.

from there southwest via the Salt River to its confluence with the Gila. The journey took three to six months and traversed the heart of Apachería.

An interesting story is the part played by cattle in these westward crossings. The mission herds founded by Kino had declined after his death, only to be revived once again by secular authority. The Spanish Crown had established land grants as far north as the middle Santa Cruz and San Pedro valleys in what is now northern Sonora and southern Arizona. White and mestizo cattlemen reoccupied the sparse range first pioneered by the Jesuits.[16]

Indian hostility, however, particularly that of the Apache, increased after the first decade of the nineteenth century and became particularly fierce after Mexican independence. The frontier was once again swept back and thousands of cattle were either left to die on the desert or to be scattered or killed by the Apache.

Members of the Cooke expedition encountered semi-wild cattle and lived off their meat[17] in December, 1846. Later expeditions also encountered and were in part sustained by wild cattle, which were apparently diminishing rapidly in numbers. Unlike the desert of the thorn forest transition, where in an earlier century wild herds multiplied, the Arizona upland desert and the Apache combined to destroy even the hardy Andalusian stock.

By 1848, when Tubac and Tumacacori were destroyed by the Apaches, only Tucson and nearby San Xavier remained of what had been Mexican civilization north of the present frontier. The cattle economy was as good as dead, and with it, Mexican settlement. This same year, however, marked the beginning of a new era as the first wave of Forty-Niners drove before them Texas and Missouri cattle. These may have been, in fact, the first cattle to arrive in any numbers on the Middle and Lower Gila. As before, the Apache continued to harass the ranchers and drovers, killing thousands of head of cattle before the final victory over this tribe years later. "Yet by way of speculation . . . these same Apaches by retarding the Spanish and Mexican advance had actually hastened later development. Huge land grants did not cover the future Arizona to complicate later settlement, as was the case in the Rio Grande Valley of New Mexico."[18]

---

[16]   R. H. Mattison, "Early Spanish and Mexican Settlements in Arizona," *New Mexico Historical Review,* Vol. 21, No. 4, 1946, pp. 285-86.

[17]   Wagoner, pp. 27-29.

[18]   *Ibid.,* p. 30.

EARLY ANGLO-AMERICAN SETTLEMENT

The pattern of Anglo-American settlement was different in most respects from the Spanish. In the first instance the influence of a church or religious order did not exist in the planting of new communities, or in the introduction of new arts and industries. Related to this was the usual disregard which typified the American's attitude toward the indigenous population. Instead of a mission church, settlement, and carefully supervised fields, the Indian was shunted aside and forgotten if possible. Only when the interests of the Indian conflicted with those of the American did the latter take notice of his existence. Perhaps most significant of all, the American never looked upon the native population as a principal source of labor.

No important white settlements were attached to Indian rancherías so that native labor could be utilized. Very few Indians found their way into the mining camps. No commensal economic relationship between the races developed as it did in Mexico. Indian crafts and industries declined as did agriculture, particularly among the Gila River Pimas after the American occupation. It was only another short step to the placement of the Indians on reservations in an attempt to wholly remove them from the white man's economy.

Another significant difference lay in the role played by the military. Whereas presidios time after time constituted the seed of an important town along the frontier of New Spain, the American military posts of southern Arizona never resulted in a civilian settlement of any permanence except for the modern-day Fort Huachuca. Thus there were no Anglo-American counterparts to the self-supporting mission or presidio, leaving only the agricultural town and mining camp as types of settlement similar to those of Spanish days.

The first towns having an American population of any importance were the already-existing but besieged Tucson and Tubac, wedged as they were between Apachería and the barren desert to the west.

Mining camps and a handful of towns that supplied them as well as the military posts that had sprung up throughout the region were the first strictly American settlements of the Sonoran Desert. The lowland towns had two basic functions. The first of these, typified by Yuma and the now-defunct Ehrenberg, was to transship supplies brought by sea and river to inland points. The second was to provide grain and forage from irrigated fields to the scattered upland mines and forts. Phoenix on the Salt, and Florence on the Gila, were two of the most important in the decades following American hegemony. These towns, laid out as they were among the mile-square fields of the U. S. rectangular survey system, were similar in many respects to the frontier pueblos of Sonora. An 1881 description of Florence bears witness to the similarities as well as the differences:

> Florence . . . has a population of about 800, several stores, two hotels, a brewery, saloons, and many handsome private residences. The streets, which are laid off toward the cardinal points of the compass, are broad, and shaded by leafy cottonwoods. Streams of water run on each side of the street, keeping the air delightfully cool and pleasant. The houses are built of sun-dried block (adobe), with shingle roofs. The adobe is the house for a warm climate; no matter how high the mercury may mount, the interior is always cool.[19]

The chronicles of early explorers and adventurers provide interesting descriptions of desert privation and danger which are today all too easily forgotten. One of these men, Daniel Ellis Conner, described the adventures of the Walker party in the valleys of the Gila and the Hassayampa rivers during the war years of 1862 and 1863:

> We traveled this desert in the night . . . on account of the heat, for the sun was pouring down. We halted for rest and water. This water was alive with little flat, scaly bugs. There was no spring here, but some tanks naturally worn under some cliffs held this fragrant water, all of which we drank before we left. We were soon in single file again. This desert was nearly devoid of vegetation. We kept our direct course until night when we were all fearfully thirsty. The dogs had either to be tied upon the packs of the mules or to be deserted and left. . . . The party's fatigued and barren-looking camp place was silent and deserted in the extreme. Men, mules, and dogs were all resigned to a famished and patient desperation. When the sun arose we were within five miles of what could easily be seen to be barren mountains. We were off at daylight and in due time reached the dry mouth of the creek that we were destined to follow, pronounced by the Indians "Haviamp". . . . We kept up this creek as the sand became more damp as we proceeded, . . . and in half an hour had quite a flood of running water at our feet. And we all did drink. There are a few who understand what real hunger means — and none who can understand and explain the cruel and murderous situation where extreme thirst is added.[20]

As with so many of the other early parties, the desert was certainly not a goal in itself but a barrier to be overcome. The Walker party founded Prescott and less than a year later, Henry Wickenburg discovered the Vulture mine near the town that bears his name. Within

---

[19]   Joseph Miller, *Arizona: The Last Frontier* (New York, 1956) p. 42.

[20]   Daniel Ellis Conner, *Joseph Reddeford Walker and the Arizona Adventure* (Norman, Okla., 1956), pp. 79-84.

another year Anglo-Americans were settling along the Salt River. This first white settlement in the Salt River Valley supplied grain and forage to the upland mining camps. Thus, approximately 330 years after the first Spanish settlement of the desert far to the south, Anglo-Americans had finally put down stakes in the desiccated but potentially rich Salt River Valley.

MINING

Near the end of the eighteenth century when Spain finally advanced into Alta California, it was Sonora and Sinaloa which more than any other region contributed settlers to this Pacific frontier.[21] This was done from a surprisingly small population base. Apache depredations and rebellion among the Pima and Yaqui had contributed to a static or declining population. Aside from a few valleys, the desert itself contained an extremely small number of whites. Late eighteenth-century colonial settlements were concentrated largely in a few upland mining districts in the Sierra Madre as well as in southern Sinaloa. A negligible white population lived to the north of the present international boundary.

In Sinaloa the white population was concentrated mainly in the south around Mazatlán, Chametla, Rosario, and Concordia. Here in 1770 there lived approximately 6,700 *gente de razón,* the majority of whom were to be found in the mining districts, particularly that of Rosario (Tajo Mine) which was also a staging point for the Plomosa and Copala mines. Culiacán alone accounted for another 1,500 white inhabitants in addition to 600 who lived on the coastal plain below that city.[22]

In northern Sinaloa, where the thorn forest begins to give way to desert, the white population declined markedly. San Felipe de Sinaloa had the largest population with an estimated 3,500 inhabitants. San Juan de Monteclaros (El Fuerte) contained approximately 1,800. These figures represent a population which was more than likely spread throughout the entire valleys of the Sinaloa and Fuerte.

In southern Sonora, Alamos stood almost alone as an important white settlement. The silver mining districts around Alamos accounted for approximately 6,280 European settlers, which means that far more than 50 percent of the white population of Sonora was concentrated

---

21   Bolton, *An Outpost of Empire.*

22   G. Pfeifer, "Sinaloa und Sonora Beitrage zur Landeskunde und Kultur geographie des nordwestlichen Mexico," *Mitt. Geog. Gesell.,* Vol. 46 (1939), p. 357.

here! Alamos alone had a population of 3,400 whites. The former importance of this town is attested to by its impressive Spanish colonial buildings, as well as by its beautiful church which faces the famous arches that line the plaza.

The Mayo and Yaqui deltas, where an estimated 25,000 Cahita Indians lived, were still avoided by the Spaniards. Thus, in Sinaloa and southern Sonora the white population held closely to the mining districts and towns of the Camino Real. The coastal desert was still avoided due to its limited opportunities.

The area north of the Yaqui delta where the desert widens to the west and the Sierra to the east is breached by the headwater affluents of the Yaqui and Sonora rivers; the white population was sparse but more widely distributed throughout the region. It usually formed a minority in a predominantly Indian population. In 1770, the Spanish were concentrated in fifty settlements whereas at least ninety-five places were listed as having Indian inhabitants — largely Lower Pima, Opata, Upper Pima, and Papago.[23]

In the Horcasitas (San Miguel) Valley, there were enumerated 981 *gente de razón* and 949 Indians. The Upper Sonora Valley contained 1,181 whites and 1,837 Indians. Ures was the chief center of population. The Lower Sonora Valley near Hermosillo (Pitic) was listed as having only 125 whites and 53 Indians. The Middle Yaqui was estimated as having about 1,800 inhabitants, practically all Indian. The Moctezuma-Nacozari region, which contained numerous mines, formed an island of white population in these eastern foothills where the Opata still retained their tribal integrity. Here there were enumerated a total of 1,567 whites and about 1,100 Indians.

To the northwest, north, and northeast of the above regions the Spanish were an even smaller minority among the missionized and civilized Indians. Here in the valleys of the Altar, Santa Cruz, and Bavispe a thin line of Spaniards and sedentary Indians kept a tenuous hold on the frontier of Apachería. In the Altar district of Pimería Alta, where the Planchas de Plata mining discovery produced an early boom, there were enumerated 330 whites among 1,398 natives. On the northern frontier around Terrenate, Cocóspera, and Buena Vista 583 whites and 764 Indians were counted. To the northeast in the Bavispe and Fronteras districts there was an estimated total of only 484 whites while the same region had an indigenous population of about 2,400.[24]

---

23   *Ibid.*, p. 358.
24   *Ibid.*, p. 359.

It can be clearly seen from these figures that the Spanish settlement of the northwestern frontier near the end of the eighteenth century was a diaphanous affair. The majority of the white colonizers were clustered in a few mining districts. Alamos was the largest but by no means the only important center. The mines of the Horcasitas, Moctezuma, and Nacozari districts formed the economic basis which accounted for their relatively large white populations. Here, exposed in the rugged western ranges of the Sierra Madre, were the rich ore bodies which were sure to attract the Spaniards. Silver primarily but also gold and much-needed mercury ores were abundant. These same mountains of middle Sonora also furnished extensive and relatively rich upland steppe providing the basis of a nascent cattle industry. There were then, in effect, two Spanish-speaking population centers at this time; one was near Alamos and another was in the upstream affluents of the Río Sonora and Río Yaqui.[25] Both of these were in reality on the eastern margin of the Sonoran Desert and not wholly within it. The important pueblos of middle Sonora such as Ures, Horcasitas, and Moctezuma were situated in the restricted desert valleys, but it was the upland steppe and the nearby mines which usually attracted their Spanish settlers.

Except for the mining districts near Altar, the desert to the west of the present-day north-south railway was avoided by white settlements. This region, which now contains the largest and fastest-growing population centers, had only a scattering of ranchos and haciendas without a single pueblo of any significance at all. The present-day sites of Hermosillo, Ciudad Obregón, and Los Mochis contained no more than a few score white inhabitants. The deltaic Culiacán, Sinaloa, and Fuerte had only a few hundred white settlers. In Sonora all the major rivers in their lower courses probably contained no more than two hundred intrepid white inhabitants. The Yaqui and Mayo Indians, by their very numbers, demonstrated the fertility and agricultural potential of the lower Fuerte, Mayo, and Yaqui rivers. Spanish settlement was, however, deterred by this same large semi-civilized population. In addition, these deltaic plains lacked the gold and silver which invariably attracted white settlement. There was no major local market for the surplus grain which these valleys could easily produce, and thus there was no incentive to develop this potential. One of the reasons advanced to support the prospective settlement of Alta California was that this area would become a market for Sonoran grain.

During the first decades of the nineteenth century and the last of

---

25   Spicer, *Cycles of Conquest,* pp. 422-34.

Spanish Colonial rule, the mining industry declined steadily. Throughout the desert and its margins, with the exception of southern Sinaloa, there was little activity in the *antiguos*[26] and less in the development of new properties. Little had transpired to make mining on this remote frontier more profitable. Transportation remained primitive with the burro being the indispensable beast of burden throughout the roadless sierras. The unfortunate monopoly which the Spanish government held on the production of mercury increased the cost of this vital raw material to the miner. Most lamentable were the continued Apache Wars and other tribal rebellions which had begun to drain the labor supply in Sonora. Not to be underestimated was the emigration of Sonoran frontiersmen and their families to Alta California — an emigration that caused a decrease in the already sparse white and mestizo population. Many of the richest mineralized districts along the Apache frontier suffered precipitous declines in population, both human and animal.[27]

Independence brought an end to the monopolistic colonial practices which had restricted mining, but gave rise to a long period of unrest which was perhaps more pernicious to the industry. Recurring civil war was compounded through foreign intervention and American presence in Texas, which drove the Apache even harder against the Sonoran mining frontier. Thus, until the end of the French intervention in the 1860's mining languished.

The years of decline had brought into existence the colorful *gambucino* (a "high-grader") who, usually alone or with the assistance of a single burro, would wander from one deserted mining property to another, stripping the most valuable ore from the mines. This practice contributed very little to the Sonoran economy during these years while doing irreparable harm to potentially valuable but deserted properties. The gambucino lives on to this day, always lending credence to the existence of the "lost mine" which is one of the basic themes of the desert. The "high-grader" brings to life the legendary riches of earlier mining epochs.

At about the time of Mexican independence, events were taking place in southern Sinaloa which were to reshape mining to the north as soon as order returned to Sonora. Among the most important of these was the arrival of Englishmen and other foreign nationals who moved quickly to replace the ejected Spanish, making investments in Sinaloa as early as 1825. The Mexican government in 1846 established

---

[26] A term used in the Sierra designating an old mine.
[27] Bolton, *An Outpost of Empire,* p. 152.

a mint at Culiacán. Overseas shipping schedules were being improved markedly throughout the first half of the century. All of this led to the reconstruction of mining on a more modern basis.

After the French intervention, a series of events occurred in rapid succession which completely altered the economic position of mining along the northwestern frontier. First among these was the elevation to power of Porfirio Díaz, an event which brought relative security to the desert south of the border. Concurrently, the United States, north of the international boundary, brought to a conclusive end the two-hundred-year Apache War. When peace returned to Apachería, miners could once more move north into Sonora. Moreover, the arrival of Americans on the frontier heralded the period of Anglo-American exploitation of Sonoran mining properties. The Porfirian regime did everything within its power to encourage the investment of foreign capital in the mines of Mexico. American engineers moved south of the border to investigate the minerals of Mexico in the first wave of what would today be called "technological assistance." From the mid-1880's, old mines as well as new were opened along the west coast of Mexico with increasing rapidity. The number of registered mining claims in Sinaloa rose from virtually nothing in 1870 to 415 in 1905 and 1,728 on the eve of the revolution in 1909. The developments in Sonora were even more striking as claims which numbered only 1,400 in 1900 reached 5,335 in 1909.[28]

The high-water mark was registered in the last years of Porfirian era. The Mexican Revolution so disrupted economic conditions that mining was no longer profitable. In the state of Sonora the number of claims fell until, in 1926, there were no more than 2,485. The effect of the civil disorder on the availability of foreign capital was particularly strong. The considerable revolutionary sympathy favoring expropriation of foreign mining properties inhibited the expansion of investment. What would under Díaz have been considered sound, became a risky venture. Within a very few years, what was thought to be the immutable mineral wealth of the Sonoran Desert south of the international boundary had lost its economic value almost entirely. Thus, political factors were in large measure responsible for both the creation and partial destruction of Mexican mining north of central Sinaloa.

Of equal importance to the development of mineral resources throughout the desert were the technological advances being made primarily in the United States. Beginning in the last decades of the nine-

---

[28] Pfeifer, "Sinaloa und Sonora Beitrage zur Landeskunde und Kultur geographie des nordwestlichen Mexico," *Mitt. Geog. Gesell.*, Vol. 46, p. 377.

teenth century, revolutionary changes brought to an end a period which began with Guzmán in 1531. Gold and silver had formed the basis of desert mining aspirations, as well as reality, for three and a half centuries. In less than thirty years this all was changed both in Mexico and the United States. Copper quickly came to replace precious metals as the backbone of mining enterprise. Today in the desert and on its margins copper accounts for over 90 percent of the region's mineral wealth. The rise of this mineral and the relative decline[29] of the precious metals was attributable to the increased demand for copper during the latter part of the nineteenth century. New uses, particularly in electricity, caused the expansion of demand for this metal. At the same time the extension of railways remedied the lack of adequate transportation facilities which had militated against the development of base-metal mining in this remote region. As transportation facilities improved, even the occasional steep decline in copper prices could not reverse the trend toward the exploitation of this metal.[30]

More direct influences, however, were at work to make copper the single most important mineral resource of the Sonoran Desert and its margins. By 1880, the majority of the important base-metal mining districts had been discovered. Ajo was perhaps the oldest, the ore there having been found about 1740 by Spanish prospectors who named the district after a garlic-like bulb which was seen nearby. There is no record, however, of the ore having been worked until 1854 when a group of Americans began shipping some particularly rich ores by muleback to the Colorado River, thence by steamboat and sailing ship to Swansea, Wales, to be smelted. By 1861 the "bonanza ores"[31] which could pay this kind of freight were no longer to be found at Ajo and the mine was abandoned.

Similarly, by 1880, the great present-day copper mines at Cananea, Clifton-Morenci, Globe, Ray, Bisbee, and Jerome had been discovered. If they contained an appreciable amount of silver, they were worked, but in 1880 these deposits were, for the most part, unappreciated and uneconomic curiosities. Gold and silver mined that year in Arizona totalled $3,700,000, whereas copper production was valued at only $426,000. While the value of precious metals remained much the same

---

[29]   A "relative" decline because from 1886 to 1916, there was in the Sonoran Desert an increase in the gold and silver production, but less than that in copper.

[30]   In 1880 the price of copper in the United States was 21 cents a pound while in 1893 the price had dropped to 10 cents. Yet the production of this metal in Sonora and Arizona was greater in the latter year than it was in 1880. C. H. Dunning, *Rock to Riches: The Story of Arizona Mines and Mining* (Phoenix, 1959).

[31]   Some Ajo ores averaged 50 percent or better. *Ibid.,* p. 46.

during the next eight years, copper production increased to $5,300,000. The year 1887 was the last year in which the value of precious metals mined in Arizona exceeded that of copper.[32] Yet 20-percent ores still formed the basis of economic copper mining operations both in Mexico and the United States. Most of this ore produced in the western United States was still shipped to Swansea.

By 1900 the value of copper mined in the Sonoran Desert and its mountainous hinterland was more than three times that of gold and silver combined, even though precious metal production had increased rapidly.[33] This advance was attributable largely to technological innovation within copper mining itself: smelters, copper concentrators, leaching plants, improved methods of handling porphyry ores, sulphide plants, the flotation process, steam shovels, and larger concentrators, larger smelters, and larger steam shovels. Each improvement helped to change worthless rock into valuable ore. The limited bonanza ore bodies were expanded to include mountains of 2-percent ore which, when worked, often uncovered new bonanzas of secondary enrichment. These ores might have gone unnoticed under relatively barren leached-out zones.

By 1910, Arizona had become the leading copper-producing state in the Union while Sonora had some years earlier assumed the same position in Mexico.[34] The well-known but little-regarded copper-mining properties were brought back into production whether or not other minerals could be economically extracted from the same ore. Railway, road, machinery, and other heavy investments were made, which probably for the first time placed the mining industry on a permanent basis.

COMMUNICATIONS

Until well into this present century, the greatest economic advance within the desert, both north and south of the border, closely followed the construction of the railways. The era of mule trains, wagon trains, and stagecoaches quickly came to an end where the rails were laid. As much as anything else it was the railway which created the low-grade copper mines and the fields of winter vegetables by lowering freight rates and providing refrigerated express trains to the eastern markets. Not since the Spanish entrada were resources created with such rapidity.

Despite the fact that the major railways both in Mexico and the United States were built over much the same terrain by the same com-

---

[32] *Ibid.,* p. 124.

[33] *Ibid.,* p. 159.

[34] Jack L. Cross, Elizabeth Shaw, and Kathleen Scheifele (eds.), *Arizona: Its People and Resources* (Tucson, 1960), p. 243.

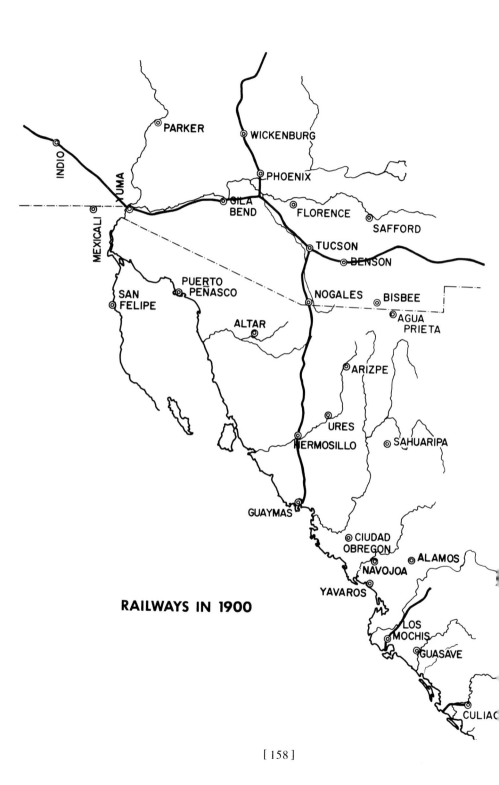

PARKER

INDIO

WICKENBURG

MEXICALI

YUMA

PHOENIX

GILA
BEND

FLORENCE

SAFFORD

TUCSON

BENSON

SAN
FELIPE

PUERTO
PEÑASCO

NOGALES

BISBEE

AGUA
PRIETA

ALTAR

ARIZPE

URES

HERMOSILLO

SAHUARIPA

GUAYMAS

CIUDAD
OBREGON

ALAMOS

NAVOJOA

YAVAROS

RAILWAYS IN 1900

LOS
MOCHIS

GUASAVE

CULIAC

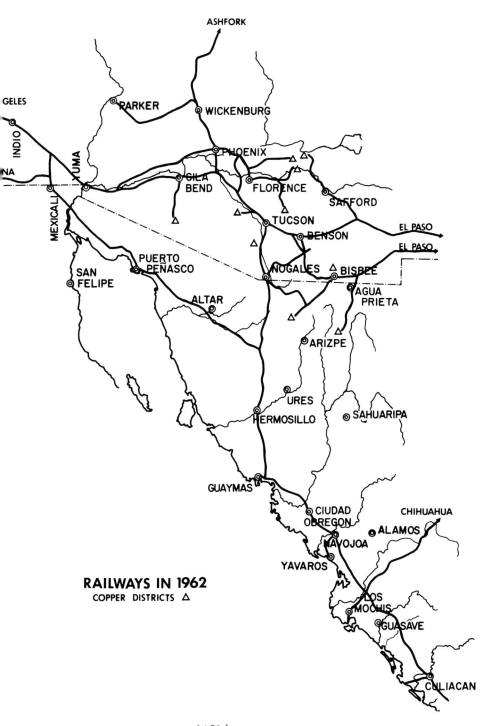

RAILWAYS IN 1962
COPPER DISTRICTS △

panies in a relatively short period of time, there are significant differences in their purpose and contribution to their respective nations. The fact that they were built by the same American companies is indicative of a significantly different national purpose served by the desert railways. An American railway in Mexico had to fulfill a strikingly different role than an American railway in the United States.

There were other differences. The final boundary line which partitioned the desert into two national sectors left the United States with a land-locked half. For this reason alone, the railway north of the border was destined to play a proportionately more decisive economic role in the years that followed. The earliest railways in the Mexican Northwest were built to connect inland towns with seaports. Indeed, the oldest railway on the Pacific Coast was built not by American but rather by English capital. Its route was that of an overseas rather than continental communication system, connecting Culiacán with the small harbor at Altata. The first to serve the Sonoran Desert, this railway was forty-five miles in length and was completed in the early 1870's. In subsequent years lines were constructed between Guaymas and Hermosillo, as well as between Topolobampo and El Fuerte. Each of these lines was a continuation of a maritime route. Only gradually were these disconnected lines joined together, forming a West-Coast railway which could compete with the Gulf of California as a major route along the Pacific.

In bold contrast were the events which led to the first railway in southern Arizona. The early ominous warnings that the United States had overextended itself territorially were swept aside in the rapid series of events which brought Texas, California, and the Oregon country into the Union. The Gold Rush took thousands of Americans to the West Coast, fulfilling that nation's "manifest destiny," and demonstrating the need for a transcontinental railway. The railway had come of age in the United States, and a line linking the Mississippi Valley with California was technologically feasible. The choice of route, however, became an issue of sectional politics in the years preceding the Civil War. These rivalries between the North (and a northern route) and the South (and a southern route) resulted in pressures which led to the purchase of the land south of the Gila River — the Gadsden Purchase — as well as a number of railway surveys which were made before there was a single stage line between California and the East. The Civil War brought to a halt all plans to link southern California with the East across the Sonoran Desert.

When railway construction finally began in the desert after the Civil War the rails were laid from California to the East. The Southern Pacific Railroad, which had linked San Francisco with Los Angeles, built southeastward from the latter city over the San Gorgonio Pass in California. The rails were laid down onto the gradually descending sand-blown plain of the western Coachella Valley. About two miles west of Indio, sea level was reached, and the construction continued southeastward over the desiccated bed of Lake Coachella down to an elevation of 263 feet below sea level. Climbing from the Salton Sink, the line was built with extreme difficulty through the sand hills that form the eastern margin of that depression. A bridge was built across the Colorado at Yuma in 1877. Three years later the first locomotive reached Tucson by a route which followed the Gila upstream to Gila Bend, but there left that river valley in order to follow the Santa Cruz Valley upstream from a point near Casa Grande. The northern bend of the Gila River was bypassed by this route. The Southern Pacific line continued eastward into the valley of the San Pedro at Benson, through Willcox and Bowie onto the high arid plains of New Mexico. It connected with the Santa Fe at Deming, New Mexico, in 1881. Thus, the Sonoran Desert's first direct railway connection with the East was completed twenty-five years after the Gila River route was selected as the best of several alternative transcontinental routes. The southern desert crossing was not, of course, the first to be completed, the Union Pacific having carried trains to the Pacific in 1869. Thus, there was a period of twelve years in which the best and quickest way to reach Tucson and other desert points was via California, no matter where one started in the East. During this same period the Apache Indians provided a further incentive for using this circuitous method of reaching the southwestern deserts. For this reason the largest single number of Arizona's early settlers were former Californians, a trend which persists to this day.[35]

On the Mexican West Coast the construction of a railway linking that distant region with the highland core of Mexico followed much the same pattern. The rails were laid from the "wrong" direction. The line connecting Guaymas with Hermosillo was extended north into the valley of the Rio Magdalena with its fruitful little oasis, and over the Encinas Pass to the border at Nogales. This community was in turn linked with the Southern Pacific at Benson in 1882. From that year until 1904 the railway from Nogales to Guaymas served mainly to connect the port of Guaymas with the rapidly developing American rail net. Guaymas served as an alternative gateway to the sea for American passengers and freight. It was, however, the purpose of the American operating

---

[35] In a recent period just under 25% of the total migrants arriving in Arizona were from California. Texas was a poor second with 7%. Arizona Development Board, *Amazing Arizona: Recent Migrations* (Phoenix, 1959), p. 12.

companies to divert as much traffic as possible to the California ports which they already served. Aside from Hermosillo and the other small places along the route from Nogales to Guaymas, Mexico was served only indirectly through El Paso over the American tracks which stretched to Nogales. There was no direct all-Mexican route from the central highlands to the Pacific Coast.

Mention has been made of the railway between Topolobampo and El Fuerte. Part of an inspired scheme to link midcontinent America to the Pacific at Topolobampo Bay[36] just south of the Río Fuerte's estuary, this railway was begun in 1885 under the name of the Kansas City, Mexico and Orient Railroad Co. Construction began across western Texas to Chihuahua while at the same time tracks were laid paralleling the Fuerte from Topolobampo.[37] The builders did not, however, correctly calculate the difficulty involved in surmounting the precipitous barrancas of the Sierra Madre, and the scheme ended in failure, after two disconnected rail links — separated by the broken cuesta over 7,000 feet in elevation — had been built.

An integral part of this magnificent plan was the settlement of hundreds of Americans at a Topolobampo Bay colony which was romantically envisaged as another San Francisco.[38] A communistic society composed largely of American settlers existed for a short period but fell victim to internal conflict and the failure of the overall plan. Most of the original Topolobampo Bay colonists drifted back to the United States, but quite a few remained, intermarrying with the Mexican population and contributing a great deal to the development of the Río Fuerte district as an agricultural center.

Part of the dream was, however, finally realized. In 1962 the last rails were laid on this trans-Sierran route, with the terminal at Los Mochis on the Pacific. A grandiose scheme has, seventy-five years later, become a reality. The logic of the railway is sounder today than it was originally, and more closely tied to Mexico. Whereas the original objective had been to shorten the shipping distance across western North America — to serve United States interests — the benefits today will accrue mostly to Mexico. The trans-Sierran extension, completed in three years by the nationalized railways, is the first new main line to be built in North America in recent years, and the only one which crosses northern Mexico from east to west.

---

[36]   Thomas A. Robertson, *A Southwestern Utopia* (Los Angeles, 1947).

[37]   *Ibid.,* p. 34.

[38]   *Ibid.,* p. 50. For a contemporary tract promoting this project, see Albert K. Owen's *Interesting Data Concerning the Harbor of Topolobampo and the State of Sinaloa* (Washington, D.C., 1883).

Many years prior to this — in 1904 — the Mexican government gave
a concession to the Southern Pacific Railroad enabling the latter to
construct a railway from Guaymas to Culiacán through Alamos and
from Culiacán southeast to Mazatlán. From that port it was eventually
to reach Guadalajara over the Sierra de Tepíc. The railway, as it was
actually built, avoided Alamos and the other ancient towns of the
Camino Real north of Culiacán because of the rugged terrain and the
lack of sanguine economic prospects for this region which had been in
decline for at least a century.

The route followed a series of marine terraces usually one to three
hundred feet above sea level, bypassing not only the broken upland
of the Camino Real but the deltaic flood plains of the coast. The
coast was avoided between Guaymas and Mazatlán. The railway circles
the deltas of the Río Yaqui, Río Mayo and Río Fuerte, bridging the
rivers and smaller streamways well inland. A railway running at right
angles to a series of streams carrying large floods from the Sierra was
costly to build and difficult to operate through the rainy season.[39]

By 1909 rails were laid down as far south as Mazatlán, but the
Revolution interrupted construction and the railway was left incomplete
until 1927. In that year Mexico City could at last compete with Los
Angeles and Chicago on an even basis in the Mexican Northwest. The
railway was seldom a financial success,[40] and the Ferrocarril Sud Pacifico,
a division of the sprawling Southern Pacific, was nationalized in 1953.
In 1954 the Ferrocarril del Pacifico received a $61 million loan from
The International Bank for Reconstruction and Development, for the
replacement of track and rolling stock. Extensive rehabilitation of the
line through re-laying of almost all of the track, repair of bridges and
freight cars, as well as the replacement of antique steam locomotives,
was imperative.

Also about 1953 a railway line was constructed across the most
inhospitable deserts west to San Luis, Mexicali, and Tijuana, giving
Mexico its first completely national rail link to Baja California. This
railway leaves the Hermosillo-Nogales line at Benjamin Hill[41] and
passes through Caborca and Puerto Peñasco en route to San Luis.
Construction west of Caborca was extremely difficult because water is
unavailable throughout most of this desert.[42]

---

[39] G. Pfeifer, "Sinaloa und Sonora Beitrage zur Landeskunde und Kultur
geographie des nordwestlichen Mexico," *Mitt. Geog. Gesell.,* Vol. 46, pp. 371-73.

[40] Osgood Hardy, "El Ferrocarril Sud Pacifico," *Pacific Historical Review,*
Vol. 20 (1951), pp. 261-70.

[41] Benjamin Hill was named for a Mexican revolutionary general.

[42] Ronald L. Ives, "The Sonoran Railroad Project," *Journal of Geography,*
Vol. 48 (1949), pp. 197-206.

Ancient and modern transportation systems mingle in the Sonoran Desert. Contrasts are especially great in the Mexican sector. Pemex service stations (above), owned by the Mexican government, have a monopoly throughout the country. The West Coast Highway, which crosses the Mexican section of the Sonoran Desert en route from Nogales to Mexico City, has modern facilities of this kind all along the way, for the buses, trucks and passenger cars of both natives and tourists. A main thoroughfare in Navojoa (right above) mirrors the past and present in one view. In primitive eastern Sonora (right center), where motor vehicles are a rarity, burros and mules are still an important though declining means of transportation. The port of Guaymas, Sonora (below), is one of the most important on the Gulf of California. Here bales of cotton await loading for shipment overseas. A bridge (bottom right) on the trans-Sierran railroad from Chihuahua City to Los Mochis, the only route that crosses northern Mexico from east to west.

— GEORGE ECKHART

— MEXICAN GOVERNMENT TOURISM DEPARTMENT

North of the border, railway building continued at a diminished rate until the 1920's, when this form of transportation began to suffer from increased competition. Not until 1887 did a railway reach Phoenix and this was no more than a short spur from the main line of the Southern Pacific at Maricopa. More surprising was the delay until 1926 of actual main-line railway connections through Arizona's capital.

The major zones of irrigated agriculture are usually well served by main-line railways due to the fortuitous coincidence which brought together favorable hydrological conditions and easy gradients. The Southern Pacific was built through the Imperial, Yuma, and Casa Grande valleys before their agricultural possibilities were even realized. Railways would have continued to operate through these basins even if irrigated agriculture had never developed. Because it did, the railroad, which at one time seemed to have a limited local potential due to the region's low population and productivity, has been successful in generating tremendous amounts of freight. Mining, more than any other single factor, has contributed to the development of branch lines. By 1900 or soon afterward, most of the important contemporary mining districts were served by railways — a service which usually meant the arduous construction of a roadbed through broken terrain and over steep gradients.

Such building has not been done without considerable cost. The construction and operation of a railway in the Sonoran Desert engenders surprising difficulties. First among these is the multiplicity of washes which necessitates the construction of miles of small bridges and culverts, whereas a single bridge would suffice in a more humid region. In addition, miles of protective levees and artificial channels must be built and maintained in order to protect rights of way. Additional levees are built in order to channel water from the spreading and braided streamways into one or two artificial channels over which the railway is constructed. These V-shaped levees are a prominent part of the man-made landscape throughout the desert wherever railways have been built. The Southern Pacific spends more on the construction and maintenance of flood-control works in its Sonoran Desert divisions than throughout the rest of its huge system. This has not always prevented catastrophic disasters such as the uncontrolled 1905 flood on the Lower Colorado which resulted in the destruction of the low-lying right of way in the below-sea-level Salton Sink and necessitated the moving of several miles of rails eastward to higher elevations. The Mexican West Coast railway is particularly vulnerable to floods due to its roadbed lying across so many streams that frequently inundate the coastal plain.

As the railway transformed the economic prospects of the desert at the turn of the century, the automobile has effected much the same metamorphosis in the last decades. The nation of Henry Ford could not fail to develop, even in this remote area, the potential of automobile transport. In addition, the international boundary does not divide the desert in this respect since paved highways stretch south of the border carrying cars and trucks the length and breadth of the entire region.

In both the United States and Mexico, cars and trucks arrived long before there were roads to carry them. This did not stop the early motorists who quickly set about making their own trails through the desert. The sparse natural vegetation, level plains, gently sloping bajadas, relatively firm surfaces, and generally dry conditions allowed the motorist to range widely throughout most of the desert without the aid of "roads." On the other hand, drifting sand, fine sandy soils, deep arroyos, ragged volcanic rock, and precipitous mountains impeded the early motorist who tried to cross the desert. He was usually aided, however, by wagon tracks which criss-crossed most of the region. Early trails, such as the Camino Real and the route of the Butterfield Stage, became in part the early "highways" of the Sonoran Desert. These trails, however, were more often avoided by the engineers who built the first genuine highways, but they remained to serve the more remote districts. To this day, sections of the old Camino Real are used to carry traffic in eastern Sonora. No part of the Camino Real in Mexico is at the present time paved.

North of the border, the end of World War I marked the beginning of the first major American highway construction program. Understandably, Arizona lagged behind many eastern states in the building of roads. However, California, and then Arizona, went ahead in the desert despite the distances and difficulties involved. The first major paved highways to be built were the east-west transcontinental routes.

There is no doubt that proximity to the United States was, and is, responsible for the important place occupied by automotive transport in northwestern Mexico. Mexico is not one of the underdeveloped countries which has vaulted from muleback to the airplane without any intervening railway and automotive stages. American innovation has quickly passed south of the border and the highway is today the principal means of technological ingress. Away from the paved highway, conditions appear to remain much the same as they have for centuries. Along the highway, refrigerated trailers haul loads of shrimp and winter vegetables, and neon lights flash the names of familiar American products. The most important transformation has been the explosive increase in the movement of people; passenger traffic formerly confined to mule and rail has taken to the highway on busses. Dilapidated local carriers are constantly being overtaken by modern trans-Sierran express busses en route from Mexico City to the border. The net flow in traffic, measured by population, is northward — in ideas and change it cannot be measured.

Thus the highway is in itself both the cause and result of a remarkable trans-frontier influence. The outcome is a situation seldom encountered in the underdeveloped world where cities usually exist as modern islands in a sea of backwardness. In the Sonoran Desert, however, the highway could be likened to a bridge across that same sea. It is this more than anything else which has brought development from the vicinal United States as well as from the more distant Mexican core. The most apparent changes during the last two decades have taken place along, and adjacent to, the newly paved highways. The earliest, longest and most important paved highway in the Mexican sector of the desert is the West Coast Inter-American Highway. It has been open to Mexico City for a little more than ten years. Like the railway, it was first completed from the American border south to Guaymas, emphasizing the impetus given by the United States to the development of communications in Mexico. Today this highway carries the economically important American tourist traffic. It remains, nevertheless, as a single artery running from the Border to central Mexico while in the United States the numerous paved highways cross and re-cross the desert, forming a closed net.

Modern highways constructed in the desert face the same hydrological problem that makes the building and maintenance of railways so difficult. Braided streamways necessitate the construction of multiple bridges and culverts which must in turn be protected by levees or grading. The multiple-lane Federal interstate highway system being constructed in the United States will soon lace the entire desert from east to west and north to south.

CHAPTER NINE

Water Resource Development

Within a desert, low and infrequent rainfall has caused many forms of life to look elsewhere than the dry surfaces of the earth for water.

Plants and those who cultivate them look not to rain-soaked soil but to water itself, which at one time — perhaps hundreds of miles away — took the form of rainfall. Xerophytic plants of the desert are adapted to collecting whatever small amount of edaphic water there is to be found, sometimes at great depths and over wide areas; they space themselves along streamways and in other situations where unusually copious quantities of water are available. Human inhabitants of the desert emulate exactly this course of action. Wild and cultivated plants, animals, and man all are directly dependent on the availability of water, usually not in the soil itself but in water brought some distance to the ultimate benefit of the recipient.

The farmer, who is the most basic link between land and man, must follow the example of natural vegetation and settle in close proximity to available water. He may remove and replace the original vegetation with plants of his choosing, but he is as subject to the dictates of water as were the desert plants he uprooted.

Unlike the rapid advance of the agriculturalist into the subhumid plains, the tropical forests, or the Arctic margins, the men who cultivate the desert face a distinct areal limit set by the quantity of water made available only at increasing difficulty from limited sources. The Sonoran Desert has not yet, and probably never will be, "transformed" by the plow in the same uniform fashion as were the grasslands to the east.

Here one may most clearly differentiate between the Sonoran Desert and the Great Plains as a social environment. On the Plains the distribution of rainfall is immediately mirrored in the amount of moisture in the soil, in agricultural possibilities, and in actual settlement and cultivation. Within the Sonoran Desert there is no such relationship. Submarginal rainfall universally prohibits dry farming,[1] placing a premium on obtaining water from a secondary source.

The inhabitants of the Sonoran Desert consume approximately 23 million acre-feet of water each year.[2] During the same average year about 250 million acre-feet of water are deposited in the form of rain, snow and other kinds of precipitation over the 333 thousand square miles which compose the desert and the watershed of the streams which flow through the desert.[3] It appears that in the long run less than one-tenth of the total distribution of annual rainfall is made available through irrigation and other uses to the inhabitants of the Sonoran Desert!

The irrigation of crops takes the overwhelming majority of water utilized within the desert. In contrast, livestock, mining, and municipal uses consume only a small fraction of the total water utilized.[4] This is estimated at approximately 6 percent in Arizona and much less than this percentage in Mexico. Thus, considerably less than one percent of the annual rainfall of the Sonoran Desert (that is, the desert plus the watersheds above the desert) is made available to livestock, or utilized in all the factories, mines, cities, and towns of the desert. The rapidly

---

[1] "Dry farming" is a system of agriculture aimed at conserving the limited amount of rainfall in semiarid districts. The term is used widely in the High Plains.

[2] These totals for the Sonoran Desert are computed from a number of Mexican and American sources. Among these should be noted: *Datos de la Región Noroeste; Panorama Económico de Sinaloa y sus Datos Estadísticos* Sinaloa, Instituto de Investigaciones Económicas del Estado (1958); *Sonora en Cifras,* Sonora, Gobierno del Estado (an annual, 1956-61); *Proyecto de Programa de Gobierno del Estado de Sonora,* Estado de Sonora (1957); *Irrigación en México,* México Comisión Nacional de Irrigación (various issues); *U. S. Census of Agriculture, 1959,* Vol. 1 (Counties), Ariz. Part 43, Calif. Part 48, U. S. Dept of Agriculture (Washington, D.C., 1959); *Reclamation Project Data; Reclamation on the Lower Colorado River,* U. S. Bureau of Reclamation (Washington, D.C., 1959); *Compilation of Surface Waters, 1950, Part 9;* and *Future Needs for Reclamation in the Western United States,* Bureau of Reclamation (Committee Print No. 14 for the Senate Select Committee on National Water Resources, 86th Cong., 2d Sess.), Washington, D.C., 1960. The statistical information contained in this chapter has been abstracted from these sources unless otherwise noted.

[3] These totals are compiled from statistical data contained in a number of sources including *Datos de la Región Noroeste;* U. S. Weather Bureau Climatic Summary of the United States (1930), Sections 18 and 26; H. V. Smith, *The Climate of Arizona* (various tables); Green, *Arizona Statewide Rainfall;* and *Climate and Man: Yearbook of Agriculture,* 1941, U. S. Dept. of Agriculture (Washington, D.C., 1941), various tables.

[4] Khalaf, p. 106.

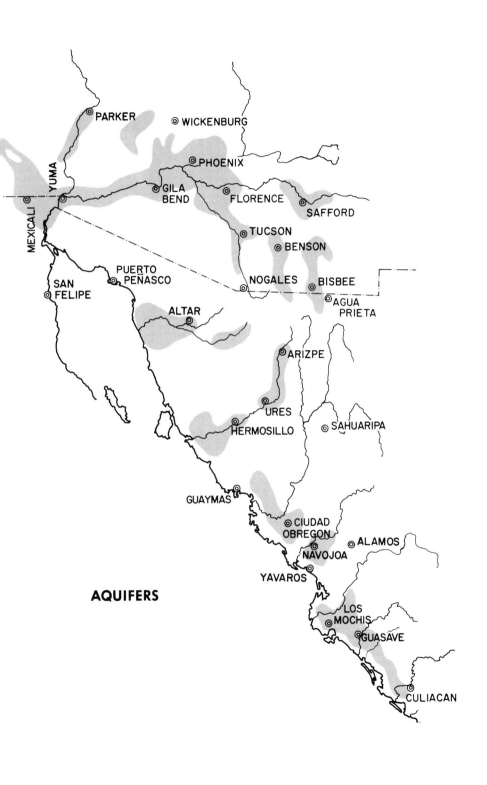

PARKER

WICKENBURG

PHOENIX

YUMA

GILA
BEND

FLORENCE

SAFFORD

MEXICALI

TUCSON

BENSON

SAN
FELIPE

PUERTO
PEÑASCO

NOGALES

BISBEE

AGUA
PRIETA

ALTAR

ARIZPE

URES

HERMOSILLO

SAHUARIPA

GUAYMAS

CIUDAD
OBREGON

ALAMOS

NAVOJOA

YAVAROS

AQUIFERS

LOS
MOCHIS

GUASAVE

CULIACAN

growing nonagricultural sectors of the economy are in themselves placing little demand against available surface water supplies.

The greatest irony is that the inhabitants of the Sonoran Desert, despite their Herculean efforts in building dams and canals, have had to rely more and more upon underground reservoirs of water. In California and Arizona the dependable supply of surface water has, for many years, been entirely appropriated. The extension of irrigated agriculture has pushed the demand for water beyond man's existing 10 percent efficiency in directly recovering rainfall. As a result, in Arizona, pumping increased threefold between 1940 and 1953. Since that year there has been no major increase in the annual amount of water pumped in Arizona, largely because the "well" has been going dry.

THE DEVELOPMENT OF GROUNDWATER

Groundwater has been made available within the district under two separate circumstances. The first of these was to supplement the development of surface water. The second was the provision of water from underground reservoirs where no significant amount of gravity water was available. Ironically, it was the development of supplemental water from the subsurface that led the way to the more general use of underground water where there was no surface water.

About ten years after the completion of Roosevelt Dam, a familiar situation developed in the Salt River Valley west of Phoenix. Gravity water used in excessive amounts for irrigation caused the groundwater table to rise to the surface resulting in the waterlogging of the land.[5] In order to rectify this, numerous wells were drilled and pumped to drain the surface, and the water was transported for irrigation downstream to the west of the waterlogged area. This was in Arizona the beginning of systematic well construction which led to the development of groundwater for irrigation, both in supplementing surface supply and in other regions where no surface water was available.

During recent times many Sonoran regions have suffered from the same turgid conditions. In the Yuma-Wellton-Mohawk area surface water from the Colorado River is diverted for irrigation. Here again, since large amounts of water are needed to maintain good soil conditions, excess water caused the water table to rise to the surface. This

---

[5]   W. T. Lee, *Underground Waters of the Salt River Valley, Arizona,* U. S. Geological Survey, Water Supply Paper No. 136 (1905), pp. 120-33, describes in detail the already high water tables that prevailed in the Salt River Valley prior to their subsequent elevation.

has been partially remedied by pumping, but only after the deposition of salts on the surface had sterilized many thousands of acres. Flushing these salts into the Colorado River has incurred the violent protest of irrigators downstream in the Mexicali district where the saline water has been threatening to sterilize additional thousands of acres.

These same conditions prevail over large areas of the Imperial Valley of California where waterlogged soils have brought excessive quantities of alkaline salts to the surface. Here the difficulties are even more profound and are complicated by the existence of the Salton Sea, which elevates water tables in its vicinity, bringing about a permanent union of subterranean and surface water.[6] This has resulted in the deposition of these salts to such a depth that one can only be reminded of a heavy snowfall. Thousands of acres have been abandoned because of this excessive moisture in what paradoxically is one of the driest parts of the desert.

There are, in addition, several less obvious purposes served by pumping. A more controlled release of gravity water can be attained when a secondary source of supply is made available. Moreover, with pumps distributed at a variety of points throughout the irrigated lands, water is much nearer the land to be served than are the surface-water supplies. Water can be supplied from pumps located near the point of utilization with a minimum of loss. When surface water is used, as much as 90 percent can be lost through evaporation and seepage before reaching the fields.[7]

In a class by itself is the widespread utilization of groundwater in areas where surface water is available in only insignificant quantities and where water-logging has never been a problem. In the United States one of the oldest, and certainly the largest, region of virtually independent groundwater development is the Lower Santa Cruz Valley, Pinal County, Arizona. Much smaller, though nevertheless characteristic of this independent development, are the Douglas and Willcox Basins of Cochise County. Other regions such as the Lower Gila, though at one time depending upon gravity water, have seen the independent development of groundwater supplies grow to dominate irrigation to the virtual exclusion of surface water along this regularly dry streambed.

In Mexico the Costa de Hermosillo is the largest region under

---

6   Khalaf, pp. 74-79.

7   There might actually occur a "water traffic jam" on the canals, laterals, and ditches when orders for water are very heavy. It might be impossible to deliver water to a given user while main arteries are filled to capacity. Yet pumps could use smaller laterals nearby to move water around the congested routes that lead from the diversion dam.

pump irrigation without the use of any surface water at all. Other developments at Caborca and in the Valle de Guaymas are similar historically to the Lower Gila where rather primitive use was being made of surface water before the advent of modern pump-irrigation practices. This early use of surface water has been largely abandoned as upstream dams have choked off any irregular supply of surface water that might have been made available to these lower valleys.

The lowering of the groundwater table occurs in areas where wells continually withdraw water from the subsurface reservoir in excess of local replenishment. The water table declines in the form of an inverted cone referred to as the cone of repression. When large quantities of water are pumped from closely spaced wells, the depression cones of such wells soon overlap and result in an irregular depression of the water table. As pumping continues in excess of recharge or replenishment, the depression continues in depth and extends outward with time, eventually resulting in a depletion of the groundwater reserves. Many of the alluvial groundwater basins throughout the American sector of the Sonoran Desert are now in advanced stages of this depletion cycle.

The areas experiencing the greatest water-level decline coincide with areas of large withdrawals. Water tables have dropped over 300 feet in several irrigated tracts within the Salt River Valley in less than two decades.

The water table decline in the Phoenix municipal area has not been so severe and is related to smaller withdrawals per unit area than in the agricultural areas. In the Lower Santa Cruz Valley there has been a decline of more than 200 feet from the original static level.[8] In nearly all the groundwater basins the decline is related to the magnitude of agricultural development. There have been rapid declines in recent years in several areas where large-scale vegetable cultivation has been carried on.[9] Visible evidence of this is to be found in several localities where fissures a mile or more in length, twenty feet in width, and forty or more feet in depth are the disfiguring result of withdrawals.

The Upper Gila Valley is one of the few fortunate agricultural areas which receive an annual recharge or replenishment of water to the subsurface reservoir. Here the Gila River is able to recharge the groundwater reservoir so that the water table fluctuates in relation to the annual amount of rainfall and runoff.[10]

In recent years there have been about 3,500 active irrigation wells

---

[8]   Khalaf, pp. 77-78.

[9]   *Ibid.,* p. 128.

[10]   Water tables everywhere within the desert fluctuate in relation to climatic conditions but unfortunately, heavy rains and runoff appear only to be able to temporarily stem a steady retreat which began with the inception of concentrated pumping.

in the Salt River and Lower Santa Cruz valleys discharging from 100 to 5,000 gallons per minute. This amounts to about 70 percent of the total groundwater pumped in the state of Arizona. Approximately 5,000 irrigation wells in the state deliver more than four million acre-feet per year. In recent years it has been necessary to deepen old wells or drill new deep wells in order to maintain large yields.

The entire water supply for the Tucson metropolitan area comes from groundwater reserves. Phoenix obtains its supply by pumping groundwater, as well as from surface water from the Verde River. The depth of wells ranges from about 200 feet to over 2,000 feet.

In Mexico the Costa de Hermosillo is the district where pump irrigation has been most thoroughly developed. About 475 wells, each pumping approximately 2,000 gallons per minute, provide water for the entire region. Here the flow of water from almost every well is, almost without exception, copious. Each well produces enough water to supply about one square mile, which is referred to in the area as an "irrigation unit." The distribution of water throughout this aquifer is so uniform that a "dry hole" is unheard of.

A fall in water tables has been the price of success. The Costa de Hermosillo has witnessed an uninterrupted decline averaging 3 feet each year since modern pumping began fifteen years ago. In the drilling of wells the government has placed an absolute upper limit on their number, as well as on their concentration. This limit was reached some years ago but has failed to stem the retreat of groundwater. It has, however, limited any accelerated declines typical of Arizona where "suitcase" farmers have indiscriminately drilled and pumped water until it is no longer available, or is excessively saline, and the land reverts to desert.

Approximately 50 percent of the total withdrawals of groundwater made in the state of Sonora are within this region. The independent Caborca and Guaymas districts produce much smaller and less uniform quantities of water from more scattered wells. Nevertheless, when taken together with the Hermosillo region, these three districts produce over 90 percent — or more than four million acre-feet — of the groundwater obtained from the state of Sonora. South of the Yaqui River pump irrigation is not regularly practiced because of ample surface water.

In the deltaic regions of the Fuerte, Sinaloa, and other rivers where irrigation, using surface water, has been carried on for a number of years, superfluous water has become a major problem, as it has along the Colorado. The results are not as devastating as in the Imperial and Yuma-Wellton-Mohawk valleys, only because the land has been under irrigation for a much shorter period of time. Most small Mexican farmers would be unable to meet the cost of the investments needed to overcome these conditions. This, however, is the exception within the desert.

On both sides of the border the extension of pump irrigation has more often meant the lowering of the water tables, complete depletion, increased salinity, and the actual lowering of the land surface including the opening of fissures that sometimes extend for miles across once productive fields. These conditions usually result in increasing the cost of water gradually until farming is abandoned on lands where surface water is not available.[11]

The watershed is a natural hydrographic unit which is as important to an understanding of water utilization as it is to a knowledge of the distribution of water resources. In the following description of water-resource development within the Sonoran Desert, the watershed is used as the primary unit of understanding. Often, however, political boundaries and economic activities divide the watershed, necessitating additional, more complex delineation of separate irrigation schemes. The description of these districts will follow the sequence of watersheds within the desert beginning in the northwest with the Lower Colorado Basin, and proceeding southeastward into the watersheds of Sonora and Sinaloa.

THE LOWER COLORADO VALLEY

The part of the Lower Colorado River Basin included within the Sonoran Desert presents a most interesting, if not unique, hydrographic diversity which is further confused by engineering works and political factors. Almost all the Colorado's streamflow originates in the Upper Basin.[12] The Gila River is a Sonoran stream but under present conditions delivers no water to the main stream of the Colorado.[13] For this reason it must be considered as having an independent, internal drainage system separate from the Colorado.

Technically, the Lower Colorado Basin also includes the valley containing the Salton Sea whose drainage is not tributary to the Colorado River, but into which the Colorado has flowed in the past. Under natural conditions this below-sea-level depression would not be included as a part of the Lower Colorado Basin because of its internal drainage, but since it receives such a large proportion of the water diverted from the Colorado River, and is an integral part of the overall Colorado River development projects, it must be considered in conjunction with the mainstream Colorado.

---

11   Dean E. Mann, *The Politics of Water in Arizona* (Tucson, 1963), p. 4.
12   Under natural condiitons 91.8 percent of the total flow comes from the Upper Basin. Khalaf, pp. 30-31. Today this is even higher.
13   *The Colorado River: A Comprehensive Report,* p. 162.

To simplify the discussion, all diversions from the right bank of the river will be surveyed as simply California or Baja California projects. Left-bank diversions from this river will be included as the first water-resource development schemes described in both Arizona and Sonora.

For centuries the Yuma Indians had been utilizing the flooding Colorado River for the irrigation of crops along its banks. Spaniards and Mexicans were, however, unable to establish permanent agricultural settlements on the irrigable land of the Lower Colorado. Not until the United States had assumed sovereignty over much of the basin was there the first recorded use of Colorado River water — in the vicinity of Blythe, California.[14] The grandiose possibility of "exporting" water from the Colorado River to the Imperial Valley of California by a simple diversion canal passing in part through Mexico was recognized even before the Civil War.[15] In the 1870's surveys were made by the federal government for the purpose of investigating flood conditions, and to determine the feasibility of diverting water to the Imperial Valley through a canal located wholly within the United States. The report was unfavorable and the construction of an international canal through Mexico which would take advantage of the dry streambed of an abandoned distributary known as Alamo Wash was finally begun in 1902.[16] The work was done by a private company which negotiated with the Mexican Government the privilege of channeling water through Mexico en route to California.

The Alamo Canal, as it was called, avoided the Algodones sandhills along the border and delivered water to the upper channel of the Alamo Wash which flows west and north toward the depressed center of the Salton Basin, offering suitable opportunities for developing auxiliary distribution structures. The canal heading from the Colorado River was cut through soft alluvium against the advice of some engineers, but was buttressed by levees. In two years' time nearly 8,000 people had settled in the valley, 700 miles of canal were in use, and 75,000 acres of land were being farmed.[17]

The Alamo Canal, however, proved difficult to operate without upstream control of the Colorado River. The channel required almost constant dredging to control silt, and protection from flood damage demanded the construction of an extensive levee system.[18] The tragic menace from floods was not fully realized until 1905 when the Colorado

14 *Ibid.,* p. 56.

15 *Ibid.*

16 *Ibid.*

17 *Reclamation Project Data,* p. 3.

18 Robert M. Brown, "The Utilization of the Colorado River," *Geographical Review,* Vol. 17 (1927), pp. 455-56.

River, while carrying a major flood from the Gila River Basin, broke through the ill-constructed heading located four miles below the international boundary. For sixteen months the Colorado poured almost its entire flow into the canal and the Alamo Wash.[19] It filled the formerly arid Salton Basin to a maximum depth of seventy-two feet, covering an area of 330,000 acres.[20] Many feared that the flood would fill the entire Salton Depression to a depth of over 300 feet. The break was finally closed with great difficulty and expense by the Southern Pacific Railroad, but only after 30,000 acres of arable land had been inundated and many farms ruined.[21] Miles of main-line track of the Southern Pacific had to be moved to higher ground. In 1907 the Colorado was turned once more toward the Gulf of California. The levees were built higher and stronger, but each year they were challenged by inundation.[22]

The difficulty of maintaining an adequate levee system was exacerbated by siltation. Each year the Colorado River was depositing over 100,000 acre-feet of silt in the region of the delta, lifting itself higher and higher.[23] Levees had to be raised each year in order to maintain a minimum of protection.

Levees constructed to protect the left-bank Yuma project on the Colorado broke several times in the first twenty years of their existence. In 1922 the levees protecting the Palo Verde Valley in California broke.[24] Defensive measures became more and more burdensome. There still remained the continued threat of another major break along the right bank of the deltaic streamway. A change in the river's course might overwhelm the entire population living at the level of the sea or below in the Imperial Valley of California and Mexico. A society whose continued existence depends upon its successful adaptation to an arid milieu is particularly vulnerable to excessive water. Delicate works constructed to convey limited amounts of water, crops which thrive under subhumid conditions, dangerously high water tables, growing seasons, and communications are all menaced by floods. In a desert, drought seldom assumes the proportions of a disaster but presents the conditions for survival. A flood is almost always a disaster.[25]

[19]   Sykes, *The Colorado Delta,* pp. 114-16, and A. P. Davis, "The New Inland Sea," *National Geographic Magazine,* Vol. 18 (1907), pp. 37-49.

[20]   *Reclamation Project Data,* p. 3.

[21]   D. T. MacDougal, "The Salton Sea," *American Journal of Science,* Vol. 39 (1915), p. 235.

[22]   *Ibid.,* pp. 231-50.

[23]   Sykes, *The Colorado Delta,* pp. 37-38, 127-68; and *Ten Rivers,* pp. 417-34.

[24]   *The Colorado River: A Comprehensive Report,* p. 58.

[25]   *Ibid.,* p. 58; *Ten Rivers,* pp. 432-33.

DAMS AND IRRIGATION

IRRIGATED DISTRICTS

(STORAGE DAMS

Much of the land in the Sonoran Desert needs only water to make it productive. The All-American Canal (left) carries water from the Colorado River across the Lower Colorado Desert to the Imperial Valley of southern California. An immense irrigated field (above) in the Imperial Valley. An intricate underground drainage and leaching system protects these fields from waterlogging and ultimate destruction by salts in the water. When such protection is insufficient, sterility results. Below, high water tables have sterilized these fields northwest of Brawley, California, in the Imperial Valley. Salt water standing in a weed-choked irrigation ditch and fields that appear to be covered with snow are the indelible stamp of alkaline deposits that result from rising water tables. In some areas, land such as this has been reclaimed and brought once again under cultivation.

The answer to these vexing problems was the construction of a single dam of unprecedented height in Boulder Canyon. The construction of Hoover Dam, authorized in 1928, was completed in 1935. This dam, impounding Lake Mead, provided the key to the development of water resources in the Lower Colorado Basin. Hoover Dam and Lake Mead are characterized to this day in superlatives, and constitute a major act of geographical surgery. The dam itself, the man-made lake, the controlled river, and the export of water and hydroelectricity have altered the natural environment extending over thousands of square miles.

The dam, constructed in the narrow Black Canyon of the Colorado, is 726 feet high.[26] The captive lake is capable of storing 32,471,000 acre-feet of water, which is slightly over two and a half times the average annual inflow of the Colorado River.[27] Above the lake is a 167,800-square-mile watershed.

The possibility of catastrophic flooding virtually ended with the completion of Hoover Dam. The reservoir acts as a huge desilting basin, retaining much of the material which elevated the delta to dangerous heights. Water can usually be retained or discharged at the discretion of those most affected. Hoover Dam assures a dependable water supply for the irrigation of an estimated 650,000 acres of land in Southern California and southwestern Arizona, as well as approximately 400,000 acres in Mexico.[28] An additional 150,000 to 250,000 acres may be brought under irrigation with full development of presently authorized projects. The wildly capricious flow of the Colorado has been replaced by a stream so dissimilar that even the name "Colorado" (red) no longer describes its lower reaches.[29]

Of almost equal importance in the overall river control scheme was a provision for the generation of electricity. Hydroelectric power was developed at Hoover Dam, not only to fill a need for power, but also to pay the major portion of the cost of construction.

To complete control of the river, it was necessary to construct a diversion dam and desilting works above the now-inadequate Laguna Dam on the lower channel of the river. The Imperial Dam and desilting basin has as its main purpose the diversion of water into the old Imperial

---

[26]   G. Barbour, "Boulder Dam and its Geographical Setting," *The Geographical Journal,* Vol. 86 (1935), pp. 498-504.

[27]   *Reclamation Project Data,* p. 52 — 12,600,000 acre-feet measured at the Grand Canyon.

[28]   *Ibid.,* pp. 52-53.

[29]   P. L. Kelingsorge, *The Boulder Canyon Project: Historical and Economic Aspects* (1941).

Canal — part of which is in Mexico — into the new All-American Canal, and the Gila Canal on the Arizona side of the river. However, it also acts as a storage dam for the drainage area between it and Parker Dam, the next storage dam upstream.

Parker Dam, with its power plant, is located about twelve miles above Parker, Arizona, and just below the confluence of the Bill Williams River with the Colorado. It was built primarily to serve the needs of the Metropolitan Water District, a water delivery district formed by five southern California counties. This district built the dam and a power plant which is necessary to lift the water in an aqueduct over the summits which have to be traversed to reach the West Coast area.[30]

Davis Dam was constructed in Pyramid Canyon, which is eighty-eight miles upstream from Parker Dam and sixty-seven miles downstream from Hoover. An earth-and-rock-fill embankment with concrete spillway, intake structure, and powerhouse, it forms the long and narrow Lake Mohave, which, like lakes Mead and Havasu, is important as a recreation center and wildlife preserve. Its waters extend to the base of Hoover Dam. Davis Dam acts as a reservoir for the irrigation of lands in Mexico, in accordance with the United States treaty with that country in 1945.[31]

Also on the Lower Colorado, just below the town of Parker, Arizona, is Headgate Rock Dam, which diverts water for the irrigation of land on the Arizona side of the river in the Colorado River Indian Reservation. Another diversion dam, Palo Verde, located just north of Blythe, California, makes water available for the irrigation of land in the vicinity of Blythe. Below the Mexican border, Morelos Dam diverts water for irrigation of Mexican farmland near San Luis.

Upstream from the Grand Canyon another major control dam has recently been completed at Glen Canyon near the Arizona-Utah boundary. This 700-foot concrete structure forms a reservoir (Lake Powell) with a capacity of 28 million acre-feet. Altogether the Colorado River constitutes the most complexly dammed and controlled river of its type in the world.

The Imperial Valley, a term which is normally applied to the southern margin of the Salton Depression, is the largest single irrigation district within the American sector of the Sonoran Desert. It ranks along

---

[30] Metropolitan Water District of California, *History and First Annual Report* (1939), pp. 7-51.

[31] *Reclamation Project Data*, pp. 599, 601; *The Colorado River: A Comprehensive Report*, pp. 164, 200, 240.

with the Salt, Yaqui, and Fuerte river valleys as one of the four most extensive desert irrigation schemes. It is, however, no more than a part of the larger All-American Canal System which encompasses the delivery of water to the Imperial and Coachella valleys.

The huge All-American Canal carries water to the southwest from the Imperial Dam on the Colorado. It winds its way through the shifting Algodones Sand Dunes along a route just north of the international boundary and then almost straight west across the southern Imperial Valley of California.

It connects with the previously constructed West Side Canal about ten miles west of Calexico and approximately eighty miles from Imperial Dam. From this point water is distributed to the north. The irrigated land of the Imperial Valley, which centers on Brawley and El Centro, has comprised a maximum of approximately 530,000 acres, located at elevations which vary from 40 feet above to 250 feet below sea level.[32]

High water tables have been a problem since the catastrophic flood which created the Salton Sea. The drilling of wells, the construction of drains, and other costly measures have lowered the water tables but only after thousands of acres of land had been sterilized by alkaline salts. Some irrigable land lying at low elevations probably never will return to cultivation.

In order to irrigate the fertile land north of the Salton Sea, the 123-mile Coachella Canal was constructed to deliver water from the All-American Canal at a point just west of the sandhills, approximately thirty-eight miles from the Imperial Dam diversion and desilting works. The Coachella Valley contains at the present time an estimated 100,000 acres of irrigated land. Approximately 80,000 acres are provided from Colorado River sources by the All-American–Coachella Canals, while the remainder is supplied by pumping.[33] The canal itself extends in a northwesterly direction until it crosses the Coachella Valley north of Indio and then continues along the west side of the valley to a terminus near the northwestern end of the Salton Sea. Irrigation is from laterals descending toward the Salton Depression from the left bank of the Coachella Canal. The network of laterals which is constructed largely underground totals an impressive 470 miles.[34]

An essential adjunct to the Coachella Valley irrigation system was

---

[32] *Reclamation Project Data,* p. 1; *U. S. Census of Agriculture, 1959,* Vol. 1 (Counties), Part 43 (California), p. 4; Table 116 gives 375,000 acres under irrigation in the Imperial Valley.

[33] *Reclamation Project Data,* pp. 2, 3.

[34] U. S. Bureau of Reclamation, *Coachella Division, All-American Canal System* (Boulder City, Nev., 1950), pp. 2-3.

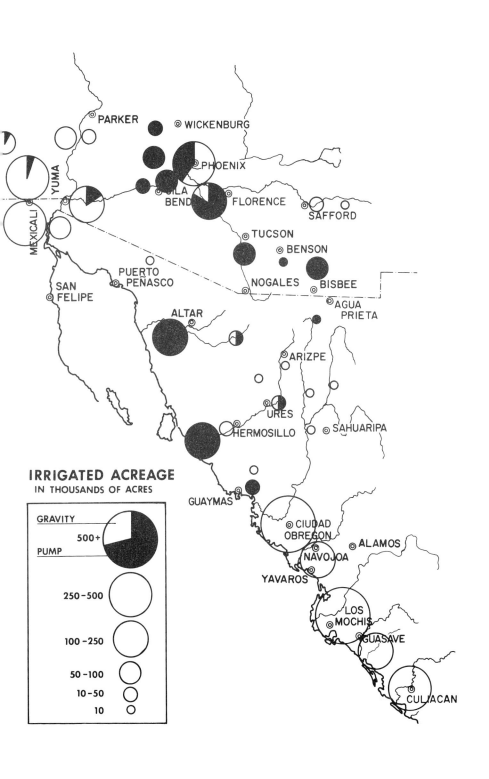

PARKER

WICKENBURG

PHOENIX

YUMA

GILA
BEND

FLORENCE

SAFFORD

MEXICALI

TUCSON

BENSON

PUERTO
PEÑASCO

NOGALES

BISBEE

SAN
FELIPE

AGUA
PRIETA

ALTAR

ARIZPE

URES

HERMOSILLO

SAHUARIPA

IRRIGATED ACREAGE
IN THOUSANDS OF ACRES

GUAYMAS

CIUDAD
OBREGON

ALAMOS

GRAVITY

500+

NAVOJOA

PUMP

YAVAROS

250–500

LOS
MOCHIS

100–250

GUASAVE

50–100

10–50

CULIACAN

10

the construction of protective dikes along the right bank of the Coachella Canal. Floodwater is retained and channeled to three major wasteways and ultimately to its natural drainageways.[35]

The Palo Verde Diversion Project is located on the west side of the Colorado River in the vicinity of Blythe, California. Diversion of water from the Colorado has always been attended by difficulties, the major problems being floods and the maintenance of satisfactory diversion conditions at the project's intake. The construction of levees, desilting basins, a diversion dam, and primarily the overall Boulder Canyon Project provide at this time a controlled flow of water for an estimated 70,000 acres of land under irrigation.[36]

The Fort Yuma Indian Reservation contains 14,620 acres of irrigable land. Almost all of this is annually under irrigation by water diverted from the All-American Canal and the Yuma Main Canal. The irrigable land is located largely between the communities of Bard and Winterhaven, California. Although located on the California bank of the Colorado River the reservation lands are an integral part of the Yuma Project, the great majority of which is located in Arizona.[37]

The Colorado River Aqueduct in southern California is the only large diversion of water destined for entirely municipal purposes within the Sonoran Desert.[38] The aqueduct was constructed by the Metropolitan Water District of Southern California in order to deliver water to Los Angeles, Long Beach, Pasadena, Anaheim, Santa Monica, and other cities in coastal California. The Metropolitan District's first objective in constructing the Colorado River Aqueduct was to supply Colorado River water for domestic, industrial, and other urban uses in the burgeoning Los Angeles conurbation.[39] Water is pumped from Lake Havasu and conveyed by the aqueduct, with the aid of huge pumps and siphons, across the desert plains and mountains to a reservoir immediately south of Riverside, California. The aqueduct has carried, over the past ten years, an average of 200,000 acre-feet of water annually — slightly less than one-third the total flow of the Salt River or more than twice the total flow of the Río Sonora.[40]

At a point south of Banning, California, a diversion which delivers water to the San Diego metropolitan area is in turn made from the

[35]   *Ibid.*, p. 3.

[36]   *Reclamation Project Data*, pp. 590-91.

[37]   *Ibid.*, p. 837, and *The Colorado River: A Comprehensive Report*, p. 265.

[38]   *The Colorado River: A Comprehensive Report*, p. 166.

[39]   Peveril Meigs, "Water Problems in the United States," *Geographical Review*, Vol. 42, (1952), pp. 362-63.

[40]   *Surface Water Supply, 1959, Part 9.*

Colorado Aqueduct. A system of pipes, tunnels, and siphons carries much-needed water to reservoirs which supply this rapidly expanding region. The route followed by the San Diego aqueduct was chosen in preference to an alternative scheme which would have diverted water from the All-American Canal at its western end.[41]

Mexicali

Immediately south of the International boundary near the Mexican city of Mexicali there is a large district under irrigation. It is in effect an integral part of the Imperial Valley Project of California, being contiguous to that scheme and having been developed concomitantly. Mexico originally received rights to water diverted from the Colorado River in exchange for the privilege of allowing American interests to construct the Alamo Canal through Mexico.[42] These same interests developed irrigated farms in Mexico, using water from this canal. The essential unity of the Mexicali and Imperial valleys was not significantly altered when the United States constructed the new All-American Canal. The Mexicali region still continues to use the Alamo Canal which receives water diverted from the Colorado River at a point one and one-half miles within the United States while making a number of diversions from the same river farther downstream.[43] This water originates entirely within the United States where it is stored behind American dams to be released as required in Mexico. The rights that the Mexicali region has to this water were guaranteed in a treaty with the United States, ratified in 1945.[44]

The irrigated district is located along the international boundary and extends south and east of Mexicali. The water is distributed to land forming part of the Colorado River's delta, which has filled the southern end of the Salton Depression, separating that tectonic trough from the Gulf of California. Water is transported with relative ease on the downgrade from the diversion point. Near the village of Bateques the water is divided into two canals which enclose the irrigable land in a triangle between them. This triangle is no more than a sector of the deltaic fan which is here utilized to facilitate the distribution of water to the alluvial

---

[41]   In a recent year nearly half of the Colorado River Aqueduct's total flow was consumed by the San Diego Metropolitan Area. This city received 82 percent of its total water supply from the aqueduct, while Los Angeles depended on this source for no more than 1.4 percent. Metropolitan Water Dist. of S. Cal., *Report for the Fiscal Year, July 1, 1950, to June 30, 1951.* Quoted in Meigs, "Water Problems in the United States," *Geographical Review,* Vol. 42, pp. 362-63.

[42]   *Reclamation Project Data,* p. 3.

[43]   *The Colorado River: A Comprehensive Report,* p. 66.

[44]   *Ibid.,* pp. 66-67.

lands filling the depression.[45] The mean elevation of the irrigated lands is approximately sea level. The land below sea level is located along the border. At the present time an estimated 400,000 acres are under irrigation in the Mexicali region.[46]

Yuma

The Yuma Region, which includes the irrigated lands of the Gila Project, has some of the oldest water rights on the Colorado. Modern irrigation, which had its beginnings here during the last years of the nineteenth century, has made great strides with the control of the Colorado and Gila rivers. The low-lying lands have benefited from flood control while additional water has been made available for the expansion of irrigation.

In the vicinity of Yuma, irrigation presents a complex pattern of numerous projects, deriving water from different sources and distributing it in a crazy-quilt pattern of canals, laterals, and ditches. This apparent irregularity is based upon the physical configuration of the Yuma region.

The town of Yuma, located at the confluence of the Gila and Colorado rivers, divides the valley land into: (1) the Lower Colorado bottomlands located between Yuma and the Mexican boundary, and (2) the Lower Gila Valley lands between Mohawk, Arizona, and Yuma, occupying both banks of the Gila and including some land along the Colorado near the confluence of the two rivers. In addition, (3) the Yuma Mesa, having an elevation approximately fifty feet higher than the valley at Yuma, extends directly south from that town to the Mexican boundary.

Each of these physical regions is the site of an irrigation scheme although each individual project may extend to some extent into a neighboring region. The Yuma Valley Project occupies principally region one, along the Colorado Valley southwest from Yuma. The Wellton-Mohawk division of the Gila Project occupies the valley lands of region two, east along the Gila River. The Yuma Mesa Division of the Gila Project occupies principally region three, the Yuma Mesa, but also delivers to the valley land along the Colorado and Gila rivers immediately east of Yuma. The small Yuma Auxiliary Project is also located on the Yuma Mesa.

The Yuma Valley Division of the Yuma Project supplies water to land of low elevation along the Arizona bank of the Colorado River

---

45 Sykes, *The Colorado Delta,* contains considerable information on the gradients, streamflow, and natural channels of this deltaic region.

46 *Reclamation Project Data,* p. 52.

between Yuma and the Mexican boundary. Since 1941 water has been diverted at the Imperial Dam and carried through the All-American Canal, and thence by the Yuma Main Canal to a siphon crossing the Colorado River to the Yuma Valley. The irrigation and drainage system has 51,936 acres within its boundaries, of which 45,000 are under irrigation.[47]

The Gila Project will ultimately furnish an irrigation water supply for 115,000 acres within the project area and for 3,406 acres in the Yuma Auxiliary Project. By 1958, works had been constructed to serve an estimated 107,000 acres. The project is divided into two divisions.[48]

The Wellton-Mohawk Division of the Gila Project begins some fifteen miles east of the city of Yuma and continues on both sides of the Gila River for about fifty miles. This division receives water from the eastern headgate of the Imperial Dam. The Gila Gravity Main Canal takes water from the desilting basin and delivers it to the Wellton-Mohawk Canal. It is then carried up the Gila Valley on a route generally parallel to the Gila River. This is done by means of three pump lifts of 31, 64, and 55 feet. An estimated 75,000 acres are under irrigation within this division.[49] High water tables and other drainage problems plague the areas of low elevation near Dome.

The Yuma Mesa Division, totaling about 35,000 acres of irrigable land, is divided into three geographically oriented units. The first of these, the Yuma Mesa Unit with over 17,000 acres under irrigation, occupies the mesa itself and extends south of Yuma toward the international boundary. The Gila Gravity Main Canal delivers water from the Imperial Dam to the Yuma Mesa pumping plant where it is lifted 52 feet. Water requirements on the sandy mesa land are greater than in the less permeable valley lands. Seepage from the mesa also creates drainage problems in the valleys below.

The North and South Gila Valley Units of the Yuma Mesa Division are located in the valley to the east and northeast of Yuma on both sides of the Gila River. Approximately 18,000 acres are under irrigation. Most of the irrigated lands in the North Gila Unit are within the North Gila Valley Irrigation District which operates and maintains the irrigation system and drainage facilities. The District comprises 7,050 acres located in the Y between the Gila and Colorado rivers. Coextensive with the South Gila unit is the Yuma Irrigation District, located on the

---

[47] *Ibid.,* pp. 837-41, and *The Colorado River: A Comprehensive Report,* p. 164.

[48] *Reclamation Project Data,* pp. 242-46.

[49] *Ibid.,* p. 242.

bottomlands south of the Gila River just east of Yuma and containing about 11,000 acres within its boundaries. The District is primarily an electric district supplying power to landowners for the operation of private wells. The water supply is from large-capacity drilled wells of between 150- and 200-foot depth.

Other Colorado River Projects

The Colorado River Indian Reservation Project was constructed and is operated by the U. S. Indian Service. Water is diverted at the Headgate Rock Dam for the irrigation of approximately 31,000 acres of bottomland, located south of Parker. About 11,000 acres are farmed by Indian owners or lessees and the remainder by White lessees. The drainage problems in this area are serious, but future expansion to an irrigated area of 100,000 acres of bottomland and 25,000 acres of mesa land is possible.[50]

Several thousand acres of scattered privately owned lands along the river are provided with water by pumping from the Colorado or from wells. Two of the larger areas are 1,600 acres below Ehrenberg and 6,500 acres in Cibola Valley. Some of the lands now under irrigation on the bottomland adjacent to the river have been acquired under squatters' rights, and title to them is in controversy.

THE SALT RIVER VALLEY

Salt River Project

Taking a leaf from the prehistoric Hohokam Indians who constructed over 125 miles of irrigation canals in the Lower Salt River Valley, were the newly-arrived Anglo-American settlers. Beginning in the year 1867 they constructed primitive diversion dams along the Lower Salt which channeled the streamflow into numerous ditches.[51] Some forty miles of these were re-excavated prehistoric canals.

Unfortunately for the farmers involved, their problems were not solved by these methods which were, in effect, not too far removed from those of the Hohokam. "During dry periods when there was little water in the river, diversion dams and canals were worthless. Conversely, during wet winter months the river often ran at flood, and simple dams were swept away in the torrent. The dams and canals offered promise, and frequently they delivered water to the lands. But as often as not the

---

50   *The Colorado River: A Comprehensive Report,* pp. 262-63.
51   *Reclamation Project Data,* p. 664.

promise went unfulfilled."[52] An early-day settler complained that "whenever there was no water in the river we had good dams."

Beginning in 1897, low runoff resulting from abnormally light rainfall in the watershed of the Salt-Verde River System brought about a series of crop failures. Livestock died and the irrigated land reverted to desert. In February 1900 a flash flood destroyed all the primitive diversion dams on the river. It appeared as if the Anglo-American settlers were facing the same fate as the Hohokam. However, legislation which was enacted in 1902 — the National Reclamation Act — provided the financial resources needed to construct an all-important storage dam on the Salt River about seventy-eight miles northeast of Phoenix. The passage of this act, however, provided its share of legal problems on privately owned lands. It was necessary to establish a basis for water rights to the floodwaters to be impounded. In order to do this, an early appropriator brought suit against a large number of landowners in the Salt River Valley. The result of this action was the famous Kent Decree which determined the water rights for every parcel of land in the Salt River Valley through exhaustive testimony regarding the historical development of irrigation in the valley. Floodwaters never before utilized because of the lack of a storage dam were distributed equally within the confines of the project regardless of the priority of appropriation.

Roosevelt Dam, which was constructed under the National Reclamation Act, was built at a narrow point just below the confluence of the Salt and its important Tonto Creek affluent. The diversion of water from the Salt was accomplished by the construction of Granite Reef Dam, located about four miles below the confluence of that river and its major tributary the Verde. Water was diverted into the old Arizona Canal on the north side of the river and into the South Canal on the south bank of the river. Numerous already existing canals were consolidated into two systems receiving water from the Arizona and South canals. Water released from Roosevelt Dam for diversion into these two canals at Granite Reef Dam followed the old channel of the Salt River. A power plant was built at the storage dam to generate electricity.

Roosevelt Dam was completed in 1911. However, in a very few years it became apparent that additional storage capacity was needed to capture the yet-dangerous floodwaters in wet years and store them for the inevitable dry years.[53] Rising water tables mentioned above presented another challenge which demanded an answer. This resulted

---

52 George Wharton James, *Reclaiming the Arid West* (New York, 1917).
53 *Reclamation Project Data,* pp. 662-65.

in an expansion of the Salt River Project which today encompasses the works described below.

Highest upstream on the Salt River is Theodore Roosevelt Dam (renamed in 1959, formerly just Roosevelt Dam). Its reservoir, Roosevelt Lake, has a capacity of 1,131,580 acre-feet, and is by far the largest reservoir of the expanded Salt-Verde system, its volume being 4 percent of Lake Mead. This volume, although small in comparison to the major Colorado River dams, is over twice the average annual flow of the Salt River.[54] Despite this fact, the economics of water utilization for agricultural purposes necessitate such high-level storage that the dam occasionally overflows. To capture this floodwater for irrigation and prevent flooding, three additional storage dams were built on the downstream Salt.

Next below Roosevelt Dam is Horse Mesa Dam, the highest of the Salt-Verde system, measuring 300 feet. This structure impounds 245,138 acre-feet in the Apache Lake reservoir which extends seventeen miles up the Salt River. Downstream, ten-mile-long Canyon Lake behind Mormon Flat Dam is capable of storing 57,852 acre-feet. The lowest and most recently constructed of the mainstream Salt River storage dams is Stewart Mountain Dam, only forty-one miles east of Phoenix. Its reservoir, Saguaro Lake, has a capacity of 69,765 acre-feet. To the north, Horseshoe Dam is the first to intercept water on the Verde River. Constructed fifty-eight miles northeast of Phoenix, it has a capacity of 142,830 acre-feet. Bartlett Dam, located downstream on the Verde, impounds 179,548 acre-feet, completing the storage capacity of the Verde River dam system. Together these two Verde River reservoirs are incapable of retaining one year's average annual streamflow.

The overall capacity of the six storage dams on the Salt-Verde System is 2,076,713 acre-feet, almost twice the average annual runoff of the two rivers.[55] After water has been stored in the six major dams, and diverted by the Granite Reef Dam into either the Arizona or Southern Canal systems, it is distributed to the Salt River Project lands. As mentioned above, the rights which the owners of this land have to the water of the Salt-Verde system were legally established before completion of the Project.[56] Flood control to this day is only a secondary consideration. Municipal uses are somewhere in between, certainly behind, that of the vested agricultural interests.

---

[54]   The Salt River's average flow at Roosevelt Dam is 649,670 acre-feet. *Reclamation Project Data,* p. 665.

[55]   *Ibid.,* The lowest that stored water ever fell since the storage dams were built was in 1940 when there were only 22,426 acre-feet in all lakes combined. This was calculated to be about three days' supply.

[56]   J. F. Griswold, *Salt River Project* (Phoenix, 1956).

— PHOENIX CHAMBER OF COMMERCE

Water in the canal leads to the ditch, which in turn leads to agricultural wealth. Upon this the economy of the Sonoran Desert has been built. In this photo a major canal delivers water to the Salt River Valley. Citrus groves dominate a landscape that was formerly a bleak desert. These groves are giving way to housing, factories, and shopping centers.

The Project contains about 236,000 acres. Of this, approximately 75,000 acres are now in urban or industrial use. Some 160,000 acres are still under cultivation — or about two-thirds of the Project — down sharply over the last decade.

Uniquely significant to the demand placed on the Salt River Project's highly developed but limited water supply is the accelerated growth of the Phoenix conurbation. The greatest urban growth is located within the irrigated lands of the Project. Every year the built-up area continuously encroaches on fields and orange groves which receive water from the Project.

It is fortunate that land taken out of agricultural production uses less water. Crops require a considerably larger amount of water per acre than the city dweller who himself uses water in prodigious quantities. Within the Salt River Project nonagricultural use of land has required about one-third as much water as does farming.

Other Salt River Valley Developments

The Salt River Project is only one part of the water-resource development in the Salt River Valley. In addition to the 160,000 acres of land presently under irrigation within the boundaries of the Project, there are on its margins a number of other irrigated districts. Most of these districts dovetail with the larger Salt River Project, and lie within the Salt River Valley and Maricopa County. Some of them, such as the Queen Creek area described below, have spread into neighboring watersheds and counties, but will be treated here as part of the overall Salt River scheme. The following districts differ most markedly from the Salt River Project in that they rely almost entirely on well water.

The Roosevelt Water Conservation District containing approximately 37,000 acres is located immediately east of the Salt River Project, and its principal source of water is from wells within the district boundaries. The district also has available some surplus gravity water from the Salt River. This surplus water was made available through a contract with the Salt River Project stipulating that the Conservation District would line the canals in its vicinity and receive in exchange a quantity of water equal to the saving in seepage achieved through this act.[57]

Farther to the southeast, the Queen Creek Irrigation District secures its entire water supply from wells. The irrigated area here has been extended in this same direction, under private ownership with water from wells, to within a few miles of the town of Florence on the Gila River. In this area to the south of the Salt River Project boundary and

---

[57]   Khalaf, pp. 138-39.

to the north of the Gila River Indian Reservation practically all of the potentially irrigable lands have been placed under irrigation, using well water.

Northwest of Phoenix a single irrigation district — the Maricopa County Municipal Water Conservation District No. 1 — delivers water to land just beyond the boundary of the Salt River Project. This district, with over 39,000 acres within its boundaries, obtains about one-quarter of its delivered water supply from the Carl Pleasant Dam and Reservoir on the Agua Fria River. The remainder is supplied by water from deep wells.

The Roosevelt Irrigation District containing 38,000 acres occupies a strip about three miles in width and twenty-four in length, extending from the Agua Fria River on the east to the Hassayampa River on the west. The district obtains its water from wells, some of which were originally drilled for drainage purposes.[58] The Buckeye Irrigation District with over 18,000 acres to the south of the Roosevelt Irrigation District is being supplied with water in a similar fashion through pumping.[59] This water contains such a high level of salt that measures must be taken to make the water utilizable for agriculture. The first non-experimental desalination plant located in the United States was constructed at Buckeye in 1960 to supply this need.

Other land situated between the organized irrigation projects and extending northward into Deer Valley and along the Agua Fria and New rivers has been developed with pumped water supplies. In some instances the development has been under corporate ownership of several thousands of acres such as that of the Goodyear Cotton Company at Litchfield Park. The total irrigated acreage within the Salt River Valley is approximately 310,000 acres.

OTHER ARIZONA DISTRICTS

The Upper Gila River Valley

The irrigated area along the Upper Gila River, most of which is just beyond the eastern margin of desert vegetation, is concentrated principally in the Safford Valley with 31,000 acres, and in the Duncan Valley with about 5,200 acres.[60] Crop irrigation in the Upper Gila was begun in about 1872. These areas have water rights to gravity flow from the river amounting to 165,000 acre-feet. The riverine lands are

---

58 *Ibid.,* p. 137.
59 *Ibid.,* p. 140.
60 U. S. Dept. of Agriculture, *Census of Agriculture: 1959,* Vol. 1, Part 43, Table 116.

dependent for water upon the unregulated flow of the Gila. Recurring shortages of water during the summer months have led to the drilling of wells to augment the supply of surface water. There are no storage dams above these Upper Gila projects.[61]

The Casa Grande Valley

The name Casa Grande Valley is given to the large irrigated region on the left bank of the Middle Gila centering on the town of Casa Grande. The irrigated land also spills over into the Lower Santa Cruz Valley. In fact, the great majority of its groundwater is withdrawn from beneath the Santa Cruz Valley while the entire surface-water supply is taken from the Gila. Both of these valleys form a limited zone of irrigation with the name "Casa Grande" used to circumvent confusion which might otherwise occur.

The overall development of irrigation in the Casa Grande Valley was based originally upon the Gila River gravity water made available to what is known as the San Carlos Project. It is located in part on the Gila River Indian Reservation near Sacaton and in part on non-Indian land lying largely within a triangular area whose apices are near Florence, Eloy, and Casa Grande. This project, with its limited surface-water rights, cannot assume the same central role as that played by the Salt River Project in the total development of water resources in that Valley.

To control the flow of water to the San Carlos Project, Coolidge Dam was built on the Gila River some 25 miles southeast of Globe. The reservoir which it forms, known as San Carlos Lake, has a capacity of 1,300,000 acre-feet; however, the maximum storage attained so far has been a little more than 800,000 acre-feet — in 1942, following one of the wettest years on record. The Gila River water supply, which varies greatly from year to year, has been supplemented with an average of 90,000 acre-feet of pumped water per year. Crop acreage is adjusted to the water supply and has varied from a minimum of 26,000 to a maximum of 46,000 acres on non-Indian or white lands. The average surface-water-irrigated acreage of Indian lands in the Project during the past ten years has been about 20,000 acres per year and approximately 30,000 acres on the white lands.

An additional storage dam on the Gila below its confluence with the San Pedro River would retain the presently wasted flood waters of this latter stream, but provide precious little water for additional acreage. Practically all the irrigable lands from the San Carlos Project area

---

[61]   In addition to the lands having gravity water rights along the Gila there is a small area to the south near Artesia having about 1,000 acres under pump irrigation.

extending southward along the Santa Cruz through the Eloy district to the Pinal-Pima County line have been developed with pump-water supplies.

West of Casa Grande in the Maricopa and Stanfield district as far south as the Papago Indian Reservation, irrigation is carried out entirely with pumped water. It is estimated that the irrigated area included within the Casa Grande Valley contains approximately 178,000 acres wholly dependent upon groundwater supplies, out of a total estimated 228,000 acres overall.[62]

Santa Cruz Valley

Irrigated development from Tucson south to the Mexican boundary has been confined primarily to the narrow strip of irrigable bottomland on both sides of the Santa Cruz River. This portion of the Santa Cruz Valley is one of the few pump areas in Arizona where the water table has not been seriously lowered through pumping. The average annual rainfall in the upper Santa Cruz watershed is capable of recharging underground supplies despite increased pumping. This is due to the fact that the irrigable acreage is limited to the narrow bottomland. The largest concentration of land under irrigation is in the Sahuarita-Continental district above Tucson.

In a relatively small way, urban development in the vicinity of Tucson has replaced agriculture and there is diminished pumping for irrigation along the Santa Cruz and Rillito bottoms. The largest area under irrigation in Pima County is northwest of Tucson in the Marana-Avra-Santa Cruz Valley district. In 1950, the area's irrigated acreage was about 32,000 acres, while the total today is estimated at about 58,000 acres. The continued growth of metropolitan Tucson places increased pressure each year on the limited underground water supply of the Santa Cruz.[63] An interesting sidelight is the fact that Tucson is the largest city in the United States wholly dependent on groundwater.

The San Pedro Valley and Cochise County

Along the San Pedro River there are a number of scattered small areas under irrigation between the Mexican boundary and Redington. Near Benson and St. David there are small diversions from the San Pedro River for several hundreds of acres. However, most of the land along the San Pedro is irrigated with pumped water. Between Redington and the mouth of the river at Winkelman small scattered areas on the bottomland are irrigated with groundwater from shallow drilled wells.

---

[62] U. S. Dept. of Agriculture, *U. S. Census of Agriculture: 1959*, Vol. 1, Part 43, Table 116.

[63] *Ibid.*, Table 116.

A few small gravity ditches diverting water from the San Pedro River still exist but the supply is supplemented with pumped water. The irrigated acreage can be only roughly estimated and probably does not total more than 5,000 acres.

Water for irrigation in Cochise County is obtained almost entirely from wells of small capacity except in the Willcox-Kansas Settlement and Bowie areas. There are in the county, including the San Pedro Valley, a total of approximately 105,000 acres under irrigation.[64] It is estimated that about one-third of the irrigated acreage is concentrated in the Willcox-Kansas Settlement areas, and south of Cochise Dry Lake. The other important irrigated areas are northwest of Willcox, along Whiteriver Draw in the southern end of the Sulphur Spring Valley, and in the Bowie-San Simon district.

Western Arizona

In western Arizona the expansion of irrigated acreage in recent years has taken place largely through the development of groundwater supplies. The area under irrigation may vary considerably from year to year in any one region but in general there has been an increase.

The districts known as Rainbow Valley and Waterman Wash are just south of the lower end of the Salt River Valley as it meets the Gila River. The approximate acreage under irrigation in Rainbow Valley, which drains west into the Gila River, is about 6,000 acres. The Waterman Wash area drains north into the Gila River and has an irrigated acreage of about 12,000 acres. Well water supplies 100 percent of the irrigated land in both districts.

The Gila River Valley from Gillespie Dam to Painted Rock Dam includes some lands adjacent to the Gila River with gravity water rights, but because of inadequate water supply this region has been dependent upon supplemental pump water for many years. Development has been mainly on the bottomlands on both sides of the Gila River and on the mesa lands west of Gila Bend. The total acreage under irrigation in this district in 1965 was estimated at 55,000 acres.

The Gila River Valley from Painted Rock Dam to the Wellton-Mohawk Project forms a separate irrigated zone. Scattered areas on both sides of the river have been developed in this district, where the irrigated acreage in 1965 has been estimated at approximately 10,000 acres, all dependent upon well water.

The district which centers on Tonopah and the area west of the Hassayampa River has developed rapidly since 1952 and is estimated

---

[64] Estimate given by Carmy Page, Cochise County Agricultural Extension Service agent.

The preparation of virgin soil south of Willcox, southeastern Arizona. Deep plowing breaks the hardpan while loosening the soil for deep-rooted plants such as alfalfa. Very heavy equipment such as is shown here is best for this purpose. The breaking of virgin soil in the American sector of the Sonoran Desert is now a rarity.

These cotton fields along the Upper Santa Cruz south of Tucson are now largely devoted to the production of forage for cattle. This field may have been cultivated (in part by cotton) since pre-Columbian times. The two pictures taken together point up the replacement of desert by cotton and cotton by other crops. This replacement may take ten years or three hundred.

to have an irrigated area of almost 25,000 acres. It is entirely pump irrigated.

In the McMullen Valley about 14,000 acres are under pump irrigation. This district extends from above Aguila in the east end of the valley to Salome at the west end. Development has been concentrated principally in the area north of Aguila.

Centennial Wash, immediately above its confluence with the Gila River, is flanked by a recently developed irrigation project which is estimated to contain about 25,000 acres. Surface water is not used in the Centennial Wash area.

DEVELOPMENT OF WATER RESOURCES IN MEXICO

In the Mexican states of Sonora and Sinaloa, modern irrigation practices using high-elevation dams, canals, laterals, and high-powered pumps have been introduced with increasing rapidity during recent years. Progress has been impressive since 1926 when the first meaningful legislation concerning the reclamation of the arid Mexican Northwest became law. The large quantities of water which formerly spread over the coastal plain in time of flood to be lost into the atmosphere, the sand, and the sea have been impounded behind dams and are diverted to the newly created reclamation colonies which line the coast. The decade of 1950–60 showed more progress than any other period in history as the development of irrigated agriculture came to equal that of the American desert. Much work remains to be done, particularly in the southern or Sinaloan portion of the desert, while continued expansion of irrigation in Sonora finds a very real limit in the scarcity of underground water and the uncertain streamflow.

The calculation of the average number of total acres under irrigation for the individual irrigation districts in Mexico presents numerous difficulties. The last fifteen years have witnessed such a rapid extension of irrigation that one- or two-year-old estimates may be far too low. In addition, the amount of water available each year fluctuates widely so that establishing an average is difficult over a short period of rapid growth. Neither official figures nor local estimates are to be entirely trusted. There is a widely held belief that official totals are overestimated. On the other hand, individual farmers often plant more land than they report to Recursos Hidráulicos.

There are in general certain factors characterizing the Mexican efforts to make water available which differ from those found north of the border. These, taken in conjunction with contrasting physical conditions, provide a noteworthy variation from the pattern set within the United States.

(1) Instead of one great river — the Colorado — and its major tributary — the Gila system — the water supply of the Mexican desert depends upon numerous smaller streams that flow straight out onto the coastal plain, roughly paralleling each other and at right angles to the Gulf of California. This means that a larger number of completely independent watershed development schemes are needed to utilize as much water as possible. It also means that potential difficulties over the allocation of water are lessened.

(2) Whereas in the American sector of the Sonoran Desert modern irrigation projects are located at elevations which range from over 3,000 feet above sea level to almost 300 feet below sea level, practically all are found between 50 and 450 feet above sea level just below the points where the mountain-born streams disgorge themselves onto the deltaic plain. The Mexicali district, Baja California, is the major exception.

(3) In Mexico, government planning, communal ownership, and other social factors combine with varying levels of technology to alter the pattern of modern water development and distribution.

(4) A somewhat lower level of technology, rural poverty, and isolation is to be seen in the continued existence of extremely primitive water-distribution methods. Brush dams and hand-excavated wells are to be found throughout the arid Mexican back country. Except on Indian reservations, these practices, where they ever existed in the United States, have been replaced.

(5) Finally, sophisticated and monumental engineering is generally absent from the Mexican water-supply projects. There is nothing to compare with Hoover Dam and the Colorado Aqueduct south of the border. Much of this, however, is a direct result of the less complex geographical handicaps to be overcome, and the smaller need to overcome them.

Sonora

San Luis on the Colorado River south of Yuma receives water from that river diverted at Morelos Dam, the only Mexican barrier on the Colorado. Water for the Morelos diversion is stored far upstream at Davis Dam under agreement with the United States. Near San Luis there are approximately 74,000 acres under irrigation from this source and an additional 5,000 acres supplied by pumps used to lower a high water table.[65] The San Luis Region is geographically a part of the Yuma Project, being contiguous with that district.

The region of Altar located on the intermittent river of the same name is a district where irrigation has been carried on since at least the last decade of the seventeenth century. Some irrigation practices to be

---

[65] *Sonora en Cifras,* 1961.

seen there today have not changed much since that time but the construction of the small Cuauhtemoc Dam has brought an estimated 8,000 acres under modern irrigation. This total is increased by an additional 5,000 acres irrigated by wells. The water is distributed by canal to the communities of Altar, Atil, and Oquitoa.

The Upper Magdalena River Valley containing the towns of Imuris, Magdalena, and Santa Ana is the scene of modern well irrigation which supplements the more primitive use of water diverted from the Río Magdalena. Out of a 14,000-acre total, there are 7,000 acres under pump irrigation. This region is along the main highway south from Nogales as it traverses this headwater tributary of the Río Concepción.

The Caborca District, including contiguous Pitiquito, is situated below the Altar and Magdalena confluence after these streams have lost most of their water. Surface irrigation from the Río Concepción is impossible for more than about 500 acres. Power-driven pumps have, however, placed an estimated 114,000 acres under irrigation, most of it since 1955. This is the largest region under irrigation in northern Sonora.

The utilization of Sonora River water has been a great disappointment to the optimists of the past. Great hopes were based upon the mistaken assumption that 200,000 or more acre-feet of water were available annually from runoff, and that as much as 500,000 acres could be irrigated from surface water alone![66] Seldom have expectations been more poorly realized.

---

66 Among the more sanguine statements based on inadequate hydrological data is the following, made in 1923:

"The total acre-feet available for storage above Hermosillo would be approximately 200,000. General conditions in this region of the State are very arid, but still the district compares favorably with Syria, whose gardens have for 4,000 years been one of the wonders of the world and whose water supply from the Abana is not greater, lacking storage, than that of Hermosillo. The dam, as projected, will be 180 feet high and 800 feet long on the top, while its bottom will be only about 200 feet long. The reservoir, when filled, will be about 10 miles long and from 1,000 to 3,000 feet wide, having the estimated capacity indicated above. The amount of electric power that can be generated has not been computed but will be very great — amply sufficient for the towns in central Sonora. This structure will be the first to be built, according to the plans of the Government engineers, in the series that will constitute the 'Sonora River Project.' Another storage dam is planned for the Sonora River and one or two for the Río San Miguel, which joins the Sonora River just above Hermosillo. Just below the junction of the two rivers there is planned a large submerged storage and diversion dam of concrete for the purpose of bringing the large underground flow of the rivers to the surface and making the water available for irrigation. The entire project, when completed, will irrigate, it is estimated, more than 500,000 acres of the fertile delta and alluvial fill lands of the Sonora River Valley." P. L. Bell and H. B. MacKenzie, *Mexican West Coast and Lower California: A Commercial and Industrial Survey*, Dept. of Commerce, 1923, pp. 105-106.

The Rodríguez Dam at the very outskirts of Hermosillo provides flood protection for that city as well as irrigation water for an estimated average of 32,000 acres, just below that city along the streamway of the Río Sonora. The Rodríguez Dam has never been filled to overflowing and in periods of drought provides much less than the average noted above. It has nevertheless increased the area under irrigation from an estimated 11,000 acres in 1926.

A more profitable venture, also developed and regulated by Recursos Hidráulicos, is the Costa de Hermosillo. Entirely dependent on well water pumped from 75 feet to 250 feet below the surface, this irrigation district has transformed an estimated 236,000 acres of the driest desert soil to one of the most highly productive agricultural regions of the Sonoran Desert. It is in fact the largest single pump-irrigated region within the desert, exceeding in size the Lower Santa Cruz Valley which it most closely resembles. Falling water tables limit further expansion of this district, while continued depletion may, in the future, cause some acreage to go out of production.

The Valle de Guaymas, an area of pump irrigation located on the deltaic plain of the intermittent Matape River just east of Empalme, is another new Sonoran project. Having approximately 32,000 acres under irrigation, the Valley de Guaymas ranks third behind the Costa de Hermosillo and Caborca in acreage under well water. Modern methods are used to supply subterranean water but an estimated average of 2,000 acres are irrigated by the annual construction and repair of primitive works to contain and distribute surface flow.

The Yaqui Valley Project, occupying the lower or coastal margins of the Yaqui River Valley, is the largest irrigation district in the state of Sonora. The development of modern irrigation here can be said to have begun in 1904 when the Díaz regime granted a concession to the Richardson Construction Company of Los Angeles to build canals distributing water from the downstream Yaqui. By 1909 this concern had completed over twenty-five miles of main canal and about fifty miles of laterals. Within a short time, it was estimated, 750,000 acres could be brought under irrigation. However, the outbreak of civil war halted construction repeatedly. In 1913 when work was suspended completely only 27,000 acres were being irrigated. Indian warfare and other political problems slowed progress so that no more than 75,000 acres were being irrigated as late as 1923. The Richardson Construction Company held at that time approximately 400,000 acres of irrigable land in the valley.

Bloody warfare between the Yaqui Indians and the Mexican Army

The Yaqui Main Canal. North of the border only the giant All-American Canal can carry this quantity of water. The dark sheet of rain in the background is a typical summer cloudburst in the Sonoran Desert. Twenty years ago this area was in the main a desert, fifty years ago a bloody battlefield. Ten miles to the south lies Ciudad Obregón, named for the revolutionary hero born in this valley.

continued as late as 1928. At that time less than 70,000 acres were under irrigation, about half by indigenous peoples and half by Mexican farmers, both of whom lived in constant peril of internecine warfare.[67] The construction of the Alvaro Obregón Dam and related works could only proceed after peaceful conditions returned to the valley. Subsequent accomplishments which have brought as much as 560,000 acres under irrigation are in truth a product of war and diplomacy as well as planning and engineering.

The Alvaro Obregón Dam, key to the development of the deltaic plain, is used to impound the Yaqui's floodwaters and distribute them as they are called for on the coast. The dam itself is situated well back in the Sierra where two low desert mountains pinch the valley before it opens out onto the coastal plain. To the north of the Lower Yaqui streamway, the Canal Colonias Yaquis delivers water principally to the Yaqui villages which line the right bank. South of the Yaqui two larger canals move water to the major zone of Mexican irrigation. The Canal Principal supplies water to the western or lower portion of the coastal plain while the Canal Alto is used to irrigate an equal area to the east, slightly higher in elevation. When the Obregón Reservoir contains enough water, these two canals supply water capable of irrigating an estimated one-quarter million acres each. Under normal conditions, however, much of the eastern zone is deprived of water.

Over 90 percent of the project's irrigable land lies south of the Yaqui. This productive zone is shown on some maps as reaching the Mayo River. However, the inability of the Obregón Dam to supply sufficient water normally precludes irrigation in the south along the north bank of the Mayo as it does in the east. The only other significant limits placed on this scheme are the rugged mountains that border the deltaic plain to the east and north as well as the high water tables and saline soils that border the Gulf for some miles inland on the west.

The construction of canals and laterals was greatly facilitated by the uniformly even and gentle gradients descending from the Hornos diversion dam near Esperanza.[68] The three major canals and other minor ones which radiate from this point flow out naturally along the alluvial fan, crossing the concentric contour lines usually at right angles. This provides a gradient sufficiently steep to move water to the fields without pumping.

The Mayo River Project, which is often considered as being a part of an overall Yaqui-Mayo scheme, lies along the left bank of the stream

---

[67]   *Sonora en Cifras,* 1961.

[68]   "Potentialidad de la Región Costera de los Estados de Sonora y Sinaloa," *Irrigación en México,* Vol. 23 (1942), pp. 89-103.

south and west of Navojoa. Water is stored at the Mocuzari Dam and then brought to an estimated 207,000 acres in a triangle between Navojoa, Huatabampo, and the Canal de Tesia. This canal supplies most of the water to the project and was engineered to follow the gentle gradient of the Mayo's deltaic fan in the same manner as that described above. The Río Mayo with its smaller streamflow has not fulfilled earlier hopes. The water supplied by the Mocuzari Dam is not adequate in the average year to supply the land which originally was put into cultivation.[69] Unlike the Yaqui Project, the Río Mayo is not flanked on the north by a canal, and several miles of desert intervene between the irrigated fields of the Yaqui and Mayo projects.[70]

Eastern Sonora

Contrasting with the modern development of hydrological resources along the coastal plains are the conditions in the upland valleys of eastern Sonora. Here, along the headwaters of streams that eventually have their waters utilized on the coast, primitive irrigation practices persist. The great efforts expended in western Sonora that have brought almost one million acres under irrigation during the last decades have not taken place in the eastern half of the state. Since 1926 only an estimated 18,600 acres have been added to the total land under irrigation in fifty municipalities located in the Eastern Sierras. Isolation and a stagnant economy are both the cause and result of the continuing backwardness seen in the underdeveloped condition of irrigated agriculture in eastern Sonora.

A knowledge of the physical conditions is paramount to the understanding of this dichotomous situation. Whereas along the coast only the availability of water limits the extent of each project, inland it is usually the absence of irrigable land located in proximity to water that limits irrigation. Wide expanses of alluvial plain occasionally interrupted by a desert mountain range are replaced, in the east, by expansive mountains divided by restricted valleys. The largest of these, the upstream Río Sonora and its tributary the San Miguel, the upstream Río Matape and the headwater tributaries of the Río Yaqui, contain only limited areas where water can be applied to irrigable land using simple methods. High-level dams, deep wells, siphons, and so forth, could possibly bring several hundred thousand acres under irrigation in eastern Sonora, but

---

69 Craig L. Dozier, "Mexico's Transformed Northwest," *Geographical Review*, Oct. 1963, p. 555.

70 México Comisión Nacional de Irrigación, "Informe final sobre el estudio económico del desarollo del riego propuesto por el uso del Río Mayo en el Estado de Sonora," *Boletín de Diciembre 1926*.

— ALFRED COHN

Two views of the Yaqui and a major tributary. The Río Bavispe (above), swollen by summer rains, fills its sandy streambed, providing water for a palustrine forest. This photo was taken near Guasavas, Sonora. The picture below is that of the downstream Yaqui near Raspadero.

— ECKHART MISSION COLLECTION, BY CHARLES C. DI PESO

only at a disproportionately high cost. In addition, most of the streamflow from the major rivers has now been appropriated on the coast.

Small arroyos descending from the eastern desert mountains present even less possibility. Valley floors are hopelessly narrow and hard rocks yield almost no water. These same conditions also impede the building of roads which has a secondary effect on the entire economy. In these ways, irrigated agriculture suffers.

The development of water resources along the Río San Miguel, an affluent of the Río Sonora system, typifies all of the headwater streams within the Eastern Highlands of Sonora. Water is utilized by a series of small pueblos that take advantage of the best hydrological conditions to be found along this intermittent streamway.

In some favored sites water is available throughout the year. This is usually where the valley fill is constricted by a sill of impermeable rock. If irrigable land is nearby, primitive dams are constructed, wells are sunk, and water is distributed to small fields. Wherever more than two or three hundred acres are under cultivation there is invariably a small nucleated oasis-pueblo. These are strung out like beads along the Río San Miguel. An agricultural census for the year 1959 enumerated the irrigated acreage for the four administrative districts along this stream-way. Although there are twenty-two settlements situated on the Río San Miguel, most of the irrigated land is adjacent to the four principal towns. A comparison of the 1959 census figures with those of a census taken in 1926, the year of the first modern Mexican irrigation act, is interesting:

Río San Miguel Irrigated Acreage

*Municipality	Primitive Gravity 1926	1959	Pump 1926	1959	Totals 1926	1959
Cucurpe	2,717	2,717	—	788	2,717	3,505
Opodepe	469	2,349	—	—	469	2,349
Rayon	2,470	2,470	—	788	2,470	3,258
Horcasitas	788	788	—	664	788	1,452
Total	6,444	8,324	—	2,240	6,444	10,564 acres

*Municipalities are listed in north-to-south order.

It is apparent that 10,564 acres is a very small percentage of a desert valley extending one hundred miles north and south through Sonora. The relatively small increase in total irrigated land from 6,444 acres in 1926 is equally significant since this covers the period of revolutionary advance in irrigation on the coastal plain.

It should also be noted that increased use of subterranean water has not resulted in the abandonment of primitive dams and other techniques used to provide surface water. Instead there has been a slow increase in land under this form of irrigation.

What is true of the Río San Miguel is also to be seen in the development of water resources along the upstream Río Sonora. In 1959 the following areas were under irrigation:

Upstream Río Sonora Irrigated Acreage, 1959

Municipality	Primitive Gravity	Pump	Total
Bacoachi	2,000	100	2,060
Arizpe	2,300	700	3,000
Banamichi	1,400	600	2,000
Huepac	700	450	1,150
San Felipe	450	250	700
Aconchi	1,000	750	1,750
Baviacora	1,250	750	2,000
Ures	1,250	4,900	6,150
Total	10,350	8,500	18,810 acres

Along the Río Sonora pump irrigation is practiced over a larger proportion of the total area of land but remains less extensive than the primitive use of surface water. Modern large-scale pumping in the vicinity of Ures accounts for more than one-half the total land under this method of irrigation. Only here has this resulted in the abandonment of early-day methods.

Irrigation practices along the headwater affluents of the generally waterless Río Matape are much the same with only an estimated 445 acres under gravity irrigation and approximately 247 acres under well water.

The more isolated Río Moctezuma, which intermittently flows into the Río Yaqui, is flanked by irrigation schemes dating back to pre-Colonial times. The methods used to exploit the limited water resources of this valley are largely those originally employed by Indian and Spanish Colonial farmers. Hand-dug wells may now be operated by pumps but in general there has been little technological advance. In this valley even more than in those mentioned above, poor communications resulting in isolation have a direct effect upon progress in water resource development. Irrigated land along the Río Moctezuma is distributed as follows:

Río Moctezuma Irrigated Acreage, 1959

Municipality	Primitive Gravity	Pump	Total
Cumpas	1,500	1,000	2,500
Moctezuma	1,100	—	1,100
S. Pedro de L.C.	400	—	400
Batuc	450	—	450
Suaqui	200	—	200
Tepupa	450	—	450
Villa Pesqueira*	400	—	400
Total	4,500	1,000	5,500 acres

*The small modern Haciendita Diversion Dam is included in the Villa Pesqueira total.

The same conditions persist along the larger Río Bavispe where primitive dams are constructed to retain floodwaters only to be washed out by the water they were built to contain. These are faithfully rebuilt, often in time to be swamped by an even larger floodtide, or to stand empty as the rains cease. To alleviate this situation La Angostura Dam was built, which also evens the flow of water to the Obregón Dam and the Yaqui delta project. There are no irrigation works attached directly to the Angostura dam. Deep wells are unheard of except in the Fronteras region near the American boundary. Hand-excavated wells provide domestic water supplies throughout other valley communities. The 1959 agricultural census gave the following totals:

Río Bavispe Irrigated Acreage, 1959

Municipality	Primitive Gravity	Pump	Total
Fronteras	—	4,000	4,000
Agua Prieta	2,300	—	2,300
Huachinera	900	—	900
Bacerac	1,750	—	1,750
Bavispe	1,850	—	1,850
Oputo	1,700	—	1,700
Huasabas	1,500	—	1,500
Other pueblos	1,000	—	1,000
Total	11,000	4,000	15,000 acres

The almost total reliance upon archaic methods is even more marked in this easternmost valley.

In the extremely rugged country bordering the upstream Yaqui, sometimes called the Río de Aros, and yet further upstream the Río Papigochic,[71] there is almost no chance for irrigation since there is little suitable land near the streamways. Such headwater affluents as the left bank Río Mulatos which descend from the humid Sierra Madre provide a disproportionate share of the water utilized on the coastal plain but only the municipalities of Arivechi and Sahuaripa are able to take advantage of this water. Together they account for less than an estimated 1,500 acres, all of this retained by annual construction and rebuilding of fragile diversion works.

Below the junction of the upstream Río Yaqui with the Río Moctezuma, but above the Obregón reservoir, only three communities utilize the water of the Río Yaqui. Bacanora and Onavas irrigate an estimated 300 acres of land using primitive methods, while Villa Pesqueira has an estimated 500 acres under irrigation.

In the rolling country separating the watersheds of the Yaqui and

---

71   There is considerable confusion regarding the use of these names.

Mayo rivers near Quiriego and Rosario about 600 acres are irrigated in an age-old fashion using the water of intermittent streams.

Sinaloa

Southward as rainfall increases the coastal plain narrows, constricting the area of potentially irrigable land while simultaneously making irrigation optional for at least some crops. However, north of Culiacán, particularly along the coast, climatic conditions which prevail in Sonora are not significantly altered, and the problem of making water available to a seasonally parched soil remains. Heavy summer runoff must be impounded to eliminate flooding and provide water for the "dry season" which usually lasts an uninterrupted eight months. This heavier summer runoff from the southern Sierra Madre, combined with the more intense solar insolation and the absence of frost in these southern latitudes, makes the possibilities of irrigation even more attractive than in Sonora. Large storage dams are particularly valuable in a region where torrential streamflow occurs perversely at the moment when seasonal rains eliminate the need for irrigation. Conversely, when water is most needed, streamflow diminishes.

The Río Fuerte irrigation scheme at the present time approximately equals the estimated 560,000 acres under irrigation on the deltaic plain of the Río Yaqui. This equality will not last for long since the Fuerte contains around twice the annual streamflow of the Yaqui and there is, in effect, no limit to the irrigable land, should water be made available to the soils of the coastal plain. At present only the left bank is under irrigation, receiving water from the Miguel Hidalgo Dam. Additional works now being constructed or planned will eventually place one million acres under irrigation, making the Fuerte Valley the largest individual irrigation scheme — exceeding the Imperial Valley of California — and the second largest river control project (after the Colorado River) in the Sonoran Desert. Like the large American projects and in large measure unlike those to the north in Mexico, the Fuerte is an integrated scheme combining electricity, road building, public health, and recreation with irrigation. All of these are grouped together under one massive basin-development program. Until additional storage facilities are constructed the Hidalgo Dam will continue, as it has in every year, to spill large quantities of water into the downstream river and the sea.

At the present time, water stored in the Hidalgo Dam is diverted near San Blas to left-bank canals, one of which delivers water as far south as the Río Sinaloa's right bank at Guasave. All of the irrigated land north of this town is within the Río Fuerte Project. This project resembles the Mexicali, Yaqui, and Mayo districts in that the land under irrigation is roughly cuneiform with the main canals taking advantage of the spreading alluvial fan radiating from near San Blas. The Canal Principal carries water almost due south to the vicinity of Guasave, distributing water to the lower elevations on its right or seaward margin. To the east another canal at an even higher altitude will irrigate an additional, intervening 80,000 acres in a triangle between San Blas, Guasave, and Naranjo. Finally, there is under construction a right-bank canal from the Fuerte River west to the Bahía de Agiabampo near the boundary between Sinaloa and Sonora. This project, when completed, will bring another 360,000 acres of alluvial plain under irrigation. A storage dam, under construction on the Fuerte above the Hidalgo Dam, will provide the needed storage capacity for the expanding Fuerte Valley Project.

The Sinaloa River Project utilizes water from both the Sinaloa and the smaller Mocorito River. For many years this project depended upon simple diversion, using a low dam that did not include storage facilities. This was supplemented by pumping well water, particularly near the town of Guasave. In 1955 these methods were sufficient to place an estimated 96,000 acres under irrigation. Since that time construction of the Jaina and Sinaloa dams on the Ocoroni-Sinaloa system, and of an additional storage dam on the Río Mocorito, have brought an overall total estimated at 220,000 acres under irrigation. It is proposed that ultimately the Sinaloa-Mocorito scheme will reclaim an estimated 320,000 acres of land.[72]

This will include almost all the land between the Sinaloa and Mocorito rivers from the towns of Sinaloa and Guamuchil to the irredeemable lands near the coast. The Río Sinaloa will, in addition, provide water to a triangular area between the main stream and its right bank tributary, the Ocoroni. This tract is located between the towns of Sinaloa, Naranjo, and the confluence of the Ocoroni and Sinaloa rivers above Guasave. The Sinaloa-Mocorito project, taken in conjunction with the larger Fuerte Project, will bring the middle coastal plain under virtually uninterrupted cultivation from the Río Mocorito north to the boundary of Sonora.

Again, in the valley of the Río Sinaloa the pattern of development seen in the projects to the north repeats itself. Water is drawn off principally to the south and distributed with facility over the alluvial fan to a cuneiform region reaching toward the Mocorito. Water from the Río Mocorito, impounded upstream, will be released and used to fill out a contiguous tract. The need for a storage dam is particularly great

---

72 It should be pointed out that, although scheduled to be only one-third the ultimate size of the Fuerte scheme, and two-thirds that of the Yaqui, the combined streamflow of the Sinaloa and Mocorito rivers, in an average year, exceeds that of the Yaqui River, which provides water for the largest project in Sonora. *Datos de la Región Noreste,* pp. 275-83.

on a stream which in an average year contains no water for a period of four months after the uncertain winter rains.[73]

The Culiacán River scheme is the southernmost of the Mexican West Coast reclamation projects which falls within the boundaries of the Sonoran Desert. From Culiacán south the coastal plain narrows rapidly, but the Culiacán project already has an estimated 271,000 acres under irrigation on both banks of the Lower Río Culiacán. Storage dams completed and under construction on the headwater Humaya and Tamazula will control summer floods and distribute them throughout the year.

The diversion dam located at Culiacán diverts water into two canals which spread out over the deltaic fan from an elevation of 115 feet. Both the northern and southern canals utilize this natural assistance to distribute water to two triangular tracts. The new dam on the Río Humaya will divert water to the northwest, and it is estimated that it will provide an additional 360,000 irrigated acres within an attenuated triangle that almost reaches the Río Moroito. This project centers on Pericos, the largest acreage being directly south of that town.

RESUME
Total Irrigated Acreage in the Sonoran Desert by Irrigation Regions

UNITED STATES	Gravity	Pump
Imperial Valley	375,000	38,000 est.
Coachella Valley	78,000	22,000
Blythe-Palo Verde	70,000	7,000 est.
Fort Yuma Indian Reservation, Calif.	15,000	
Yuma and Gila Projects	125,000	27,000
Colorado River Indian Reservation, Arizona	31,000	supplemental
Cibola and Ehrenberg	9,000	
Salt River Valley	182,000	132,000
Safford-Artesia	30,000	1,000
Duncan	5,000	
Casa Grande	50,000	178,000
Santa Cruz Valley		
(Pima and Santa Cruz counties)		63,000
San Pedro Valley		5,000
Rainbow Valley and Waterman Wash		18,000
Gila River from Gillespie Dam to		
Painted Rock Dam		55,000
Gila River from Painted Rock Dam to		
Wellton-Mohawk Project		10,000
Tonopah		25,000
McMullen Valley		14,000
Centennial Wash		25,000
Subtotal, American Sector	970,000	620,000

[73] The Mocorito has never flowed during the month of May since records have been kept at Guasave. *Ibid.,* pp. 332-36.

MEXICO	Gravity	Pump
Mexicali	380,000	20,000 est.
San Luis, Río Colorado	74,000	5,000
Sonoita		
Rio Altar	8,000	5,000
Caborca		114,000
Imuris, Santa Ana, Magdalena, Trincheras	7,000	7,200
Costa de Hermosillo		236,000
Hermosillo (Rodríguez Dam)	32,000	supplemental
Valle de Guaymas	2,000	32,000
Río Yaqui	570,000	supplemental
Río Mayo	207,000	supplemental
Río Fuerte	600,000	supplemental
Río Sinaloa ⎱ Río Mocorito ⎰	230,000	supplemental
Río Culiacán	272,000	supplemental
Eastern Sonora	35,900	19,200
Valle del San Miguel	8,600	5,400
Valle del Sonora	10,000	8,500
La Colorado and Mazatán	500	300
Valle del Moctezuma	4,000	1,000
Valle del Bavispe	11,000	4,000
Sahuaripa and Upper Yaqui	1,500	
Middle Yaqui (Onavas and Bacanora)	300	
Subtotal, Mexican Sector	2,417,900	438,400
TOTAL, SONORAN DESERT	3,387,900	1,058,400

CHAPTER TEN

The Native Economy

There exists nothing which could be described as the "economy of the Sonoran Desert." There is no single hegemonic factor capable of uniting the loosely interrelated economies which exist within or touch upon this major physical division of North America. Nor does the sovereignty that Mexico and the United States share within the desert necessarily signify the existence of two economies, based upon the resources of the desert, one in Mexico and one in the United States. There is within the Sonoran Desert an amalgam of economic activities representing many dimensions in time and space. Through the years, a series of temporarily dominant economic systems has both created and destroyed resources only to find that other economies may either resurrect or ignore, improve or degrade what was formerly of value.

Even before the period of Spanish colonial rule, the indigenous population of the region engaged in a variety of economic activities exploiting diverse resources. There were the nonagricultural Guasave and Seri tribes who fished the rivers and coastal lagoons, as well as the Gulf, and who also utilized the roots, fruit, small animals, and insects which the desert provided.

Many of these same desert resources were ignored by the Cahita Indians, among others, who relied principally upon agriculture apparently unaided by systematic irrigation and not supplemented by seasonal nomadism. For the Opata, permanent irrigation imposed a more restricted geographical range of economic activity while allowing greater independence from the vicissitudes of nature. Each of these tribes lived in close proximity to nature and isolated from one another in static subsistence economies. Even then they made use of such a variety of resources that no single land-man relationship existed giving rise to any all-pervasive "desert resource."

The arrival of the Spaniard within the desert did not mold these individual economies into any "colonial pattern." Instead of achieving transformation and homogeneity, the Spanish colonial mode of life was only superimposed, with widely different effectiveness, on the indigenous economies, many of which continued to exist. From that time on each economic advance, every significant innovation, has added to the complexity of economic enterprise and resource development.

Today the Sonoran Desert is divided between two nations. The economy of each half is no more than an integral though geographically remote part of the larger national economies of Mexico and the United States. The startling disparity in standards of living to be witnessed across this international boundary is dependent mainly upon the existence of two national economies whose levels of development are widely separated.[1] The desert does not exist as a separate economic region within either national economy.

The American sector of the desert is only a small part of the large American free-trade area. Its generally high level of economic development relies disproportionately upon military and other federal expenditures, such as the construction of highways and dams. Being part of a continental power, the American desert states may take advantage of what their unique climate and other contrasting resources offer the nation as a whole.

There is no doubt that the higher standard of living within the desert north of the international boundary mirrors the generally higher level of material well-being found in the United States. This, in turn, is based upon a population that possesses generally high standards of education and technology. Despite the originally diverse national, racial, and religious composition of the American people, there has evolved a national homogeneity far greater than that possessed by most countries.

---

1   Within recent years there has been an increasingly copious flow of material concerning levels of development. This reflects the fundamental change in the international political situation since the Second World War. "The very large and steadily increasing economic inequalities between developed and underdeveloped countries . . . are flagrant realities and form a basic cause of the international tension in our present world." Gunnar Myrdal, *Rich Lands and Poor: The Road to World Prosperity*, rev. ed. (New York, 1957). This work, as well as Colin Clark, *The Conditions of Economic Progress* (London, 1951), Ragnar Nurske, *Problems of Capital Formation in Underdeveloped Countries* (New York, 1953), S. H. Frankel *The Economic Impact on Under-Developed Societies* (Cambridge, Mass., 1953), A. W. Lewis, *The Theory of Economic Growth* (London, 1955), and P. T. Bauer and B. S. Yamey, *The Economics of Underdeveloped Countries* (Chicago, 1957), are a few of the many studies that investigate this economic dichotomy. B. J. Higgins, *Economic Development: Principles, Problems and Policies* (New York, 1959), devotes pp. 67-74 to a case study of Mexico as an underdeveloped country.

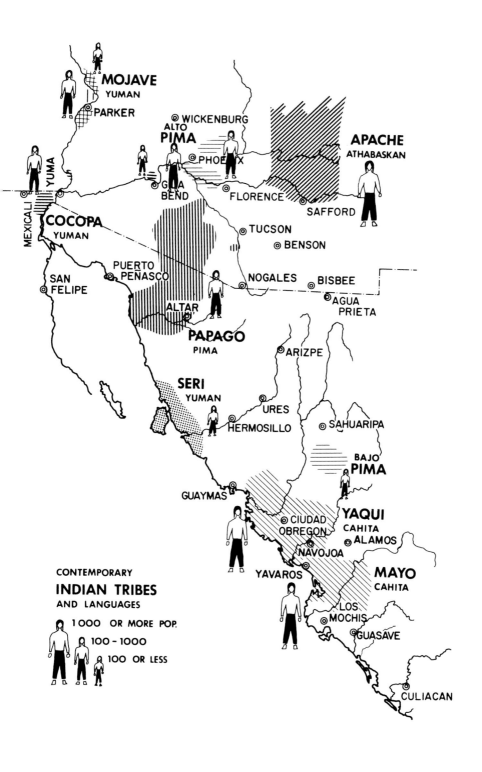

MOJAVE
YUMAN
◉ PARKER

◉ WICKENBURG

ALTO
PIMA
◉ PHOENIX

APACHE
ATHABASKAN

YUMA

◉ FLORENCE

GILA
BEND

◉ SAFFORD

MEXICALI

COCOPA
YUMAN

◉ TUCSON
◉ BENSON

PUERTO
PEÑASCO

SAN
FELIPE

◉ NOGALES   ◉ BISBEE

◉ AGUA
PRIETA

ALTAR

PAPAGO
PIMA

◉ ARIZPE

SERI
YUMAN

◉ URES

◉ SAHUARIPA

HERMOSILLO

BAJO
PIMA

GUAYMAS

◉ CIUDAD
OBREGON

YAQUI
CAHITA
◉ ALAMOS

◉ NAVOJOA

CONTEMPORARY
INDIAN TRIBES
AND LANGUAGES

YAVAROS

MAYO
CAHITA

1000 OR MORE POP.

100 - 1000

100 OR LESS

LOS
MOCHIS

◉ GUASAVE

◉ CULIACAN

In Mexico, national totality is only slowly being achieved through education and racial integration, and the gradual replacement of the native tongues by Spanish. Large Indian minorities are far from being completely absorbed in Mexican cultural and economic life. "The nation is . . . divided almost evenly between those who have a standard of living about the same as that of the Indian in the Colonial period, and another half which is better endowed economically."[2]

This relatively even division does not exist in such bold relief throughout the arid Northwest where standards of living are generally higher everywhere, and some Spanish is understood and spoken by virtually everyone. There exists, nevertheless, a minority which is racially, economically, and linguistically Indian in character.

THE CAHITAN ECONOMY

The most numerous group of aborigines to maintain any degree of national integrity are the Cahita Indians. For this reason they will be dealt with as the principal example of a continuing native economy. Occupying lands which had little to offer the Spaniard, and successfully resisting the first Spanish attempts at conquest, such tribes as the Zuaque, Mayo, and Yaqui were left outside the destructive encomiendas. Before measures could be taken to exploit these natives they were entrusted to the Jesuit fathers and only then did the indigenous population which occupied the great alluvial floodplains of modern Sinaloa and Sonora (the Sinaloa, Fuerte, Mayo and Yaqui rivers) come under the direct influence of the Spanish colonial economy.[3] Thus the single largest native language group of northern Mexico came into contact with an already "Mexicanized" economy south of the Río Sinaloa.[4] The Cahita tribes that occupied the southernmost valleys were, in the ensuing years, absorbed by this same Mexican population, thus losing their national identity. The Sinaloa, Tehueco, and Zuaque tribes, among others, ceased to exist as such and their culture came to be considered Mexican. The question of how much advanced was the economy of the Spanish-speaking sons over that of the Cahita-speaking fathers will probably never be answered, but present-day evidence indicates extremely gradual change. In Mexico the adoption of the Spanish language by an indigenous group seldom betokened any forward economic leap.

---

2 Howard F. Cline, *The United States and Mexico* (Cambridge, Mass., 1953), p. 75. See also Nathan Whetten, *Rural Mexico* (Chicago, 1949), pp. 52-57.
3 Sauer, *The Distribution of Aboriginal Tribes*, p. 2.
4 *Ibid.*, p. 24

At the same time the Mayo and Yaqui continued to resist complete absorption into the "Mexican" economy while adopting most of the material innovations introduced by the Jesuits.[5]

These priests introduced the metal hoe. They brought horses and burros and introduced the Yaqui to the plow. Cattle, goats, sheep, fruit trees, and vegetables provided a wealth of new agricultural products. Wheat was advanced as the ideal winter-sown grain to balance corn. The delta of the Yaqui became the granary for the new settlements in Pimería and later California.[6] This was done through the expansion of irrigated agriculture.[7]

The economic continuity of these Cahita communities located on the deltaic lands of the Mayo and Yaqui rivers must be attributed to their sedentary modes of life. The native population usually occupies even until today the same villages which were inhabited at the time of the first Spanish entrada. They farm the "same fixed area of land," and the "manner of subsistence has either not changed or the change is of a determinable nature."[8]

The fertility of the land occupied by the Indians appears to be little changed.[9] Almost all the land farmed was "equally available to the tools, crops, and tillage of the aboriginal [as well as] the present inhabitants."[10] Farming was and is supplemented by hunting, fishing, and gathering in the large areas of "wild and non-tillable land which surround most of the agricultural tracts then as now. Extensive stock raising has been introduced but it has in large measure only replaced the more intensive hunting and gathering practiced by the pre-Columbian aborigines."[11] Only in those areas where modern irrigated agriculture has impinged upon native land has this aboriginal pattern been altered significantly.

Among the Cahita, cultivated agriculture is the principal occupation. The first and one of the most difficult tasks presented to the native

---

[5]   Edward H. Spicer, *Potam, A Yaqui Village in Sonora* (American Anthropological Assn., Memoir 77, 1954), p. 26.

[6]   *Ibid.*, pp. 26-27.

[7]   Ralph L. Beals, *The Contemporary Culture of the Cahita Indians,* Bureau of American Ethnology Bull. 142 (Washington, D.C., 1945), p. 5.

[8]   Sauer, *The Aboriginal Population of Northwestern Mexico,* p. 5. Beals, n. 7 *supra,* p. 2, states that "the foundation of many Yaqui and Mayo towns (villages) still in existence seems to coincide with the establishment of missions in the early seventeenth century although data are inadequate." This viewpoint tends to conflict with that of the above which expresses a prior settlement, but both authors agree on the permanancy of Cahita settlement.

[9]   Sauer, *The Aboriginal Population of Northwestern Mexico,* p. 9.

[10]   *Ibid.,* p. 4.

[11]   *Ibid.*

farmer is clearing the land.[12] For the Yaqui, whose settlements are scattered chiefly along the north bank of the Yaqui River, it means clearing the "dense, almost jungle-like" riverine thorn forest as well as the sparse desert thorn trees and cactus.[13]

Native irrigation is accomplished through a variety of methods depending upon the availability of water. Along the larger rivers where water is available throughout much of the year canals have been constructed by the native population to distribute water to tribal lands. In many canals the entry of water depends on the height of the river although weirs of stakes and brush are sometimes used to divert the water.[14] Floods, which occur frequently, wreak havoc, destroying these primitive diversion dams. They are rebuilt, but seldom in time to capture the needed water before the desert streamway runs dry.[15]

Often, however, the community effort required to construct even these primitive diversion dams and shallow canals is not to be found among the Cahita.[16] Instead fields are laid out on the lower river terraces or dry oxbows which are slightly below the coastal plain but higher than the average flood level of the nearest streamway. During a local rain, water drains into these fields from adjacent higher elevations. Sometimes the drainage is aided by natural *bajillos* which are small independent and reticulate streamways. They give the appearance of a system of narrow, shallow, and meandering irrigation ditches, each about three or four feet wide and one or two feet deep.[17] Fields are located across or adjacent to the bajillo. The deciding factor in field location is not the arroyo or river itself but the presence of the bajillo.

Where nature has not provided these miniature streamways, the native agriculturalists will build a small canal. These canals, which are seldom more than one quarter of a mile in length, are dug back at right angles from the arroyo and at right angles to the land gradient. They are made two to three feet in width and one to two feet in depth, closely imitating nature. The dirt removed is thrown on the low side to increase effectiveness. Some of the older irrigation ditches have been

---

[12]   W. C. Holden and others, "Studies of the Yaqui Indians of Sonora, Mexico," Texas Technological College *Bulletin*, Vol. 12, No. 1 (1936), p. 117.

[13]   Spicer, *Potam, A Yaqui Village in Sonora*, pp. 41-42.

[14]   *Ibid.*, p. 5.

[15]   A very similar riverine environment is discussed in F. B. Kniffen, "The Primitive Cultural Landscape of the Colorado Delta," *Lower California Studies, III: University of California Publications in Geography* (1931), pp. 43-66.

[16]   Charles J. Erasmus, "The Economic Life of a Mayo Village." Unpublished M.A. thesis, University of California. (Berkeley, 1948), pp. 11, 69.

[17]   *Ibid.*, pp. 68-69.

— ARIZONA HIGHWAYS

The Yaqui Indians, despite their bellicose appearance and proven historic fierceness in battle, are in fact sedentary agriculturists. The herd of goats is not nomadic, and well-kept fences protect small gardens.

eroded into deep barrancas. This usually necessitates the abandonment of adjacent land.[18]

The irrigated fields are partitioned into roughly square plots. The size of these ranges from approximately one quarter to three or four acres, with the average probably less than one acre.[19] Each individual field is surrounded by an earth bank called a *bordo*. The bordos range in height from one foot to three feet. Where the land is fairly flat larger plots are enclosed and the bordos are smaller in height. The canals or bajillos lead into the fields, the purpose being to flood as much of the land as possible. After a good local rain the fields become small lakes contained within these low dikes. It may take as long as a week for this water to soak into the soil or completely evaporate. In a region where rainfall comes in quick and sporadic downpours, resulting in rapid runoff, the use of bordos is well adapted to these conditions. They succeed where probably no other primitive method would, although it is true that after a very heavy rain the bordos enclosing the fields in the direct path of a bajillo are usually destroyed. The more common problem is to capture sufficient runoff to flood the fields to capacity.[20]

Bordos are universal within the native agricultural region along the Río Mayo and are used in conjunction with the more sophisticated canals drawing water from the river when it is running high. Since the construction of the Mocuzari Dam, the Río Mayo seldom carries enough water to fill the old canals, and many of these areas have been abandoned. More often, however, the old fields have been incorporated into the Río Mayo Project.

Inland and to the south, between the Mayo and Fuerte rivers, bordos are used in association with the numerous subsequent arroyos. In the vicinity of Masiacas, fields surrounded by bordos are irrigated by canals leading from primitively constructed diversion dams thrown across these smaller arroyos.

In the native agricultural zone along the north bank of the Yaqui River, water is supplied to the fields by a wide variety of methods. The modern Colonias Yaquis Canal supplies larger quantities of water to native agriculturalists in the easternmost Yaqui settlements. This canal, constructed by the Mexican government, should not be included in a survey of "native" agriculture. It is significant, however, that this and other major irrigation works on the river which distribute water to

---

[18]   *Ibid.*, p. 7.

[19]   Holden and others, "Studies of the Yaqui Indians of Sonora, Mexico," Texas Technological College *Bulletin*, Vol. 12, No. 1, p. 117, and Erasmus, p. 72.

[20]   Erasmus, p. 72.

Mexican farms have taken so much of the river's water that there is, among the western Yaqui settlements, an increasing dependence on aboriginal dry or flood farming.

A number of crops are grown without irrigation where the roots do not need to penetrate very deeply into the deltaic soil to reach water. Particularly during the winter when there is little or no water in the Yaqui's distributaries and evapotranspiration is low, crops are planted which may survive on the infrequent winter rainfall. Wheat and the deep-rooted legumes are grown under these conditions with varying degrees of success.

Among the Yaqui, many of the older canals have fallen into disuse. Even when there is considerable water in the river most of these canals are high and dry. Carrying water by hand is commonly practiced in the spring of the year. The source of this water is the occasional waterhole in the streamway or shallow wells which are dug deeper as the dry season sets in.[21] Sometimes the water is carried a mile or two in order to irrigate miniature fields measuring seldom more than 8 by 12 feet and surrounded by bordos only a few inches high.[22] Onions, garlic, tobacco, sugar cane, and tomatoes are occasionally irrigated in this manner.

After the first summer rains, crops are planted which may mature without irrigation. If the summer rains are relatively heavy and the alluvial soils have high water tables, corn is successfully harvested despite the desiccating heat. Plowing is done in January or February and again in June. Planting is postponed until after the first soaking rain; cultivation is normally done only once after sowing.[23]

Throughout every village during almost any year, crop failures occur on at least some lands, irrigated or not. Lack of water is almost always the reason for a small or non-remunerative harvest.[24] A flood will of course destroy the entire crop.

Water supply for native lands depends upon: (1) the proximity to a major river or arroyo; (2) the level of the annual flood (an excessive flood being as pernicious to agriculture as a drought); (3) rainfall in the immediate area; (4) the level of water tables and the amount of retained moisture in the soil; and (5) the measures undertaken by the native agriculturalist to insure against drought and flood.

---

[21]   Beals, *The Contemporary Culture of the Cahita Indians,* p. 43.

[22]   Holden and Others, "Studies of the Yaqui Indians of Sonora, Mexico," Texas Technological College *Bulletin,* Vol. 12, No. 1, p. 119.

[23]   *Ibid.,* pp. 119-20.

[24]   Spicer comments that in Potam territory crop failures have occurred "at different points . . . every year for the past fifteen years, and lack of water is always given as the cause." Spicer, *Potam, A Yaqui Village in Sonora,* p. 43.

It must be noted that the water supply available to Cahita farmers is extremely variable. In January of 1949 a flood swept through the aboriginal lands along the lower Yaqui and Mayo rivers, causing great destruction to winter-sown crops. This flood followed severe droughts which had persisted through the previous years. Suffering was compounded.[25] Good harvests on these native lands located well away from the major rivers usually coincide with disastrous floods on those rivers. A "cash surplus crop" seems to be harvested about once every ten years, and this too seems to correspond to the frequency of major floods.[26]

It has been observed that annual variation in the amount of water available to Cahita agriculture has resulted in chronic food shortages, considerable shifting in the location of fields, and antagonisms toward the Mexicans who are accused of expropriating water formerly available to native farmers.[27]

The Cahita farmer practices crop rotation and leaves fields fallow but not by intention. All harvesting is done by hand. The farmers save their own seed, usually selling the best because of its high price.[28] All agriculture is limited to annuals except for a few enterprising natives who have planted fruit trees. Mangoes, pomegranates, oranges, and even an occasional date palm are to be seen, usually in close proximity to the village.[29] The absence of aboreal crops, despite their being apparently well adapted to a benign climate and a water table which can be reached by penetrating roots, must be attributed to strictly cultural factors.

Cahita land is never fertilized intentionally. Sedimentation and the casual intrusion of livestock provide the only significant fertilization, and the value of both is doubtful.

Incalculable damage to crops is caused by numerous pests both wild and domestic. Dogs, cattle, goats, and burros join jackrabbits and other rodents in devouring much needed food supplies while still in the fields. Barbed wire is strung by those who can afford it. Otherwise fences are constructed according to age-old methods. Stakes are driven into the ground and straight poles are stretched between them. These poles have been gleaned from the thorny vegetation of the district and

---

25   *Datos de la Región Noroeste,* No. 10, p. 105.

26   Erasmus, p. 87.

27   Spicer, *Potam, A Yaqui Village,* pp. 43-44.

28   *Ibid.*

29   In Tenia village (Mayo), one native family was reported to have had an orchard containing 4 orange, 1 fig, 3 grapefruit, 3 lemon, 2 lime, 3 plum, and 2 pomegranate trees. Erasmus (p. 80) commented that this was unusual and that the other Indians came to purchase this fruit.

Only the sturdy barbwire fences differentiate these farms from those which the first Spaniards found in the Yaqui villages of Potam and Vicam. Native materials are used almost exclusively. The economy and neatness of these villages compares favorably with poorer Mexicanized agricultural settlements.

when erected, form a natural substitute for barbed wire. These fences, however, do not impede the passage of jackrabbits and other small species. Dogs and coyotes provide the best form of control for these pests.[30] Birds are frightened away by small boys. The Cahita have no remedy for the depredations of insects.

Land tenure is tribal. The right to secure new land for cultivation is obtained through petitioning the tribal council.[31] Except where Mexican irrigation projects have impinged on Cahita land, there is usually more than enough *monte* (uncultivated peripheral land) available for clearing.[32] Cultivated land is in fact a small proportion of the total lands of an average community.[33] Spicer, in his detailed study of Potam, states that land is abundant in Potam territory, there being "more than enough land to go around for the present residents. No record or map of the fields are kept by the village governors."[34] Once a parcel of land has been cultivated, the use of such land remains within the family and passes to a man's widow upon his death.[35]

Tribal land tenure is one of the central themes of Mexican history, and its significance in the social geography of the arid Northwest will be discussed in some detail. At this moment it should suffice to note that Mayo farmers cultivate an average of no more than 3.5 acres apiece despite the fact that for any individual farmer the amount of land available is, for all purposes, unlimited. Furthermore, very rarely is more than one-half of a family's land allocation under cultivation. Some *campesinos* never request any land at all, subsisting largely on their small collection of animals, as well as through gathering.[36]

Most of the above failings are common throughout those areas of the world where tribal land tenure prevails. In addition, the native farmer finds that this form of land tenure precludes the establishment of individual credit so essential to modern agriculture.

The pattern followed within what yet remains of the native Cahita agricultural economy is that of the aboriginal Western Hemisphere. The crops planted are harvested for subsistence and the most important

---

30   Erasmus, p. 87, enumerates a number of native pest controls which include the beating of cans, the erection of scarecrows, the stringing of jackrabbit intestines along the fences and across the fields, and the making of snares.

31   Beals, *The Contemporary Culture of the Cahita Indians*, p. 9.

32   Spicer, *Potam, A Yaqui Village in Sonora*, p. 43.

33   *Ibid.*, p. 43, and also Holden and Others, "Studies of the Yaqui Indians of Sonora, Mexico," Texas Technological College *Bulletin*, Vol. 12, No. 1, p. 119.

34   Spicer, *Potam, A Yaqui Village in Sonora*, p. 43.

35   *Ibid.*

36   Erasmus, pp. 87–88.

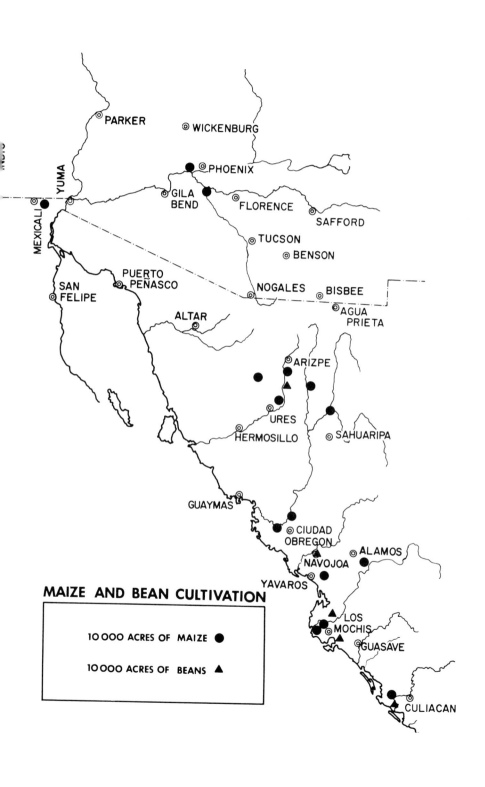

PARKER

⊚ WICKENBURG

● ⊚ PHOENIX

⊚ GILA
BEND ● ⊚ FLORENCE

YUMA ⊚ SAFFORD

MEXICALI ⊚ ●

⊚ TUCSON

⊚ BENSON

PUERTO
PEÑASCO

SAN
FELIPE ⊚ NOGALES ⊚ BISBEE
⊚

⊚ AGUA
PRIETA

ALTAR ⊚

⊚ ARIZPE
● ▲ ●

URES ●

HERMOSILLO ⊚ ⊚ SAHUARIPA

GUAYMAS ⊚

● ⊚ CIUDAD
OBREGON

▲ ● ALAMOS
NAVOJOA

YAVAROS ⊚

MAIZE AND BEAN CULTIVATION

▲ LOS
MOCHIS
⊚

▲ ⊚ GUASAVE

10 000 ACRES OF MAIZE	●
10 000 ACRES OF BEANS	▲

● ⊚ CULIACAN
▲

are those which were planted in the Sonoran Desert before the first Spanish incursions—such as corn, numerous varieties of beans, and squash.

The principal native-grown crop is, without question, corn. It is the one crop grown by almost all Cahita farmers, and is planted in both winter and summer. The winter crop is sown on a limited number of acres since it is less successful than that planted in the summer. The spring months provide neither the requisite heat nor water. During this season most fields lie fallow.

The major planting of corn is made after the first soaking rains of the summer, either in July or August. These rains alone are usually not able to sustain this crop and irrigation is resorted to during the decreasing rains of September and October. Growth is rapid during these months and the crop is ready to be harvested in November. During this time squash and other crops have been planted between the rows, and these are also harvested.[37] Insect pests, weeds, and the lack of water do irreparable damage to the crop.

The native varieties of corn produce small yields, but the Cahita have been loathe to "experiment" with new varieties. The harvest usually amounts to less than one bushel an acre, and five bushels would be considered a "very good" crop.[38] Considering the small area planted it is not difficult to calculate the low per-capita income each farmer realizes from this, his major economic activity.

Beans are the second most important crop, and are planted in both winter and summer. The black-eyed bean is planted at the same time as summer-sown corn. The summer-planted crop continues to bear through much of September and October, and constitutes a major factor in the Cahita diet, as it does throughout Indian Mexico.

Several kinds of crops may occupy a single row and on a single acre there may be found a dozen different crops. Corn and sweet sorghum are grown together. Watermelon, cantaloupes, and gourds are planted in the same fields in January and February. Tobacco is planted alongside beans and other crops. Beals observed that one entire tobacco crop consisted of thirty-two plants, enough for the farmer and no more.[39] Tomatoes are only occasionally planted, which is surprising considering their commercial importance on adjacent Mexican farms. When planted, they are scattered in the familiar fashion among other plants. Chile peppers of all sizes, colors, and shapes are grown both for consumption

---

[37]   *Ibid.* pp. 121-22.

[38]   Holden and Others, Texas Technological College *Bulletin*, Vol. 12, No. 1, p. 124, and Erasmus, pp. 87-88.

[39]   Beals, *The Aboriginal Culture of the Cahita Indians*, p. 117.

and sale. These have been an important part of the indigenous economy from time immemorial.

The pattern of agriculture so far described reflects an unmistakable influence; that of the aborigine prior to the Spanish entrada. The foregoing crops are native to the Western Hemisphere.[40] They are not ground-covering and lend themselves nicely to interspersed cropping. All may be harvested quite readily by hand. Grown together and in small quantities, this combination of crops exemplifies subsistence agriculture, little changed from pre-Columbian times.

An intrusive pattern of agriculture contrasts sharply with the above. Crops are more often grown for cash. They are grown singly, usually covering the ground. Most of the plants were introduced from the Eastern Hemisphere, and are often more difficult to harvest. Seasonally, these crops balance the native species.

The most important European-introduced crop is wheat, which is planted in November and December. Water retained in the soil and the meager winter rains often provide the only moisture for this crop. Wheat is irrigated only if there is sufficient water in the streamways to enter the canals, or if local rains cause water to flow in the bajillos. Since most of the rivers are either empty or very low during the winter months, irrigation cannot be depended upon.

The generally cloudless skies which yield little rain do, however, encourage the rapid maturation of wheat. It is harvested in May and June under ideal conditions. Yields are irregularly low but have been improved.[41] Harvesting is done with a sickle or a small scythe. A roughly circular piece of ground which has been moistened and made hard serves as a threshing floor, and horses which are owned by the native farmer are driven over the floor as they have been for centuries in the Iberian Peninsula. Otherwise the grain is beaten by native families using mesquite poles. Almost all of the wheat is sold since the Cahita diet does not usually include wheat flour.

After wheat, the most important introduced crop is the *garbanzo* bean (chick pea) which is usually sold to Mexican middlemen who in turn export large quantities of the crop mainly to Spain and Cuba. It is planted by some of the natives in November or December and is harvested in May or June.[42]

Sesame seed is grown as a cash crop when the Indian farmer is

[40]   Sauer, *Agricultural Origins and Dispersals* (New York, 1952), pp. 62-71.
[41]   Holden and Others, Texas Technological College *Bulletin*, Vol. 12, No. 1, p. 123.
[42]   Erasmus, pp. 76-77.

provided with the seed. Much the same can be said for safflower which is extremely well adapted to dry farming, and has been promoted among the Mexicans by the cotton brokers as a good autumn crop to balance cotton.

Cotton itself is not grown by the Cahita farmer. This is interesting because according to Pérez de Ribas it was grown at the time of the Jesuit entrada.[43] Doubly interesting is the fact that cotton has recently become the single most important source of income elsewhere on the Yaqui, Mayo, and Fuerte deltas. Many Cahita Indians find employment in the Mexican cotton fields but do not plant the crop on their own land. Cotton lends itself to *monocultura*, "bigness," and systematized credit. Cahita agriculture is incompatible with all of this. It must be concluded, therefore, that when a Cahita farmer becomes a cotton planter within the Mexican market economy he is no longer a "native" agriculturist.

Among the Mayo and Yaqui no other introduction from the Old World has so altered the aboriginal way of life and land-use pattern as the keeping of livestock. Cattle, goats, sheep, pigs, and chickens are found in every Cahita village. Horses and burros owned by natives are utilized as beasts of burden. Without these animals it is doubtful that the native settlements could have retained their economic self-sufficiency in the face of colonial pressures. The altered land-man relationship brought about by the introduction of livestock has ironically contributed to the native population's continuing resistance to complete economic absorption. These animals have so apparently improved the economic possibilities presented by the coastal desert that complete absorption of this never-too-numerous group has been postponed for almost four centuries.[44] Self-sufficient and relatively independent subsistence agriculture has proved successful in forestalling what may, of course, be the ultimate "Mexicanization" of this society.

Cattle rank as the most important animal among the Cahita. Most Indian families have at least one cow but seldom more than five, although a few may have as many as fifty head. Cattle are not bought, sold, or butchered on a schedule. Disease and drought take a high toll and usually determine whether a herd increases or decreases. Beef is certainly not a regular item in the native diet, which consists normally of little more than tortillas, beans, chiles and coffee. The cows are milked but no milk is sold outside the community. Cheese is made by almost all those who own cows and it is regarded as a necessity in a diet which

---

[43]   Holden and Others, Texas Technological College *Bulletin*, Vol. 12, No. 1, p. 120.
[44]   Spicer, *Potam, A Yaqui Village in Sonora*, p. 45.

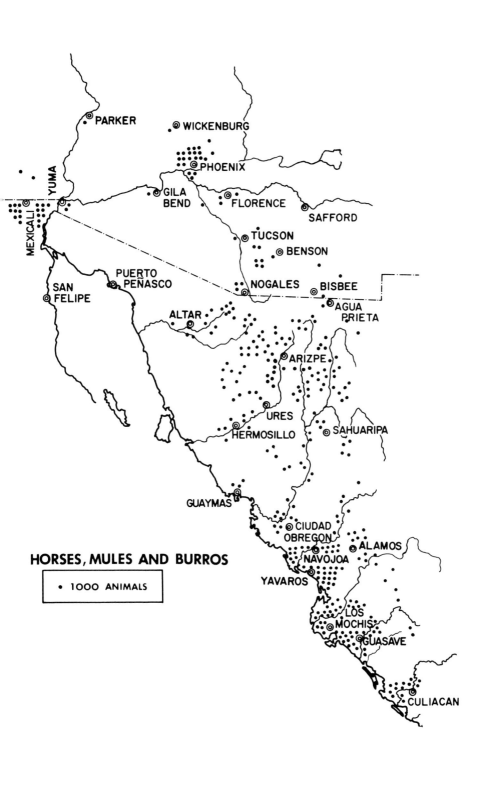

HORSES, MULES AND BURROS

• 1000 ANIMALS

PARKER
WICKENBURG
PHOENIX
GILA BEND
FLORENCE
SAFFORD
YUMA
MEXICALI
TUCSON
BENSON
PUERTO PEÑASCO
SAN FELIPE
NOGALES
BISBEE
AGUA PRIETA
ALTAR
ARIZPE
URES
HERMOSILLO
SAHUARIPA
GUAYMAS
CIUDAD OBREGON
ALAMOS
NAVOJOA
YAVAROS
LOS MOCHIS
GUASAVE
CULIACAN

departs, at least in this regard, from the aboriginal pattern. Some cattle are sold outside the native settlements to Mexican field hands at the time of the cotton and tomato harvests when money is available.[45]

For the most part cattle must depend upon browsing, since grass is only seasonally available along the waterways. The extremely unlikely cholla cactus is devoured by the cattle whose noses come to resemble pin-cushions. Forage crops are conspicuous by their absence. Native fields rarely ever produce even enough fodder for the draft animals.[46] The water supply for cattle is critical during the prolonged dry season, particularly that following the uncertain winter rains. Wells are dug to furnish these poor beasts with water but there is usually a considerable loss of cattle despite desperate efforts.[47]

Among the Cahita, a large proportion of the families keep sheep and goats. There is a greater concentration of these two animals among the natives than among the neighboring Mexican population. Sheep are kept for their wool and seldom eaten. Neither animal is regularly sold. A few pigs wander about the Cahita villages devouring cactus roots, mesquite beans, and waste. These animals are usually sold to the Mexicans, since both the Mayo and Yaqui have a belief that pigs were once human. Thus, pork and pork lard are not eaten.[48]

In transport, the Mayo and Yaqui follow sixteenth-century Spanish patterns rather than aboriginal modes. Not manpower, but horses, an occasional mule, and especially burros are used to carry goods. The majority of the Cahita use burros for draft animals. Horses are used to herd cattle.[49] Since horses and mules will not forage in the desert and burros will, the latter are more common in the villages. There are still large numbers of wild burros despite the encroachment of modern irrigation along the rivers which has caused a dimunition in their numbers.[50]

The gathering of wild plants, which undoubtedly had a more important place in the economy of the pre-Columbian Cahita, is still practiced today. A study of the Mayo village of Tenia revealed that from a total of 114 plants growing within close proximity to that village, 92 were utilized in some fashion or another.[51] Of these, 24 plants had varying

---

45   *Ibid.*
46   Erasmus, pp. 87-88.
47   *Ibid.,* pp. 95-96.
48   Beals, *The Contemporary Culture of the Cahita Indians,* p. 10.
49   *Ibid.,* p. 39.
50   There was a time within living memory when large numbers of wild burros were to be found throughout the entire Sonoran Desert. Today they are largely confined to the Mexican sector. See *Arizona, The Grand Canyon State: A State Guide* (revised ed. 1956), pp. 56-58.
51   Erasmus, p. 57.

Cahita dwellings — the one above under construction. Ownership of a truck by a Yaqui Indian is uncommon but not unknown. Modern machinery is in fact accepted before innovation in architecture and crop selection.

degrees of importance in the native diet. Some of these were eaten right in the field when encountered while others required careful preparation. At no time of the year do the Cahita live entirely from wild plant products. Gathering never more than supplements agriculture.

The fruit of the giant pitahaya and *echo,* a pitahaya-like cactus, are harvested in the summer. The berry of the thornless jito tree ripens in June and is eaten after drying. During September and October the *tuna,* which is the fruit of the *nopal* (prickly pear), ripens. It is relished as highly as the pitahaya. Numerous other wild plants are gathered, usually during and just after the summer rainy season.[52] During the late winter and spring the maguey (agave) is relied upon both for food and drink. It is the wild plant with the greatest commercial value for from it both mescal and tequila are produced.[53] The gathering of the plant, and the preparing and marketing of the mescal are a considerable enterprise.

The "bean" of the mesquite tree which anciently was most important in the Cahita economy is today considered an inferior food and resorted to only in an emergency.[54]

Aside from the twenty-four desert plants that are utilized for food, numerous others find a wide variety of uses in the hands of the Cahita gatherer. Thirty-six are used medicinally for both men and animals. Thirty-four trees and shrubs are used for building purposes (the carrizo, a riverine cane, being put to a particularly large number of uses).[55] Nine are utilized for dye, glue, poison, soap, and other chemical purposes; six are used as brush for fences; four find use as twine; while four are cut in the field and carried home as food for animals. Finally, three have certain religious uses.[56]

In the Mayo villages deer, tree rats, rabbits, and iguanas are caught and eaten. Honey is gathered during the summer.[57] Despite their proximity to the sea, few Cahita Indians make any use of it at all. There are very few Yaqui fishermen.[58] A few Mayos fish for shark, shrimp, and *lisa* (a general term used for river fish). Such fishing is done from shore with nets on a very small scale. Neither Mayo nor Yaqui have boats,

---

[52]   *Ibid.,* pp. 57-67.

[53]   *Ibid.,* pp. 63, 67. These two are the most popular alcoholic beverages consumed in northwestern Mexico.

[54]   Beals, *The Aboriginal Culture of the Cahita Indians,* p. 13. Also Beals, *The Contemporary Culture of the Cahita Indians,* p. 10.

[55]   Spicer, *Potam, A Yaqui Village in Sonora,* p. 42.

[56]   Erasmus, pp. 55-57.

[57]   *Ibid.,* pp. 50-52.

[58]   Spicer, *Potam, A Yaqui Village in Sonora,* p. 40.

but they occasionally fish with plant poison in the bays and estuaries. Oysters are sometimes gathered.[59]

OTHER NATIVE INDUSTRIES

Other native industries are limited — probably more so today than ever before as the more dynamic Mexican economy of the coastal desert has destroyed, through competition, many of the self-sufficient aspects of the former native way of life. The huge irrigation projects of the Yaqui, Mayo, and Fuerte deltas provide both permanent and seasonal employment, inducing the native farmer to desert his subsistence activities and join the Mexican exchange economy. The burgeoning towns provide an even greater inducement to leave the village and the ancient way of life. The lure of cash to be gotten in exchange for labor in the Mexican fields nearby draws the Cahita away from his meager farm, and from his gathering. Crafts have, in particular, suffered from deculturation. Being unable to produce goods capable of competing in the national economy, the native craftsman finds that even his isolated village is swamped by machine-made products as well as machines themselves. Beals says, "The sewing machine is ubiquitous among the Mayo."[60] The sewing machine may be purchased only with cash.

Not only sewing machines but corn must be purchased. "At nearly all times of the year the village [Tenia] must purchase its food staples."[61] Cooking utensils and farm implements must also be purchased, since their manufacture has almost entirely ceased.[62] The native textile industry, which at one time was virtually self-sufficient from the production of fibers to the looming and dyeing (with native vegetable dyes) of cloth is in precipitous decline. As has been mentioned, the planting of cotton has been abandoned. Practically all the loom weaving done by the Cahita at present is found among the Mayo and is confined to only three classes of articles — blankets, sashes, and bags. The first two are of native wool and the last is of native maguey fiber. The continued manufacture of these three articles rests on their acceptance outside the villages. The Yaqui do practically no weaving although earlier it must have been common. Hrdlicka noted in 1904 that Yaqui manufacture of cotton and

---

[59]   Beals, *The Contemporary Culture of the Cahita Indians*, p. 14, and Erasmus, p. 54.

[60]   Beals, *The Contemporary Culture of the Cahita Indians*, p. 22.

[61]   Erasmus, p. 182.

[62]   Holden and others, Texas Technological College *Bulletin*, Vol. 12, No. 1, p. 124.

woolen fabrics had declined greatly at the time of his visit.[63] Competition from manufactured goods had even then begun to destroy native craftsmanship, and with it the Cahita subsistence economy.

What remains of the native textile industry is located in certain villages which manifest some degree of specialization. Bacavachi, for example, makes large numbers of excellent serapes but only a few blankets, although these are of excellent quality. Masiaca makes virtually no serapes but many poor-quality blankets. The making of sashes is a village industry at Masiaca. Here also the fiber of the maguey is used to weave *morrales* (small bags). Men do nothing but gather the leaves of the maguey and extract fiber while women spin and weave.[64] The men who cut the maguey plant often combine this with the preparation of mescal.[65] Hammocks and saddle pads are made by the Mayo. Aside from the ordinary textile techniques, the Mayo weave hats, baskets, mats, and nets. The most common baskets are made from carrizo gathered locally; smaller baskets are made from palm fiber and willow branches. The Yaqui today make almost no baskets. Circular casting nets are made by a few men and used locally.[66]

Another declining industry is pottery, which is fashioned from inferior local clays extracted from the sandy mesa soil.[67] The related manufacture of adobe bricks is carried on outside almost every village. However, it and the other building trades are certainly not flourishing. Native craftsmen are only able to compete in the construction of the poorest shelters, since they lack much of the equipment and ability needed to construct the type of buildings erected in the expanding towns. The manufacture of primitive furniture is an economic activity engaged in by a few Cahita craftsmen.[68] Carpentry of all kinds is not an important native industry.

Next to agriculture and the various food gathering activities, the collecting of firewood employs probably the largest number of Cahita workers. Firewood is sold in the Mexican towns where there is still a large market for it, the winter months naturally being the most active period for this industry. The burning of shell to make lime is an important activity in the coastal villages.[69] Thus, one of the largest markets for firewood is the native lime works.

---

63   Aleš Hrdlička, *Notes on the Indians of Sonora, Mexico* (Lancaster, Pa., 1904).

64   Beals, *The Contemporary Culture of the Cahita Indians*, p. 33.

65   Erasmus, p. 135.

66   Beals, *The Contemporary Culture of the Cahita Indians*, p. 36.

67   *Ibid.*, p. 39.

68   *Ibid.*, p. 45.

69   Erasmus, p. 134.

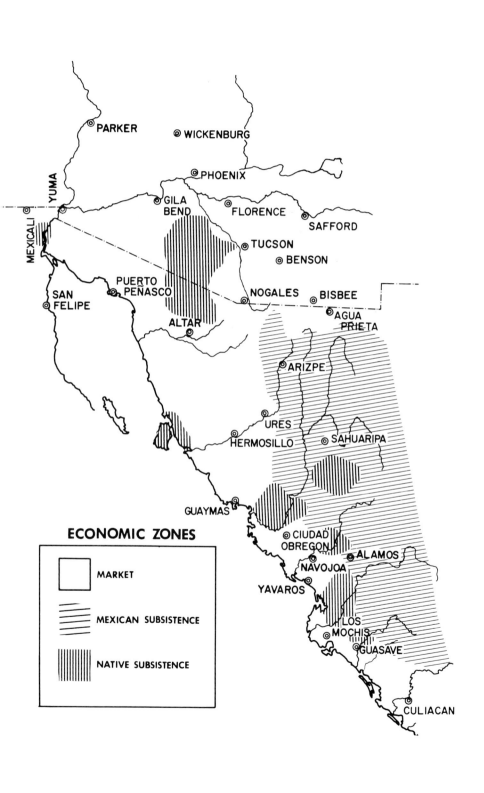

PARKER

WICKENBURG

PHOENIX

YUMA

MEXICALI

GILA
BEND

FLORENCE

SAFFORD

TUCSON

BENSON

PUERTO
PEÑASCO

NOGALES

BISBEE

SAN
FELIPE

AGUA
PRIETA

ALTAR

ARIZPE

URES

HERMOSILLO

SAHUARIPA

GUAYMAS

ECONOMIC ZONES

CIUDAD
OBREGON

ALAMOS

NAVOJOA

YAVAROS

MARKET

MEXICAN SUBSISTENCE

LOS
MOCHIS

GUASAVE

NATIVE SUBSISTENCE

CULIACAN

As is often the case, the competition between the native and "colonial" economies focuses on the land itself. The static native economy, with neither the resources nor the institutions needed to compete must give way areally to more productive uses. Much land has already been expropriated, and as irrigation projects are extended, particularly along the north bank of the Río Fuerte, the tribal lands will be once again narrowed to the least promising desert along the Sonora-Sinaloa boundary. The natives will be given the opportunity to form ejidos and collectively occupy the irrigated land which formerly belonged to the tribe (this they have usually refused to do). The mestizos will probably settle on most of it, if past experience is a guide, since individual Indians find it difficult to engage in the irrigated agriculture of the project.

Those who do not take up the irrigated lands will find that their former way of life has been irrevocably altered by the stripping away of desert and thorn forest vegetation. The monte which provided so much is being cut back. Gathering, the raising of livestock, the collection of the numerous other resources that the desert provided will be much less. Firewood for use in the making of lime will become scarce. The natural growth of maguey, pitahaya, and other plants will be uprooted and with it a cornerstone of native industry. The native can only react and with limited ability to the progress and colonizing advance of the intrusive economy.

CHAPTER ELEVEN

The Mexican Economy

          The arid mountains and plains stretching south of the international boundary support an economy which is geographically isolated from the central plateaus of Mexico. The Sierre Madre Occidental has, throughout history, existed as a barrier to the economic expansion of those who controlled the rich heartland of Mexico. The Aztec, Spanish, and Mexican economies have, until recently, failed to integrate the Sonoran Desert with the trans-Sierra core.

          The year 1927 might well mark the beginning of regional economic integration since that year saw the completion of the railway linking Mexico City with the border at Nogales, while the previous year witnessed the enaction of the first comprehensive legislation dealing with the development of water resources in the Mexican Northwest. These years also saw the termination of the civil conflict that since 1910 had brought terrible destruction to Mexico, and out of which the nation passed from feudalism to an embryonic modern industrial state.

          To place undue emphasis on these few years in the late 1920's would exaggerate their importance as an historical "turning point." Both the water-resources plan and the completion of the West Coast railway at this time were in large measure the result of the waning Mexican Revolution which had, for over fifteen years, stopped all actual progress in this direction while instituting a high level of faith in national economic planning.

          Undue emphasis placed on the importance of these years would also overlook locational realities affecting the desert. First, the Southern Pacific of Mexico was an American railway built to unite the West Coast of Mexico with the United States, not with Mexico City. America's economic sphere of influence within the Sonoran Desert did not, indeed, disappear when the last rails were laid across the Sierra.

In addition, there were geographical limitations on both the railway and the irrigation schemes which were the keys to Mexico's economic expansion into the desert Northwest. The coastal plain provided the best route for the construction of the railway, while the same wide expanse of arid but potentially productive soil was the obvious site for large-scale irrigation projects. This meant that one physical subregion of the desert had been selected for development while another had been written off. The latter region was the desert basin-and-foothill province of eastern Sonora and Sinaloa. Such formerly important places as Sinaloa, El Fuerte, Alamos, Ures, and Arizpe were to be left out of the era that began in the late 1920's. These towns of the Camino Real, located for the most part in the narrow valleys to the east of the western-most ranges of the coastal Sierras, had been avoided by the railway. Their confined valleys offered no room for the expansion of irrigated agriculture.[1]

Thus, the bi-partite economic division of Mexico's *región noroeste* came into being. Dams were built across the Sonora, Yaqui, Mayo, Fuerte, Sinaloa, and Culiacán rivers at various points on their lower courses, and canals were extended out onto the alluvial plain of the coast. The irrigated fields lay on either side of the main line of the Southern Pacific and those rails were soon paralleled by the paved highway which also connected Nogales with the capital.

Towns such as Hermosillo, Cajeme (now Ciudad Obregón), Navojoa, and Los Mochis, which were situated within the irrigation projects, grew as their agricultural hinterlands expanded. Paved highways were built to link these burgeoning centers with the Gulf Coast. Airfields were constructed to bring these cities into a national system of airways. Hotels, banks, commercial branch offices, and regional federal agencies were established. This expansion brought further growth in a self-fulfilling series of related events. The highways brought tourists from the United States and the *industria del turismo* so important to the Mexican economy was added to the economic gains of the coastal plain. Guaymas enlarged its shipping facilities as West Coast agriculture developed an exportable surplus. Shrimp and excursion fishing at this port expanded as the paved highway to the north provided a fast route to the United States. Both a railway and a paved highway were constructed, linking this rapidly developing zone with Mexicali and Tijuana. Pump irrigation was put into practice on the coast west of Hermosillo and in the desert near Caborca. All of these developments took place on the coastal plain.

Meanwhile, the old towns of the upstream Sonora, Yaqui, Mayo,

---

1   Sauer, *Road to Cibola*.

Seafood — especially shrimp — the exportable surplus of Mexican West Coast agriculture, excursion fishing, and tourism in general are all important items in the economy of Guaymas — the most important port on the Gulf of California. In this photo shrimp boats, docking and packing facilities are to be seen in the foreground. Across the bay is the center of Guaymas, distinguished by its old church and commercial buildings.

and Fuerte rivers languished. Roads were only slowly improved, irrigation was not extended, and except for a few war years, the mines which had been a source of income for centuries, declined. There are no railways and no airfields throughout most of eastern Sonora and Sinaloa. In fact aside from some electrification there has been no significant economic advance in the eastern desert basins and foothills region which at one time was the most prosperous area of the Sonoran Desert. The east has seen a relative decline which has made it, in many respects, the most economically underdeveloped sector of the entire desert. Even the native agricultural zones described above are less isolated, having been able to obtain, through their position on the coastal plain, greater access to the regions of intensive development, and through this at least an awareness of their own backwardness. The isolation is so complete in eastern Sonora that this awareness which must precede economic development barely exists.[2]

This region represents what President Avila Camacho meant when he pointed out, in the mid-1940's, that of twenty-two million Mexicans only six million were "really part of the economic system." The other sixteen million, he noted, lived in almost complete isolation from the exchange economy and from each other. Avila Camacho believed "they are isolated because they are poor and they are poor because they are isolated."[3] At the time Camacho spoke a much larger portion of Mexico's Northwest fell into this category. Today only mountainous eastern Sonora and Sinaloa suffer from this vicious economic circle.

There are then, within the Sonoran Desert, south of the international boundary, two distinct levels of economic development — one representative of the emerging post-revolutionary Mexico of paved highways, railways, and large irrigation projects; the other representing the period prior to the revolution, lacking all of the above.

The modern economy exists as part of the Mexican national economy and is able to draw upon the resources of other regions. The economy of coastal Sonora and Sinaloa was developed as part of a national policy. The considerable investments upon which recent growth has been maintained were derived from outside sources. This has allowed the modern economy to assume an active role in its relationship with the desert environment.

The backward regions to the east contrast in every respect with the above. Their subsistence economy is unable to draw upon outside

---

[2]   Whetten, pp. 8-10.

[3]   C. L. White, "Whither South America: Population and Natural Resources," *The Journal of Geography,* Vol. 60, (1961), p. 108.

resources although some limited amounts of cash and credit are available. It resembles the native economy in that aside from some governmental investments it is largely self-sufficient in maintaining a very low level of regional income. More than this, the eastern regions, as well as the native economic zones, contrast with the coast by following a more passive role in their relationship with nature. They have been unable to transform the desert into a more tractable milieu.

Only on the coast within the zones of modern water-resource development has the characteristic menace of drought been controlled. Not that a limited supply of water has been replaced by an unlimited supply, but that the lack of water has been eliminated as a cause of crop failure. Today, in contrast it is the occasional heavy rain or flood which is more often the cause of crop damage. Floods which wash out irrigation ditches, fill canals with silt, and destroy roads, combine with rains which delay the time of planting or harvesting to constitute the primary threat to a highly controlled environment.

Long periods of below-average rainfall over the watersheds of the rivers which supply water to the coast lower the level of water in the reservoirs, and thus allow the farmers to limit the number of acres to be planted. The kind of drought which destroys Cahita and Papago crops has been eliminated as the major cause of crop failure. No other proof is needed of man's ability to take the active role in his relationship with the elements and successfully alter his environment than this. The native agriculturalist, regularly plagued by drought and seldom harmed by flood, is a creature of the desert. The large-scale Mexican farmer, whose greatest fear is excessive rain and flood, has in effect created his own environment and has become victim of it. The storage dams are less successful in controlling excessive water than they are in circumventing drought. In addition, as the railway and highway have opened new markets for perishable crops, high operating costs have caused the most remunerative crops such as cotton to come to the fore, along with tomatoes and other vegetable crops particularly susceptible to the vagaries of weather. Rainfall and even frost constitute little threat to the subsistence farmer, who, independent of the market economy, is able to delay planting and harvesting without regard to conditions in California's Central Valley or elsewhere. Fifteen different crops grown for one's own consumption provide a degree of insurance against failure not possible in the specialized and commercial Mexican farms.

Large-scale irrigated agriculture within the Sonoran Desert's Mexican sector is both the major economic activity and that part of the economy showing the greatest gains over the past two decades. In this respect, Mexico's Northwest at the present time resembles Arizona's economy at about the time Mexico began its development of water resources (1926). These most recent gains in irrigated agriculture are predicated upon several basic realities of Mexican economic life.

In order to attain the higher standard of living which Mexico hopes to achieve through industrialization, the importation of staple foods had to be limited. Purchases of food products abroad cut deeply into the foreign exchange needed by Mexico to insure the industrial raw materials and machinery which has made her remarkable economic growth possible.

Agricultural self-sufficiency is not readily attainable in a country which has traditionally been unable to feed itself. Agriculturally, Mexico is for the most part too dry, too wet, or too rugged. Add to this the fact that Mexico has one of the world's highest rates of population growth and the magnitude of this problem becomes apparent. The Sonoran Desert, which is crossed by numerous rivers rising in the Sierra Madre, was an obvious choice for the early development of large-scale irrigated agriculture. Not only was this desert a potential bread basket but its seasonal range of temperature offered to the irrigator a wide variety of crops, and therefore a degree of economic flexibility found in few other regions. Wheat, rice, cotton, sugarcane, and winter vegetables could be grown in addition to corn and beans. Wheat could be cultivated in such quantities that Mexico could materially diminish her reliance on imports. The Republic is at the present time nearly self-sufficient in this commodity. Rice production could also be increased, further diminishing the need to import grains.

In contrast, cotton was already being exported and the expanding home market was saturated by the older producing districts such as Laguna. The world market, however, presented Mexico with the possibility to earn vital foreign exchange. Across the Pacific, Japan's expanding economy waited as the logical market for Sonoran cotton. Thus, through increasing the production of these crops Mexico could gain additional foreign exchange while lessening the need for it.

Sugarcane and winter vegetables provided another alternative for penetrating foreign markets. Winter vegetables could be sold north of the border well inside the practical limits placed on shipping perishable products.

The decision was made to go ahead in this region and from that moment national policies have forged an important role for Mexico's arid Northwest. The state of Sonora, for example, has increased its irrigated acreage approximately 14 percent annually[4] since the first year

---

[4]   *Sonora en Cifras*, 1960.

of the modern Mexican irrigation program. The Sonoran Desert now produces over one-half of Mexico's wheat and has assumed overwhelming leadership in the production of cotton. These formerly arid soils have been perhaps the most significant contributor to the agricultural development of Mexico which has with "prodigious effort," resulted in an increase of food production in that country over a twenty-year period of approximately 4 percent per year.[5]

THE AGRICULTURAL ECONOMY OF THE COAST

Almost the entire agricultural product of the desert south of the international boundary comes from a limited number of large irrigated oases near the coast. In 1926 most of these were in existence but their irrigation was mainly by primitive and uncontrolled means. Only the region of Mexicali benefited from large-scale multipurpose irrigation and this was no more than a fortuitous byproduct of American efforts in the Imperial Valley. Some districts, such as the Costa de Hermosillo and Caborca, which depend upon pump irrigation, were developed only after the inception of the overall program.

Today the regions of Mexicali, Yaqui, and El Fuerte stand out as the largest of these oases. None of the three regions clearly leads as the principal producer of a wide variety of crops, but each, due to some climatic or locational factor, heads the list of intra-desert regions in at least one of the major commodities. Although any field may produce two crops annually, wheat and cotton — the most widely planted crops — have growing seasons which are mutually exclusive. The farmers must choose one or the other. Collectively, these choices usually result in the selection of either wheat, cotton, or some other single crop, as the principal commodity grown within each district. Furthermore, once the area has begun to specialize, the investments needed to plant, cultivate, harvest, and process the crop are so large that the region is further compelled to continue the production of the most remunerative single crop. Highly organized and mechanized agriculture within a market economy is subject not only to the historical *la monocultura* but to a high degree of geographic inertia.

Cotton has during the last fifteen years replaced wheat as the most important commodity grown within Mexico's sector of the Sonoran Desert, despite the rapidly increasing cultivation of the latter crop. The success which cotton has achieved rests in large measure upon the

---

[5] Harrison Brown, "Life in the Americas during the Next Century," *The Annals of the American Academy of Political and Social Science,* Vol. 316 (1958), p. 14.

coincidental outbreak of the Korean War at the time thousands of acres were coming under irrigation for the first time, and cotton was the first crop planted.[6] The world price spiralled upward, providing further incentive to drill wells. It was during this time that the Costa de Hermosillo was developed. Farmers were able to buy hundreds of acres of desert, drill wells, buy pumps, machinery, and seed, and pay for their entire investment with the proceeds of one or two crops. Farmers to the south, in the Yaqui, Mayo, and Fuerte valleys turned to cotton without regard to the more humid conditions and summer rain which interrupts the picking. Farmers in Mexicali planted cotton despite the poorer soils, taking advantage of the drier atmospheric conditions which promote the development of cotton bolls. New land was staked out in Caborca and the Valle de Guaymas with cotton in mind. The profits from this single crop during a few short years gave more impetus to the development of agriculture in the Mexican Northwest than any other economic factor aside from irrigation itself.

By the mid-1950's the Sonoran Desert had assumed first position among the major Mexican cotton-producing districts by a wide margin.[7] The state of Sonora was the largest single producer of cotton among the Mexican states, with the irrigated Sonoran oases harvesting approximately one-half of the entire national production of 2,100,000 bales. Due to this expansion in the Sonoran Desert, Mexico had shouldered aside Pakistan, Egypt, and Brazil to become the world's fifth-largest cotton-producing nation, ranking behind the United States, the Soviet Union, China, and India.[8]

Not only have cotton acreages been increased but the yields per acre have been significantly improved. Insect and weed control have been in part responsible for this. Nitrogen fertilizers, which are now used on at least 95 percent of the fields planted to cotton also must be given credit.[9]

Today the region of Mexicali reigns as the desert's largest cotton-producing district, with an average of approximately 300,000 acres devoted to this crop. Cotton dominates the economy of the Mexicali district as it does nowhere except perhaps at San Luis and Caborca.

---

[6] C. A. Cook, "Mexico Grows more Cotton and Wheat with expanded Irrigation," *Foreign Agriculture*, Vol. 19 (1955), p. 7.

[7] Earlier accounts of the cultivation of cotton in Mexico such as L. A. Garlock, "Cotton in the Economy of Mexico," *Economic Geography*, Vol. 20 (1944), pp. 70-77, have little value today. The entire pattern of cultivation has shifted to the arid west.

[8] *Commodities Yearbook 1966*, p. 127.

[9] In 1954 only an estimated 9 percent of the total cotton crop received any fertilizer. *Sonora en Cifras*, 1961.

Loading bales of cotton in the Mexicali district. This is just one link in the economic chain that leads from stored or pumped water to foreign exchange credited to Mexican accounts in Tokyo, Frankfurt, Milan, and other cities. The Sonoran Desert contributes disproportionately to the excellent balance of payments enjoyed by Mexico. The peso is as strong as any currency in the world.

These smaller cotton-growing regions have much the same climate as Mexicali.

The modern production of cotton in Mexicali is probably as old as that of the oldest cotton district in the desert. The large tracts of land owned and operated by the American companies, which built the old Imperial Canal through Mexico, planted several thousand acres of land to cotton in 1910. Mexicali was in that year a dusty border town of less than a thousand inhabitants,[10] labor being provided mainly through the importation of Chinese coolies. World War I provided the market conditions which resulted in the first 100,000-bale crop in 1920. *Braceros* (literally, "arms," corresponding to the American hired "hands" —farm workers) streamed north from the southern Mexican states, replacing the Chinese and spilling over into the cotton fields of the Imperial Valley. At that time there were only three small gins in Mexicali and the majority of the crop was taken to Calexico to be ginned. Further-more, all of the cotton grown in the Mexicali district was purchased by American cotton merchants who had offices in Calexico.

After 1920, cotton production (which collapsed in the Imperial Valley) declined but continued to be the single most important source of income to the Mexicali district, largely because there existed no alternative crop.[11]

World War II and the Korean War pushed production to new heights. In 1955 Mexicali produced 447,000 bales and since that time production has been maintained at about 300,000 bales. The success of cotton, which dominates the economy of Mexicali, is best attested to be the growth of that city from a population of 4,000 in 1920 to approximately 200,000. At the present time, Mexicali gins all its own cotton and ships the majority of the crop through Ensenada to Japan, with California ports as alternate outlets.

The Costa de Hermosillo, founded on cotton, has seen recent diversification as the Mexican government has pressed for national self-sufficiency in wheat. International complications, over which Mexico has almost no control, have also worked within recent years to limit the continued expansion of cotton acreages. Cotton surpluses in the United States, continued expansion of world cotton production, competition from synthetic fibers, and many other factors have worked against the Mexican cotton farmer. In particular, the subsidies paid to the American

---

10 George F. Deasy and Peter Gerhard, "Settlements in Baja California, 1768-1930," *Geographical Review*, Vol. 34 (1944), pp. 581-86.

11 In the late thirties under President Cárdenas the irrigated lands of Mexicali were expropriated and distributed to the workers. Whetten, p. 128.

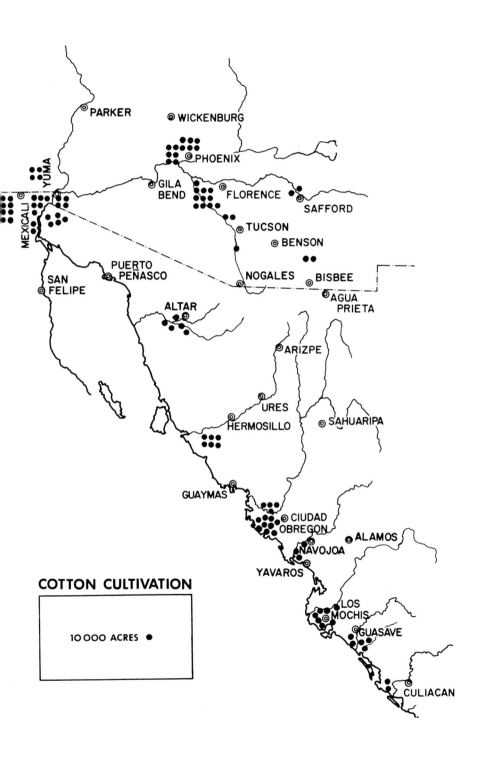

PARKER

WICKENBURG

PHOENIX

YUMA

MEXICALI

GILA
BEND

FLORENCE

SAFFORD

TUCSON

BENSON

SAN
FELIPE

PUERTO
PENASCO

NOGALES

BISBEE

AGUA
PRIETA

ALTAR

ARIZPE

URES

HERMOSILLO

SAHUARIPA

GUAYMAS

CIUDAD
OBREGON

ALAMOS

NAVOJOA

YAVAROS

LOS
MOCHIS

GUASAVE

CULIACAN

COTTON CULTIVATION

10 000 ACRES ●

cotton farmer contrast with the export tax paid by the Mexican producer. In the Yaqui and Mayo valleys of southern Sonora, cotton shares first place with wheat. Further south in the Fuerte Valley not only wheat but sugarcane, rice, tomatoes, and winter vegetables challenge cotton for each irrigated acre due to a more benign winter, but even here cotton maintains its primacy as a cash crop. A warm spring, combined with the earlier and more intense summer rainy season, encourages the earlier planting and picking of cotton in the state of Sinaloa and this, in turn, provides a marketable cotton at a season when supplies are low.

Only in the far south, in the district of Culiacán, is cotton displaced almost completely by tomatoes, rice, sugarcane, and winter vegetables.

Cotton Acreages, Mexican Sector, Sonoran Desert, 1966[12]

Mexicali	290,000	Caborca	45,000
Yaqui	130,000	Mayo	30,000
Fuerte	70,000	Culiacán	20,000
Hermosillo	55,000	Guaymas	10,000
Guasave*	50,000	Eastern Sonora	5,000
San Luis	50,000	Guamuchil	5,000
		Total	760,000

*Guasave is actually part of the overall Fuerte Valley irrigation scheme

Cotton in the region of Mexicali and throughout the state of Sonora is considered a summer crop. Planting begins in the Yaqui Valley in April and proceeds north through the month of May. Picking takes place mainly after the summer rains from September to December. As mentioned previously, cotton is a winter crop in northern Sinaloa. Planting begins in November or December, with the harvest mainly in June.

The cultivation costs for cotton are higher per unit-area than for wheat or most field crops. It requires the employment of large numbers of workers on the land itself and in related local industries. Cotton is for this reason disproportionately important to the overall economic structure of each oasis community.

In addition, cotton, with its numerous insect enemies, requires large volumes of insecticides, fertilizers, and herbicides. Sales and service

---

12   This and the following tables were compiled from many sources including México, Secretaria de Economía, Dirección General de Estadística, *Tercer Censo Agrícola, Ganadero y Ejidal* (1957); for Sonora, Sinaloa, and Baja California, *Sonora en Cifras,* 1961; Raul Ibáñez and others, *Panorama Económico de Sinaloa y sus Datos Estadísticos* (Instituto de Investigaciones Económicas del Estado de Sinaloa, Culiacán, Sinaloa, 1958); the Asociación de Productores de Algodón del Noroeste, A. C. Ciudad Obregón, Sonora, report of March 15, 1967; and U. S. Dept. of Agriculture, *Foreign Agriculture Circular.* This is not a complete list but includes the more important sources.

of agricultural machinery, which in its widest sense even includes airplanes used to dust cotton, all give employment in the cotton-producing districts. Gins and oil mills spring up, contributing further to the local economy.

A typical cotton farm of 600 acres on the Costa de Hermosillo may employ eight or ten families on a year-round basis. During the thinning, hoeing, and picking seasons additional labor is employed. Picking is done by hand despite the fact that much human labor has in general been replaced by machines. This reliance on hand picking is due in large measure to the warm climate which allows continued vegetative growth of cotton necessitating three or more separate pickings.[13] South of Hermosillo summer rains interrupt the picking process, making the use of machines even more ineffective. The relatively low cost of labor but certainly not the "backwardness" of Mexican cotton farmers further inhibits the mechanization of cotton picking.

The greatest costs incurred in the production of cotton are those of irrigation and insecticides which have recently been about the same. Because of the large investments the cost of raising cotton is inflexibly high. For this reason the price markedly affects the number of acres planted.

During recent years wheat has closely rivaled cotton as the most widely planted crop in the desert, south of the border. In 1966 this crop occupied an estimated 1,030,000 acres.

Wheat Acreages, Mexican Sector, Sonoran Desert, 1966

Yaqui	320,000	Eastern Sonora	45,000
Hermosillo	210,000	Guaymas	25,000
Fuerte	115,000	Caborca	20,000
Guasave	100,000	Guamuchil	10,000
Mayo	90,000	Culiacán	10,000
Mexicali	80,000	San Luis	5,000
		Total	1,030,000

The value of the crop, however, has fallen far below that of cotton in every year since 1950. Only in the state of Sonora does wheat really challenge cotton for first position among the irrigated crops. The Lower Yaqui Valley has been since Colonial times the bread basket of the arid Northwest, and leads all other districts in the production of wheat. The Costa de Hermosillo, another Sonoran project, ranks second despite its being smaller in overall size than either Mexicali or the Fuerte Valley.

Given enough water, climatic conditions are almost ideal for the

---

[13] No cotton-picking machine has yet been built which can successfully comb the field several times without destroying the undeveloped bolls.

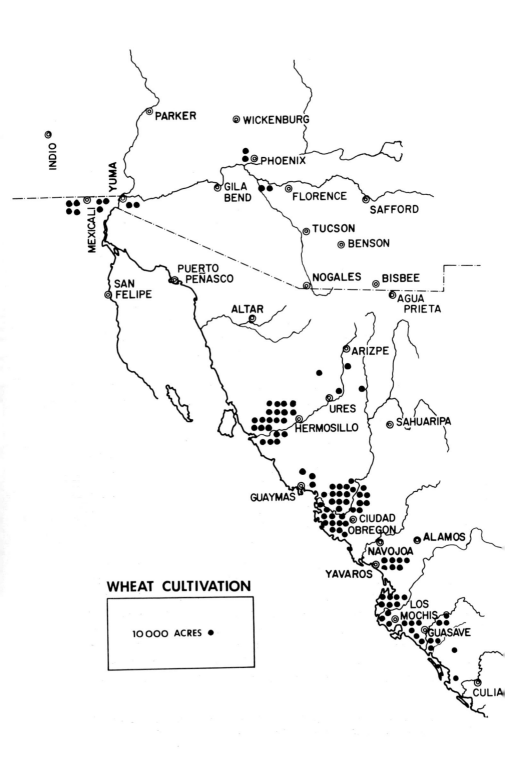

WHEAT CULTIVATION

10 000 ACRES ●

Preparing a huge wheat field on the Costa de Hermosillo. Such enormous fields are typical of this recently developed area. Although founded on cotton, the Costa has seen much diversification as the Mexican government pressed its drive for self-sufficiency in wheat. During recent years, wheat has been second only to cotton in the number of acres planted in the Mexican sector of the Sonoran Desert.

cultivation of wheat. Planted in November and December, wheat matures after the uncertain winter rains. The harvest begins in the Fuerte Valley in April and is terminated by June in Hermosillo. Wheat is a highly mechanized crop, employing very few locally in comparison to cotton. The importance of this crop should not, however, be underestimated. Next to cotton it has shown, over the last fifteen years, the greatest absolute increase in both acres planted and crop value.[14]

A greatly increased yield per irrigated acre has, next to the expanded acreage itself, been the most noteworthy factor in West Coast wheat farming. Until the end of the Second World War there had been virtually no effective agricultural research done within the Mexican half of the desert. In addition, very little of what had been accomplished elsewhere was made available to Mexican farmers. In 1943 the Rockefeller Foundation, in cooperation with the Ministry of Agriculture, began a program of agricultural investigations aimed at increasing the production of food crops.[15] As a result of that work practically all the wheat, as well as corn and beans, produced on the West Coast are varieties bred or introduced through this cooperative effort. Additional increases in wheat yields have been achieved through control of insects and plant diseases. Fertilizers, little used throughout much of Mexico, have found in the Sonoran Desert's irrigated land an important market. Increased yields also result from the more regulated flow of water achieved through the larger river-control schemes instituted since 1949. Between 1950 and 1957 Mexico's production of wheat doubled, making the country self-sufficient, at least for the short run, in this important commodity. Almost all of this increase came from the irrigated Sonoran districts.[16]

Rice, which has for many years been a major product on the deltaic lands of southern Sonora and northern Sinaloa is, next to wheat, the most important grain and the fifth most important single crop grown in the Mexican desert.[17] The cultivation of rice, like all other crops, is subject to the highly competitive demand for irrigated land. Until 1949 rice led all other crops in value among those grown in Sonora.[18] In the

---

[14] The greatest advance in the cultivation of wheat followed the fall in the price of cotton.

[15] Combined Mexican Working Party, The Johns Hopkins University, *The Economic Development of Mexico* (Baltimore, 1953).

[16] Dozier, "Mexico's Transformed Northwest," *Geographical Review,* Oct. 1963, p. 560.

[17] Cotton, wheat, tomatoes, sugar cane, rice, in that order.

[18] Rice, 44 million pesos; wheat, 39 million; cotton, 19 million, *Sonora en Cifras,* 1960.

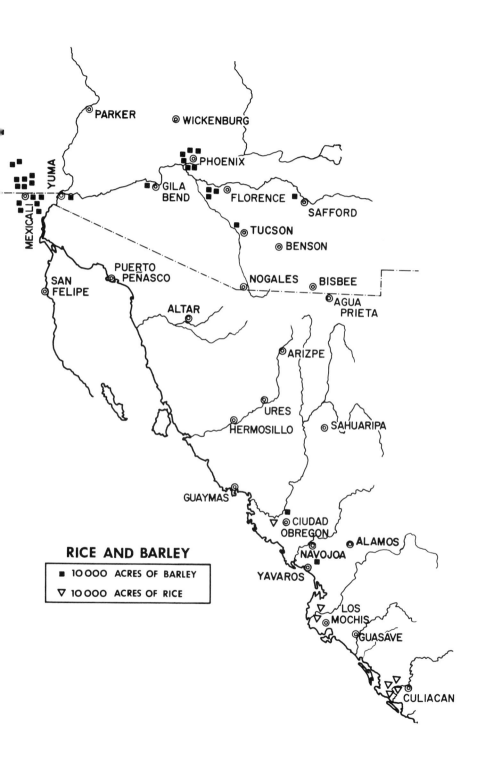

PARKER

◎ WICKENBURG

YUMA

◎ PHOENIX

MEXICALI

◎ GILA
BEND

◎ FLORENCE

SAFFORD

TUCSON

◎ BENSON

PUERTO
◎ PENASCO

NOGALES

BISBEE

SAN
FELIPE

ALTAR

AGUA
PRIETA

◎ ARIZPE

URES

HERMOSILLO

◎ SAHUARIPA

GUAYMAS

▽ ◎ CIUDAD
OBREGON

◎ ALAMOS

NAVOJOA

YAVAROS

RICE AND BARLEY

■ 10 000 ACRES OF BARLEY
▽ 10 000 ACRES OF RICE

▽ LOS
▽ ◎ MOCHIS

◎ GUASAVE

▽ ▽
▽
▽ ◎ CULIACAN

following year, a high percentage of land which had been planted in rice was appropriated by cotton and later wheat as well as other crops.

The decline in rice acreage has been precipitous and is attributable largely to the increased price of cotton. This points up an important element in the economic geography of a low-latitude desert. Once water is made available and the land is planted in cash crops, a higher degree of competition among crops exists than in any other region.[19] Since the controlled climate of an irrigated desert provides a greater choice of crop possibilities, there are more competitors. In addition, the high, fixed costs of this "created" environment force the agriculturalist to reappraise more often his cost-price relationship with regard to this longer list of alternative crops.

With rice — a particularly "thirsty" plant — water is the critical factor. Thus, the crop must be highly remunerative in order to justify the large expenditure of water.[20] In the region of the Fuerte near Los Mochis and Guasave, therefore, rice production assumes larger proportions than in southern Sonora and is even more important south of the Sinaloa River where it occupies the largest acreage on the coastal plain below Culiacán.[21]

Although corn is the uncontested leader among all Mexican crops, forming the cornerstone of the Indian and mestizo diet, it is today of secondary importance among those crops grown in the Mexican Northwest. The cultivation of corn probably never was as important in the arid and Spanish North as it was in the more densely populated Indian South of Mexico. Cultural factors as well as climate combined to limit the amount of corn planted in the Sonoran Desert. It was cultivated mainly in the upland valleys and by the Indians on the coastal plain. The method used was usually that of *temporal* farming — the seed being planted after the first summer rains brought water to the fields. This type of farming was adopted from the Indians by the white settlers in the isolated valleys of eastern Sonora.

Today the cultivation of corn follows these Colonial and indigenous patterns. The largest part of the crop is grown in eastern Sonora. Until just recently, it has been planted with reluctance in the major zones of irrigated agriculture along the coast.[22] However, within recent years, it

---

[19]   Provided that these crops do not, as in the case of cotton, necessitate a large investment in machinery.

[20]   Ibáñez and others, p. 31.

[21]   *Ibid.,* p. 33.

[22]   In the state of Sinaloa in 1957 only 45,000 acres of corn were cultivated within the lands of the major irrigation projects while temporary and dry farming accounted for slightly over 250,000 acres planted to this crop. Ibáñez and others, p. 34.

has been increasingly planted on cotton lands, particularly in the Yaqui Valley district, thus achieving a better balanced, two-crop harvest.

Elsewhere, it is a subsistence crop whose value does not fluctuate violently with market conditions. For this reason the cultivation of corn has been more stable. The acreage planted to this crop in the desert is the same today as it was in 1942 and probably no different from what was planted at the beginning of the nineteenth century.[23] In the valleys of northern Sinaloa it is grown by the poor *ejidatario* and Indian farmers. Corn is only the sixth most important agricultural product within the Mexican zone.

What has been said about corn can be repeated for beans. Although a crop of relatively small importance in the Mexican half of the desert, beans are, among the great mass of Mexicans, a staple food second only to corn. Beans are grown generally where corn is grown and by the same small farmers. Whereas corn is mainly a summer crop, beans may be planted at almost any time of the year, but are generally planted in spring and autumn, with the harvest being consumed locally, there being no shipments to other Mexican states.

The barley crop is closely tied to the production of beer and other malt products which have shown a remarkable increase in consumption due to the higher standard of living. The Yaqui Valley and Mexicali lead all other regions in this crop. Unlike the irrigated areas north of the border, barley is not grown as an animal feed.

Sesame seed and garbanzo beans are two introduced crops which have for many years been grown for cash by the smaller farmers of northern Sinaloa and, to a lesser degree, by the farmers of southern Sonora. Both crops are grown mainly for export, with the garbanzos going mainly to Cuba and Spain. Neither crop has shared in the increased acreages of the district; indeed the garbanzo has even had an overall decline in plantings.

Oilseeds such as sesame and safflower can be grown using "dry-farming"[24] methods in the rolling land of the thorn forest transition. Temporal fields belonging to ejidatarios are also planted to these crops. The garbanzo, on the other hand, is grown largely within the river-control projects near the towns of Los Mochis, Guasave, and Guamuchil.

Among the cultivated crops of the Mexican half of the Sonoran Desert the tomato stands third (behind cotton and wheat), exceeding sugarcane — the fourth-ranking crop — by a wide margin. The tomato is, in turn, only one of a number of winter vegetables grown in the southern, relatively frostfree margin of the desert. Over 90 percent of

---

[23] *Sonora en Cifras.*
[24] Farming without irrigation in a semiarid environment.

the overall Mexican West Coast vegetable acreage is cultivated in the valleys of Sinaloa.

Tomatoes were first grown for export in the valleys of Sinaloa at the turn of this century. Among the original growers were some of the survivors of the American colony at Topolobampo. Prior to 1905, tomatoes were shipped from Mazatlán and other Sinaloa ports to Los Angeles and San Francisco by slow and unrefrigerated boats — with understandably poor results. The first carload shipments were made by rail to Nogales from Bacum (in the Yaqui Valley) and Los Mochis in the years immediately prior to the Revolution.

In 1910 and 1911 frosts destroyed the crop along the Yaqui and tomatoes have never regained any importance in this valley. The unsettled political conditions of the Costa during the decade of 1910–1920 limited exports, but the latter year saw the first 1,000-car shipment to the border. In that year 15,000 acres of tomatoes were planted in the irrigated districts of Sinaloa.[25]

Early growers found that tomatoes grown in coastal Sinaloa ripened mainly in February and March, two months ahead of Florida, California, and Arizona. In fact, some tomatoes could be grown to ripen in November or December. The occasional year of killing frosts in the southern United States causes increased demand for Mexican tomatoes and other winter vegetables. In these years planting is extremely profitable as prices rise. The harvest may be prolonged until well into April.

Over a period of sixty years tomatoes have been the most consistently profitable vegetable crop and account for over three-fourths of the total acreage.[26] Tomatoes are grown within the large projects by farmers who plant an average of between 100 and 200 acres in this crop, although some *campos* are much larger. Many of these large-scale farmers own their own airplanes and buy insecticide and fertilizer by the "carload." There is a disproportionately high number of Americans, Spaniards, Britons, Cubans, and other foreigners among these tomato planters.

During recent years there have been significant innovations and improvements in the harvesting, packing, refrigeration, and transportation of tomatoes and other winter vegetables. Nearly all are now graded and packed by experienced workers in modern, well-equipped sheds. The green tomatoes are run over sizing machines and sorting tables

---

25   Bell and MacKenzie, pp. 147-48.

26   In 1959-60, 58,600 acres of ground tomatoes and 10,000 acres of staked tomatoes were planted. Closer spacing and fewer grade defects mean that an acre of staked tomatoes will yield four to five times as many tomatoes of export quality as an acre of ground tomatoes. Thus, vine-ripened tomatoes represent about 40 percent of the total exports.

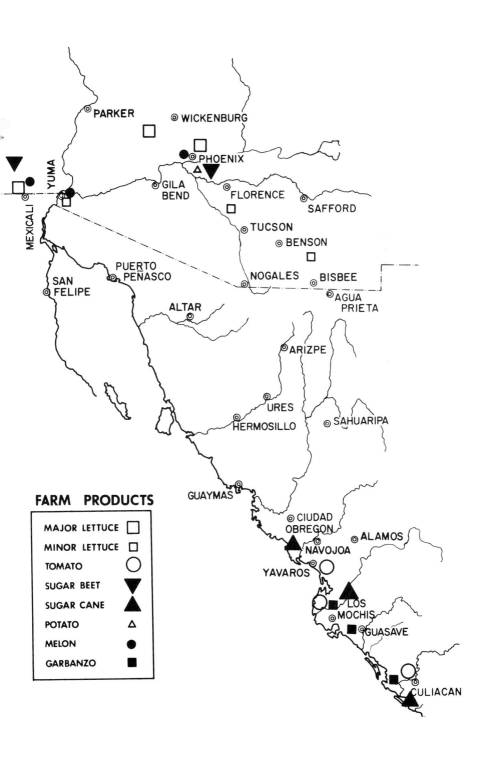

FARM PRODUCTS

MAJOR LETTUCE	□
MINOR LETTUCE	◻
TOMATO	○
SUGAR BEET	▼
SUGAR CANE	▲
POTATO	△
MELON	●
GARBANZO	■

PARKER

◎ WICKENBURG

● ◎ PHOENIX

△ ▼

◎ GILA
BEND

◎ FLORENCE

SAFFORD

◎ TUCSON

◎ BENSON

MEXICALI

YUMA

PUERTO
◎ PEÑASCO

NOGALES ◎ BISBEE

◎ AGUA
PRIETA

SAN
◎ FELIPE

◎ ALTAR

◎ ARIZPE

◎ URES

◎ HERMOSILLO

◎ SAHUARIPA

◎ GUAYMAS

◎ CIUDAD
OBREGON

◎ ALAMOS

▲ NAVOJOA

YAVAROS ◎

○

◎ MOCHIS

▲ LOS
■ MOCHIS

◎ GUASAVE

○

■ CULIACAN ▲

before being individually wrapped. Several packing sheds have been constructed where vine-ripened tomatoes are pre-cooled before being shipped in refrigerated railway cars or trucks.

The paved highway from Culiacán to Nogales has cut the shipping time in half. The distance by highway is 652 miles and the trucks arrive in 18 hours. The railway, however, continues to provide a cheaper alternative, and by this means vine-ripened tomatoes have been shipped as far east as Detroit, although most are marketed west of Kansas City. Western Canada provides yet another market for Sinaloa tomatoes. The new highway and railway just completed across the Sierra from Mazatlán to Durango also make available another market in Texas and the Mississippi Valley.[27]

Of possibly greater significance still is the increasing demand each year of the domestic market. Most of the towns and cities of Mexico are only beginning to be well supplied with fresh vegetables. The highway system in Mexico is being continually improved, incomes are rising, and the population is increasing rapidly. The Mexican population's increased buying power presents a great opportunity to those who make their living growing vegetables in the irrigated fields around Culiacán and Los Mochis.

The principal hazards to the winter vegetable grower are frosts, excessive rains, plant diseases, and insects. Frost damage can be severe. In February 1956, for example, nearly all the vegetables on the coastal plain were destroyed. Under normal conditions the rainy season, which ends in early September, presents no problem to the winter vegetable grower. It is, however, the unusually heavy rains, which may occur in January or February, that cause considerable damage. In 1949 and again in 1960 there was extensive rain damage to all winter vegetables. Flooding resulted in a complete crop loss along the rivers in southern Sonora and northern Sinaloa. Irrigation canals were washed out and field work was interrupted. Repairs on irrigation ditches had to be made before other work could progress. There was much replanting and harvests were delayed until American varieties were already in the markets.

---

[27] The distance from Culiacán to Laredo over this route is 869 miles, only 217 miles more than to Nogales. This means that a truckload of tomatoes bound for Texas moves south from Culiacán to Mazatlán before passing northeast to Texas. Interestingly enough, this places the southernmost growing regions in closer proximity to this north-of-the-border market. It may in fact promote the development of a winter vegetable industry in southern Sinaloa (outside the desert) where the frost danger is virtually nonexistent. Another improvement in transportation which will affect this important West Coast industry is the completion of the long-dreamed-of railway between Los Mochis and Chihuahua.

Aside from Culiacán, the valley of the Fuerte in Sinaloa, and the Yaqui and Mayo valleys in Sonora produce tomatoes. The region of Huatabampo (Mayo) produces good winter tomatoes but suffers damaging frost approximately once in every five years, a rate about twice that of Culiacán.

At the present time, a wide variety of winter vegetables are grown and exported to the United States and Canada. Bell peppers, cantaloupes, and watermelons occupy, after tomatoes, the largest acreage. There have been no significant changes during recent years in the quantities of these crops harvested.

Within the Sonoran Desert the production of sugarcane is limited to the valleys between the Río Fuerte and Río Culiacán where it is grown on land irrigated by the large projects. Since sugarcane is a "factory crop" it is grown only in close proximity to the large, well-equipped sugar mills. There is one located at Los Mochis and two at Culiacán.

Historically, sugarcane has played a pre-eminent part in the development of Sinaloa (no sugarcane is grown in Sonora) as it has in so many parts of the American tropics. The great agricultural potential of the deltaic soils of the Lower Fuerte and Culiacán were first developed by the sugar planters. Since the turn of the century other crops have taken over much of the land first planted to sugarcane but it was sugar that first demonstrated the possibilities of large-scale irrigated agriculture on the alluvial soils of northern Sinaloa. For most of this century the expansion of the sugar industry on Mexico's West Coast has been impeded by revolution, land expropriation, lack of capital and credit, as well as by limited water. Plant disease and numerous other factors have also halted the continued development of the sugar industry which has fallen behind cotton, wheat, and winter vegetables in these valleys.[28]

Although sugarcane has probably been grown for centuries in small plots along the rivers of Sinaloa, it was the development of the large sugar properties such as the United Sugar Company of Los Mochis that made sugar the core of Sinaloa's economy during the Porfirian era.[29]

Prior to this time, white settlement hugged the Sierra to the east along the Camino Real. Towns such as Alamos and El Fuerte were the principal centers of commerce, though agriculture was of little importance. The Díaz years resulted in an extension of agriculture on to the coastal plain as existing haciendas were greatly expanded and new

---

[28] Pfeifer, "Sinaloa und Sonora Beitrage zur Landeskunde und Kultur geographie des nordwestlichen Mexico," *Mitt. Geog. Gesell.,* Vol. 46, pp. 405-27.
[29] *Ibid.*

properties established. This paralleled a rapid growth in Mexico's economic development which in turn is inevitably accompanied at this stage by an even more rapid increase in the consumption of sugar. Between 1900 and 1908 Mexican consumption of refined sugar increased faster than an impressive 60 percent increase in national production. By the latter year, Sinaloa had increased its production to rank second only to the state of Vera Cruz. It was during the Porfirian years that foreign investment flowed into the sugar plantations. As far as Sinaloa was concerned, much credit is due to the ill-fated Topolobampo community which brought interest and investors to the Fuerte even after its complete demise in 1892. During the nineties, a large mill was erected at Los Mochis by American interests beginning a rapid climb to dominance in sugar by American capital, gradually encroaching upon the unmechanized Fuerte hacendados. As an example, tractors were introduced to the United Sugar Company properties prior to the Revolution; some, driven by steam and fueled by pitahaya wood, proved very satisfactory.[30] Irrigation was at first accomplished mainly by primitive diversions from the Fuerte River although some modern pumps powered by both steam and gasoline were installed along the banks of the Fuerte prior to the Revolution.

The Revolution resulted not only in years of economic disorder but also in the expropriation of the large sugar properties.[31] These were then handed over to ejiditarios who had no other alternative than to continue their contracts for the delivery of cane with the mills which remained in the possession of their original owners. These small growers in general were unable to obtain necessary financing for the cultivation of sugar and turned to subsistence farming. The long growth period makes financing of sugarcane particularly difficult.

Sugarcane is one of the thirstier crops grown in the region — requiring an estimated five feet of water annually — and was, until the completion of the storage dams on the Fuerte and Sinaloa rivers, subject to water shortages. These factors have all combined over the last fifty years to inhibit the expansion of sugarcane acreages, with the result that sugarcane is just one of a number of important crops, even in the Los Mochis and Culiacán districts. Recently, however, there has been renewed interest in sugar, caused in part by the estrangement of Cuba and the United States. Sugarcane yields per acre have doubled on some of the Fuerte lands since the regularization of water supply following the completion of the Hidalgo Dam. All of this has caused renewed

---

30   Bell and MacKenzie, pp. 111-12.
31   Whetten, p. 128.

interest and confidence in cane sugar, and recent harvests have been the largest in history.

Sugarcane is planted during the summer rainy season in August or September, with the first crop being harvested eighteen months later. The cultivation of sugarcane, like most other crops grown in the Mexican sector of the Sonoran Desert, is highly mechanized while still requiring large numbers of agricultural workers. Tractors and trucks have generally replaced teams and wagons, but planting and cutting is still done by hand. Thus sugarcane resembles cotton in its reliance on both heavy machinery as well as cheap labor.

Overall, the Fuerte Valley contrasts with the irrigated districts to the north in that frost does not menace the most sensitive crops. Because of this and the larger amount of water available, the Fuerte presents a much more flexible set of agricultural conditions. Winter vegetables as well as tropical crops can be grown in addition to all the crops grown in the Mayo, Yaqui, and Hermosillo districts. To the north the degree of diversity is limited by the occasional sub-freezing temperatures.

The original introduction of livestock revolutionized the region's economy and for several centuries provided the cornerstone of desert land use. It was through cattle, in particular, that the sparse Sonoran vegetation was best utilized and made available economically. Extensive land utilization through cattle was in fact one of the few alternatives open to the early settler. Sparse natural vegetation and the lack of water were factors limiting the expansion of pastoralism but often absolutely precluded any other activity.

The care of livestock became a way of life, and it is well known that when any economic activity is classified as "a way of life" it has lost its strictly economic character. In the arid Northwest of Mexico a value has been placed upon ranching which goes far beyond the economic value of the animals raised. The average Mexican agriculturist, although he has probably turned to irrigated farming, still places a disproportionate value on the extensive use of desert land through cattle.[32] To the north, across the border, the American cattleman has found a new desert land-value relationship through livestock which is truly economic. This has not taken place in Mexico. The result is a much wider gap

---

[32] In 1950 the agricultural census of livestock in the state of Sonora gives cattle a total value of 725 million pesos. Yet these same cattle produced appoximately 50 million pesos worth of meat and 34 million pesos worth of milk. Disregarding milk, which is obtained largely through robbing beef calves of their natural food, it is curious to note a value of 725 million pesos placed on an animal population which produces a total of only 50 million pesos worth of animal products each year. Estado de Sonora, *Proyecto Programa de Gobierno del Estado de Sonora* (Hermosillo, 1957), p. 117.

between the two countries in the utilization of land for pastoral activities than there is in irrigated farming.

The distribution of cattle in Mexico's arid Northwest mirrors the availability of palatable vegetation in proximity to water. Desert vegetation does not regularly include grasses except in riverine areas and other widely separated upland locations. Cattle must resort to browsing which usually provides little forage indeed.[33]

In the extremely dry region west of the Nogales-Guaymas highway where rainfall totals less than 5 inches annually there exist large tracts that for all practical purposes support no cattle.[34] Only in the weeks following particularly heavy rains are cattle moved onto these ranges. The Caborca-Altar-Santa Ana region is the only major area where cattle are raised on a permanent basis.[35]

East of this highway in the desert foothills of eastern Sonora there is an appreciable increase in rainfall, improved vegetation, and larger numbers of cattle. Where rainfall averages between 10 and 15 inches there is a permanent range. The principal valleys that penetrate this eastern region provide a little improved pasture, cultivated feed, and water. Three-quarters of the state's range cattle are to be found in this region which, of course, encompasses large areas outside that having strictly desert vegetation.[36] Here, indeed, is an area particularly well adapted to cattle breeding. It contains a number of areas which have been classified as *zonas de concentración* (zones of concentrated cattle ranching — a term devised by the Dirección General de Estudios Económicos). By far the largest of these zones centers on Cananea and includes the *municipios* of Santa Cruz, Arizpe, and Imuris. In a recent year this zone included almost two-thirds of Sonora's purebred cattle, mostly Herefords. This concentration of fine cattle is due largely to the history of foreign ownership of ranches, including the huge Green holdings (recently expropriated by the Mexican government). Almost all of this area is, however, outside the Sonoran Desert and the range is an encino-ocotillo-grassland community.

The lower elevations to the south and southeast support fewer cattle but include a number of the zonas de concentración. The San Miguel, middle Sonora, Moctezuma, Nacozari, and Bavispe river valleys,

---

[33]　Robert R. Humphrey, *Arizona Range Grasses, Their Description, Forage Value and Management,* University of Arizona Agricultural Experiment Station, Bull. No. 298 (Tucson, 1958). The description of conditions in the desert southwest of Arizona might also suffice for western Sonora.

[34]　Sonora, *Proyecto de Programa de Gobierno del Estado de Sonora,* p. 119.

[35]　*Ibid.,* pp. 109-10.

[36]　*Ibid.,* p. 119.

Cattle being driven down the dry streamway of a Río Moctezuma affluent near Moctezuma, Sonora. Irrigated fields in the distance and at the lower left contain circular threshing platforms similar to those of medieval Spain. The cattle drive mirrors the nineteenth-century frontier. This picture is as much history as current events.

as well as the surrounding mountains, are able to support large numbers of cattle.[37]

The southern coastal desert which merges with the thorn forest of eastern and central Sinaloa is not heavily grazed by cattle but does contain, along the major river valleys, a much larger number of cattle than the region as a whole.[38] This does not mean, however, that a modern cattle-feeding industry, based upon forage crops grown on irrigated lands, has developed. Despite the recent increase in the planting of alfalfa, sudan grass, and other forage crops, there is nothing resembling the cattle feeding which takes place in the Salt River Valley of Arizona. Cattle die by the thousands in the desert during each drought, both from thirst and hunger. These animals, which could either be provided for in the desert or brought to market, are left to die instead.

Beset by numerous problems, the desert cattle ranch of northwestern Mexico is not a great deal different from what it was a century ago. The car and truck have lessened the isolation somewhat, but primitive roads continue to hinder communications over much of the desert range.

Aside from the semiarid highlands near the border, the Mexican West Coast supports a population of largely degenerate *criollo* (in this case, "indigenous") cattle, almost all of which are in part descendents of the first Spanish cows driven into this region from Nayarit and Chihuahua. It is interesting to note that the horns of those in the foothills of the Sierra are noticeably longer. In contrast, near the highways many have some of the characteristics of northern European breeds. Except along the international highway, the range is almost entirely without fences and modern cattle-breeding techniques are either unknown or ignored.

Every square mile of desert that is capable of supporting cattle also supports large numbers of unproductive horses and burros. The latter include an indeterminably large population of wild burros which have, for the most part, disappeared north of the border. Domesticated and partially domesticated horses, mules, and burros which number an estimated 100,000 head in Sonora alone are more numerous today than in years past[39] — this despite their being replaced by cars, trucks, tractors, and other agricultural machinery. These virtually useless animals do incalculable damage to the natural vegetation upon which cattle feed, particularly in those periods of abnormally low rainfall.

---

[37]   *Ibid.,* pp. 117-19.
[38]   Ibáñez and others, p. 39.
[39]   *Sonora en Cifras.*

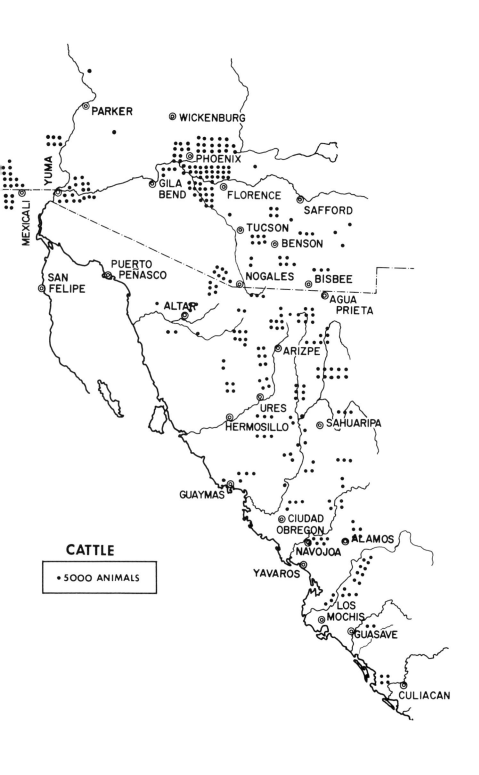

CATTLE

• 5000 ANIMALS

Closely related to this problem is that of overgrazing. Throughout most of the desert there is a complete lack of adjustment in the relationship between the number of cattle and the carrying capacity of the range. This relationship reaches the critical point twice each year during the prolonged dry seasons and again after the summer rains have begun. Overgrazing destroys the *agostadero*[40] before it has reached maturity, depriving the animals of a major source of food during the latter months of the year. There is almost no attempt by the ranchers to control seasonally the number of cattle on the range or in any other way protect the widely scattered agostaderos.[41]

Usually it is the scarcity of water that forces the ranchers to move their thirsty herds on to pastures that should be protected until maturity. Under any circumstances it is hunger and thirst which threaten entire herds, compelling the Mexican cattle rancher to take costly measures insuring no more than temporary survival. In those areas where rainfall measures less than 8 or 10 inches, cattle ranching is seldom more than survival, for the animals and rancher alike. Sources of drinking water are widely separated and unsure throughout the entire desert. The poor rancher is often unable to drill wells, install pumps, and construct tanks where they are most needed. After a long rainless period the pastures near the few remaining waterholes are completely destroyed and the cattle die anyway.

Even more dangerous to the herds is the fact that long rainless periods so diminish green vegetation that starvation is common. When this condition is advanced, no amount of shifting from one district to another will save cattle. "Droughts" of this kind will destroy from 10 to 20 percent of the desert herds.[42] The ranchers seldom are able to purchase feed to save starving herds simply because there is none to be found. The only remedy is to improve pastures through irrigation or seeding and to cultivate alfalfa, sorghums, and other forage crops as well as to manufacture ensilage.[43]

Alfalfa is the leading forage crop in the Mexican half of the desert, although it ranks seventh among all cultivated crops, a position that compares quite unfavorably with the important position occupied by this crop in Arizona.[44] This is despite the fact that growing conditions

---

[40] *Agostadero* is the term used to describe the summer pastures which develop rapidly after the first seasonal rains.

[41] Estado de Sonora, Consejo de Planeación Económica y Social, *Memoria Sesión Plenaria de Abril 20 de 1958* (Hermosillo, 1958) — hereafter cited as *Memoria Sesión de 1958.*

[42] *Sonora en Cifras,* 1961.

[43] *Memoria Sesión de 1958.*

[44] Alfalfa ranks third behind cotton and the combined total of all vegetable crops in Arizona.

are almost ideal. The Fuerte Valley farmer is able to make ten or twelve cuttings annually compared to the six or eight which are common in the irrigated valleys north of the border.[45]

Primitive communications, close proximity to the United States, and economic policies of the Mexican government combine to create an unfavorable cattle market whose depressing characteristics exceed all other factors.

Perhaps the last real cattle drives in North America bring cattle from the region of Sahuaripa and beyond to the railhead at Cananea. These cattle are driven over terrain which trucks travel with great effort or not at all, and those animals that survive the two hundred or more miles are sold as skeleton-like creatures to American buyers who pay a per-pound duty at the border. These emaciated animals are then fattened, and are able quickly to put on weight at low cost.

The existence of such marketing procedures leads to additional problems for the Mexican cattle industry. Only the younger, more healthy specimens are able to survive such treatment and these animals alone command a price in the export market. The domestic market is left with only poor-quality stock. At this point the Mexican government enters the picture by placing extremely low ceiling prices on meat. Probably all the cattle would be exported to the United States, except that the government will either embargo completely or grant export permits only on the condition that the cattlemen sell a fixed quota of their animals in the local market. Naturally they cannot afford to feed them for these low prices and the demand for forage crops is consequently limited. In addition, the poor quality of meat marketed at home is understandably the result of the old and low-grade animals which find their way to slaughter. This vicious economic circle impoverishes the cattlemen, degrades the stock, limits the production of forage crops, and lowers both the quantity and quality of meat consumed locally. Revolutionary policies designed by the government to make meat available at low prices to lower income groups may be effective elsewhere in Mexico but near the border, and in an arid district, the results have been catastrophic.

THE URBAN ECONOMY

The manufacturing industries of Sonora, northern Sinaloa, and the Mexicali district mirror the regional preoccupation with agriculture and the general level of national economic development.

---

[45] Ibáñez and others, pp. 38-40; *Arizona Agriculture, 1961* (University of Arizona Agricultural Experiment Station, Tucson), p. 2.

Mexico still occupies a lower rung on the ladder of industrialization and its national income is yet relatively low. This means that many heavy or highly sophisticated industries have either not developed or are concentrated only in Mexico City or in one or two other nationally important centers. It also means that light industries, particularly those which produce food and other low-cost necessities, assume a disproportionately important role among those industries which have been established in the Sonoran Desert. The rapid development of irrigated agriculture happened to coincide with Mexico's early rapid expansion of light consumer industry. It is thus natural to find an intimate relationship between the primary economic activity of the region — agriculture — and its newly created industries. A 1958 economic census for the state of Sonora showed that 2,237 were engaged in an industry directly associated with local agriculture and ranching, out of a total ascertainable industrial employment of 5,418.[46] This same proportion is to be found in Mexicali and northern Sinaloa. For the state of Sonora the total number of workers in manufacturing industry, whether agriculturally related or not, amounts to less than 3 percent of the state's total labor force.

Throughout the Mexican half of the desert, cotton gins and cottonseed oil mills have been established by private enterprise, and today constitute the largest single industry. Almost every cotton-growing district has its cotton gin, numbering an estimated seventy-five for the region as a whole. Such major centers as Mexicali, Hermosillo, and Ciudad Obregón have several each.[47]

The second-ranking industry, flour milling, is equally well distributed throughout the desert. This industry competes in a national as well as local market. It would probably be larger if it did not suffer through price discrimination in the national market.

The shrimp and meat-packing industry ranks third in the state of Sonora with several hundred workers. In the state of Sinaloa, as well as at Guaymas, Sonora, shrimp canneries employ large numbers of workers. Taken together, meat packing and shrimp canneries constitute the third largest regional industry.

Modern meat packing began when the border was closed to Mexican cattle due to foot and mouth disease.[48] To aid the local cattlemen, the national government constructed five packing plants at Agua Prieta, Cananea, Magdalena, Guaymas, and Hermosillo. When the border was

---

[46]   Actually, this 1958 Census lists 6,941 industrial workers but 1,523 are included under "various" leaving 5,418 categorized workers. *Sonora en Cifras,* 1960.

[47]   Rodríguez Adame, pp. 5-9; *Sonora en Cifras,* 1958.

[48]   Earl B. Shaw, "Mexico's Foot and Mouth Disease Problem," *Economic Geography,* Vol. 25, No. 1 (1949), pp. 1-12.

The port of Guaymas (above) is home to a large shrimp boat fleet (background) and numerous sport fishing boats such as the one at anchor. On the far shore stands one of several shrimp-packing plants. Below, the major power plant at Guaymas is located at tidewater and is supplied by tanker with oil from Támpico via the Panama Canal.

again opened in 1955 these packing plants could no longer operate economically and all were closed except the one at Magdalena.[49] Today these plants, built in the late 1940s and early 1950s, and modern in most respects, stand idle.

Breweries and bottling plants constitute the fourth most important industry, and the first industry among those not directly dependent upon local agricultural resources. The high relative position reflects the importance of such consumer industries in underdeveloped countries. It is also not surprising that these products are popular, considering local climatic conditions.

Foundries, small machine shops, garages, and light engineering occupy fifth place among regional industries. In reality this may be one of the most underdeveloped industrial groups, for it is basically a service industry and has lagged behind the demand placed upon it. While almost all of the desert's communications and industry have been mechanized within the last few years, the region has only in part been able to service this vast and growing network.

Although having little in common, cement manufacturing and ice making are, within the desert, vital auxiliary industries, because the specific type of regional food product is exceedingly dependent on these manufactures. Cement is indispensable to the construction of dams, ditches and other irrigation works, while ice is used in immense quantities to preserve winter vegetables and shrimp. Most medium-size towns, such as Guaymas, Navojoa, and Los Mochis, as well as the larger cities have other light manufacturing industries.

The small-scale manufacture of tile, adobe brick, soap, and lime continues from Colonial times in all towns of any consequence. In addition, each of these communities has workers employed in printing, the baking of bread and tortillas, as well as in the manufacture of numerous small and simple articles such as crude furniture, boxes and other containers.

A few towns have developed larger-scale industries which are not universal. Some are closely tied to local agricultural specialties such as the sugar mill in Los Mochis and the two near Culiacán. The fruit-and-vegetable canning plant at Los Mochis should be included in this category, as well as the plants which manufacture insecticides at Hermosillo, Ciudad Obregón, and Mexicali. Chicken farming, processing, and canning at Guaymas has developed as a local industry which could well have importance for northwest Mexico as a whole. Other industries are

---

[49]   *Arizona Agriculture, 1955,* p. 8.

Hermosillo, the capital of Sonora. Its cathedral and government buildings in the distance are surrounded by nineteenth-century buildings (middle ground). The low adobe buildings are, in turn, surrounded by both wealthy suburbs and the poorest slums.

Navojoa's impressive church dominates this growing Río Mayo community.

Views of four major cities in Sonora and Sinaloa.

The tile sidewalk, church, and modern buildings of Guaymas face the harbor.

Typical of northwestern Mexico's architecture is the new hospital at Guasave.

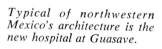

indirectly tied to agriculture — for example, the sorting, handling and packing of food products before they cross into the United States at such border towns as Nogales and Mexicali.

In a class by themselves are the canneries mentioned above at Guaymas, Topolobampo, Puerto Peñasco, San Felipe, and Yavaros. Guaymas alone employs 300 workers in the canneries, and well over one thousand fishermen find at least part-time employment in the port. Several hundred work in ice plants and other related industries. Such places as Puerto Peñasco and San Felipe, Baja California, isolated as they are in the driest western desert, are even more dependent upon the catching and processing of shrimp.

The more than 300 commercial fishing boats which are registered in Sonoran Desert ports provide employment for several hundred more workers engaged in building, fitting, and repairing these small craft. Many other types of boats including dugout canoes are built, mainly in Guaymas.

All of the above industries provide, however, no more than auxiliary services to the basic agriculture, ranching, and fishing which are the pillars of Mexican West Coast economic development. No single regional industry of significance has developed independent of these basic, resource-oriented activities. Unlike the desert north of the border, manufacturing based upon any other local resource has failed to develop.

The more explosive population growth of the last decade is not based on industry but on the immigration of *campesinos* or peons, who come in large numbers from the over-populated rural districts with the hope of finding employment in the cities. Seldom fulfilling this hope, the unemployed congregate on the hillsides and railway property around the edges of Hermosillo, Ciudad Obregón, and other cities. The most depressing slums are found in the largest and most rapidly growing city, Mexicali. Here live thousands of braceros, many hoping for employment in the fields of California, now closed to them. They make their homes in shacks made of packing cases, flattened tin cans, cardboard, ocotillo stems, and tar paper. These structures suffer greatly in comparison with native Indian architecture.

The largest cities are located in or within close proximity to the major irrigated districts. Aside from Hermosillo and Guaymas they owe both their beginnings and their recent growth to local agriculture. The relative size of cities such as Ciudad Obregón, Navojoa, and Los Mochis reflects more than anything else the magnitude of local agricultural production.

Hermosillo grew as a presidio, state capital, and regional market disproportionately large in relation to its contiguous irrigated lands which to this day are no greater in extent than 30,000 acres. Much of

— GEORGE ECKHART

The village of Oquitoa in the Altar Valley could from appearances be an oasis settlement in the Sahara south. A trip of less than one hundred miles from the U. S.-Mexico border brings about an astounding change in the cultural landscape.

An agricultural settlement in the Valle de Guaymas near Empalme, Sonora. Farm workers and their large families live in structures like these below. In the center of the photo is a reed mat (petate) house similar to true aboriginal architecture, undoubtedly built by an Indian or an Indian family. The lessons of native architecture were only partially learned by the builders of the house on the right.

— ORME LEWIS, JR.

Hermosillo's recent growth is attributable, however, to the successful drilling of wells on the coast approximately fifty miles west of the city. This agricultural wealth, in combination with the town's earlier functions, has given Hermosillo within the last fifteen years a wider economic base. In this, Hermosillo has to some extent reversed the normal evolution of agricultural market towns by having a relatively well-developed urban structure before the "first seed was planted."

Guaymas developed as the most important port north of Mazatlán. Despite the "backwater" characteristics of the Gulf and its limited hinterland, Guaymas was for many years the terminus of the Southern Pacific. Even when the railway was completed south to Mazatlán and beyond, Guaymas was the head of effective navigation on the Gulf, due to the inland route followed by the rails north of Guaymas. Despite the construction of the railway to Mexicali through Puerto Peñasco, Guaymas has not forfeited its position, since Puerto Peñasco is incapable of handling all but the very smallest sea-going vessels. Recently the growth of Guaymas has been encouraged by the development of the Valle de Guaymas, an important irrigated district northeast of the railway town of Empalme.[50] Thus, in Guaymas, as in Hermosillo, agriculture came along later to further the growth of a town whose economy was already based on other functions.

Within the major Mexican communities, commercial activities such as retail stores, wholesale houses, and markets comprise the single largest occupational group. Navojoa, for example, functions as a market town for the irrigated delta of the Río Mayo, including among its economic satellites Etchojoa, Huatabampo, and Alamos. However, Navojoa lacks the multitude of more specialized financial institutions to be found in Ciudad Obregón, forty-four miles to the north. Complex financial and administrative functions for the entire southern part of Sonora are centered in Ciudad Obregón. In this respect, Navojoa is itself a satellite of the larger Río Yaqui community. This functional overlap, which is highly exaggerated in more densely populated and humid regions, has developed only with the increased population and wealth of the irrigated coast. The railway, but more importantly the paved highways, have made it possible.

In addition to the urban functions already outlined, each of the

---

[50] Empalme, the Spanish word for junction, is an eastern satellite of Guaymas lying on low ground. It is here rather than at Guaymas itself that the railway from Nogales reaches sea level over slight gradients. A causeway connects Empalme with the docks at Guaymas. It is this short railway from Guaymas to Empalme that makes the latter a junction. Empalme is the site of important railway shops.

Two public market scenes in northwestern Mexico. The one above is typical of the covered markets of the larger towns and cities, while the one below typifies the uncovered and occasional markets of the smaller and isolated villages. As in Central America, West Africa, and other developing areas, women play a disproportionate part in retail commerce.

desert towns south of the international boundary has, to a greater or lesser extent, other industries underlying its recent growth. Construction projects furnish employment for thousands of workers throughout the desert. This industry is centered in the major towns but contributes its services to the nearby zones of "agricultural colonization." The drilling of wells, the building and maintenance of irrigation ditches and farm roads are inconspicuous compared to the more spectacular construction of dams, power plants, and highways.

The contribution made to the desert economy by military and educational institutions is relatively small. Little is spent within the desert on the military; there are no large naval bases, forts or airfields. Hermosillo is the seat of a small university — the University of Sonora — and there are technical schools in Mexicali and Ciudad Obregón.

Tourism is an increasingly important factor in the economy, directly or indirectly providing jobs for several incalculable thousands. The Port of Guaymas is the only town in the region which is in itself an important holiday center. The 260 miles of paved highway between Nogales and this port carry hundreds of American cars, many pulling pleasure boats fixed on trailers. This parade of boats through the desert is a curious spectacle which is evidence of the new active role taken by an affluent and leisure-oriented society in its relationship with the desert. A resident of Phoenix does not consider the 460 miles between his home and Guaymas as being an unduly arduous weekend trip, even while towing a boat.[51]

In Guaymas deep-sea fishing boats are rented for daily excursions Three miles west of the port, Bocachibampo Bay has developed as a seaside resort with a number of fine hotels, while a little to the northwest, even more ambitious development has been taking place at San Carlos Bay. The highway north of the port is lined with motels and trailer parks, giving the entire area the neon-lighted appearance of the entrance to an American city. A great deal of American capital has gone into Guaymas and the visible results are to be seen most clearly along the highway and at Bocachibampo and San Carlos bays.[52] In this respect there is a clearly defined "American Quarter" quite reminiscent of the "French Quarter" of a North African city. The heart of Guaymas remains much as it was at the beginning of the century with its Colonial Spanish style plaza, church, and commercial houses. The waterfront which is relatively free of American tourists, gives the appearance of a Mediterranean seaport.

---

[51] Arizona is the improbable first-ranking state in per-capita boat ownership. These boats are operated almost entirely on man-made reservoirs or in Mexico
[52] "Sunny Sonora, Mexico," *Sunset,* Jan. 1961, p. 52.

Puerto Peñasco, which the Americans call Rocky Point,[53] has an even more isolated American colony at Cholla Bay, five miles west of the port. Here several hundred Americans spend a good part of the year partaking of marine pleasures. The Cholla Bay settlement is an ugly, unplanned and ramshackle line of shacks and trailers about which neither Mexico nor the United States can take any pride whatsoever. Aside from the water, its only possible attraction lies in its proximity to Phoenix through Sonoita over paved highways. Daily these roads carry numbers of cars and boat trailers.

Probably the single most important aspect of Mexico's West Coast tourist industry has nothing to do with local amenities but concerns the long inter-American highway stretching south for hundreds of miles through the desert. This paved highway, since it was opened up in 1953, has carried thousands of American tourists south to Guadalajara and Mexico City. Hotels, restaurants, and service stations line the route and form clusters at the edges of the major cities. It is impossible to assess the importance of this "industry" to the desert economy as a whole. Nevertheless, it is interesting to note that tourism is assuming an important place in the local economy at about the same relative time as it did in the economic development of Arizona.

A very different kind of tourist industry exists in the border towns. It will be discussed in the chapter on political geography.

THE ECONOMY OF EASTERN SONORA

The seemingly "endless series of enormous ridges"[54] which contain the roughly parallel north-south valleys of eastern Sonora, including the Río Sonora and its major tributary the Río San Miguel, the Río Yaqui and its headwater tributaries the Río Moctezuma and the Río Bavispe, enclose the most completely self-contained economy to be found in the Sonoran Desert. Here is the last remnant of Colonial New Spain on the Pacific.

Although the great majority of people who inhabit this eastern region live in villages lining the intermittent streams, it is the rugged desert mountains which give this area its distinctive stamp. The broad plains of the desert to the west are replaced by narrow winding valleys and massive mountains. Communications are maintained over tortuous mountain tracks such as that between Ures and Moctezuma called

---

[53] Puerto Peñasco, Rocky Port, is used interchangeably with Punto Peñasco or Rocky Point. It takes its name from a lava flow which forms part of the coastline enclosing a small inlet that serves as a harbor for commercial fishing boats.

[54] Kroeber, p. 177.

A trip through eastern Sonora is still an endurance test. Primitive roads cross steep ridges only to terminate at bridgeless streams — in this case the Río Bavispe at Guasavas, Sonora. Then once again you traverse more virtually uninhabited upland. Finally one arrives at an oasis with its palm trees. The photo at bottom is of the plaza in the old capital of Ures.

Cattle ranching in eastern Sonora is in many ways the same as it was two hundred years ago. Longhorn cattle and cattle drives hundreds of miles long still exist. The top picture was taken at Moctezuma as cattle driven from Sahuaripa find water in the narrow and shallow Río Moctezuma. Many of these thirsty animals will not survive the drive to market. Caballeros (below) herd Brahma cattle during a roundup. The improvement of stock continues through continuous importation. The wide open desert, however, encourages the degeneration of breeds. Poor pasture and water wreak havoc on imported breeds. A ranch corral between Opodepe and Rayón in the San Miguel Valley is shown in the bottom picture. Native palm is used in the construction.

— CHUCK ABBOTT

— GEORGE ECKHART

[281]

El Camino del Monstruo de Plomo which is as fearsome as its name.[55] Most of the eastern villages were formerly Pima Bajo, Opata, and Jova Indian settlements.[56] As has been mentioned, the seventeenth century witnessed the establishment of Jesuit missions in these villages. During the succeeding centuries, the transformation of Indian to Mexican was so successful that today there is no "official" Indian population in these valleys[57] although the great majority of the people show some Indian racial characteristics.

The riverine village is the social and economic structure basic to this isolated region. Each village is in large measure a self-sufficient productive unit. Each is in every sense of the word an "oasis." At the time of the Spanish *entrada* almost every Indian settlement in these valleys was situated near the river on the partially evacuated basin fill.[58] The fields were planted on the alluvium where water could be diverted from the river with little effort. This nearly uniform pattern of occupance continues to this day, resulting in a similarity of village and economic types that varies only slightly from settlement to settlement and from valley to valley.

The description of Huepac on the Río Sonora could, with only minor alterations, be that of almost any village on these rivers of eastern Sonora:

> The terrace on which Huepac is situated rises abruptly some fifty feet above the flood plain of the Sonora River which here has an altitude of nearly 2,000 feet. Normally the river shifts about on a bed of sand and gravel, about one-fourth mile wide on the average, between low cut banks, but occasionally floods cover most of the flood plain. Floods in summer are frequent; those in winter are less frequent but more severe. On occasion, heavy rains in the headwaters wash away crops, livestock, fences and fertile agricultural land and deposit much sand and gravel on fields once valuable.[59]

The village itself stands for the most part above the highest flood crest.

In Huepac, as well as in almost every other village, the fields are strung out along the intermittent river both above and below the major settlement. The best lands near the village have been worked for many

---

55 The "Road of the Lead Monster," named for a local mine.

56 Sauer, *"The Aboriginal Population of Northwestern Mexico,* and Kroeber, pp. 39-40. This isolated area in eastern Sonora is almost coextensive with the aboriginal domain of the Opata and Jova (except in the middle Yaqui where the Pima Bajo lived). This is set out in Sauer *The Distribution of Aboriginal Tribes,* pp. 50-51 and Map.

57 Sauer, *The Aboriginal Population of Northwestern Mexico,* pp. 26-29.

58 Sauer, *The Distribution of Aboriginal Tribes,* p. 50.

59 Leslie Hewes, "Huepac, An Agricultural Village of Sonora, Mexico," *Economic Geography,* Vol. 11 (1935), p. 284.

Eastern Sonora as it is today. Primitive as distinguished from ancient building techniques are not the rule but are nevertheless common. Medieval milling techniques and plumbing are being replaced but are still prevalent. Washday in eighth-century Morocco or twentieth-century Moctezuma? These scenes are very slowly passing from the western Sierra Madre — but only very slowly.

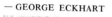

years. In Huepac, Moctezuma, and other places these are known as the *tierras de la misión*.

"An individual owning property along the river may dig an irrigation ditch as he sees fit; but most ditches serve a number of properties and their use is regulated by commissioners."[60] These ditches are seldom more than a mile in length and are carefully constructed and cared for. During the rainless months of autumn and spring, the Río Sonora frequently is dry both above and below Huepac. However, in the immediate vicinity of the village there is always water in the river due to welling up from below. This means that with the construction of primitive brush dams a little water can be led into the ditches at all times of the year "although some of the outer lands may suffer from water scarcity."[61] The irrigable land of Huepac and other villages is limited by the existence of settlements upstream. During the dry seasons these communities may claim most of the water which finds its way to the surface.[62] Only about half of the irrigable land of Huepac can be certain of enough water in a dry year.[63]

Temporales (fields depending upon seasonal rains and unregulated runoff) are found adjoining the irrigated tracts. These fields are located usually at the mouths of arroyos which disgorge from the desert mountains.[64] It is upon the irrigated fields, temporales, and surrounding monte that each individual settlement must depend. The settlements are to this day largely self-sufficient.

The two or three square miles of irrigated land are the core of each settlement's agricultural self-sufficiency.[65] Each farmer seldom has more than ten acres of tillable land, but he is often able to plant two crops each year which effectively doubles his acreage. It is in fact the double cropping of wheat and corn on the same land that provides the margin of economic survival for the village.

During recent years the utter abject poverty which persists throughout much of rural Mexico has not been an important factor in these valleys. Since the Revolution[66] most of the peasant farmers receive

---

[60]   *Ibid.*, p. 288.

[61]   *Ibid.* Conditions almost identical to this were noted in field work in the spring of 1958 and again in the spring of 1961 at Cumpas, Moctezuma, and Arizpe.

[62]   *Ibid.*, pp. 288-89.

[63]   *Ibid.*, p. 291.

[64]   Both *temporal* and a variety of irrigation methods date back to pre-Colonial times in these valleys. Carter, p. 112.

[65]   Mexico, *Censo de Sonora, Tercer Censo Agricola Ganadero y Ejidal*, 1957.

[66]   The nearly twenty years of civil war drained this area as much as any other in Mexico. The economic effects are to be seen in the ruined and abandoned houses and fields. Hewes comments on this in his 1931 article. This condition continued to exist in the summer of 1961.

— E. TAD NICHOLS

Colonial architecture of eastern Sonora. The one-story, flat-roof, adobe house built around a patio, which is typical of this area, can be seen in these photos. In the lower right of the bottom picture is the domed roof of the mission church.

— SOUTHWEST MUSEUM, LOS ANGELES

a good deal more than the "three tortillas in the morning, three tortillas at noon, and three at night" which is the average diet in much of rural Mexico.[67] Malnutrition, however, often does result from protein deficiency. The peon, though he may keep a cow and a few chickens, usually sells the milk and eggs to buy mescal. The primitive lime works which were discussed as a native industry on the Costa also exist in these valleys. They produce lime which, though ostensibly used to soften corn for tortillas, is in fact fulfilling a need for calcium. The intense sunshine of the desert does alleviate, however, any Vitamin D deficiency. Alimentary dwarfism and other extreme results of chronic hunger are uncommon in the valleys of eastern Sonora. The self-sufficient economy of this region is better able than most areas of rural Mexico to feed itself. Dietary deficiencies are more often caused by the inability of the agriculturalist to utilize what he has produced, such as beef cattle and milk, rather than his, or his land's incapacity to produce. The cities of the coast harbor in their slums more victims of malnutrition than the isolated and poverty-stricken valleys. Nevertheless one unavoidable truth is the realization that the international boundary between the American Southwest and Mexico is a frontier of hunger.

In these valleys of eastern Sonora the most important crop is wheat which is usually irrigated, but some is planted with only the hope of receiving above-normal rainfall. Corn, which follows wheat on much of the irrigated land, is planted after the first summer rains and is watered from the rising rivers in July and August. Corn, more often than wheat, is grown on temporal land, the harvest taking place in late autumn in time to permit the planting of wheat in the same field.[68]

Beans are planted at almost any time of the year but most commonly in the late winter. This crop is harvested in time to plant summer corn. "Crops other than wheat, corn and beans rarely, if ever, occupy an entire field, but are found interspersed in small irregular patches among corn and other crops. An attempted self-sufficiency in the holdings has resulted in this patchwork."[69] These small fields of chiles, melons, tobacco, and other interspersed plants are not in any significant respect dissimilar from those of the Yaqui and Mayo Indians of the coastal plain. It has been said that this type of agriculture was being practiced by the Lower Pima and Opata at the time of the first entrada.[70] The

67   Josue de Castro, *The Geography of Hunger* (Boston, 1952), p. 100.
68   Hewes, "Huepac: An Agricultural Village of Sonora, Mexico," *Economic Geography,* Vol. 11, p. 287.
69   *Ibid.,* p. 290.
70   Sauer, in *The Aboriginal Population of Northwestern Mexico,* gives for the aboriginal Opata and Jova tribes a population of 65,000 — an indication of the successful and intensive agriculture practiced by these people.

A magnificent aerial photo of the old capital of Arispe, Sonora. The block-faulted basin-range mountain apparently barren of vegetation, the deeply eroded river terrace, irrigated fields, dry streamway, rectangular pueblo plan, mission church, and patios — as much as any other, this picture tells the whole story.

pattern of local irrigated agriculture is based on the methodical utilization of streamflow in a carefully tended system of canals and ditches. It appears also to be an aboriginal legacy. The earliest inhabitants of these eastern valleys utilized a variety of sophisticated methods to bring water to their fields.[71] Thus it must be assumed that aside from the introduction of wheat, the utilization of land in cultivated agriculture by the contemporary Mexicans in these isolated valleys is little changed from the aboriginal pattern.

The round threshing platforms which are still to be seen in Spain are prominent elements in the cultural landscape of these valleys. To this day beasts are driven upon the circular platform in the age-old fashion of Mediterranean Europe.[72]

Ranching, which has been described in general terms for eastern Sonora, is of course important to each individual village. The desert land of each municipio is divided into a number of large ranchos whose owners may have title to some irrigated land in the valley. There is, however, almost no effort on the part of the cattlemen to raise forage crops in these fields for their often starving herds. Near the villages, cattle, horses, and burros forage in the dry river beds and along the fence rows. These belong to small ejidatarios and other farmers. The great majority of farmers keep cattle and other livestock whose products supplement subsistence farming.

Roads penetrate the region only with great difficulty. No satisfactory route exists across the Sierra to Chihuahua, although there are plans to remedy this. The roads which wind their way over the massive desert mountains to the coast carry few vehicles. No railways penetrate the headwater valleys of the Sonora and Yaqui rivers aside from the one which reaches the railhead at Nacozari. There is no important airfield in the entire region. Under these conditions it is understandable how the economy has remained relatively static from Colonial times.[73] Manufacturing, except for the crude fabrication of domestic artifacts, does not exist. Mining, which in the past was instrumental in the "Mexicanization" of the region, is carried on solely on a small scale. Deposits of tungsten, gold, silver, copper, lead, zinc, molybdenum and other minerals might well be economically exploited if communications were improved.

---

[71] A. F. Bandelier, *Final Report of Investigations Among the Indians of the Southwestern United States Carried on Mainly in the Years from 1880 to 1895.* (Papers of the Archaeological Institute of America, American Series No. 4, Cambridge, Mass., 1892), p. 410.

[72] One farmer was seen threshing wheat by driving a tractor over the platform, effecting a remarkable compromise between "modern" and ancient.

[73] Whetten, p. 8.

CHAPTER TWELVE

The American Economy

The American sector of the Sonoran Desert has a much higher level of economic development than the region to the south of the international boundary. The contrast between the two halves, though it may be startling, represents a relative condition. It is a popular illusion to assume an absolutely "modern" economy in the United States and a permanently "backward" economy in Mexico. The foregoing description of conditions in Mexico demonstrates that aside from the isolated valleys of eastern Sonora, there is little in Mexico's Northwest which could be described as static. What does exist is a relatively higher level of development in the deserts of Arizona and California, based upon an earlier start and perhaps a slightly faster average rate of economic growth within this century.

The "ancestral poverty" of Indian Mexico has weighed heavily against the rapid emergence of any Mexican region. In contrast, the arid American Southwest "had no past to bury."[1] Its first Anglo-American settlements coincided with a dynamic expansion of the national economy, and its first settlers represented a relatively homogeneous phalanx of youthful and technologically oriented people with a Northern European background. The sparse indigenous population presented no lasting barrier to progress.

The American desert contains an economy which is in many ways unique but certainly not isolated or self-contained. It is no more than part of the highly integrated American national economy. However,

---

[1] "Arizona Hitches its Future to Ideas and Industry," *Business Week*, June 23, 1956, pp. 114-28, and "Hungry Workers, Ripe Crops and the Nonexistent Mexican Border," *The Reporter*, April 13, 1954, p. 28.

The two largest cities of the desert, Phoenix and Tucson — photographed from the air — fill wide basins from mountain range to mountain range. The amount of space devoted to parking in both cities is apparent. The top left picture depicts the binodal core of Phoenix looking north up Central Avenue; that at bottom left shows a mixed office, apartment, and hotel complex which constitutes the north node of Phoenix. Below, central Tucson looking south-west. The main residential and business expansion has been to the east — due in part to the small mountains seen in the central background — and Tucson's population center is now several miles east of the central business district.

it is differentiated through climate from neighboring regions, and because of this the Sonoran Desert is able to contribute in a unique manner to a highly specialized continental economy. In other respects the recent evolution of the American desert economy has mirrored what has taken place elsewhere in the United States. Probably the most important of these, as they affect the desert, have been the increased affluence of the American people, their greater mobility, an increased role played by the federal government, and a number of technological breakthroughs. Among the latter there must be included universal low-cost air conditioning which has ameliorated the region's single greatest climatic disadvantage — high summer temperatures. This has resulted in a greater number of people willing to work in the desert and a consequent increase in the industrial establishments willing to locate plants and other facilities in the region.[2]

Because of these events in the desert to the north of the border, climatic amenities and other intangibles have replaced mining, irrigated farming, and the extensive use of desert vegetation for livestock grazing as the region's most important resources. These earlier economic activities, based upon tangible resources, have however, continued to expand, often undergoing revolutionary changes.

AGRICULTURE

Except for the growth of the livestock-feeding industry, agriculture in Sonoran Desert areas has failed since the middle 1950's to produce any significant increase in production and income. Water shortages, cotton acreage controls, and urban encroachment have each contributed to a leveling off in crop income. Rapid progress in desert agriculture during the period between the Second World War and the Korean conflict gave Arizona the greatest rate of gain in agriculture income among the fifty states of the Union.[3] This increase, which included income from livestock as well as field crops, took place in the southern and southwestern deserts — not in the central or northern parts of the state.

Irrigated agriculture in the southern desert and semiarid counties

2 "Why the Big Boom in the Desert States," *U. S. News and World Report,* October 11, 1957, p. 76.

3 In the period 1946-54 crop income in Arizona increased from an annual $163,200,000 to $269,600,000, or 65% increase. By 1964 this income had increased only slightly to $282,600,000, or only 5% more. This leveling off reflects what has transpired in the desert areas of both Arizona and southeastern California. *Arizona Statistical Review,* various years.

of Maricopa, Pinal, Yuma, Cochise, Pima, and Graham accounts for more than 90 percent of Arizona's total field-crop acreage.[4] Natural conditions, as well as agricultural methods, resemble in broad outline those found in the major irrigated zones south of the border. Large, highly mechanized farms which are similar to those of the Costa are character- istic not only of southern Arizona but of the Imperial and Coachella valleys of California as well. Throughout the desert, intense heat and long growing seasons mean that the same crops are cultivated and that double cropping may be practiced. Insects, frost, and flood provide the principal hazards to irrigated farming as they do south of the border. The cost of overcoming these hazards is the largest expense aside from irrigation itself. Fertilizers are used in even larger quantities than in Mexico's Northwest. Some crops such as winter vegetables are labor intensive, and Mexican nationals and Mexican-Americans have tradi- tionally provided the largest source of field workers. Thus, even the ethnic background of the agricultural labor is the same.[5]

Much of this is — at the time of writing — in a state of flux: cotton picking machinery, which now accounts for 92 percent of the harvest, has eliminated the need for large numbers of seasonal workers.[6] In 1962, for example, for the first time there were no contract Mexican nationals employed in the Arizona cotton harvest. Only 7,700 seasonal workers of all backgrounds were hired in 1962, whereas 13,600 were employed the year before.[7] The great monthly variation in labor demand with its autumnal peak is a thing of the past. Regular hired workers are a larger percentage each year of total agricultural employment.

The number of braceros employed in desert agriculture has declined precipitously. Federal legislation enacted in 1963 had by 1965 terminated completely the importation of Mexican labor on temporary work per- mits. The consequences have been felt mainly in the Imperial, Coachella, and Yuma valleys where the reliance upon braceros was the greatest.

Everything considered, the greatest contrast between agriculture in the Mexican and American sectors of the Sonoran Desert is not to be found in the utilization of labor, agricultural methods, crops planted, or rate of growth in acreage. It is, instead, in the smaller relative impor-

---

[4] *Ibid.*, 1961 edition, p. 2. One economist commented that "Arizona has 73 million acres. From the standpoint of economics you could throw away 70 million of them," *Business Week*, June 23, 1956, p. 117.

[5] "Tossed Salad," *Newsweek*, Feb. 20, 1961, p. 26. "Violence in the Oasis," *Time*, Feb. 17, 1961, p. 18.

[6] Arizona Employment Security Commission, *Farm Labor Report, 1963*, p. iv.

[7] *Ibid.*, pp. 18-19.

tance of agriculture in the overall economic structure of the American desert. Neither cotton nor any other crop is king any longer in the desert north of the border.

*   *   *

When irrigated, the desert soils of southern Arizona and California provide almost ideal conditions for the cultivation of cotton. As in Mexico, cotton is the major crop grown on the irrigated lands and provides the greatest source of income throughout the region. Cotton is the economic yardstick by which other crops are judged. There is usually a greater potential return from this crop and it would perhaps be even more widely grown were it not for federal controls on cotton acreage.[8]

When the first Spaniards entered what is now Arizona, they found the Pima Indians growing cotton in the Gila Valley.[9] In 1912 cotton was reintroduced to the Salt River Valley. This was two years after the first sizeable cotton acreage was planted in the Imperial Valley. There the crop was an immediate success and 28,000 acres were planted in 1913.

The expanding automobile tire industry precipitated a demand for long-staple cotton which could be grown more successfully in the Sonoran Desert than anywhere in the traditional Cotton Belt. In 1916 a major tire and rubber company acquired several thousand acres of potential cotton land in the Salt River Project several miles west of Phoenix.[10] For a few years, only American-Egyptian cotton was grown. The war-born demand immediately brought on a cotton boom. Within two years every possible acre which could be diverted from something else was planted to cotton. Among other things most of the Salt River Valley's 60,000 dairy cows were sold and the pastures and fields of hay were converted to cotton growing. Dairying has never regained its former relative status.

By 1920 the Pima variety of long-staple cotton was planted on 180,000 acres in Arizona alone. However, the end of the war saw the narrowing of the price differential between Pima and short-staple varieties. Many farmers turned to the upland short staples which would produce more heavily. With expanding irrigation cultivation of cotton was extended to the Casa Grande Valley (Pinal County) which in time replaced the Salt River Valley as the chief Arizona cotton-producing

---

8 The federal government, through price supports and acreage allotments, completely controls the amount of cotton produced in Arizona and California.

9 Castetter and Bell, *Pima and Papago Indian Agriculture,* p. 57.

10 Paul Litchfield, chief executive of the Goodyear Tire and Rubber, in 1916 planted several thousand acres of cotton near what was to become Litchfield Park.

In the desert, cotton-picking machinery harvests over 90 percent of the crop north of the border. In Mexico, hand-picking prevails. This is not due to any supposed backwardness but is the result of purely economic factors. Labor costs and climatic conditions combine in Mexico to preserve manual labor in cotton fields though adequate capital exists to mechanize the entire picking process in a one- or two-year period.

district. At the same time cotton came to be the most important single crop in the Imperial and Coachella valleys. Its cultivation was extended into the smaller irrigated districts throughout the desert, such as the Santa Cruz Valley (Pima County) where it today dominates cultivated agriculture as it does nowhere else in the desert with the exception perhaps of the Casa Grande Valley. Cotton is one of a number of important crops in the Yuma district but suffers through competition with alfalfa, feed grains, winter vegetables, and citrus fruit. Yuma's irrigated agriculture depends less upon cotton than any other American desert region.[11]

The production of cotton in the Sonoran Desert of southern Arizona and California has varied with economic conditions, having its greatest periods of expansion during the war years. The greatest acreage ever cultivated was in the year 1953 as a result of Korean War demand.

All the while an independent trend has set in which has resulted in the exchange of basic crops between the South and Southwest. The livestock industry of the Southwest, based upon extensive rangelands, has gradually lost ground to the South where smaller stock farms with better pastures are proving to be very efficient. On the other hand, cotton growing is moving from the South to the Southwest. Texas, California, New Mexico, and Arizona each year produce more than one-half of the nation's cotton. Much of this is due to government policies, particularly acreage allotments and support prices, but the underlying element is the almost ideal climatic conditions which prevail in the irrigated fields of the arid West. Throughout the decade of the 1950's, Arizona produced more cotton per acre than any other producing state. In 1954 when the national average yield per acre was 341 pounds, Arizona's average was 1,039 pounds per acre. This production record was achieved entirely within the Sonoran Desert and on its semiarid margins. During this period California ranked second with the Imperial, Coachella and Palo Verde valleys contributing to the high average yields. At the time of writing these yields are threatened by the pink bollworm but measures are under way which should curb this threat.

Not only are yields high but they are increasing. The end of the Korean War brought over-production and acreage controls. This has continued to the present time. The production of cotton in Arizona has fallen by nearly 100,000 acres since 1960. The Imperial Valley has been limited to as little as 40,000 acres in recent years.[12] This forced growers

---

11   *Arizona Agriculture, 1960*, p. 10.

12   This 40,000 acres, however, produced 88,000 bales, the largest yield per acre in the Valley's history to that time. This compares with the 21,000 bales raised in 1921 on about the same acreage, or an increase from 250 pounds of lint cotton to over 1,000 pounds in that period.

to use their best land for cotton in order to get maximum returns from their shrinking fields. The general use of insecticides and fertilizers, plus better farm practices and the elimination of water shortages, which were common before the All-American Canal was built, all contributed to this improved yield, which is higher than that of Mexico. As in Mexico, the production of cotton contributes disproportionately to the regional economy by necessitating the establishment of cotton gins and other ancillary agencies.

The cultivation of vegetables on the irrigated lands of the Sonoran Desert is the second-ranking agricultural industry. Although vegetables occupy less acreage than feed grains and alfalfa they produce more income for the desert farmers. Approximately 150,000 acres of irrigated land are planted to vegetable crops each year in the valleys of southern Arizona and southeastern California. Aside from irrigation itself, the large-scale cultivation of vegetables in the Southwest has been made possible by one of the most intricately organized and coordinated transportation systems which specializes in providing rapid movement of perishables to the centers of consumption in California, the Middle West, and East. Both major railways and a large number of trucking companies have refrigerated cars and trailers which are capable of hauling the entire desert crop with a minimum of difficulty through the blazing heat to eastern markets. This same system handles in addition more than 10,000 carloads of perishables from Mexico.

As tomatoes dominate the vegetable crop in Mexico, so lettuce accounts for more than half the American desert vegetable industry. The growing of lettuce is markedly concentrated in a few districts. This concentration is the result of climatic factors which combine with marketing condiitons and other economic elements to necessitate the selection of a few specialized areas for the production of lettuce. Since there is in reality only one American market — the entire nation — each prospective grower must try to produce a lettuce crop at an advantageous time of the year. As an example, the recently developed higher elevation lettuce-growing district at Willcox, Arizona, was the result of a decision made in 1957 by a consortium of Salinas, California, growers and a Chicago packer to develop a lettuce-growing district that would market a crop late in May and June after the lower-elevation crops which are largely picked during the first three months of the year. This would take advantage of a better price during this period. These men also desired a district which could produce a second crop on the same land to be marketed in September and October. A one-year test at Kansas Settlement near Willcox Playa, at an elevation of 4,000 feet, demonstrated that this area had both the requisite climate and underground water for the establishment of a major lettuce-growing district.

The next year wells were drilled, 7,000 acres of land cleared, lettuce planted, a million-dollar refrigerated processing plant erected, a labor camp accommodating 1,400 workers constructed, and several miles of railway track laid. In one year Willcox became a major desert lettuce-growing district.

The Imperial Valley has from the beginning led all other desert lettuce-producing areas. For the ninety-day period from mid-December to mid-March, this below-sea-level region markets 80 percent of the United States lettuce crop harvested during these months. A second crop may be grown in the autumn of the year, but the land is generally put to other uses.

The Salt River Valley, at an elevation of 1,000 feet, is a leading area of specialized lettuce growing in Arizona with an estimated 21,000 acres planted to this crop in 1965-66. Some 11,000 acres were harvested in the spring, and approximately the same in the autumn. The Yuma lettuce, grown at about 100 feet elevation, is harvested at the same time as the Imperial Valley crop. An estimated 20,000 acres were picked in the winter of 1965-66. Aguila, west of Phoenix at 2,300 feet, has two harvesting seasons, early spring and autumn. This region in 1965 produced 2,000 acres of lettuce evenly divided between these seasons. Other lettuce-growing districts are in the Santa Cruz (Red Rock), Coachella, and Palo Verde valleys.

New lettuce varieties and other improved techniques have increased yields 150 percent since the 1920's when the crop was threatened by blight. Technological changes in the industry, such as the adoption of vacuum cooling for the quick preservation of fresh lettuce, have made it possible for the cultivation of lettuce to become more specialized and localized.

Cantaloupes and watermelons are grown side by side with lettuce in the major vegetable-growing zones, providing the second most important vegetable and "truck" crop. Cantaloupe production is not increasing, due primarily to the decreasing acreage devoted to this crop in the Imperial Valley. Yuma is now the leading cantaloupe-producing area in the Southwest. The Yuma-Imperial area climate, with its high light and heat intensity, is favorable for the production of quality melons. Theba, Arizona, and the Coachella, Palo Verde, and Salt River valleys are also melon-growing areas, but they have declined in importance.

Carrots, a crop of smaller significance, are concentrated in the Imperial, Coachella, and Salt River valleys. The harvest takes place in the low-elevation Imperial and Coachella districts from November until April with most of the shipments being made in January. The Phoenix

Onions, cabbage, and lettuce under cultivation in the Salt River Valley. These seasonal and labor-intensive vegetable crops underpin Arizona's agricultural economy. Despite increasing mechanization, low-paid labor is seemingly as indispensable north of the border as it is to the south.

district follows with shipments in May and early June. The "field-factory" is the predominant agricultural method used in the harvesting of carrots as well as other vegetable crops.

In recent years potatoes have become the third most remunerative vegetable crop in Arizona; they are of major importance to agriculture in the Phoenix region. Whereas most other vegetable crops have declined or shown no increase in value, potatoes are a noteworthy exception. They have even greater significance in the Coachella Valley where they support an expanding California market.

Only in the Imperial Valley are tomatoes of any importance. This is one of the significant contrasts between the Mexican and American halves of the Sonoran Desert. It has been demonstrated that tomatoes grown as a winter vegetable suffer increasingly pernicious frost damage north of the Fuerte Valley, so that production is limited to the coast south of the Yaqui. The Imperial Valley, despite its "almost frostfree" climate, does not allow competition with coastal Sinaloa in the production of winter tomatoes.

The foregoing account of Sonoran Desert vegetable production is far from complete. Thirty different kinds of fresh vegetables are grown commercially and shipped to northern markets. Onions and celery have occupied greater acreages in the recent past. Sweet corn is important as are garlic and asparagus. Cabbage and radishes fill hundreds of cars shipped to the East.

The relatively frostfree climate of the low-elevation deserts has encouraged the planting of citrus fruit and other frost-sensitive tree crops. Navel oranges are grown in the higher elevations of the Salt River Valley, and are harvested during November and December for shipment throughout the United States. The increased planting of Valencia oranges is attributable to a favorable market for the fresh fruit during later months into the spring. Improved methods of protecting Valencia oranges from low temperatures have encouraged expanded plantings in the Salt River Valley and on the Yuma Mesa. This latter area is particularly favored. Good air drainage from this sandy terrace into the valley below gives natural protection against frost. This is supplemented in the best-managed groves through the effective use of wind machines and smudge pots which encourage the circulation of air. The Arizona Valencia oranges are harvested and marketed during March, April, and May before the California crop is available in the markets.

Commercial lemon groves have expanded very rapidly on the relatively warm Yuma Mesa which produces high yields. Grapefruit is also grown in all the major citrus zones, but is concentrated in the Salt River

Tree crops, citrus and dates have been of particular importance to the desert areas of southern Arizona and California. The Sonoran Desert provides a limited and complementary sub-tropical agricultural region for the world's largest mid-latitude market.

Valley. The existing acreages of grapefruit are supplying good-quality fruit from October to June with the great majority of the crop being harvested in the spring months when quality is best.

During recent years a significant shift has taken place in the cultivation of citrus fruit in Arizona. The early dominance of the Salt River Valley has been challenged by the Yuma district. By 1958, some 42 percent of Arizona's citrus acreage was located near Yuma. In 1964-65, for the first time, Yuma surpassed Maricopa County in the production of oranges, lemons, and grapefruit, with approximately 50 percent of Arizona's total. Urban encroachment upon mature groves in the Phoenix area has contributed to the relative decline. At the same time, federal laws have created an opportunity for tax shelter in new plantings. Most of these have taken place in the Yuma Mesa district. As in the case of cotton allotments, federal law has resulted in a changed pattern of land utilization. All together, the American sector of the Sonoran Desert, including the Coachella Valley, has within it something slightly under fifty square miles of citrus groves — more than twenty times that of the Mexican desert to the south, a fact certainly attributable to political and economic reasons rather than geography.

Table grapes have been planted on irrigated land in the Yuma and Salt River areas. Dates have been grown in the Imperial, Coachella, Yuma, and Salt River valleys since the turn of the century. The low atmospheric moisture in the Imperial-Coachella valleys and the Yuma district has been an asset for the development of this truly desert crop.

As mentioned above, the production and distribution of crops have, within recent years, been affected by urban sprawl. Thousands of acres formerly devoted to the production of citrus fruit and other tree crops, as well as vegetables, have been turned over to real estate developers. The growth of Phoenix has been particularly devastating to the fields and groves which surround this oasis community. The decades following the completion of Roosevelt Dam witnessed the expansion of citrus groves in the immediate vicinity of Phoenix. Many of these trees were torn up to make room for tract housing only a very few years after they came into production. This process continues at an even faster rate today but many of the individual trees are saved, since their shade and fruit provide an inducement to the buyer of the subdivided property.

Another desert crop requiring both large numbers of field workers and a heavy investment in machinery and plant is sugar beets. They have been grown largely in the Imperial Valley of California where they rank behind cotton and lettuce as the most important crop. The beet harvest in April follows the lettuce harvest and precedes the heavy work in the melon and cotton fields. Beet thinning during the early winter months comes before the lettuce harvest, thus allowing a better year-round utilization of labor.

Arizona, however, will soon also produce sugar beets, since in 1963 the Department of Agriculture authorized a 20,000-acre allotment of sugar beets for Arizona. A beet-sugar factory has been built south of Chandler, and contracts have been signed with farmers to plant sugar beets for harvest in 1967. As in the Imperial Valley, farmers who are located within a reasonable hauling distance of the sugar factory – such as south and east of Mesa-Tempe – may find the production of sugar beets somewhat more profitable than barley, sorghum, or alfalfa, although much less valuable than cotton. But the acreage of the more profitable crops – cotton and sugar beets – is limited by government controls. Both crops would occupy a greater percentage of Arizona if these restrictions were dropped. Thus, the Sonoran Desert produces under irrigation both cane and beet sugar, in two widely separated and specialized districts.

Seed crops also occupy a place of importance in the agricultural economy of the desert. Alfalfa seed is grown in the Imperial, Yuma, and Salt River valleys.[13] Arizona is the nation's largest producer of sugar beet seed, almost all of Arizona beet seed being produced in Maricopa County.[14] The Yuma district has for many years produced practically the entire United States crop of Bermuda grass seed. During recent years approximately 3,000 acres of small grains and 8,000 acres of sorghum seeds were produced in the irrigated zones of southern Arizona.[15]

Unlike northwestern Mexico, wheat has until recently never been an important crop in the irrigated fields of the American Southwest. Before 1950 wheat in Arizona was seldom planted on more than a very few thousand acres. But in 1965 this crop occupied 26,000 acres.[16]

The rapid growth of Phoenix, Tucson, and other cities in the Southwest, including those of coastal Southern California, has encouraged the amazing development of an urban horticultural industry in Arizona. This considerable enterprise is today of greater economic importance to the state than lettuce or any other single agricultural product aside from cotton and livestock. Urban horticulture concentrates on the breeding and raising of grass for lawns, cacti, palm trees, citrus trees as evergreens, both evergreen and deciduous shade trees, and shrubs with both tropical

---

13 *Arizona Agriculture, 1960,* p. 15.
14 *Arizona Agriculture, 1957,* p. 16.
15 *Ibid.*
16 *Arizona Agriculture, 1966,* back cover.

and mid-latitude origins. Native and exotic plants propagated in local nurseries are to be found everywhere throughout the built-up areas of desert. Tree planting has, since the early days of the American West, been nothing less than a patriotic duty. This fervor is exaggerated in the Sonoran Desert, which has seen both the early destruction of native trees along the stream courses and the subsequent introduction of shade trees in the towns. Lawns are maintained only with great difficulty although new varieties of Bermuda grass developed in the desert are able to withstand the desiccating heat. The nursery industries are concentrated in the environs of the larger towns.

The livestock industry of the American sector of the Sonoran Desert is in some respects similar to that found south of the border. However, in several extremely significant particulars it departs from the Mexican pattern. Cattle predominate over all other domesticated animals in the desert north of the international boundary as they do to the south. The utilization of desert land does not differ except that a greater number of wells and more barbed wire allow better distribution and control of cattle on the range.

The 1959 agricultural census enumerates approximately the same number of cattle in the desert north of the border as coeval to the south. But in the north the breeds are generally better and the management of both animals and range is better than that practiced by the Mexican cattlemen. However, as in Mexico, beef cattle in southern Arizona and southeastern California rank second only to cotton in the economic structure of agriculture.

The northern half of the Sonoran Desert has a greater proportion of its total area receiving less than 5 inches of rainfall. As is the case in Mexico, these extremely arid reaches are unable to support a permanent cattle population. Cattlemen are able, however, to move their stock into some of this desert after the seasonal rains. In Arizona, it is more often in the late winter and spring, whereas in Mexico it is commonly after the summer rains which are usually more intense south of the border. The sparse vegetation and waterless expanse of the Lower Colorado Valley Desert which supports the least number of cattle in the state of Sonora contains the fewest range cattle in the American Desert. Imperial, Yuma, western Pima, Maricopa, southern Mohave, and eastern Riverside counties have only small areas which are able to support any cattle on a permanent basis. Here more than one hundred acres are needed in any season to provide forage for one cow.

The most significant departure from desert land utilization as practiced in Mexico is the development of cattle-feeding operations in

A private dwelling in Phoenix, a golf course at the foot of famous Camelback Mountain, and a canal bringing water to both illustrate an important part of the human ecology of the American desert. Housing and tourism depend upon water. Water is the product of money generated in large measure by jobs, many of which are based upon construction and tourism.

— PHOENIX CHAMBER OF COMMERCE PHOTOS

the zones of irrigated agriculture.[17] The number of cattle in Arizona — slightly less than one million — has not changed materially since the turn of the century, although the number of range cattle has decreased and the number of other cattle such as feeders in commercial feed lots has increased. In almost every year since World War II there have been more cattle marketed out of desert feed lots than there were in the previous year. In 1965, 639,000 cattle were sold from feed lots in Arizona.[18]

The feed lots are concentrated in the Salt River, Casa Grande, Yuma, and Imperial valleys. The growth of this specialized form of agriculture is closely associated with the higher productivity of the irrigated districts and the increased population and affluence of the Southwest and California. Governmental restrictions on cotton acreage have resulted in the search for an alternative to the planting of this highly remunerative crop. The cultivation of hay and feed grains in conjunction with cattle feeding has in large part provided an answer to this problem.

The largest feed lots are operated independently of farming but in some proximity to the fields which produce forage. Feeder cattle find their way to Arizona and the Imperial Valley from much of the South and West as well as Mexico.[19] An average of about 80 percent of Arizona's cattle is marketed in California, particularly in the Los Angeles area.[20] Despite the great distances involved, the desert cattle industry is inextricably tied to climatic and economic conditions in the High Plains states and the Midwest.[21] It is also linked to the value of feed grains, freight rates, the cost of water, and the controls on cotton acreage. More than anything else, it is subject to the vicissitudes of the cattle market and economic conditions in general. Thus, the Arizona desert cattleman is far removed from the isolated ranchero of Sonora for whom cattle are a way of life from which there seems to be no alternative.

Hay — chiefly alfalfa — and feed grains are grown mainly in areas where gravity water is available and where pump lifts are less than 250 feet, since low water costs are essential to the farmer who cultivates forage crops.[22] Alfalfa has for a century been the principal forage crop in the irrigated fields of Arizona, but it more than any other crop suffers

---

17   *Ten Rivers*, II, pp. 434-35.
18   *Arizona Agriculture, 1966*, p. 21. This figure is for the entire state but the great majority of the feed lots are in the desert south of the state.
19   *Arizona Agriculture, 1961*, p. 17.
20   *Ibid.*, pp. 8-9.
21   *Arizona Agriculture, 1959*, pp. 16-17.
22   *Arizona Agriculture, 1956*, pp. 12-13.

Cattle continue to provide an essential pillar of support to the desert economy. In the Arizona and California sectors of the desert, extensive use of the dry range is being replaced in importance by cattle feeding in large lots. The latter is concentrated in the Salt, Casa Grande, Gila, and Imperial valleys.

from water shortages. When water is in short supply, the farmer will give his cotton fields priority, and the hay crops will receive only what is left over.[23] In this way, an alfalfa field which may have a potential of eight cuttings annually is limited to four or less. The production of alfalfa throughout the region has fallen from about 280,000 acres in 1959 to approximately 220,000 acres at the time of writing.[24] The value of alfalfa is difficult to ascertain because such a high percentage of the total crop is fed on the farm and because it is impossible to assess its soil-enriching features in ordinary economic terms.

Production of feed grains in southern Arizona and the Imperial Valley is related both to the cattle-feeding industry and to government cotton acreage allotments. Since the advent of these latter restrictions (1954), barley and grain sorghum production in Arizona has increased more than 200 percent.[25] For the first time in the history of Anglo-American agriculture, corn has become an important crop. Like alfalfa, much of these grains are used on the farm for feed.

Climatic conditions and a controlled supply of water in the Sonoran Desert result in the highest barley yields in the United States. Early autumn plantings are frequently used as winter pasture for sheep and cattle. Barley may be grazed once or twice and still be harvested as grain.

Sorghum planted in early summer produces the highest yields in the United States despite the extreme heat. This means that sorghum can be, and is, grown with barley in a program of double cropping. Maricopa, Imperial, and Pinal counties lead all other areas in the production of these feed grains.

Unlike Mexico, and despite setbacks, dairy farming is an important agricultural enterprise in the American part of the desert. It is concentrated in the irrigated valleys, particularly the Salt River. Intense summer heat has a depressing effect on milk production and breeding efficiency, but the irrigated districts are the only areas in which the same location provides sufficient feed and a ready market for milk. Despite handicaps, dairying has made an impressive comeback in Arizona and is surpassed by only three states in average annual milk production per cow.

High temperatures eliminate the need for costly housing and other precautions which are an integral part of dairying elsewhere in the United States. Dairy cows are maintained in the open except for the

---

[23]   *Ibid.,* 1957, p. 13.
[24]   U. S. Department of Agriculture, *Census of Agriculture, 1959,* Vol. 1, Part 43, Table 1b.
[25]   *Arizona Agriculture, 1966,* back cover.

construction of sunshades. Alfalfa provides the basic diet for dairy cattle although a variety of other feeds are consumed by desert herds. Cottonseed meal is fed to cattle, providing another integrating factor within the highly organized oasis economy. Corn, grain sorghum, sudan grass, and other roughage supplement these feeds.

Aside from Maricopa County, dairy cattle are concentrated in the Imperial and Coachella valleys of California, and the Casa Grande, Santa Cruz, San Pedro, Verde, and other valleys of Arizona. The dairy herds of Imperial and Riverside counties in California provide for the Los Angeles and San Diego milksheds.

From the foregoing account of agriculture in the Sonoran Desert of the southwestern United States a number of conclusions may be drawn: (1) Productivity — per unit area — of irrigated land is extremely high even for such unlikely desert enterprises as dairying; (2) the overall growth of agriculture does not have the spectacular characteristics of the adolescent expansion to be seen south of the border; (3) an improvement in the rate of growth cannot be expected in the near future because of the critical limitation of water and the expansion of built-up areas into the irrigated countryside; (4) the organization of agriculture both within each irrigated zone and between the entire desert and the rest of the country is complex, mechanized, and highly integrated.

MANUFACTURING

Although the industrial strength of the United States is still concentrated mainly in the region to the east of the Great Plains, during recent years there has been an accelerated movement westward to the Pacific of both population and industry. The greatest growth on the Pacific has been in Southern California. Arizona has been a "bridge state" in this rapid development. A parallel might be drawn between the Sonoran Desert's position and that of the deserts of Central Asia in Russia's expansion to the Pacific. Similarities, such as the early importance of military posts, agriculture, and mining in the development of the "bridge" are all striking. Understandably perhaps, other economic activities were slow to materialize. Nevertheless, military bases, agriculture, and mining demanded the establishment of ancillary service industries. At first these were mainly within the retail and wholesale trade categories but included construction as well as small engineering and mechanical industries, and the like.

Meanwhile, the desert climate was gaining a reputation for being beneficial to persons suffering from respiratory and arthritic ailments. Tucson and Phoenix in particular attracted thousands of ailing people from the East, many of whom were highly skilled but sometimes convalescent workers, technicians, and managers. There also came into existence an amenity and climatically oriented potential labor pool.[26] This latent labor force was available and was made use of, particularly during the rapid expansion of industry which began with the Second World War. This expansion attracted industry not dependent on mining, cotton, cattle, or any other local primary or raw material. It was the desert climate, more than any intangible factor, which encouraged the government to have established in the Sonoran Desert of Arizona a large number of air bases and associated aircraft industries. The mutually essential resources were the clear skies and low humidity, upon which no definite economic value had previously been placed.[27]

Closely related to this was the more direct effect of climate upon what was to develop into Arizona's third major industry — tourism. The same "winterless" climate was a most significant element in the evolution of Phoenix, Tucson, Palm Springs, Wickenburg, and other places into winter resorts. The permanent population also increased.[28]

The "bridge" had finally become a goal in itself. Such seemingly unrelated elements as irrigated agriculture, copper mining, the military, convalescents, and tourism established the economic and population base upon which manufacturing and other more complex activities could be built. The result was startling; nonagricultural employment in Arizona, the overwhelming proportion of which is in the southern desert, has risen during the years since 1945 faster than any other state in the Union with the possible exception of Nevada. Manufacturing has risen even more rapidly than nonagricultural employment as a whole, running counter to the national trend.

In the more than two decades since America's entry into World War II, manufacturing has emerged as the single largest source of income to the inhabitants of the Arizona desert.[29] This is not to infer that the region should be included as a part of a new "Manufacturing Belt." Any estimate of employment in manufacturing for the entire Sonoran Desert north of the border would at present still amount to no more than 70,000 workers. Arizona still ranks near the bottom of the list of states in manufacturing employment. While the United States as a whole in 1966 employed approximately 30 percent of its total nonagricultural

26   *Arizona Highways,* April, 1957.
27   *Business Week,* June 23, 1956, p. 118.
28   Edward L. Ullman, "Amenities as a Factor of Regional Growth," *Geographical Review,* Vol. 445 (1954), pp. 119-32.
29   *Arizona Statistical Review, 1961,* p. 2.

Factories constitute some of the best modern architecture in the Phoenix area. An electronics plant representative of some twenty others lies below the "shoulder and head" of Camelback Mountain. This plant is within the irrigated acreage of the Salt River Project and represents one of the major replacements of irrigated agriculture.

— ARIZONA PHOTOGRAPHIC ASSOCIATES, INC.

A plant producing navigation and other electronic products in the desert north of Phoenix. The lower bajada with its scant vegetation provides ample space for a modern "horizontal" plant. This vegetation as it positions itself along normally dry desert streamways is apparent.

workers in manufacturing, the state of Arizona had only 18 percent of its nonagricultural work force in manufacturing.[30] Nevertheless manufacturing is still the fastest rising segment of the desert economy, with the possible exception of financial services and public administration.

The Phoenix and Tucson metropolitan areas account for an estimated 85 percent of the desert's manufacturing employment. The Phoenix metropolitan area employs over 34,000 workers in manufacturing while in Tucson the figure is in excess of 8,000. Each year this binodal concentration represents a greater proportion of the region's entire economic development.[31] It is in these two oasis communities that the newest and largest of the region's manufacturing industries are concentrated. These industries which manufacture aircraft and aircraft parts, missiles, electrical and electronic components for aircraft, telecommunication and computers, such as semiconductors and integrated circuits, dominate this fastest-growing segment of the desert economy. Approximately 18,000 of the region's total employed population are engaged in the aerospace industry, as well as the closely related electronics industry.

The Phoenix metropolitan area is the center of the electronics industry although some manufacturing takes place in Tucson. Large facilities dedicated to the manufacture of integrated circuits, semiconductors, computers, and other electronic systems are situated on almost all sides of the central city. They are universally modern, air conditioned, and well landscaped. The largest transistor manufacturing plant employs 6,000 workers, the majority being women who are well adapted to the fabrication of these minuscule products. During recent years, this type of manufacturing activity has shown the most rapid growth in employment — mainly by a few large firms.

These aerospace and electronics industries demand disproportionately large numbers of engineers and technicians. It has been estimated that one-fourth of all manufacturing employees in the Phoenix area are scientists, engineers, or skilled technicians.[32] The competition for these skills has been fierce as the United States has pressed forward its various space programs. Technologically oriented industries which located plants in Phoenix or Tucson usually found that critically skilled positions could be filled more quickly here than elsewhere. For example, the vice president of one Phoenix electronics manufacturing firm stated

---

[30]   *Ibid.*, 1966, p. 14.

[31]   "Arizona Hitches its Future to Ideas and Industry," *Business Week*, June 23, 1956, p. 117.

[32]   "Why the Big Boom in the Desert States," *U. S. News and World Report*, Oct. 11, 1957, p. 81.

Various aspects of the Phoenix area's economy are to be seen in these photos. Electronics constitutes the largest single manufacturing industry. Women such as these provide the larger part of the labor force, contributing to a potentially serious socio-economic imbalance. The aerial photo of midtown Phoenix shows numerous buildings that are dedicated to retail trade, finance, and medical purposes. Taken together, these still represent the "real business" of Phoenix, though manufacturing is making a strong assault on this primacy.

that his firm found it possible "to recruit high level staff members for Phoenix assignments when equally qualified people could not be found for an assignment in other areas of the country."[33] Climate and other desert amenities appear to be the principal factors in the relative success that Phoenix in particular has achieved in filling critical occupational categories. Phoenix, as well as Seattle, Boston, Denver, Dallas, Minneapolis, Houston, Los Angeles, the San Francisco Bay area, and a number of communities in Florida and New Jersey, have become the principal new centers to which electronics and aeronautical engineers gravitate. The majority of these areas have a benign climate or are inordinately well supplied with educational facilities or other amenities.

The wide and empty desert plains provide the necessary space for long airport runways. At the other extreme, the products of the electronics factories are often so small and the raw material requirements so negligible with regard to bulk that the high transportation costs of the intermountain West fail to affect adversely their establishment in southern Arizona.[34] Indeed, the location of Phoenix — less than 400 miles from the Southern California complex of aircraft and electronic industries — is an actual advantage. It could be maintained that the growth of these industries in Phoenix and Tucson represents the development of a Southern California industrial satellite in the desert. Geographical limits which would restrict the location of such "thirsty" industries as steel making, chemicals, or paper, have little bearing on electronics and allied manufacturers who have chosen the desert as a site for their new factories.

Not to be underestimated is the part played by the federal government in the development of manufacturing in this region. The United States government is the largest purchaser of electronic and aeronautical equipment, and the existence of military installations within the area is a significant advantage to local manufacturers. The size of these military establishments challenges the imagination. For example, Davis-Monthan Air Force Base at Tucson is an investment ten times larger than that of the six storage dams in the Salt River Project.[35] It is all too easy to fail in estimating the relative importance of a large modern military establishment to the overall economic development of this region. Fort Huachuca southeast of Tucson is an old cavalry post chosen to be the electronics proving ground for the U. S. Army. The convenience of having

---

33   *Industrial Development,* December, 1957, p. 18.
34   "Why the Big Boom in the Desert States," *U. S. News and World Report,* Oct. 11, 1957, p. 80.
35   *Ibid.,* and Griswold, *Salt River Project.*

In the desert, manufacturing takes on diverse forms. Outside Brawley, California, a beet sugar refinery advertises its low elevation. A turbine-engine factory in Phoenix displays a tremendous variety of complex fixtures outside the main building.

products tested at Fort Huachuca has been an important factor in the development of an electronics industry in Arizona. Dry atmospheric conditions and isolation determined the selection of this fort as a major American testing laboratory. In turn, large electronics manufacturers established themselves in the desert. This has helped to draw other smaller and more specialized manufacturers into the region. The effect is cumulative.

As the electronic and aircraft industries are associated with each other and with government installations in the desert, the primary metal and metal-products industries are interwoven into the specialized local manufacturing pattern. The great majority of the region's metal industries were established under wartime pressures and their continued existence depends in large measure on government contracts and policies.

On the southwestern edge of Phoenix is one of the largest aluminum extrusion plants in the United States. Built during World War II for strategic reasons, it has only since then found its economic *raison d'être*. This plant was the final step in the process which turned Arkansas and Caribbean bauxite into aluminum ingots in the low-cost hydro-electric power zone of the Pacific Northwest, which in turn shipped the ingots to Phoenix for extrusion and partial fabrication. The selection of Phoenix was based on its proximity to the burgeoning airframe industries of Southern California, Kansas, Oklahoma, and Texas, as well as on its protected inland location. The end of the war resulted in the closing of this huge factory, but renewed hostilities in Korea and elsewhere were instrumental in its being reopened. The plant, which includes a modern tube mill, continues to be well located in relation to aircraft and missile makers throughout the Southwest. Phoenix and Tucson alone provide a local market which did not exist during World War II. Today, however, the petroleum, trucking, and automobile industries consume more aluminum than ever before. California and the Southwest have higher per-capita interest in these industries than any other region of the United States. Residential and commercial building as well as the construction of house and truck trailers occupy a similar position in these areas of expanding population. Primary aluminum is less dependent today on the defense and armament industry than the average of all desert industries.

Fabricated and machined metal parts, castings and erections in aluminum, but primarily in steel, constitute an important industry. The tool-and-die industry is essential to local aircraft and electrical firms. Irrigation, electrical power, natural gas, and highways demand steel pipe and structural forms. An indigenous steel-fabrication industry largely centering on Phoenix has grown to supply these demands. This was probably bound to happen in a region so far removed from the American manufacturing belt.

Food processing and kindred agriculturally related activities, which south of the border rank first among desert industries, have a prominent place in Arizona and southeastern California. They have, however, been displaced from a position of primacy which they held prior to 1941. Approximately 8,000 workers find employment in food- and cotton-processing industries.[36]

The food and fiber manufacturing category contrasts with the foregoing electrical, mechanical, and metal-working industries not only in its earlier establishment but also in the generally smaller size, slower growth rate and wider geographical distribution of the individual concerns. Whereas the former are almost entirely concentrated in Tucson and the Phoenix metropolitan area, food processing takes place throughout the region.

Cotton gins and cottonseed-oil mills dot the irrigated valleys of the American desert as they do in Mexico, but are understandably concentrated in the major cotton-producing zones — the Salt River, Casa Grande, and Imperial valleys. Brawley, El Centro, and Calipatria in Imperial County, California, Glendale, Litchfield Park, Chandler, Gilbert, and Mesa in Maricopa County, Coolidge, Stanfield, Casa Grande and Eloy in Pinal County, Marana and Sahuarita in Pima County, Somerton in Yuma County, and Safford in Graham County, Arizona, are smaller communities in which cotton gins and cottonseed-oil mills are the primary and sometimes only manufacturing activities.[37] Most of these establishments are operated by the same international concerns that are to be found in the cotton-producing districts of Mexico's Sonoran Desert.

Except for one under construction the only large packing house in the region is at Phoenix but many small slaughter houses are scattered throughout the desert. Most of the desert's considerable livestock population is slaughtered and processed in Coastal California packing houses.

Flour mills are not as important in the desert economy of the American sector because the limited cultivation of wheat and relatively small population have not warranted their establishment in any numbers. The largest mills are in the Phoenix conurbation and concentrate primarily on the milling of feed grains for cattle. For this reason these mills should perhaps be considered as an integral part of the cattle-feeding industry.

Bakeries, bottling plants, and some other small food processors are to be found in almost every desert community. A regional specialty

[36]   Arizona Development Board, *Arizona Directory of Manufacturers, 1960*, p. 2.

[37]   Western Resources Conference, *The Western Resources Handbook, 1956*, Boulder, Colo., 63-64, pp. 601.

reflecting the nearness to Mexico is the preparation of food typical of that country. Several hundred workers are employed in a number of Arizona towns.[38] This food is consumed locally and shipped to all parts of the country in canned and frozen form.

Probably the most direct effect which climate has had on local industry was the early development of factories making air-conditioning devices. Today, more than 1,000 workers are employed in this activity, with Phoenix the principal manufacturing center and Tucson ranking second. The evaporative air-cooling equipment so effective in areas of low humidity is still the most common product, despite a gradual replacement by refrigeration units. It is perhaps typical of Americans not to suffer too long anywhere. The first Anglo settlers in the desert began to tinker with air conditioning, and by the 1920's an effective low-cost cooling device was being made locally. Over 99 percent of the dwellings in Phoenix have either evaporative coolers or refrigeration.

Next to the allied aerospace electronics and aluminum industries, the fastest-growing manufacturing category is the clothing industry. Unlike air conditioning, it is not home grown. Its existence is the result of decisions by a number of small clothing manufacturers in New York, Chicago, and Los Angeles to move their activities to Arizona. Climate may have indirectly affected the choice of Phoenix and Tucson as prospective plant sites but other factors such as the availability of labor at relatively low wages probably weigh more heavily in the equation. For some, Southwestern and Mexican motifs were used to stimulate a style-conscious market for Arizona clothing manufacturers. Chambers of Commerce, hotels, and shopkeepers have worked in conjunction with the apparel industry to establish in Phoenix and Tucson an important and growing industry, a rival for the older producing areas. At the present time there are an estimated 3,500 workers, mainly women, employed locally in more than thirty factories.[39] These are usually modern and air conditioned, contrasting greatly with conditions in the East. There is yet no connection between local cotton and the manufacture of clothing, as the intervening textile industry has failed to develop, except for one small plant located, interestingly enough, on the Colorado River Indian Reservation and constructed under government auspices.

The chemical industry, with its high consumption of water, has avoided the desert except when local markets have proved so alluring

---

38   Arizona Development Board, *Arizona Directory of Manufacturers, 1960*, pp. 39-41.
39   *Arizona Directory of Manufacturers, 1960*, pp. 9-12.

— RAY MANLEY PHOTOGRAPHY

Astronomical observations and movie making are growing desert industries both in large measure due to and dependent upon climatic conditions. The summit of Kitt Peak (above) in the Quinlan Mountains southwest of Tucson is the home of Kitt Peak National Observatory, including the world's largest solar telescope (foreground), and of several telescopes of the University of Arizona's Steward Observatory. Though outdoor scenes for movies, such as this "Western" below, have long been filmed in the desert, the addition of sound stages now permits the filming of an entire movie or television series, thus contributing an ever-increasing number of dollars to the desert economy.

— RAY MANLEY PHOTOGRAPHY

that even this handicap has not stood in the way. An early example of this was the establishment nine miles south of Benson of what has become the largest single plant for the manufacture of dynamite in America. A group of the larger Arizona mines formed a consortium which built the plant at Benson in order to lower the price of this explosive which they consume in such large quantities.[40] A plant manufacturing rocket fuel is located outside Mesa.

Insecticides and fertilizer, which are manufactured locally — largely in the Phoenix metropolitan area — serve a local market. Insect infestations have seen a historical increase as modern farmers, through irrigation and the introduction of a variety of cultivated plants, have created in this hot desert a series of irrigated "insect incubators." To combat this, more and more is spent each year on insecticides. A specialized service industry has grown up around the fumigation of dwellings, and the spraying and aerial dusting of crops.[41]

The increase in the manufacture of building materials reflects the rapid growth of Phoenix, Tucson, Yuma, and other desert communities. The Phoenix metropolitan area alone has had a total rate of construction which exceeds most cities whose metropolitan areas have twice or three times the population. During several recent years the Phoenix area has seen constructed as many as 17,000 residential dwelling units annually, putting it in the same general class as Philadelphia and Detroit, and much higher than Boston, Cleveland, and St. Louis.[42] Tucson, which has witnessed the building of an average of more than 4,000 dwellings each year, ranks with the majority of those cities whose metropolitan population approximates one-half to three-quarters of a million population, or at least twice that of Tucson. As one might suspect, the number of workers employed in construction is almost double the national average. Since 1962 a downturn in the construction of housing, the result of excessively optimistic construction in prior years, has caused layoffs in this industry. Yet almost one in every ten nonagricultural workers is engaged in constructing not only dwellings but the new power plants, factories, office buildings, motels, and multilane highways which have spread across the desert.

Distance alone accounts for much of this higher per-capita employment in construction. Longer highways and power lines are necessitated by these distances. The drought and heat which characterize the desert

---

40   Dunning, *Rock to Riches*, p. 206.

41   *Arizona Agriculture, 1961*, p. 8.

42   In 1965 this rate fell to 5,700 units due to the cumulative effects of several years of overbuilding. Valley National Bank, *Arizona Progress*, April, 1966.

both increase and decrease the magnitude of construction needed to develop the region. Irrigation accounts for a large proportion of the region's total works, which of course would be unnecessary under a humid climatic regime. On the other hand, heating plants are smaller and the cost of constructed dwellings is less.[43]

Large regional manufacturing industries have grown up in association with construction. Isolation, which results in high transportation costs, necessitated the early development of a cement industry in proximity to the largest markets. There are two large plants, one located at Rillito outside Tucson and another at Clarkdale in the Verde Valley. Limestone is available in the vicinity of each plant. Gypsum is shipped from Winkelman, Arizona.[44]

The manufacture of wood products associated with the construction industry takes place throughout the expanding desert towns and constitutes an important industry. The Phoenix area alone employs several hundred workers in the fabrication of millwork and other wood products. In general, however, wood constitutes a smaller percentage of construction materials utilized in the desert Southwest.

MINING

In an earlier chapter the development of the regional mining industry was traced through the early days of the technological revolutions which made low-grade ores available for exploitation. Involved in the interesting story of these momentous changes, one is apt to overlook the essential human base of mining.

The individual miner has always been the key to successful mining operations despite the prevailing philosophy that in "the desert men are cheaper than timbers." At the turn of the century the majority of Arizona copper miners were Cornishmen called "Cousin Jacks,"[45] who brought into practice an ancient knowledge of mining acquired in Cornwall. Working with them were Mexicans who moved north to take advantage of higher wages. The collapse of mining in Mexico after the beginning of civil disorders in 1910, combined with the labor shortage and increased demand for copper following the outbreak of World War I, caused the immigration of many additional Mexican miners during the second decade of the century.[46]

---

[43] Some types of plants may cost only 50 percent of what they would in a cold winter climate. *Newsweek,* Feb. 13, 1956, p. 80.
[44] Arizona Development Board, *Amazing Arizona: Natural Resources,* p. 6.
[45] Dunning, p. 101.
[46] *Ibid.,* pp. 167-68.

At the present time, mining in the American sector of the Sonoran Desert has reached a state of maturity. The era of the bonanza is past. Development today is more than ever before concerned with large-scale extraction of the abundant low-grade ores which characterize the desert and its margins. Twenty-five years ago, today's average ore would have been considered waste rock.[47] Open-pit mining has become an ever-larger proportion of the total mining industry. Rising costs have, in many districts, caused the cessation of operations underground although the recent development of the San Manuel District counters this trend.

The relative importance of the precious metals has continued to decline in relation to copper.[48] There have been no important developments in petroleum and uranium, two mineral products which have achieved prominence in Arizona, California, and through much of the western United States. Lead, zinc, and other base metals have played only a small part in the continuing evolution of desert mining. Only molybdenum, extracted as a byproduct in the majority of the copper-mining operations, has shown a recent gain in importance. Some manganese ore is mined in the western desert mountains.[49]

Within the desert, mining is more than ever before concentrated in the state of Arizona, with the Mexican and California sectors registering a relative decline. In Arizona, mining has shown a tendency to move down into the desert southwest, forsaking its mountain stronghold. The development of large ore bodies at the Pima, Mission and Esperanza mines southwest of Tucson and at San Manuel, thirty air miles northeast of Tucson, have made that city the center of the fastest-growing mining region in the United States. The mines southwest of Tucson are still mainly under development and will, when in full production, be among the largest in the United States. These developments typify the willingness of modern mining companies to invest tens of millions in removing overburden, etc. prior to producing their first ton of copper. Continued activity at the Silver Bell and Ajo mines combine with the aforementioned properties to make Pima County the largest producer of minerals in Arizona. The Ajo District has been within recent years second only to Morenci in eastern Arizona as the largest copper producer in the state.

Second to Pima County in the Arizona mining industry is Pinal, a desert county where copper also reigns. San Manuel is actually located

---

[47]   Cross, Shaw, and Scheifele, pp. 248-51.

[48]   Arizona Dept. of Mineral Resources, *Twenty-First Annual Report* (Phoenix, 1960), p. 6.

[49]   *Ibid.,* p. 12.

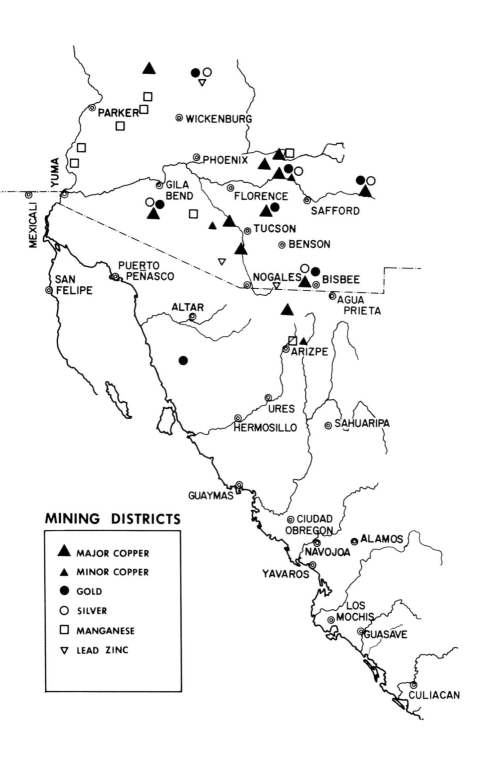

PARKER

WICKENBURG

YUMA

MEXICALI

PHOENIX

GILA
BEND

FLORENCE

SAFFORD

TUCSON

BENSON

PUERTO
PEÑASCO

NOGALES

BISBEE

SAN
FELIPE

ALTAR

AGUA
PRIETA

ARIZPE

URES

HERMOSILLO

SAHUARIPA

GUAYMAS

MINING DISTRICTS

- ▲ MAJOR COPPER
- ▲ MINOR COPPER
- ● GOLD
- ○ SILVER
- □ MANGANESE
- ▽ LEAD ZINC

CIUDAD
OBREGON

ALAMOS

NAVOJOA

YAVAROS

LOS
MOCHIS

GUASAVE

CULIACAN

Two of the giant new open-pit mining operations southwest of Tucson that have helped make Pima County, Arizona, the world's fastest-growing copper-producing region. The cost of removing the overburden alone from the huge mine in the center exceeded the value of minerals recovered from all but a handful of the early-day bonanzas.

in this county as are the important producers at Ray and Superior. The old townsite of Ray was recently evacuated as open-pit operations were extended into the town itself. A new town has been constructed at Kearny. All of these mines produce gold and silver recovered as byproducts from what are basically copper ores.

The isolated Bagdad mine in Yavapai County is another large producer of copper, although its ores are economically marginal.[50] In contrast to this are the "bonanza" mines at Jerome and Bisbee. These mining districts located outside the Sonoran Desert itself have in the past contributed disproportionately to the Arizona mining industry. The great United Verde mine at Jerome was closed in 1953 after seventy-five years of production. The ore body was worked out but only after it had produced a monumental tonnage of copper as well as gold and silver. The Bisbee mines continue to produce copper ore in considerable quantities while also recovering gold, silver, lead, and zinc. Here as elsewhere, open-pit operations have come to dominate the extraction of ore.[51] In Mohave County near Kingman a major copper deposit is being developed, providing an important stimulus to that county's long-somnolent economy.

In Gila County the Miami-Inspiration Copper District has been for fifty years a major producer of this metal, and led all other Arizona districts from World War I until the Depression of the 1930's. At the present time three large mines in the Globe-Miami area are responsible for the county's continued prosperity.[52] Obtaining water for mining and smelting operations is an ever-present problem — it was critical to the development of the Ajo mines — while necessitating costly works elsewhere throughout the arid mining districts. The fortuitous discovery of ample water near Ajo was the *sine qua non* of that area's development as a major producing district.[53] In contrast, the Miami-Inspiration District has taken advantage of flooding in an early-day mine to supply, through pumping, the modern smelter.[54]

At present, copper and other mining operations in southern Arizona are more productive than ever before in the history of the industry. Copper production has increased from 281,000 short tons in 1940, to 403,000 in 1950, and to 703,000 tons in 1965. Local wars, political

---

[50]   Dunning, p. 254.

[51]   Frank J. Tuck, *Stories of Arizona Copper Mines: The Bog, Low Grade, and the Bonanzas* (Phoenix: Arizona Dept. of Mineral Resources, 1957), pp. 55-63.

[52]   William H. Kerns, Frank J. Kelly, and D. H. Mullen, "The Mineral Industry of Arizona," *Bureau of Mines Minerals Yearbook* (Washington, D.C., 1959), p. 20.

[53]   Dunning, pp. 171-72.

[54]   Tuck, *Stories of Arizona Copper Mines,* p. 20.

Large investments, mainly American, have resulted in mining developments in Mexico similar to those north of the border. The low-grade copper ore of Sonora is processed in the 16,000-ton flotation plant at Cananea, Sonora. One hundred percent of this plant's production is shipped to the United States.

uncertainty, and labor unrest in the Congo (Katanga), Zambia, and Chile have contributed to copper production declines and subsequent price increases. Meanwhile, manufacturing has grown at an even faster rate, replacing mining, irrigated crops, and livestock as the principal economic activity of the state. Mining and agriculture, along with tourism, should continue to be important sources of local income but their ability to assume the lead once again over manufacturing as the first-ranking desert industry is probably impossible.

However, it must not be overlooked that supplemental industries including construction, utilities, wholesale and retail trade, financial professional and nonprofessional services, transportation, and public administration constitute the largest and most rapidly growing sector of the American desert economy. In Arizona as a whole, approximately two-thirds of the labor force is employed in these categories. These groups are relatively more important in Arizona than they are in the national economy. The desert no longer supports a colonial economy based upon the production of raw materials in association with self-sufficient agriculture. The growth of basic industries such as tourism, mining, agriculture, and manufacturing has been followed by an even more rapid growth of supplemental industries.

POWER

The production of electricity in the Sonoran Desert has both led and followed the economic development of the area. The mines and smelters were early and large consumers of electricity, and they remain as the single largest individual market for electricity. In time, however, they were joined by a multitude of other large power consumers. In the irrigated districts the power needed for lifting water from deep wells is generally provided by electricity. That water is a product of electric power is not as well known or advertised as electricity being the product of water.

In the desert almost all of the usual utilizers of electric power are present. One interesting variation, however, is air conditioning which places exceedingly heavy demands on generators during the heat of summer. This seasonal load coincides with the greatest demand for irrigation water, creating a definite peak load during the summer months — in contrast with most regions of the United States where winter peaks are common. For this reason, there are plans under way which will link the Phoenix region with the Columbia River power-generating facilities via a 750,000-volt transmission system focusing upon Hoover Dam. Surplus power will flow south in the summer and north in the winter.

Both steam and hydroelectric power are generated in numerous

With the completion of the dam at Glen Canyon, the development of hydro-
electric power on the Lower Colorado has probably reached its climax. Two or
three potential dam sites exist in the Grand Canyon area and below, but
conservationist opposition is adamant. Each year that passes provides alternate
power sources lessening the relative need for hydroelectric power. The photos
are of the power installations at Parker and Hoover dams (left above, and
right) on the Colorado, and of the Sahuaro Lake reservoir — which also serves
as an important recreation area — on the Salt River.

locations throughout the American sector of the desert. The federal government has been a prime mover in the development of hydroelectricity. Beginning with installations on the Salt River at Roosevelt Dam and on the Gila River at Coolidge Dam, the federal government has proceeded in dam after dam to harness the water power of the lower Colorado River Basin.

Major generating facilities are located at Glen Canyon, Hoover, Davis, and Parker dams. At the time of writing, the Glen Canyon generating facilities are still under construction. Downstream, Hoover, Davis, and Parker dams provide power principally for southern California and Nevada, as well as for central and southern Arizona users. The explosive growth of the Los Angeles, San Diego, Las Vegas, Phoenix, and Tucson areas has necessitated a great expansion in power generation only part of which is, of course, hydroelectric.

Steam generating plants are located principally in the major metropolitan areas and are, in the majority, privately owned, contrasting with the public hydroelectric power-generating facilities. Even here, however, much power is purchased by outlying farmers (in the Phoenix area) and by mines and smelters (in the Tucson area). The thermal electric power is derived almost entirely from natural gas supplied by pipeline from West Texas and New Mexico.

*   *   *

At this point agriculture, manufacturing, construction, mining, and power have been discussed and their contribution to the desert economy noted. In every case this contribution is significant if not indispensable to the economic well-being of the area. Yet, taken together, these primary industrial categories do not employ one-half the civilian labor force in Arizona. The 1960 census pointed out that 52.1 percent of Arizona's labor force was employed in trade, services (including financial), and public administration. Taking into consideration the fact that these are statistics for all of Arizona, rather than for the desert alone, the assumption can be made that almost exactly half of the desert's labor force is employed in these categories. For the United States as a whole, the corresponding total is 45.9 percent. Thus, despite the undoubted importance of cattle, cotton, copper, winter vegetables, electronics, aircraft, construction, transportation, and electricity, the desert is disproportionately supported by tertiary or supplemental industries. This has become increasingly true over the years; the Arizona figures for trade, services, and public administration in 1910, 1930, and 1950 are, respectively, 26.1, 38.4, and 48.5 percent. In spite of the greater productivity of farm, mine, and factory, ancillary services are more important today than ever before.

CHAPTER THIRTEEN

Political Factors

Between 1848 and the present, the United States and Mexico divided a parched wilderness between themselves, apportioned its limited waters, and subjugated its indigenous people to the authority of law. In many respects the desert itself was altered to conform to this political pattern. Mexico and the United States during this period proceeded at differing rates to build roads, lay rails, sink wells, dig ditches, string fences and establish towns, so that their authority would unite the desert frontier with their respective core areas, and at the same time make the desert a more productive region. This period of more than a century witnessed the most intense and successful efforts toward total Mexicanization as well as the first and equally successful steps toward "Anglo" Americanization of this outlying realm.

Today when one crosses the border there is an immediate and visible change from the United States to Mexico. American institutions, architecture, economic levels, English speech, Protestantism, and the racial types of northwestern Europe are, in general, replaced at the frontier by contrasting Mexican characteristics. This, of course, was not true when the boundary was first drawn. Certainly less than one thousand Americans lived north of the frontier within the desert. A more numerous Mexican population had manifested only intermittent and decreasing control of its northwestern frontier over the preceding century.

In 1848 the entire desert was in reality a no-man's land between the effective political power of either the United States or Mexico — power which rested in the more humid areas to the east and south. Only occasional pueblos and forts acted as sensitive nerve ganglia, transmitting the frustrations and failures of this arid frontier to the distant national core areas. There existed an uneasy peace with the more numerous sedentary tribes such as the Yaqui and Yuma, and open warfare with the nomadic Apache.

That the United States should so rapidly overcome the determined resistance of the native population where the Spanish and Mexicans had failed can only be understood as success in a conflict where one contender was an expansive and materialistic nation engaged in one of the world's epic mass migrations while the other had for over two hundred years done no better than maintain a defensive equilibrium against the aboriginal population. It has been observed that the rapid American march reveals "the advantage of an expanding economic frontier working from an immediate base over a defensive frontier operating a long distance from the centers of resources and population. The Anglo-American lever had a long power arm and a short weight arm."[1] The result was that the Anglo-American advance stopped only when it reached the line of effective Spanish-Mexican colonization.

The desert itself presented an even more powerful adversary in the two-nation attempt to occupy the region effectively. The lack of water and resultant agricultural poverty, great distance, and isolation limited settlement, economic development, and finally, national interest in the area.

Events and innovation have pressed hard against the indigenous cultures as well as against the emptiness of the desert itself. Undirected national aspiration, technology, and birth rates have had more effect on the frontier than the direct policies of central governments. As in the earliest days when neither arid desolation nor the Apache were intimidated by the treaty makers and boundary markers, today the equally real pressures along the same frontier are not removed by strictly political means.

The evolution of the modern frontier since its creation has been the substitution of one conflict for another. One cannot look to the land itself as a cause of frontier pressures. Aside from the failure of the United States to achieve an outlet on the Gulf of California, the desert land offers little in the way of contrast north or south of the border. It is the differing social characteristics and national goals of the two neighboring people that have given the desert frontier its continuing problems.

The Gadsden Purchase in 1854 was the last contiguous addition to the continental territory of the United States. America had completed, territorially at least, its "manifest destiny."

By most accepted standards the border west of the Continental Divide is well located. Except for the short Colorado River boundary south of Yuma, the frontier is of the simplest geometric type.

---

[1] Herbert E. Bolton, *Wider Horizons in American History* (New York, 1939), p. 87.

Whatever political difficulties have elsewhere developed along this type of boundary have been avoided here due to the extremely sparse population. Potentially troublesome areas, conditions such as the trans-frontier flow of water from the Colorado River to the Imperial Valley of California, and the valleys of the Santa Cruz and Sonoita rivers, both of which cross and re-cross the border, have not developed into areas of major international conflict over water rights. Over much of the desert the long straight lines of demarcation pass untrammelled and hence uncontested.

The frontier, however, is much more than a line. In spite of its apparently rigid character it must act as membranous tissue against which social and economic pressures play, and through which some of these same forces must pass. The Mexican-American border is, in this respect, subject to greater pressures than the average. One pressure is economic in nature. A cogent argument could be made that there is no other national frontier that separates neighboring countries with such differing absolute levels of economic development.[2] This economic contrast is felt across the border in both directions. One could in fact hypothesize multiple economic frontiers of land, labor, and capital, none of which corresponds to the actual boundary. Mexico's relatively low level of economic development, labor costs, and capitalization are felt north of the border where the reverse conditions prevail. Mexican bracero labor has regularly crossed in large numbers into the irrigated valleys of southern Arizona and the Imperial Valley, forming what is in effect a Mexican labor province. The international boundary has little deterred the passage of laborers north to work primarily in American agriculture.[3] At the time of writing, braceros or Mexican nationals under contract have been excluded from American fields by Congressional order. It is much too early to assess what the lasting effect of this change in policy will be. Nevertheless, Mexican workers permanently resident in the United States continue to harvest a majority of the crops grown in the irrigated fields of southern Arizona and the Imperial Valley.

Somewhere well north of the border, Mexican labor, by diminishing its influence, establishes an economic frontier: that of labor cost. American capital, on the other hand, flows south of the border in the form of machines and vehicles which profoundly influence the economy of Mexico. Near the frontier this influence is most directly felt, raising

---

[2] D. W. Fryer, "World Income and Types of Economies: The Pattern of World Economic Development," *Economic Geography,* Vol. 34 (1958), pp. 283-303. Recently, there have been published investigations into this area of study too numerous to cite.

[3] "Hungry Workers, Ripe Crops and the Nonexistent Mexican Border," *The Reporter,* April 3, 1954.

wages to the highest levels in Mexico and lowering costs through mechanization.

Much of this seemingly natural interplay between adjacent economies has taken the form of contraband and illegal immigration. With such great economic contrasts, these are continuing problems, but less than one might expect to encounter on a narrow line where the "developed" meets the "underdeveloped" world.

THE MEXICAN-AMERICAN BOUNDARY

The Mexican-American border which extends for nearly two thousand miles, first along the Rio Grande River and then west to the Pacific just south of San Diego, divides the Sonoran Desert into two relatively equal parts.

The western, or Sonoran Desert, portion of the boundary was first defined in the Treaty of Guadalupe Hidalgo in 1848 and for the most part followed the Gila River west to the confluence of that river with the Colorado River.[4] West of the Colorado, the boundary followed the line between Upper and Lower California. This latter division between the two Californias was defined as a "straight line drawn from the middle of the Rio Gila, where it unites with the Colorado, to a point on the coast of the Pacific Ocean, distant one marine league due south of the southernmost point of the Port of San Diego."[5] This boundary, as it was delineated west from the Colorado River, remains to this day as the international frontier between these two countries.

East of the Colorado River the international boundary crossing the desert was changed by the Treaty of 1853 between the two countries. This "Gadsden Purchase" moved the line south from the Gila to the present town of Nogales, thus including within the Sonoran Desert territory of the United States its first Mexican population in the pueblos of Tucson and Tubac.[6]

The need for writing this second treaty in 1853 resulted from the

---

4   It is interesting to note that the treaty makers took care that "no tax or contribution . . . be levied upon vessels or persons navigating [the Gila] . . . except in the case of landing upon one of their shores." Article 7 of treaty between the United States and Mexico concluded at Guadalupe Hidalgo Feb. 2, 1848. Needless to say, this passage mirrors the sanguine hopes of the treaty makers for navigation on the intermittent Gila, which have certainly never been fulfilled.

5   Article 5 of the Treaty of Guadalupe Hidalgo, Feb. 2, 1848.

6   In exact terms the boundary was located at the parallel of 31°20′ at a point 100 miles west of the Rio Grande where it proceeds due west to the 111th meridian of longitude west of Greenwich, "thence in a straight line to a point on the Colorado River twenty English miles below the junction of the Gila and Colorado Rivers; thence up the middle of the said river Colorado until it intersects the present line between the United States and Mexico." Article 1 of the Treaty between the United States and Mexico concluded at the City of Mexico, Dec. 30, 1853.

difficulties and disputes which arose in the original survey and demarcation of the boundary,[7] a survey which left unresolved the thorniest problems of the borderlands. The boundary of 1848 brought the United States, for the first time, into official contact with the Western Apache frontier. Article 11 of the treaty committed the United States to prevent Indian raids into northern Mexico, but was very vague in the necessary positive demarcation between El Paso and the Gila River, the heart of Apachería.[8] The treaty stipulated no longitude or latitude; it merely declared that the boundary from El Paso to the Gila should coincide with a line drawn on a map, which was "an 1847 reprint of an 1828 plagiarism, of an 1826 reproduction of part of an unsurveyed 1822 publication."[9] Its inaccuracy was amply demonstrated when the survey party found that the map had placed El Paso thirty-four miles north of its actual location.[10] This meant the loss to the United States of some three million acres in the Mesilla Valley west of El Paso, one of the most practical railway routes to the Pacific.

This error alone would probably have been enough to require the negotiation of a second treaty without the pressing complications brought about by Apache raids and sectional conflict over a southern transcontinental railway route.[11] The treaty as finally ratified was the result of a compromise after six different boundaries had been proposed to the United States Senate. Although Senate debate had mentioned a port on the Gulf of California, on no occasion had the Mexican government agreed to such a provision, since an American salient reaching the Gulf would, of course, have separated Central Mexico physically from Baja California. In fact, as the border was drawn, the only remaining route left to Mexico which connected the central provinces with Baja California was the narrow, almost waterless Camino del Diablo. The effect of the treaty on Mexican West Coast communications was loudly denounced in Mexico City and, along with other humiliating features of the treaty, led directly to the impeachment and banishment of Santa Ana, the Mexican president.[12]

---

[7] John R. Bartlett, *Personal Narrative* . . . . 2 vols. (New York, 1854).

[8] Frank C. Lockwood, "The Gadsden Treaty," *Arizona Quarterly*, Vol. 2 (1946), pp. 5-16.

[9] George P. Hammond, ed., *The Treaty of Guadalupe Hidalgo* (Berkeley, 1949), p. 70.

[10] U. S. Senate, *Report of the United States and Mexican Boundary Survey*, 32d Cong., 1st Sess., Sen. Exec. Report No. 345 (Washington, D.C., 1852), Vol. 9, Nos. 61, 81, etc. The documentary material on the American section of the Commission is voluminous and contains elaborate descriptions of the topography, climate, vegetation, and people of the region through which the survey was run.

[11] Paul N. Garber, *The Gadsden Treaty* (Philadelphia, 1923), pp. 20-21.

[12] A. M. Carreño, *La Diplomacia Extraordinaria entre México y Estados Unidos, 1789–1947* (2 vols.; México, D.F., 1951), Chapters 2 and 5.

Thus, the widespread belief that America's failure to obtain an outpost on the Gulf of California was a result of ignorance about geography among the treaty writers (or because of the surveyors' thirst for water or alcohol as has been opined) is unfounded. However, as the treaty was finally drawn, the United States achieved its goal: obtaining the territory needed for a relatively low-elevation crossing of the Continental Divide.

As settlers began to occupy lands adjacent to the boundary and as the sovereignty of the United States and Mexico replaced that of the Apache, disputes arose over the exact location of the boundary line. Smuggling, filibustering, and the continued presence of nomadic tribes added to the problems.[13] The more familiar border problems associated with dense settlement replaced by degrees those of desolation. The development of ranches, mines, irrigated farms, towns, and military establishments along the border has, in due course, caused increased pressures and frictions undreamed of one hundred years ago.

EARLY PROBLEMS OF SOVEREIGNTY

The Mexican-American border divided the territories of several desert tribes: the Cocopas and Yumas of the Colorado River, the Papagos and Pimas in the Arizona Upland Desert, and the nomadic Apache who moved between valley and mountain on their foraging activities.

The advent of American sovereignty in the northern desert at first had little effect on either Indian or Mexican. The Mexican authorities had hoped for assistance in their conflict with the Apaches who recognized no boundaries, tribal or national. American intervention was at first hesitant and at cross purposes with Mexican intentions. This was particularly evident during the period between the Mexican War and 1854 when there was uncertainty over the location of the boundary. Wandering brigades of regular and discharged American soldiers, Forty-Niners, and other immigrant groups came into frequent contact with Mexican settlers waging defensive warfare against the Apache.

The desert frontier acted as a magnet for Mexican and American renegades who quickly descended to the economic level of activities of the Apache. The Mexican and American authorities, in an attempt to cope with chaos, enlisted the support of other tribes who, in turn, played Mexican against American, occasionally raiding white settlements

---

[13]   Charles A. Timm, *The International Boundary Commission, United States and Mexico* (Austin, Texas, 1941), p. 24.

themselves. Survivors were often uncertain whether their assailants had been Mexican outlaws, Apaches, or other Indian renegades. This mistaken identity resulted in punitive forays which crossed the frontier at will.

In the decade immediately following the final marking of the boundary (1854-1864), civil war broke out in both nations, bringing complete anarchy to the border region. In 1854 the French filibusterer Comte Gaston Raousset de Boulbon foreshadowed the French intervention when he and his followers captured Guaymas only to be decisively defeated by the Sonoran defenders.[14]

This action as well as that of William Walker in Baja California[15] may have inspired the 1857 filibustering expedition led by Henry A. Crabb, an American.[16] Entering Arizona from California, he and one hundred well-armed followers marched into Sonora, crossing the border at Sonoita oasis. Hoping to take advantage of the chaos and factionalism in Sonoran politics by throwing his small army into one camp or another, and by this acquire a large tract of land near the border, he lost all when the Sonoran governor rallied the people to the defense of Mexican soil. He and his followers were exterminated in the Battle of Caborca after a siege of several days. Meanwhile, another party of Anglos set out from Tucson to lift the siege, but arrived too late and came close to following Crabb's men to a desert grave.[17]

The extension of American frontiers to the Pacific Coast also placed the Sonoran Desert on the checkerboard of American sectional conflict. Although the region was sparsely populated with settlers, most of whom were either unfamiliar or uninterested in the slavery question, it did not lack geographical importance, particularly to the South. The only available access the Confederacy had to California was through the Southwestern desert. Grand strategy dictated a Southern advance on California with the hope of bringing that state into the Confederacy, and with it the wavering states of Utah and Missouri.

Added to this was the belief that the Southwestern territories and California could supply much of the gold needed to finance the war. Confederate success in the Southwest would also have meant access

---

[14] Almada, pp. 326-27, 389-404.

[15] Pablo L. Martínez, *A History of Lower California,* trans. by Ethel D. Turner (México, D.F., 1960), pp. 373-78.

[16] Rufus K. Wyllys, *Henry A. Crabb: A Tragedy of the Sonoran Frontier* (Berkeley, 1940).

[17] History leaves us with conflicting accounts of this incident. The truth probably is to be found somewhere between the sympathetic accounts of R. J. Hinton, *The Handbook of Arizona, 1877,* pp. 36-40, and the Mexican nationalist version in Almada, pp. 388-89.

to the Pacific and complete Southern control of the Mexican border with whatever advantages this position of leverage might have had over Mexican and European neutrality. Conversely, it was imperative that the Union forces who had considerable popular support in California should not let this come to pass.

Meanwhile, the discovery of gold along the Lower Gila in 1858, and the opening up of the copper mines at Ajo the year before, brought more Americans into the borderlands, increasing friction between them, the Mexicans and the aboriginal people.[18]

If the outcome of the Crabb debacle had not already accomplished it, the outbreak of the American Civil War in 1861 probably brought to an end any further American incursions against Mexican soil. This however did not bring peace to Mexican Sonora. The French took this opportunity to renew their interest in the Mexican West Coast which was part of their overall plan for Mexican domination. There was even an armed intervention by English marines, who occupied for a short time in 1862 the port of Guaymas.[19]

The first Confederate advance across the Great Divide brought panic to the scattered and sparsely populated forts and pueblos in the area north of the border. Their small garrisons abandoned and burned the recently established Forts Mohave, Breckenridge, and Buchanan. Only Fort Yuma remained.[20] The Apaches, encouraged in their belief that earlier attacks had been responsible for the withdrawal of American forces, reacted to these events by accelerating their raids in a territory which was left without military protection.

The advance of Confederate forces across the desert was halted by the news of the arrival of California volunteers at Fort Yuma. One short engagement — the so-called "Battle of Picacho Pass" — was fought at Picacho just northwest of Tucson. The harassment from Apache bands who were more interested in the color of one's skin than one's uniform further encouraged the Confederate departure. These events left the few remaining settlers at the mercy of the Apache bands who extended their attacks once more into Mexico, where civil war also flamed. Over most of the Sonoran Desert the whites had, in effect, abandoned their claims of sovereignty. The desert once more became western Apachería.

A small Union army moved against the Apaches with all the forces

---

18 W. Eugene Hollon, *The Southwest: Old & New* (New York, 1961), pp. 190-92.

19 Almada, p. 386.

20 Raymond S. Brandes, *Frontier Military Posts of Arizona* (Globe, Ariz., 1960), pp. 1-8.

available, determined to wage a war of extermination against this tribe.[21] A relentless war, lasting two years, freed the American sector, at least temporarily, from the Apache but in reality only drove these Indians south into chaotic Sonora. As time went on, the Apaches learned to use the international border as alternate refuge from either American or Mexican forces.

In order to terminate forays across the border and to eliminate the use of the international frontier as a sanctuary, the governments of Mexico and the United States concluded in 1882 a treaty permitting regular soldiers from either country to pursue marauding Indians across the boundary into each other's territory.[22] Three years later this proviso allowed General Crook to follow Geronimo and his Apaches into Mexico where they were finally hunted down and forced to surrender in May of 1886.[23] This marked the end of the Indian frontier in the United States, but Sonora had much more to hear from the Indian.

THE FRONTIER OF CAPITALISM

The end of the Apache Wars closely coincided with the beginnings of a new era along the desert frontier. The railway age was upon the American Southwest in 1881 when the Southern Pacific was completed from California to New Mexico. The railway was in fact instrumental in ending the Apache menace. Isolation, great distances, and broken terrain — the traditional allies of the Apaches — were all diminished as effective hindrances to the complete control of the land by the Anglo-Americans. The railway had, of course, a wider significance, becoming the single most important factor in the political geography of the desert.

The Southern Pacific was the product of the industrial United States which had grown from adolescence in the first two decades after the Civil War. The railway was an indispensable agent of that industrialization, bringing raw materials to the factory and distributing settlers and machines so that distant satellites could grow and prosper, generating more traffic, markets, and raw-material flow. The railways of western America, focusing on such cities as Chicago, Omaha, St. Louis, and Kansas City, reached out to the remotest corners of the country, tying together diverse economies, colonizing and exploiting the varying natural resources.

---

[21] Hollon, pp. 229-32.
[22] Treaty concluded on July 29, 1889, between the United States and Mexico.
[23] Cross and others, pp. 49-51.

Industrialization also thrust the United States upon the world. America began to flex its international muscles; overseas expansion — ("Imperialism" has never been an acceptable term to Americans for American territorial expansion) — became a burning political issue. The Caribbean and Mexico were resurrected as likely spheres of American influence. The Pacific became a third prospect.

The later nineteenth and early twentieth centuries saw the completion of the American railway net, brought to early maturity the industrialization of the American economy, and placed America on the world political stage.

On the arid plains and bajadas of the American Southwest these inexorable political and economic tides were not always apparent but were no less real. The age of the railway, industrial capitalism, and overseas expansion was at hand and each of these aspects manifested its effect upon the border. The last frontier of the Apache became the borderlands of Capitalism within the decade of the eighties.

In complete contrast to this was Mexico. Virtually railwayless, possessing a pre-industrialized economy and a feudal social structure, Catholic and Indian Mexico had advanced little since Colonial times. Mexico did, however, have a new president who was to give his name to an epochal period; the Age of Díaz (1877-1910). By encouraging foreign investment and ownership of Mexican land and capital, the Republic during the next thirty years built railways, developed mines and factories, paid old debts, and encouraged renewed confidence in Mexico. To accomplish this, Díaz brought political order by suppressing all domestic opposition to his policies.

From Europe and the United States there began in the eighties a flow of men and machines which marked the beginning of the Mexican Industrial Revolution. Along the frontier, however, the economic development of Mexico during this period was so subject to political factors arising north of the border that one must consider them at this time.

Geography placed Baja California, Sonora, and Sinaloa within the growing economic sphere of the United States, particularly the state of California. These west-coast Mexican states face the Gulf of California, one of the least-traveled bodies of water on the earth's surface. Thus, European influence, particularly investment, has always been surpassed by American interests who possess a locational advantage. One enters Mexico from the United States across the gently sloping intermontane and coastal plains leading southeast to Mazatlán and beyond. No natural barriers thus separate the important routeways of the American Southwest from those leading to the important centers of Sonora and Sinaloa. In striking contrast, the central highland core of the Mexican Republic is separated by the barrancas of the Sierra Madre Occidental — mountains which have always acted as one of the most effective barriers to communications in western North America.

Only in this perspective can it be seen how the Apache frontier became the borderlands of Capitalism when, under Díaz, Mexico was in fact unified for the first time. It has been observed that

> it is not until the Juarez Period (1856-72) that we can properly begin to speak of a Mexican nation. Until then it was little more than a conglomeration of regions loosely bound together and at war with one another. It was left for Díaz to consolidate the Mexican nation.[24]

Freed from banditry and internecine civil war, Mexico opened its doors to foreign influence and investment, and geography conspired to draw the Mexican West Coast into the burgeoning sphere of late nineteenth-century American capitalism.

In Arizona the railway and mining interests quickly came to dominate the economy of the state. These interests achieved ascendancy in a region where distance presented the greatest challenge and geology the highest rewards. Across the arid bajadas south of the border the same challenge and rewards awaited the enterprising American who was quick to react.

Before the Mexican Revolution brought this capitalistic period to an end, the international boundary between the states of Sonora and Arizona alone was crossed by four American-owned railway lines. Taken together, they constituted over 95 percent of the trackage within the Mexican desert region and had an equally disproportionate influence on the economic development of the area.

To the east, the first railway ran south across the semiarid uplands connecting the American-owned copper mines at Nacozari with the smelter at Douglas, Arizona. The eighty-two mile line was built to serve no regional purpose other than the mines at Nacozari. Two more lines starting at the border converged on the American-owned copper mines at Cananea. The easternmost line was constructed across the boundary at Naco; the western line was extended from Nogales. Neither Nacozari nor Cananea was linked by rail with Hermosillo or any other Mexican town. Since these isolated settlements were no more than trans-frontier segments of the American "copper economy," there was little commerce between them and the interior of Mexico, and even less reason for American interests to encourage that commerce. If the Mexicans were

---

[24] Frank Tannenbaum, *Mexico: The Struggle for Peace and Bread* (New York, 1950), p. 46.

interested in what the Americans were doing south of the border, they were free to use the mule and wagon tracks dating back to Father Kino's time.

These copper-mining communities, as well as the intervening stations between them and the border, were as closely linked to the United States as they were isolated from the rest of Mexico. They existed as economic outliers of the United States, owned and governed by American capital. The Cananea Consolidated Copper Co., Phelps Dodge, and other American interests enjoyed a degree of extraterritoriality which made a mockery of the international boundary. These American mine and railway salients in Mexico were not only free from centers of Mexican control such as Hermosillo, but local authority was equally isolated from Mexico City, which was in turn sympathetic to foreign enterprise.

In 1906 these "capitulations" were brought to the attention of all Mexico when the situation took a critical turn. The Cananea mines — the largest single enterprise in Sonora — employed approximately 5,400 Mexicans and 2,200 American nationals at discriminatory wages. This premium paid for American labor was "justified" by the governor of Sonora as being the fair compensation for the American miners who were "more constant, more determined, and more productive for the enterprise and in no way should it be understood that the American workers' better pay was the result of national spirit."[25] When the Mexican workers went out on strike, violence erupted and much of Cananea was put to the torch. In the rioting, armed American guards and Mexican militia (*rurales*) killed twenty-three Mexican workers, losing four of their own number.[26] The governor of Sonora, in his attempt to reestablish order, dispatched soldiers from Hermosillo over the tortuous track that led to Cananea. Before they could arrive he insured victory over the strikers by accompanying at least fifty heavily armed American irregulars (identified as "Rangers")[27] as they crossed the border at Naco, Arizona. An American "invasion" of Mexico supported by the Mexican government throws a good deal of light on the real significance of the international boundary and places considerable suspicion on the real sovereignty of the Mexican nation during this period. The extraterritorial status of Americans and American capital was certainly most complete in the isolated enclaves of American enterprise along the border, particularly where American-owned railways reached south from border stations to American-owned enterprises inside Mexico.

---

25   Almada, p. 354.
26   *Ibid.*, p. 352.
27   *Ibid.*, p. 353.

The fourth American railway was to have the most profound impact on the political geography of the Mexican West Coast. The Southern Pacific of Mexico, built by American interests, and owned and operated by the railway which dominated communications through the American desert to the north, acted as the agent through which a rather benevolent form of American economic imperialism was extended south along the West Coast Corridor. This salient of American capitalism in the desert was for over forty years (1884-1927) the only railway link between the Mexican West Coast and the outside world.[28]

By virtue of this uncontested position, the economic interests of the United States held an insurmountable advantage over either Mexican or foreign rivals in tapping the resources of this region. The great delay in opening up a railway line over the Sierra Madre, uniting the core area of Mexico with the outlying Northwest, tended to perpetuate American influence, and conversely, this influence was blamed for the failure to complete rapidly this vital link. The rugged *quebradas* of the Sierra de Tepic were no deeper than the economic and political chasm which continued to develop between the arid littoral and the uplands while American influence extended itself along the Southern Pacific lines. Whether or not this railway was guilty of separatist actions that, in effect, were a form of economic filibustering, is dependent upon one's point of view.

It is important to note that the existence of this disjointed railway acted as a catalytic ingredient in the rapid development of the economy of the Mexican Northwest. Even its prolonged disassociation with the Mesa Central and Mexico City probably elevated standards of living as the detached region became economically more American and less Mexican. Over this railway there entered thousands of Americans, both immigrants and transients, who carried south their more advanced technology. At the same time the precarious desert economy was not flooded with cheap peon labor from the southern states.

The Southern Pacific also played a vital role during the years of revolution. This detached railway leading south from Nogales to Mazatlán, but little further, meant that there developed in effect a separate theater of war where the complete control of this railway, as well as the ports of Guaymas and Mazatlán (the Southern Pacific's only outlets to the sea) were essential to the effective occupation of the north-western coastal plain. It should be added that control of the border

---

[28] In 1884 the line between Nogales and Guaymas was completed. The year 1927 marked the opening of service to Mexico City. John W. F. Dulles, *Yesterday in Mexico: A Chronicle of the Revolution, 1919–1936* (Austin, Texas, 1960), p. 290.

stations, such as Nogales, Agua Prieta, and Naco was essential to maintain dominance in the west.

Because of its window on the United States, largely provided by the Southern Pacific of Mexico, as well as its protective isolation, the desert state of Sonora existed independently throughout most of the revolutionary years, producing the most successful armies in Mexico, four of whose military leaders — de la Huerta, Obregón, Calles, and Rodríguez — occupied the presidency.[29] This vicinal American influence, and the superiority of Sonoran soldiery, are the subject of continuing debate.

It must be noted that strategically the Sonoran Desert became the "heartland" of Mexico. Sonoran generals leading Sonoran armies became the dominant factor in revolutionary politics. After the fall of Mexico City to Sonoran and Yaqui soldiers in August of 1914,[30] the remaining years of the revolution were characterized as conflicts among Sonorans, or between Sonora and military forces from other regions, chiefly the northern states of Chihuahua and Coahuila. So completely did the politicians and armies of the northwestern desert come to dominate the revolutionary period that effective control of Sonora was often balanced against the control of the remaining states, including the capital.[31] On other occasions, Sonora existed as a secessionist state which federal forces were unable to subdue.[32]

How much of this revolutionary independence was due to the superior military skill and other tangibles, and how much distance, terrain, and other more strictly geographical factors entered the equation cannot be answered. The hard-fought battles at Ojitos in the Sierra between Chihuahua and Sonora,[33] the battles of Sasabe, Naco, and Agua Prieta,[34] the repeated battles waged at Guaymas and Mazatlán, as well as the constant guerrilla warfare along the tracks of the Southern Pacific,[35] point to the strategic importance that lay in the control of the limited number of routes into the Sonoran Desert — the border points, the port cities, and the all-important West Coast railway. (It is a little-known fact that "for the first time in history in April 1914, a plane was used for warfare when Constitutionalist Captain Gustavo

---

29   In this respect Sonora and the isolated western deserts resembled Savoy and Piedmont in the Italian Wars of Unification, or Morocco in the Spanish Civil War.

30   Dulles, p. 9.

31   *Ibid.,* p. 8.

32   *Ibid.,* pp. 24, 46, 438-39, 452.

33   *Ibid.,* pp. 5, 454.

34   *Ibid.,* pp. 14, 452.

35   *Ibid.,* pp. 7, 8, 75-76, 439.

Salinas . . . flew the *Sonora* over the sea near Topolobampo, Sinaloa, in order to drop bombs on Victoriano Huerta. . . . These same flyers used the *Sonora* to bomb the Federals at Mazatlán.")[36]

There were many important campaigns launched from the desert fastness of Sonora but no outside force was able to control all of this area or even small districts for any length of time.[37] The control of the border and the port cities throughout Mexico was one of the continuing strategic factors during the period of the Revolution.

The border between the two countries was the scene of considerable activity during the revolutionary period when Mexico delivered herself from feudalism. Although the United States remained officially aloof through most of the revolution, the American government played favorites through diplomatic channels. Along the desert frontier embargoes were placed on arms, food, and horses, only to be withdrawn when the situation south of the border changed to what was believed to be America's advantage.[38] Military forces representing favored revolutionary factions were allowed to cross the frontier, use the facilities of the Southern Pacific to parallel the border, and then recross into Mexico.[39] When forces under the command of other less-favored generals crossed the border they were classified as "bandit" raiders, and cries similar to those of the "Alamo" and "Maine" were heard throughout the country. The most famous of these forays was Pancho Villa's attack through the Sierra on Columbus, N.M., in March of 1916 which precipitated American countermeasures resulting in an invasion of Mexican soil.

American border towns were the receiving points for thousands of refugees, the sites of numerous exile councils, and the staging areas for re-invasion by these same groups. The most serious and inflammatory border problem during the years of revolution was the occasional raid or "incident" involving the two nationalities.[40] One of these, a pitched battle, took place in Nogales in 1918 between Negro American soldiers and Mexican revolutionaries.[41]

BORDER TOWNS

The most apparent and lasting effect that the existence of a major political boundary has had on the social geography of the Sonoran Desert

---

[36] *Ibid.,* pp. 452-53. Francis McCullagh, *Red Mexico* (London, 1928), describes the destruction of bridges and stations along Southern Pacific tracks.

[37] Dulles, p. 76.

[38] Cline, p. 181.

[39] *Ibid.,* p. 174.

[40] Tannenbaum, pp. 261-65.

[41] Almada, pp. 508-509.

has been the rapid growth of "border towns." The term "border town" has, in American usage, come to signify one of that class of communities strung out along the American-Mexican boundary and as a generic term is almost never used to describe a settlement which happens to lie on the boundary between the United States and Canada. In fact, the northern boundary of the United States is most usually referred to as "the boundary" while the line separating the latter country from Mexico is almost always termed "the border." It has been observed that the distinction stems from the fact that there has been a great deal more friction between the United States and Mexico than with Canada.[42] Lawlessness and trans-frontier conflict have resulted in the American adoption of the word "border" from the English usage where it has been more specifically applied to the boundary and adjoining districts between Scotland and England. The word "border" usually implies the existence of a border zone where unsettled conditions prevail. A "border town" has this same connotation.

The existence of a border which is more zonal than linear finds expression in Mexican usage as well. The mixture of "decultured" Mexicans with similar Anglo elements in the border towns has resulted in a class termed *pochos,* literally meaning "faded."[43] Mexicans who live within the border zone are regarded by their countrymen as having lost much of their nationality. The semantics of the "border" reflect its reality.

Of the many border towns within the desert only one existed prior to treaties establishing the international boundary. The minuscle oasis of Sonoita, established as the far western mission outpost of Pimería Alta by Father Kino in the last years of the seventeenth century, happened to lie about one mile south of the Gadsden Boundary, which made it a border town. All the other border towns within the desert date from the period after the final boundary survey was complete. These towns, although some of their sites may have been previously occupied by straggling rancherías, owe their existence to their location along the international boundary, although it is possible, of course, that had the boundary not been established at its present location some settlement might have developed on the same site. However, all of these settlements owe their growth and present size to the international boundary. To generalize further about border towns is to invite contradiction since each settlement is unique. Only the distinct border-town phenomenon, as it exists along the boundary between these two countries, and the

---

42   Walter Prescott Webb, *The Great Frontier* (Boston, 1952), p. 2 ff.
43   Cline, p. 110.

CALEXICO
MEXICALI
YUMA
SAN
LUIS
LUKEVILLE
SONOITA
SASABE
NOGALES
BISBEE
DOUGLAS
NOGALES
NACO
AGUA
PRIETA

BORDER TOWNS

universal need for water which all desert communities face, encourages generalization. Aside from these two factors, and the disproportionate growth of these communities in recent years, little can be said about one which is true for the majority of the others.

Each settlement is binodal in character, having a Mexican and American center. The size of these two cores, divided by the boundary, may vary greatly. The Mexican half is always the larger in population, if not the most impressive in appearance. The two towns may be contiguous so that the boundary line itself is virtually indistinguishable from the air. This is the case in Nogales and Mexicali-Calexico. On the other hand, there is sometimes a "no-man's land" from several hundred yards to a mile or more in width between the built-up areas of the two communities, such as can be seen in Agua Prieta-Douglas or Sonoita-Lukeville.

Functional symmetry or the lack of it in these border towns of the desert exceeds any morphological considerations in variety and interest. Each binodal community exists to some varying degree because of international factors. Trade is the most important. Governmental activities usually take second place ahead of all others, including manufacturing. A good example of this is Nogales, Arizona-Sonora, which is the border point on both the main line of the West Coast railway and the most heavily traveled highway crossing the desert frontier. In both communities wholesale and retail trade, as well as related transport occupations, employ many more workers than all other categories combined.[44]

The dominance of these commercial activities within the economy of Ambos Nogales ("Both Nogales")[45] is in large measure the result of political division. Large numbers are engaged in bulk-breaking activities necessitated by the border. Estimates of the foreign destination of goods handled by both Mexican and American enterprises exceed 75 percent, and attest to the essentially international character of Nogales' commerce.[46] Wholesale trade dominates in spite of the fact that Mexican and American tourists vastly swell retail trade. Thus, the position of Nogales, as the chief portal to the Mexican West Coast, as well as that region's gate to the United States, makes this border town a wholesale

---

[44]   Arizona Development Board, *Nogales and Santa Cruz County* (no date, actually 1960), p. 17; Almada, pp. 5-7.

[45]   "Both Nogales" is a term used by the natives of the twin towns along with "Los Dos Nogales," the latter being the original name of the settlement. It was so called because of two walnut trees — *nogales* — which stood close to each other on either side of the boundary. These names are once again applicable, but for a different reason. Granger, pp. 320-21.

[46]   Arizona Development Board, *Nogales and Santa Cruz County*, p. 10.

center of considerable importance, ranking second to Phoenix within Arizona.[47]

Unlike almost all the other desert settlements ("desert settlements" are here interpreted as settlements which exist primarily to serve the desert region), the size of Nogales does not depend upon local irrigated agriculture — for this plays almost no part in the economic functions of this town. Being international, the commercial area served is very wide, and to understand the underlying forces dominating the commerce of these border communities, one must go first to the heart of the world-wide division between the developed and the underdeveloped nations. Nogales, Arizona, representing the former, exports machinery, transport equipment, and petroleum products. It also exports large quantities of seed, fertilizer, and insecticides, which mirror the agricultural economy of its Mexican trade partner. Nogales, Sonora, receives these in exchange for the primary products of fisheries, farms, ranches, and mines.[48]

In spite of political division, the essential economic unity of the two halves cannot be overemphasized. In some respects, this mutual interdependence is greater in Ambos Nogales than that found between the north and south sides of a politically unified community. The reliance upon diurnal immigrant labor by Nogales, Arizona, enterprises and upon international markets for products sold in shops on either side of the border is close to complete.

The international policies of both nations have a commanding effect on the two communities' economies. Strategic stockpiling, embargoes, tariffs, quotas, subsidies, and quarantines such as that placed on cattle for fear of foot-and-mouth disease directly affect the prosperity of Nogales and all other border towns within the region. The most recent of these was the cutback by the U. S. government in the fall of 1965 in the quota of liquor imports allowed to individual tourists reentering the U. S. This currently is having adverse effects on the Nogales economy. All these are factors over which regional interests have only limited and indirect influence if they have any influence at all.

The unity of these politically divided towns is nowhere more clearly visible than in the free-trade zones which surround each Mexican border community. Most American goods may enter the Mexican border town without duty, but if they are transshipped to the interior, they must pass customs inspection. This is accomplished by stationing inspectors along the desert roads that lead south. At least one, and sometimes a series of two or three customs stations are located at intervals beginning just

---

[47] U. S. Bureau of the Census, *Census of Business, 1962.*
[48] Arizona Development Board, *Nogales and Santa Cruz County,* pp. 10-11.

outside the town limits. These are lonely stations that suddenly appear out of the burro bush and mesquite. All vehicles are required to stop for inspection. American tourists must show papers permitting the temporary importation of their cars, a requirement that is not necessary at the boundary itself. Mexican nationals, driving cars or trucks with Mexican markings, must prove whether ownership of the vehicle is in the interior of the country, or if the car is owned in the border town and is dutiable. These multiple stations may impede, but certainly do not choke off, contraband, which is a major "industry" along the border.

The very existence of the free-trade zones surrounding even the smallest border towns, the customs stations, and the continued contraband, are all the result of the unsurpassed economic pressures on this most sharply delineated boundary between the developed and underdeveloped worlds. Where labor costs may increase tenfold within a distance of ten miles, where standards of living, although more difficult to measure, vary somewhat less sharply, where levels of technology and mechanization show such contrast that methods already obsolescent in the United States have yet to be introduced into Mexico, some form of economic buffer area is necessary. The free-trade zone was chosen by the Mexican government to serve this purpose, and it acts as an economic midway station in what would otherwise be a no-man's land between countries with widely separated levels of economic development.

Among the remaining border towns located within the Sonoran Desert region there are both similarity to and variance from the Nogales pattern. Naco and Douglas-Agua Prieta are like Nogales in that they are situated outside the desert itself but are intimately associated as border towns with an economy which is desert oriented. They differ from Nogales in that mining (particularly copper) dominates their economies.[49] Douglas is, in fact, the child of the Bisbee mines, and its situation was determined by the proximity of these mines, the availability of water, and transcontinental rail connections, which meant fuel for the copper smelter, its chief industry.[50] The twenty-mile-wide Sulphur Spring Valley was chosen as the best location for the smelter, but the exact site of Douglas was chosen because of its position on the international boundary.

Its Mexican twin, Agua Prieta, has the usual commercial relationship with Douglas,[51] but instead of good communications with the rest

---

[49]   Thomas J. McCleneghan and Philip G. Olson, *Douglas, Arizona: An Economic Report* (University of Arizona Bureau of Business and Public Research, Special Study No. 13, Tucson, 1957), pp. 1-11.

[50]   Glenn S. Dumke, "Douglas: Border Town," *Pacific Historical Review*, Vol. 17 (1948), pp. 283-98.

[51]   *Ibid.*, p. 290.

— RAY MANLEY PHOTOGRAPHY

Aerial and low-level photographs of the border crossing at Nogales showing the modern customs buildings on both sides. The railway leading into Mexico crosses the line at a 45-degree angle from the bottom left. The gull-wing structure in both photos is the Mexican immigration building.

— BILL SEARS

of the state of Sonora and the Mexican West Coast, it must rely on a more local hinterland.[52] Mention has been made of the Nacozari railway. Cattle play an important part in its economy for Agua Prieta is backed by lush semiarid plains and mountains which reach south and east into Chihuahua. It is this position commanding the best of two east-west routes over the Sierra that has given Agua Prieta its strategic position. This route may, in the future, have important economic consequences for Agua Prieta, but at the present it is little traveled because it lacks a good paved road.

Naco, Arizona-Sonora, though much smaller, is tied to copper and cattle in the same way as Douglas-Agua Prieta. Its importance as a border town fluctuates with the economics of these products, notably the former. A fall in the price of copper, or a new United States government policy concerning this commodity, affects the mines at both Bisbee and Cananea, an effect which is rapidly mirrored in Naco.

Through the more desolate countryside west of Nogales, the international boundary stretches through the least-populated region of the Sonoran Desert to meet the Colorado River at San Luis, Arizona-Sonora. The population is limited by the rainfall, which decreases in this direction, San Luis receiving only 2.3 inches annually. In spite of these arid conditions which leave the border virtually uninhabited, there have developed three border towns; Sasabe, Sonoita-Lukeville, and San Luis, Arizona-Sonora. Sasabe is the smallest of these binodal settlements, having only local significance. Situated on the edge of Papaguería, its population is in part tri-lingual.

Sonoita-Lukeville was mentioned before as being unique in that it existed before the boundary survey. It is the site of a prehistoric Indian settlement that depended upon the intermittent waters of the Río Sonoita, which, though its flow is largely underground, comes to the surface above Sonoita village. Papago Indians utilized this water for irrigation as did their Mexican descendants.[53] It achieved momentary attention during the California gold rush when it was the last sure source of water along the infamous track which rightly came to be known as the Camino del Diablo. West of the Sonoita oasis one could, until a few years ago, still come across the bleached bones of the unlucky argonauts who found only dust instead of water in the Tinajas Altas (Spanish for "high jars"— a series of tanks or water-filled hollows high on the side of a desert

---

[52]   There have been high hopes for the completion of the railway south from Nacozari to Cd. Obregón, making Douglas-Agua Prieta "The Gateway to Mexico." At the time of writing there is little hope.

[53]   Ronald L. Ives, "The Origin of the Sonoita Townsite, Sonora, Mexico," *American Antiquity* (1941), pp. 20-28.

The border crossing at Sonoita-Lukeville is traversed by tens of thousands of tourists and weekend vacationers every year. The customs house is a familiar sight upon entering Mexico. A mile from the crossing is the only pre-Guadalupe Hidalgo Treaty border town and genuine oasis — Sonoita. It is interesting that the oldest border town today depends mainly on east-west communications from the interior to Baja California. The photo below illustrates this by depicting a service to the California-bound bracero. To the American fisherman, the United States customs house marks a milestone on the way home.

— NATIONAL PARK SERVICE PHOTOS

mountain range of the same name). For more than 135 miles between Sonoita and Yuma, this arid, lifeless track crossed no streams, and what water there was available was to be found in these natural rock cavities whose supply was replenished occasionally by infrequent showers. This is one more reason why Sonoita is different from other border towns. Its primary importance has always been as a station along a roughly east-west route paralleling the frontier, rather than being a border crossing point. Within the last five years, a paved highway has been completed from Hermosillo west to Mexicali, and Sonoita again occupies the position of being the last stop before one travels what is perhaps the most deserted stretch of paved highway in North America. Sonoita is also on the highway to Puerto Peñasco (Rocky Point), to which thousands of American tourists, fishermen, and boaters travel each year. Ironically, this makes the outlying oasis of Sonoita one of only two towns in the state of Sonora (the other being Navojoa) where two paved roads cross.[54] Lukeville, Arizona, is no more than a straggling line of houses back from the customs station.

San Luis, Arizona-Sonora, on the Colorado is yet a different type of border town. Here the boundary passes through this valley with its rich deltaic and mesa soils which have been brought under cultivation through the control and distribution of the Colorado's water. San Luis, Sonora, is the chief center of an agricultural area having the same name and comprising an estimated 74,000 acres. The chief function of San Luis is to provide market, mill, and railway for local irrigation agriculture, but the town also achieves prominence as a "typical border town" because of the nearness of Yuma with its military establishments. San Luis, Arizona, its undernourished twin, is the southernmost settlement in the rich Yuma-Somerton-Gadsden agricultural district.

By far the largest of these politically bifurcated desert communities is Mexicali-Calexico. Mexicali, whose rapidly growing population exceeds 200,000 inhabitants, is the capital of the state of Baja California and is unique among all border towns, Mexican or American, in being a state capital. This is interpreted by some Mexican nationalists as being the complete surrender of at least one state to *pochismo*. More accurately, it is the intelligent recognition that only in the extreme north of this arid peninsular state, adjacent to the border, has the availability of water encouraged the increase of population upon which political power depends.

Mexicali and the state of Baja California are more closely asso-

---

[54]   Even Hermosillo cannot claim this distinction. This points to what probably is the greatest economic shortcoming of Mexico's Northwest — the lack of good roads.

ciated with, and dependent upon, the United States than any other community in Mexico. The all-important water which has allowed the growth and prosperity of the Colorado Basin south of the international boundary originates entirely within the United States. The remarkable growth of Mexican agriculture and industry within the region is entirely dependent upon the language of the treaty provisions dealing with water utilization between the two countries.[55] Without this treaty guaranteeing the availability of water to Mexico, and the works constructed to deliver it, the Mexicali region would suffer immeasurably from both the vicissitudes of nature and Washington. Planned and continued growth would be impossible. Mexicali and the Colorado Delta south of the border would have remained, or would revert to, desert. The dependence is complete.

Through Mexicali, in the years since the establishment of the West Coast railway, there have passed more braceros on their way to the fields and factories of California than have left Mexico through any other single exit. A large measure of the commodities produced in the Mexicali region is either consumed in the United States or shipped from San Diego and other West Coast ports. Perhaps no other single Mexican district is so affected by American capital which continually invests in the machines and improved agricultural technology, that are the models for domestically owned enterprise. However, in all of the above cases, this influence is rapidly decreasing.

The close association with and dependence of the region south of the border upon California and the United States may also be explained by the fact that almost two thousand miles of road separate peninsular California from Mexico City. In addition, the dynamic growth of California during recent decades has swept the Mexican border into its social sphere in the same way that its influence has buffeted the economy and population structure of the Southwestern states. The Mexican lament, "So far from God, so near the United States," finds its most exaggerated reality along the border between Mexico and California. Volcanic Los Angeles, which has reached northeast to Owens Valley, east to the Colorado River, and with the recent bond issue, once again north five hundred miles to the Feather River in the largest single water-supply project in history, must look constantly for new sources of water. Coastal Southern California, whose population will exceed twenty million (if estimates are correct) by the year 1980, covets the water of the Colorado. Modern engineering has allowed it to tap these waters, probably the only time on record that a society has taken huge quantities

---

[55] *The Colorado: A Comprehensive Report,* p. 67.

of water from a desert (Parker Dam, annual rainfall 5.04 inches) to distribute within a humid area (Los Angeles annual rainfall, 14.76 inches)! The continued existence of the Mexicali region is dependent upon the safeguards written into the treaty of 1944 between the two nations.[56] Mexicali is itself a creature of international politics in the same way that its fields are a product of the Colorado River.

Calexico, Mexicali's undersized twin, is subject to many of the same problems resulting from the international boundary. Its fortunes are tied to those of the Imperial Valley and California's position in the struggle for Colorado River water. It is, in many ways, more of a small market town than a "typical" border town. Its international functions appear to be grafted on to its local *raison d'être*. Whereas Mexicali is the capital of a state which was brought into separate existence in order to maintain a nation's position on the Pacific, Calexico has been, and is, in contrast, a prosperous but unsuccessful aspirant to the county seat of Imperial County, California.

The one overriding characteristic of the border town is its dependence upon international trade between the two countries. Within recent years the movement of food products northward has dominated a rising volume of Mexican exports to the United States. In contrast, Mexico has been importing less through its western desert frontier than in the 1950's. As mentioned before, Mexican imports mirror the needs of a rapidly developing economy. Machinery and vehicles account for approximately two-thirds of Mexico's imports through the Arizona Customs District. Despite the growth of a domestic auto industry resulting in a decreased importation of passenger cars, this commodity group continues to dominate Mexican imports from the western United States. In this category, agricultural machinery ranks first, being over twice that of the total for autos, trucks, buses, and parts. Of small but increasing importance is the importation of air-conditioning and air-cooling equipment, most of it manufactured in Arizona. Food products amount to only about 5 percent of total Mexican imports, while dairy products have shown recent increases typical of demand in countries undergoing a rapid rise in standards of living. The importation of feed and fodder has increased but remains low as cattlemen south of the border continue to follow historical patterns. An increasingly significant import has been natural and liquefied petroleum gases, another sign of an increased standard of living within an area far removed from Mexican centers of petroleum production. Since 1960 the importation of fertilizers from Arizona points

---

[56]   *Ibid.*

has increased, while pesticides have decreased slightly. In every case it must be remembered that the demand for American products in Mexico's Northwest is affected not only by the domestic ability to supply needs but also by increased competition from overseas suppliers through the ports of Guaymas, Topolobampo, and Mazatlán.

American imports across this desert frontier have, in contrast, increased during almost every year in the last decade. During the fifties, winter vegetables gained primacy. Since 1960, seafood, mainly shrimp, has led all imports through Arizona and California border points, until today it comprises about one-half the total dollar volume of all imports. With the reopening of the border to cattle (following the foot-and-mouth disease eradication campaign in Mexico) imports have risen until cattle today rank third behind seafood and winter vegetables. In this latter category fresh tomatoes in season constitute the bulk of vegetable imports. All vegetables and fruits including cantaloupes have shown slight declines since 1960. One should not interpret this as having any more than short-term significance since both demand in the United States and land under irrigation in northern Sinaloa continue to increase. All non-food items constitute only about 5 percent of total American imports — nearly the exact converse of the largely nonagricultural exports to Mexico.

Another contrast in the flow of goods to the north and south of the border is the marked seasonal variation in American imports which does not occur in exports, the flow of goods southward having little or no seasonal change. The time of greatest imports has always been in the late winter and spring. This is due to the overlapping shipping seasons in shrimp, vegetables, cantaloupe, and cattle. The spring peak in the import of fresh vegetables is reinforced by the coincidence of heavy imports of cattle, while the increased imports of autumn are the result of simultaneous shipments of cattle and shrimp. The import of all three major commodities is low or nonexistent during the summer months. All of this is once again due to the basic contrast between agricultural northwest Mexico and its nonagricultural trading partner.

THE COLORADO RIVER CONFLICT

One of the knottiest problems of political geography within the Sonoran Desert merits close examination. The Colorado River, which drains the northwestern one-third of the Sonoran Desert is, for a very short part of its course, the boundary between the United States and Mexico. Through its entire course within the desert it is a boundary between either American or Mexican states. The very real drawbacks and possible political consequences of selecting a river as a boundary are well known.[57] The Colorado River presents enough unique and immensely significant problems fraught with emotion to merit careful investigation.

When political boundaries were first introduced to the region in 1848 the banks of the Colorado lacked any permanent white settlement. The valley of the Colorado presented one of the most difficult environments to early settlers. The chief concern of the treaty makers when the treaties of 1848 and 1853 were negotiated was the preservation and protection of navigation rights on the Colorado River.[58] In these early treaties no provisions at all were made from the apportionment and control of water for irrigation. There was in fact no need for regulation at that time since only the most limited use was made of the Colorado's water, and that for the watering of livestock and some primitive irrigation, mainly by the Yuma Indians.

The navigable aspects of the Colorado were important to the treaty makers since these concerned trans-desert communications to California. The thought of other impending conflicts was as remote as glacial ice in an uninhabitated, and largely unwanted, desert. The day when virtually every gallon of the Colorado's water would be negotiated for, apportioned, analyzed for quality, and delivered to hundreds of thousands of consumers within the desert, and millions more in coastal Southern California, was within the lives of their own offspring but not even remotely within their own imagination.

International Aspects of the Colorado River

The political implications of using the water of the internationalized Colorado for irrigation came to light officially only after the turn of the century. Only at this time was the direct effect of physical geography upon the apportionment of the Colorado's water realized. In 1902 the first major effort to divert water from the Colorado was effected through an abandoned distributary of this river which traverses Mexican territory but empties into the Salton Basin in California. In delineating a boundary along a straight line between the mouth of the Gila River and the southern margin of San Diego Bay, the treaty makers had crossed and recrossed this most advantageous channel leading to the irrigable lands of the Imperial Valley. The close proximity of the Colorado's delta to the Salton trough became, through political accident, a source of possible conflict.

---

[57] H. W. Weigert, *The Principles of Political Geography* (New York, 1957), pp. 97-100.

[58] Article 4 of the Treaty between the United States and Mexico concluded at the City of Mexico, 30 December 1854 — the "Gadsden Treaty."

Until well into the twentieth century both governments continued to consider the Colorado only in terms of navigation,[59] while the local settlers were busily diverting ever more of the Colorado's water. There still existed no international agreement or treaty providing for the diversion of this water or for the maintenance of navigation in the border regions as envisaged in the early treaties. There existed no international guarantee that water already diverted by the expanding population of the Mexicali-Imperial Valley would remain theirs.[60]

With or without a treaty, water was being withdrawn, and navigation was being interfered with, both through the lack of water and the construction of the Laguna Dam above Yuma. Both Mexican and American interests in the low-lying irrigated lands were in jeopardy until some permanent allocation of water was completed between the two countries. However, the water taken from the Colorado had in itself created the political forces that would perpetuate the already existing diversion. Water meant wealth and increased population in the valley. The principal vested interest of this expanding population was the Colorado's water. Navigation on the Colorado, which never was of great significance, gave way to irrigation as the latter assumed greater economic importance.

The curious position of Mexico in the Lower Colorado Valley remained unaltered. She continued to receive water which for all practical purposes originated entirely within the United States. At the same time, the irrigated lands of California's Imperial Valley received their water only through Mexico's consent. This standoff ended as the United States, through the construction of the All-American Canal, terminated its reliance upon Mexico's Alamo Canal for the delivery of water. Extended droughts throughout the decade of the 1930's brought about a critical situation on the Lower Colorado. It was apparent that some kind of international understanding was needed on what finally was recognized as a limited amount of water. A treaty ratified in 1944 between the two countries confirmed the annual delivery to Mexico of 1,500,000 acre-feet "from any and all sources" within the Colorado Valley.

Until 1961 the language of this treaty appeared to be adequate, and Mexico constructed the Morelos diversion dam, assuring the flow of water to fields in the Mexicali district. In that year, however, the

---

[59] A Captain Edgar Jadwin reported to Congress in 1903 that irrigation had been undertaken by two companies, but that "these companies have not as yet taken out sufficient water to materially interfere with navigation. Fortunately the period of the year when the land requires the greatest amount of irrigation coincides with the time of higher water on the river." Timm, p. 192.

[60] *The Colorado: A Comprehensive Report,* p. 66.

just-completed Wellton-Mohawk reclamation project began draining salt water into the Colorado from salt-impregnated land within the project. The new American irrigation system was leaching salt water out of the soil and dumping it into the main stream above the Morelos Dam diversion. The salt content of the Colorado at the border rose from a tolerable 800 parts per million to more than 6,000 ppm. Land in the Mexicali Valley was threatened with permanent damage. Demonstrations erupted and Mexican officials in the area demanded action against "aggressive" American irrigation policy. Although the treaty stated that water was to be delivered from "any and all sources," the State Department realized that the U. S. was vulnerable under international law. In 1965 an agreement was reached between the two governments whereby the U. S. will build a thirteen-mile canal to divert brackish water leached from the Wellton-Lower Gila lands and deliver it to a point below the Morelos Dam where it will flow directly into the Gulf of California. (At the time of writing this canal was under construction.)

Thus, the 1.5 million acre-feet of water that is to be delivered annually to Mexico is interpreted as being water suitable for irrigation and not waste water unutilizable by American irrigators, since the entire available supply of Colorado water was appropriated north of the border.

The Arizona-California Controversy

The recognition of the Colorado's inability to supply all the demands placed upon it for water has led to one of the most bitter and extended interstate conflicts in the history of water law, not between Mexico and the United States, but between Arizona and California.

Laws concerning water rights in America were based originally upon the English Common Law of the seventeenth century; it was the law of the kingdom and not the empire. "Since England was a humid country with numerous small streams and abundant rainfall there had been no occasion for irrigation within the islands; consequently the English Common Law had not developed to meet the needs of the institution of irrigation. . . ."[61] However, "Had England been an arid country instead of a humid one, it is safe to say that the common law . . . would have followed the needs of an arid region,"[62] it being absurd to apply the water law of a humid region to a desert.

This was recognized by the Supreme Court of the Territory of Arizona in 1888 when it stated that "up to about a third of a century

---

[61]   Webb, *The Great Plains,* p. 432.

[62]   C. R. Van Hise, *The Conservation of Natural Resources in the United States,* quoted in *ibid.,* p. 385.

ago . . . the territory of Arizona had been subject to the laws and customs of Mexico, and the common law had been unknown; and that law has never been, and is not now, suited to the conditions that exist here, so far as the same applies to the uses of water."[63] The Mexicans and Spanish before them had recognized Roman civil law which was in turn suited to the needs of irrigators in the Mediterranean Basin. Arizona and California courts have consistently reaffirmed the continuity of Roman, Spanish, and Mexican law in their jurisdictions.

Arizona, among other western states, accepted the diversion of water from a stream for "beneficial" use regardless of the dimunition of that stream. The water could be used on either riparian or nonriparian lands whereas the common law would leave all land not immediately adjacent to the stream "high and dry." The "Arid Region Doctrine" granted to the first appropriator an exclusive right "and to later appropriators rights conditioned upon the prior rights of those who have gone before." Not to use the water is to forfeit the privilege of using it. All states, from Texas and the Missouri River west, have in one way or another adopted the "Arid Region Doctrine." It is generally conceded that this doctrine has been the necessary legal condition allowing the most rational application of gravity water to irrigable fields. Without it most irrigation projects would have had to make the land conform to the law — an impossibility. Western water law was an outgrowth of the realization that in a humid region value is attached to land alone, but in the desert value inheres in the land only as water is made available to it. In effect, it is water alone that has value, for it is the scarce or limited factor. Within the desert, miles of greasewood without water remain virtually valueless. The orderly distribution of water was to become as vitally important in a desert society as the distribution of land had been in the Mississippi Valley.

However, the configuration of the Lower Colorado River Basin, the river's irregular flow, and other factors, such as the total expropriation of the Gila River's water by Arizona, has led to numerous complications. Since the most easily irrigable land lies on the California margin of the river, Arizona has feared the total appropriation of the Colorado's water by California interests. Under the Arid Region Doctrine nothing seemed to prevent this.

The Colorado River and its tributaries drain an area of 244,000 square miles in seven states and Mexico. The river has, on several occasions, been declared navigable, thus placing its main stream under

---

[63] Clesson S. Kinney, *A Treatise on the Law of Irrigation* (San Francisco, 1912), p. 1012.

federal control. Its waters can only be distributed in accordance with federal law. Tributaries have, on the other hand, remained under the jurisdiction of the various states. This confused pattern has persistently defied any permanent solution to the problem of apportioning equitably the Colorado's waters which are distributed to the irrigation ditches and, for all practical purposes, are used up and unavailable to any other agency. Compared to this, navigation rights, which have been one of the thorniest problems of multiple jurisdiction in Europe, pale to insignificance. The quality of river water used for any purpose other than irrigation may be changed downstream, but until it reaches the sea it exists as a renewable resource. A river whose waters are entirely consumed by irrigation resembles a limited body of ore, and the conflicts along that river are those of the mining camp. There is no room for compromise. An improvement in the position of any one party means a consequent diminution in the sum of the remainder.

Despite continuing successful appropriation of water in the Lower Basin, floods and siltation remained a constant menace to the valley. Millions of dollars spent for levees brought only partial and temporary respite from danger. The answer to the recurring flood-silt-flood cycle was the multipurpose Hoover Dam. Only this would allow the eventual total utilization of the Colorado's water. In so doing, however, the tempo of conflict would quicken. Arizona's gain had to mean California's loss. A solution so daring met with active resistance from the states of the Upper Basin; the headwater states, Colorado, Wyoming, New Mexico, and Utah, feared that a controlled lower river would stimulate its development, and hasten the appropriation of water by the Lower Basin States at the permanent expense of later upstream development. A deadlock between the upper states, where 91 percent of the Colorado's water originated, and the lower states, where it could most readily be utilized, was broken in 1921 by federal and state legislation, which authorized the negotiation of the first interstate river compact.

The commission authorized to apportion the waters of the river among the seven states reached a compromise which equally divided what the negotiators wrongly assumed to be about 75 percent of the Colorado River system water supply between the Upper and the Lower basins. Each basin is apportioned in perpetuity 7,500,000 acre-feet annually of the waters of the Colorado River system defined by the compact as the Colorado River and its tributaries in the United States. (Provisions were made for allocating to each basin the burden of any treaty that might later be negotiated between the United States and Mexico.)

Six states promptly ratified the Colorado River Compact in 1923.

Arizona refused. Its principal reason was the Gila River which was included as a tributary of the "Colorado River System" as defined in the Compact, but whose waters had already been appropriated and been put to use entirely within the state of Arizona. For Arizona to admit the inclusion of the Gila River, with nearly two million acre-feet, would result in the diminution of Arizona's claim to mainstream water.

While Arizona remained out of the Compact, the federal government went ahead with the Boulder Canyon Project Act, authorizing construction of Hoover Dam and the All-American Canal to serve the Imperial-Coachella Valley. California's right to appropriate ever more water from the Colorado was limited to 4,400,000 acre-feet under further legislation. This limitation was brought about by the fear of all other interested parties that the geographical position of California would be so favorable after the completion of Hoover Dam that only strong legislation could keep the entire Colorado from flowing into the below-sea-level desert valleys, and onto the coastal plain of Los Angeles.

In attempts to halt California's diversion of water in excess of the limitation, Arizona tried and failed on three separate occasions during the thirties to have the courts set aside the Compact.

Finally, Arizona approved a contract with the United States for the delivery to that state of no more than 2,800,000 acre-feet annually from the "Colorado River System." The contract itself expressly left undetermined the exact meaning of "Colorado River System" and the controversies among the states. On the basis of this contract, Arizona sued California in 1952. Arizona claimed that the 2.8 million acre-feet were all in the main stream and did not include the water of the Gila River. Arizona's argument came to rest on the simple contention that since water does not flow upstream, the Upper Basin is wholly unconcerned, and so is the Compact, with the Lower Basin tributaries.[64]

California counterclaimed that due to prior right of "beneficial consumptive use,"[65] any losses due to evaporation or lack of sufficient supply during years of drought should not affect its entitlement to 4.4 million acre-feet; Arizona contended that any shortages should be suffered on a pro-rata basis.

After years of testimony, the Special Master submitted his report

---

[64] In 1944 Arizona passed statutes purporting to ratify the Colorado River Compact.

[65] Charles E. Corker, "The Issues in Arizona v. California," in *Resources Development: Frontiers for Research,* Franklin S. Pollak, ed. (Western Resources Conference, 1959; Boulder, Colo., 1960). Beneficial consumptive use has been defined as "the difference between water diverted and water which returns to the main stream after use for irrigation." P. 91 ff.

to the Supreme Court, and this was made public in May, 1960. Briefly, the report recommended that:

1. Arizona's definition of consumptive use, e.g., diversion less return flow, be upheld.
2. Waters of the mainstream below Lake Mead be divided, and the Gila and all other tributaries below Lake Mead be excluded.
3. The Mexican Treaty obligation of 1,500,000 acre-feet annually should get first call. This sum should be borne by the Lower Basin, but, when the surplus above 7,500,000 is insufficient to meet this draft, the Upper Basin would be called upon to share the deficiency on a 50-50 basis.
4. Arizona be granted 2,800,000 acre-feet annually, and Nevada 300,-000, and that California be limited to 4,400,000 acre-feet, or nearly 1,000,000 acre-feet less than it is now diverting from the mainstream.
5. Water in excess of 7,500,000 acre-feet, and the treaty obligation of 1,500,000 acre-feet, be divided equally between Arizona and California.
6. If Nevada signs a contract with the federal government to develop an irrigation project, it should share in any surplus water to the extent of 4 percent, which would reduce Arizona's share of the surplus to 46 percent.
7. If the flow below Lake Mead is insufficient to meet allocations, the water should be divided on the same percentage basis as allocated: Arizona to get 28/75ths; California 44/75ths; and Nevada 3/75ths.
8. Prior rights of Indian tribes should be scrupulously observed.

The Supreme Court in its final decision substantially upheld the 1960 report in favor of Arizona. Of primary importance was the opinion that the water from which California could calculate its share of the Colorado River was in the mainstream only. The waters of the Gila River were reserved to Arizona, significantly reducing the amount claimable by California as surplus.

The court's decision, however, places the entire Arid Region Doctrine in jeopardy since "prior appropriation for beneficial consumptive use" is conditioned by the contention that "all water rights are appurtenant to the public domain and may be privately acquired only by affirmative legislation of Congress."[66]

That there is not enough water in the Colorado River to satisfy the claims of the Upper Basin states, Mexico, the newly confirmed grant of 2,800,000 acre-feet to Arizona, and the 300,000 acre-feet to Nevada, while at the same time supplying California with enough water for existing projects is quite apparent.

---

[66]   Corker in *ibid.*, p. 102.

If the total net usable supply available to the three Lower Basin states is in fact only 5,850,000 acre-feet in an average year while the allocation of water to the three states is 7,500,000 acre-feet, none of these states will be able to obtain their allocation from the river. In a normal year the 5,850,000 acre-feet or less would be divided on the basis outlined in Section Seven of the court's preliminary report. This could mean that California might receive no more than approximately 3,200,000 acre-feet whereas she presently obtains 5,378,000 acre-feet for existing projects. This would mean that approximately 200,000 acres of irrigated land (or its equivalent) would revert to desert if no alternative supply of water is made available.

The Central Arizona Project

With the final legal obstacle surmounted, Arizona is pressing for enactment of the Central Arizona Project. The need for this complex water-delivery system is based upon the declining water tables of central and southern Arizona. With over 4,000,000 acre-feet being withdrawn annually, most of which is not subject to replenishment even in years of above-average rainfall, Arizona must look to the Colorado River to supplement a dwindling supply. Without Colorado River water, irrigated acreage in Arizona will decline by one-third in the next decade.[67]

As presently constituted, the project would draw 1,200,000 acre-feet from Lake Havasu and by the use of pumps, elevate that water 985 feet. The power for this would come from the proposed Hualapai Canyon Dam in the Grand Canyon National Monument. The water would then be carried 240 miles by siphon and canal to an additional reservoir just above the existing Granite Reef Dam on the Salt River. A portion of this water would be supplied to the farms and municipalities of the Salt River Valley, freeing approximately 500,000 acre-feet of water to the Casa Grande Valley where depletion through pumping is in a critically advanced state. This would be accomplished by construction of a new canal seventy-five miles in length to the vicinity of Picacho. To complete the project, dams would be built on the upstream San Pedro and at the Buttes damsite on the Gila. Eventually, Colorado River water would be delivered to Tucson, a total distance of 375 miles from Lake Havasu. About one-third of the power produced at Hualapai Canyon Dam would be needed to lift Colorado River water the 985 feet to central Arizona. Of the 1,200,000 acre-feet diverted, an estimated 814,000 acre-feet would be used for agricultural purposes, and 256,000

---

[67] U. S. House of Representatives, *The Central Arizona Project,* Hearings, 82nd Congress, 1st Sess. (Washington, D.C., 1951), Part I, page 68.

acre-feet for municipal and industrial uses. About 120,000 acre-feet would be lost to evaporation and seepage.

The merits of the project have been argued vehemently pro and con, exponents of the latter position contending that the Central Arizona Project would be (as Mann quotes) a "gift to land boomers who profligately wasted the precious underground water resources by over-expanding and now wish to be bailed out by the federal government . . . a gigantic raid on the public treasury amounting to billions of dollars."[68] This may or may not be true. It is, however, incontestable that the Central Arizona Project is an attempt to remedy a withdrawal of largely irreplaceable underground water exceeding 4,000,000 acre-feet by bringing 1,200,000 acre-feet of Colorado River water to the central valleys of Arizona. In other words, it is proposed to remedy an overdraft of underground water by an overdraft of Colorado River water. It is, at best, a partial answer to a problem which will be paid for by the abandonment of irrigated land elsewhere, since all the Colorado River's water, like the underground water of Arizona, is at the present time utilized to a level above average annual replenishment. Only with the addition of water to the mainstream Colorado from some other basin — such as the Columbia or Yukon — can all of the present demands be met. Already proposals along this line are meeting stiff opposition from Pacific Northwest congressmen.

---

[68]   Mann, p. 143.

CHAPTER FOURTEEN

A Pattern of Settlement

From the earliest times the struggle for land has been perhaps the central theme of Mexican history in the arid Northwest as well as elsewhere. Failure in this conflict has usually resulted in peonage, migration, or genocide. This has in turn shaped the population's distribution and composition. The more recent and most familiar episodes in this epic struggle began with the independence of Mexico, developed after the entrance of the United States and American capital into the region, and reached a climax during the Mexican Revolution. Earlier antagonists were replaced by new forces on both sides of the border, but the seeds of conflict were sown long before.

Among the natives of the Mesa Central, land hunger and tribal conflict predated the first Spanish entrada. A well-defined system of tenure based upon Aztec hegemony existed, bringing both order and slavery to the majority of the Mesa's Indian population. The Spaniards, through the encomienda, "exported" a similar system of feudal land tenure to the outlying frontier.[1] Through the centuries, Aztec rule was exchanged for Spanish, the encomienda became the hacienda, but the landless Indian remained the base of a seemingly eternal Mexican social pyramid. The conditions of *latifundismo* determined the distribution, settlement, and utilization of land, first in the densely populated core, and later along the expanding frontier. Great rural estates aspiring for self-suffi-ciency, seeking arable land and water, as well as wood and pasturage, moved north with the frontier. Native people, who may or may not have been previously missionized, were distributed among the hacendados,

---

[1] Whetten, pp. 79-85.

and their villages incorporated into the haciendas. Many of the haciendas, which seldom contained less than 2,500 acres,[2] were so large that they were divided into several ranchos or estancias.[3] Even with such subdivision, most of the haciendas were too vast to be developed intensively, and extensive tracts were left entirely unused.[4] Throughout Mexico the concentration of land in a very few hands shaped the evolution of agriculture, industry, and commerce.

On the northern frontier, diminishing rainfall and a sparser population placed limits on the economic development of the hacienda (or on any other system of land tenure). Only the introduction of domestic animals facilitated the expansion of large landholdings — cattle ranches — into regions where remunerative exploitation would otherwise have been confined to the limited riverine areas suitable to irrigation under primitive conditions. Thus the introduction of livestock allowed the extension of an already long-established pattern of settlement and tenure into a marginal region. The competition for land which already existed among the sedentary tribes of Sinaloa and Sonora was extended from the irrigable tracts to the intervening uplands as the cattle ranching of white men gave these areas resource status.

Despite the success of the cattlemen, many of the larger tribes continued to remain intractable and largely outside the haciendas. The populous Cahita in particular failed to be absorbed by the haciendas which exploited the desert vegetation. Colonial cattlemen had to rely on transient white or mestizo labor which, due to its scarcity, demanded the highest wages in New Spain. Haciendas were unable to prosper where labor was mobile and relatively well paid. In Sonora a great deal of potential rangeland never fell inside the limits of the *latifundias* but remained either outside the northern and northwestern frontiers of the province, or within the native enclaves. The irrigable valley land necessary to the development of feudal self-sufficiency was stoutly defended by both Indian and missionary from the hacendados. Lacking Indian labor which could be impressed into serfdom within the haciendas, and pushing hard against the natural limit of land suitable for cattle raising, the arid "western slope contained [in 1910] the smallest number of haciendas among all the natural regions in Mexico."[5]

In 1910 there were in Sinaloa (excluding the *distrito* of Mazatlán)

---

2   McBride, p. 25.
3   Frank Tannenbaum, *The Mexican Agrarian Revolution* (New York, 1929), p. 106.
4   McBride, p. 27.
5   *Ibid.*, p. 81.

— DAVID A. HENDERSON

On the northern frontier, where diminishing rainfall and a sparser population combined to limit the economic development of the hacienda, only the introduction of cattle facilitated the expansion of large landholdings. These large holdings have nearly all been broken up, but most land is still privately owned, and small subsistence ranchos like the modest one pictured here are common.

no more than 37 haciendas concentrated primarily in the Culiacán, Sinaloa, and Fuerte valleys. In this same year there were 265 smaller holdings still larger than 2,500 acres; these properties averaged approximately 13,000 acres each. Much of this land was of little agricultural value so that the smaller tracts provided little more than subsistence for a few families.[6]

In Sonora where the encomienda was never an effective agent of native suppression, and the natural vegetation provided even less incentive for the development of haciendas, large landholdings were fewer than in Sinaloa, there being no more than 77 properties which, in 1910, exceeded 2,500 acres.[7] In contrast, the number of even smaller subsistence holdings on the northern frontier was relatively large, despite the arid conditions which necessitated more extensive agricultural methods. As early as 1810 there were in the province of Sonora as many as 356 ranchos (a term applied to individually owned properties which vary greatly in size, but which generally refers to a relatively small rural property worked by the owner himself with the aid of his immediate family). This constituted an exception to the general distribution of small holdings which were concentrated on the Mesa Central, scattered among the great colonial latifundias.

Mexican independence resulted in the transference of many haciendas to creole or mestizo ownership, but did not destroy the large holdings. The social disorders did, however, free prospective settlers for the northern frontier and the newly independent Mexican government gave additional incentive in the form of legislation for the distribution of land to colonizers. Though the new laws wisely specified large tracts, since a larger area would be necessary to support a family in an arid district, the grants were by Sonoran standards small holdings. At the same time the secularization of mission lands acted as a magnet, drawing prospective small holders to the irrigated valleys of central Sonora. These comprised a disproportionately large number of white adventurers who were attracted to the frontier's mining and rangeland resources. They bypassed the more densely settled Sinaloa with its encomienda-born mestizo population, as well as the coastal lands of the Yaqui and Mayo Indians. Central and southern Mexico yielded few Indian and mestizo colonizers to Sonora, for this large group had neither the resources nor the inclination to migrate.

Thus in the years before the Gadsden Purchase the present-day composition of the desert's population had begun to take form. Sinaloa,

---

6   *Ibid.*, p. 148.

7   *Ibid.*, pp. 148-49.

with its three-century-old history of racial integration, was largely mestizo. Sonora, which had effectively assimilated only two large native popula- tions, the Pima and Opata, during a much shorter colonial history, was to a greater extent white, the mestizo population being concentrated in the former Opata lands and in the mountains adjacent to Sinaloa (near Alamos). On the other hand, the Lower Mayo and Yaqui contained the largest concentration of unassimilated Indians within the frontiers of effective Mexican occupation. To the north, beyond the last presidios on the borders of Pimería and Apachería, lay a desert region which soon came to be called Arizona. In 1854, it was still "Indian country," having only an extremely small Spanish-speaking white and mestizo population concentrated in the middle Santa Cruz Valley south of Tucson. The Mexicans in Arizona were from the first year of American sovereignty a minority group, first among an Indian majority and later in a rising tide of Anglo-American immigration. Thus, the contemporary racial and national composition of the Sonoran Desert's population was roughly outlined in the mid-nineteenth century. A century later population studies show the following breakdown:

Estimated Present Racial Composition of the Sonoran Desert[8]
(percentage)

	Sinaloa	Sonora	Arizona
Indian	1	14	2
White	1	42	89
Mestizo	98	42	5
Negro	0	0	4

Thus Indians, though represented throughout the three states, are concentrated in southern Sonora. The European or white population increases proportionately northward throughout the desert. In both in- stances the international boundary does not delineate a clearly defined racial frontier. Interestingly, it is the mixed or mestizo population which is delineated by the border. Both Mexican states are clearly mestizo or becoming so, while Arizona is not. Southern Arizona might have become so had it not been for the deluge of white migrants from the middlewestern and western states that has continued down to the present

---

[8] These figures can only be considered as rough approximations. The 14% Indian total for Sonora was arrived at by using the 1930 census. Since then the Mexican government for political reasons has succeeded in diminishing the Indian population statistically to an unrealistically low proportion of the population. In Arizona only the four desert counties are here included. The Arizona Mexican minority was estimated at slightly under 11% of the total (using the 1960 census of Spanish surnames), and it in turn was divided and apportioned equally to the white and mestizo categories. The criterion used was the almost equal division of white and mestizo in the neighboring state of Sonora (42.54%, 41.04%).

time. In Arizona, the constant assimilation of the Indian into the mestizo, the mestizo with the Anglo-American, and high birth rates do not contravene the overall proportional growth of white Arizonans, giving the American desert its white complexion. Finally, the Negroes are confined to the American desert.

Much of the recent and usually bloody history of land redistribution in Mexico has little affected the arid Northwest. The liberal Constitutional reforms of 1857 were in part aimed at forcing the economic development of the large Indian element situated chiefly in central and southern Mexico, with the hope of raising the Indians from their communal lethargy while "offering the incentive of individual proprietorship."[9] In Sonora and Sinaloa where the population was composed mainly of Spaniards or Spanish-speaking mestizos, there was a favorable response to the reforms, many of which had already been accomplished. In a report dated 1849 it was pointed out that the inhabitants of Sinaloan and Sonoran pueblos had in the main acquired title to land that they occupied which formerly belonged to the *municipios*. "To these people the reform measure meant but a confirmation of titles to lands which they had long held practically as their own. Individual property was no novelty to them."[10] The unwillingness of the Indian population to comply with the constitutional reforms demanding the division of communal property was not characteristic of this frontier.

In addition, the continuing conflicts between the haciendas and the threatened communal lands of the pueblos were less intense than those which characterized the struggle for land in the interior. Haciendas were fewer and their owners less wealthy and powerful. At the same time the pueblos, many of which were founded under colonial law, held good titles to their land, there being relatively few untitled Indian *congregaciones*[11] and *rancherías* within the region which had not taken advantage of earlier laws permitting the legal documentation of aboriginal titles. To the south where Indian lands were communally owned without title, the struggle between the pueblos and the powerful hacendados was fiercely waged.

On the Sonoran frontier, the formation of small rural properties from communal holdings was carried forward largely without incident, and in the period between 1877 and 1893 Sonora led all other states

---

9   McBride, p. 133.

10   *Ibid.*, p. 134.

11   The *congregación* was a term originally applied to Indian communities grouped into relatively permanent settlements by the Spaniards. Later it was used to refer to many of the villages in which the land was held in common. See Whetten, p. 42.

in Mexico, allotting 4,501 individual titles to land formerly held in common, each parcel averaging 130 acres in size.[12]

Additional land within the public domain was granted to colonists. Sonora, in the period 1866–1883, disposed of more land to private interests in this manner than any other state, with Sinaloa and Baja California not far behind.[13]

During this period, the opening of Mexican land to foreign ownership was accelerated. As early as 1824 the northern frontier was thrown open to alien settlement, which was so "successful" that Texas rapidly filled with American colonists. In 1837 Mexico attempted to pay its large foreign debts in public land. From that time on the national government carried forward a policy which did virtually everything it could to further the alien ownership of Mexican land. Huge tracts were granted to companies who did no more than survey land throughout the arid North. In Sonora one individual company received 4,500,000 acres in several concessions.[14]

The rise to power of Porfirio Díaz and the arrival of railway companies accelerated the concession of land to foreign interests. Foreign land companies followed the railways into the irrigable lands of the Yaqui and Fuerte deltas.[15] Foreign companies secured huge irrigable acreages in the Mexicali district. Southwestern "cattle barons" extended their property lines across the international boundary so that title to northern Sonora was held in such far-removed places as New York, San Francisco, and Kansas City.[16]

As late as 1928 a survey of national and foreign ownership of land in Sinaloa and Sonora revealed that a disturbingly large percentage of the more valuable properties in the two entities was held by American and other foreign interests. The geographical distribution of these Ameri-

---

[12]   McBride, p. 93.

[13]   *Ibid.,* p. 95.

[14]   McBride, p. 149. This huge grant amounted to one-third of the land surveyed by this concern.

[15]   The Richardson Construction Co. on the Lower Yaqui and the United Sugar Co. at Los Mochis were the two largest landholding companies within the irrigated zones of the desert.

[16]   Among the large American landowners holding land in Sonora and Sinaloa in the year 1902 were the following:

Sonora Land and Cattle Co.	1,290,000 acres
M. M. Sherman of Kansas City	500,000 acres
Sinaloa and Sonora Irrigation Co.	400,000 acres
Richardson Construction Co.	400,000 acres
West Coast Cattle Co.	225,000 acres
W. Bennett & Sons, Nogales	75,000 acres
Green Cattle Co.	(six large holdings)

Pfeifer, *Mitt. Geog. Gesell.,* Vol. 46, pp. 380-84.

can-owned lands, concentrated as they were in Sonora near the frontier, was a source of growing anxiety to those Mexicans who wished to preserve their national integrity. Often, as in the case of the Green holdings, huge tracts of land were deeded to the owners of mineral properties close by the border, creating a veritable independent and self-sufficient transfrontier march. With their own stores, mines, railways, farms, and pastures encompassing hundreds of square miles, the Green properties centering on Cananea could only be likened to a feudal duchy.

This was one of the conditions (such as that previously described at Cananea) which led directly to the Mexican Revolution starting in 1910, and resulted in the revolutionary constitution of 1917 which cast doubt on all lands acquired by foreigners after 1876, on the theory that the Díaz government had fraudulently given away the nation's patrimony. The constitution forbade the further sale of land to aliens in a zone 100 kilometers wide along the international boundaries and 50 kilometers wide along the maritime frontiers.[17] At the same time it provided for redistribution of land taken from the largest holdings. These would then be handed over to communal farmers or ejidatarios.[18]

Although the expropriation of large foreign holdings was clearly set forth in the Constitution, the sheer magnitude of the operation, as well as the United States' strongly enunciated opposition, kept this from being an immediate reality. The anti-foreign policy pursued by the Mexican government did, however, indirectly result in the forced sale of many large holdings. The Green properties were finally expropriated in 1960. However, American ownership of land continues in proximity to the border and along the coast. Considerable interest has been shown by American and other aliens in the irrigated lands at Caborca, the Costa de Hermosillo, and in the Yaqui, Mayo, and Fuerte districts. Ownership is concealed through "dummy" Mexican corporations or other means. These holdings are officially termed *pequeñas propiedades,* being less than 150 hectares in size.[19] The larger tracts of nonirrigated land held by aliens are today a much smaller proportion of the total foreign land ownership than at any earlier time during this century. The well-managed irrigated pequeñas propiedades owned by foreigners at the present time are looked upon favorably by the Mexican government.

The creation of communal farms or *ejidos* through the redistribution of large estates or out of the national domain has been the greatest

---

17   Whetten, pp. 118-19.

18   E. N. Simpson, *The Ejido: Mexico's Way Out* (Chapel Hill, N.C., 1937), p. 65.

19   *Pequeñas propiedades* are small holdings by individuals. One hundred and fifty acres of irrigated land, usually planted to cotton, is the maximum legal limit of private land-ownership under the Mexican Constitution. Whetten, p. 134.

departure from pre-revolutionary land policy. It has been carried forward with varying degrees of vigor during the last forty years. For a number of reasons the ejido has had less success in establishing itself in the Sonoran Desert than elsewhere in Mexico.

Pastoral activities and other extensive uses of arid land do not lend themselves to this form of tenure. In the irrigated districts, small private holdings are more common than elsewhere in Mexico and "land hunger" is less acute. This is directly attributable to the earlier successes achieved in colonization of vacant land as well as in the division and secularization of pueblo and mission lands. The small proprietor already existed in relatively large numbers while there were, aside from the foreign holdings, relatively few large properties occupying the irrigable land of the desert. Since there were few haciendas there was little irrigable land available to communize.

Exceptions to this were the Fuerte and Mexicali valleys where large holdings based upon peculiar circumstances provided opportunities for the creation of ejidos. In both cases, large foreign landowners dominated an economically vulnerable monoculture — in the first case, sugarcane, and in the latter, cotton. Worldwide depression provided the background for the expropriation of temporarily unprofitable farms in these valleys.

An even greater handicap was and is the lack of capital available to ejidatarios. Modern irrigated farming, as it has evolved on the West Coast, requires a capitalization far beyond the communal farmer's resources or credit. Thus, the ejido is a proportionately less significant part of Sonoran irrigated agriculture. The national, regional, and local totals of ejido membership are as follows:

Ejido Membership and Distribution by Irrigated Zones, 1957[20]

	Number Ejidos	Number Ejidatarios	% of Total Irrig. District in Ejidos
Total Mexico	1,204	151,970	41.46
Total Northwest	213	20,911	33.27
Mexicali	73	5,557	42.00
Rio Altar	14	151	25.17
Costa de Hermosillo	1	71	.26
Colonias Yaquis	7	1,010	100.00
Yaqui	29	5,260	33.28
Mayo	35	5,053	36.76
Culiacán	54	3,809	25.09

Of more recent importance was the enactment in 1947 of a new Federal Colonization Law which has been put into effect widely since

[20] Mexico, Secretaría de Económica, *Tercer Censo Agrícola, Ganadero y Ejidal, 1957.* Information is not available for the Río Fuerte District where there are probably as many ejidos as there are in the Rio Yaqui.

1958. Any twenty-five workers who have no land, and find none available locally for collectivization into an ejido, may be resettled into what is called a *colonia*. Unlike the ejido, these colonias are located at some distance from the original villages of the colonistas. The arid Northwest has, with the opening up of large-scale irrigation projects, attracted numerous colonistas from the crowded south. Colonias differ from the ejidos in that the land is owned outright and not in common.[21]

Despite the differences in land tenure, wheat, cotton, or rice dominates in a given area regardless of type. Sugarcane in the Fuerte district is confined to the ejidos serving the mill at Los Mochis. Otherwise, if there is any relationship between the kind of crop grown and the type of tenure, it is usually indirect — such as the poorer soils and water supply on some ejido lands. As one observer has remarked:

> Other things being equal (soils, drainage, roads and the like), it is hardly possible to distinguish from land use where one form of tenure ends and another begins, and this applies to the quality of the crop as well as to the kind. One factor is undoubtedly the practice of illegal renting of adjacent ejido lands by *particulares* and operating all as a unit.[22]

THE POPULATION OF NORTHWESTERN MEXICO

As late as 1935, Sauer could write, in reference to the northwest coast of Mexico, that

> the aboriginal population between [the] Gila and the Rio Grande de Santiago [was] in excess of half a million, almost three-fourths of the number now living in this part of Mexico. Bit by bit the theme has obtruded itself that aboriginal rural populations and present ones are much the same. This I believe is not a sensational conclusion, but a quite natural one.
>
> Populations in such a country as Mexico cannot be expected to conform to the growth which our western civilization has experienced. The fields which feed the people today are the same that were farmed aboriginally, the flood plains and colluvial slopes were as amenable to primitive planting — stick and hoe — as they are to the simple plow and metal hoe of the present cultivator. On those lands there is no problem of fertilizing or crop rotation. No crops have been introduced that yield more food than native crops; indeed the crops are still primarily the immemorial crops of the Indians. Changes in tillage have taken place but they do not mean more intensive tillage.

---

[21] Kathryn Wylie, "Mexico's Agrarian Reform," *Foreign Agriculture* (1961), pp. 17-18.

[22] Dozier, "Mexico's Transformed Northwest," *The Geographical Review* (Oct. 1963).

If Indian families were small, whereas present Mexican families are large, a disparity would be introduced into the two scenes. Such evidence as we have indicates that fecundity was about the same as at the present. Nor is there evidence that health conditions have improved . . . We know of no diseases that have disappeared, but of numerous ones that have been introduced. There remains the possibility of intertribal wars as a possible depressant of aboriginal population but . . . there is no record of serious hostilities. There is a static quality to the population scene; once, and now, again the land of [coastal northwestern Mexico] has been filled in similar manner by human habitations; between the two periods lie a disastrous decline and slow recuperation.[23]

Thus, as Sauer viewed the distribution and density of population 405 years after Guzmán's entrada, there was little to say that had not been recorded in the earliest chronicles. The occupation and utilization of the semiarid and desert coast was much the same after four centuries. Any agricultural innovation introduced by the Spaniards was more than compensated for by the introduction of European diseases which almost immediately assumed plague proportions, devastating native populations and leading to famine. When populations finally stabilized at a lower level there was, according to Sauer, slow growth to what he considered the relatively static 1935 level, which was approximately a quarter larger than the aboriginal population.

Assuming that Sauer's total aboriginal population estimates are correct[24] and that the "disastrous decline" stabilized at one half the original level one hundred years after the first entrada, the "slow recuperation" lasting for approximately 300 years proceeded at a rate of less than one-half of one percent annually, or a net increase of less than 5 per thousand annually.

If these estimates are close to being correct, and the assumed birth rate of forty per one thousand which Sauer cites as a reasonable estimate for aboriginal births is also approximately correct, and that throughout the three-hundred-year numerical recuperation to the 1935 population level there were more regional immigrants than emigrants — a reasonable assumption on a frontier — then death rates had to exceed thirty-five per one thousand annually and may have exceeded forty, depending upon the net increases registered through immigration.

The picture is one of an "underdeveloped" society which has for centuries utilized the same land, producing much the same crops, in the same way — where deaths balance births and the population increases

---

[23] Sauer, *The Aboriginal Population of Northwestern Mexico.*
[24] *Ibid.*, pp. 3-8.

only very slowly. These conditions persisted until at least 1935 in the Pacific Northwest of Mexico, and for that matter, throughout Mexico, signifying little or no demographic difference between the arid Northwest and Mexico as a whole, or even Latin America considered as an entity.

The picture today is significantly changed. The "large families among the aboriginal inhabitants" which Sauer conjectures were about the same as those in 1935[25] have become even larger. The state of Sonora leads all Mexican states in fecundity with 57.3 births per thousand, while Baja California registers 49.5 and Sinaloa falls slightly below the national average of 46.9 with 44.9 births per thousand.

The decline in death rates throughout the arid Northwest is more precipitous than the national average which is in itself a monument to public health and other recent advances in hygiene and medicine.[26] Baja California with an 8.3 death rate is the lowest among the Mexican states while Sinaloa follows with only 8.6. Sonora's rate is slightly below the national average (12.9), standing at 12.2 per thousand.[27]

The net internal increase in population (registered in births over deaths) is everywhere throughout the coastal desert states higher than the remarkable 34 per thousand national average. Sonora leads all states with 45.1 per thousand. Here is a figure certainly nine times the conjectured three-hundred-year average ending in 1935. It may well be fifteen, twenty, or many more times the long-term average rate of internal population growth registered in the northwestern frontier provinces after populations began to increase once again, probably in the seventeenth century.

In addition, the net gain in population through immigration which was probably small throughout this period has become an important part of the region's expanding population. Immigration is encouraged by a comparatively greater regional economic advance, which in turn has resulted in higher standards of living, attracting people from other parts of Mexico. In the preceding chapters, the recent marked growth of urban and rural economies has been discussed, stressing the fact that agriculture is largely responsible for both the increase in rural and urban

---

25   *Ibid.,* p. 3.

26   Sauer writes concerning the regional conditions in 1935: "Modern hygiene and medical service scarcely touches the population of today. Raw, bacillus-laden cow's milk is now widely used in feeding infants and small children. Contagious diseases take a heavy toll of children, especially measles and diphtheria in certain sections, also typhoid and smallpox, all of which are probably Old World introductions." *Ibid.*

27   Despite the much higher total population, the states of Sonora and Sinaloa registered fewer deaths in 1957 (14,363) than they did in 1940 (15,152).

Two street scenes in the all-too-hot and dry adobe villages of eastern Sonora — Batuc above, and Arispe below. The lack of trees and resulting shade despite hundreds of years of settlement defies explanation.

populations through immigration. It is a picture which contrasts startlingly with that sketched by Professor Sauer. The fields are no longer "the same as those that were farmed aboriginally." Those areas that were "amenable to primitive planting – stick and hoe – as they are to the simple plow and metal hoe" of 1935 are still being farmed, but so are hundreds of thousands of desert acres that receive their water from huge dams and deep wells installed since that year. There is still "no problem of fertilizing or crop rotation" but fields are being fertilized and crops are rotated as well as dusted for insects and weed infestations.

Sauer commented in 1935 that "no crops have been introduced that yield more food than the native crops"; but it seems doubtful if he fully appreciated the importance of wheat as a winter crop in the Sonoran Desert (which allowed more effective double cropping), or the improved utilization of desert vegetation only possible through the Spanish-introduced domestic animals. Nevertheless, granting his original point, he is referring to an economy composed of subsistence farmers. Crops, in a market economy, certainly need not be food crops to provide more food for the farmer. The great recent increases in cotton acreages provide more food for more people than if the same acres had been planted in maize. He also was referring to an economy in which other income-producing industries were almost nonexistent. All basically urban economic activities must have been considered by Sauer to be of insignificant proportions in that year. But now, in addition to agriculture, railways, shipping, tourism, and shrimp canneries also provide food to the desert's inhabitants.

The truth lies in the fact that for three hundred years until about the time of Sauer's notable observations, the population of the Sonoran Desert, and its southern margin, was relatively stable at about the aboriginal level. Death rates were closely equated with birth rates; and a static economy based on subsistence agriculture barely provided the alimentary base of this sparsely populated region. *In fine,* populations were not increased through either immigration or internal growth, nor were the populated areas within the region significantly different from early days, though there had been revolutionary changes such as the destruction caused by the first entradas, the depopulation through the early encomiendas, the continued ravages of epidemic disease which marred the mission settlements, the rise and fall of mining camps, the introduction of animals and new crops, the devastation of the Apache wars and the other native uprisings, and the coming of the railway. In the generation since that year there has come into existence an entirely new social geography based on a rapidly developing economy tied to irrigation and modern transport.

Two views of the shabbily constructed slums of Hermosillo that serve as reception centers for the rural dispossessed. The top picture shows the narrow, irrigated fields of the Río Sonora in no way dissimilar to those of remote Arispe.

THE AMERICAN CONDITION

In the United States, the distribution of desert land is not the overriding political issue that it is in Mexico. In 1848 and 1854 the United States obtained free title to the arid lands of Arizona and California. At that time there were in existence only a few Spanish and Mexican land grants — chiefly south of Tubac — in addition to the undocumented "title" held by Indian tribes to their land. Thus the federal government was given at that time not only sovereignty over, but title to, the ceded desert land. In over one hundred years the situation has not changed radically. At present in Arizona the federal and state governments — either outright or in trust — hold title to almost 85 percent of the state, leaving only 15 percent of the state's land privately owned.[28]

Much of the federal land is contained within forest and wildlife preserves, and national parks and monuments; military bases and bombing ranges cover additional tracts throughout the desert. Thousands of square miles of arid land are leased out for grazing. The great majority of state-owned lands are also leased to livestock interests. Much of the privately-owned land is located in some of the most productive areas, but surprisingly large tracts of federal, state, and Indian land are to be found nearby under irrigation. Indian reservation land is often in close proximity to the growing cities. The Anglo-American population is concentrated on the privately-held irrigated land which is usually contiguous to the Indian reservations. The reservations were originally delineated to encompass the most productive of those tribal lands under some form of irrigation. From the very beginning of Anglo-American settlement, Indians and Anglos have lived in close proximity along the Santa Cruz, Salt, Gila, and Colorado rivers. Despite recent population growth, the ownership of land as well as the distribution and racial composition of the population were fairly well established in these valleys as early as 1854.

South of the border a similar situation existed until about 1926, the first year of the modern Mexican irrigation act. Since then an agricultural revolution has resulted in a major shift of population towards the coast. An explosive growth in population as well as greater mobility have destroyed any concept of a relatively static population and settlement pattern so apparent to Sauer in 1935.[29]

In a similar fashion beginning about 1940 a significant change

---

[28] *Arizona Statistical Review, 1965,* p. 32.
[29] Sauer, *The Aboriginal Population of Northwestern Mexico,* pp. 3-8.

transpired north of the border which in twenty-five years multiplied the population more than threefold. This took place when an already highly mobile population was encouraged by a number of disparate yet inter-related events to take up residence in and around Phoenix, Tucson, Yuma, and elsewhere in the desert. Though the war, the government, aviation, air conditioning, and continuing prosperity have all been given credit for the explosive growth of recent years, it should not be forgotten that the dam builders and well drillers had by 1940 created an artificial environment supporting, for example, in the irrigated Salt River Valley oasis, a population density of approximately 400 people per square mile of Salt River Project land. However, in the years after 1940 this popula-tion increased until at the present time in the Salt River Valley there is a population density of 2,000 per square mile of irrigated and built-up land. (New Jersey, the most densely populated American state, in 1960 had 800.2 inhabitants per square mile!)

It must be observed that until these revolutionary changes took place the aboriginal pattern of population greatly influenced the distribu-tion of white settlers. The Spaniard with his reliance on the labor of sedentary Indian tribes settled in those areas where this human resource could be exploited. At the beginning of the twentieth century the Spanish-speaking population of the desert was concentrated in those areas which had a relatively high level of culture immediately before the first entradas. The English-speaking population found sufficient room for its limited agricultural activities on land unoccupied by indigenous people. Even after the completion of the Salt River Project in 1911 the population grew only slowly and there was seemingly enough land for all. For the most part, the whites exploited water resources which the Indians had never, during historic times, utilized, and in general did not encroach on land cultivated by natives. However, the great growth in population following the outbreak of World War II submerged the small native population and destroyed any static equilibrium which might have existed formerly between white and native areas. Not that the reservations have been physically affected, but their population no longer constitutes a cohesive minority and their cultural and racial integrity is being rapidly destroyed. Despite all the interest that anthropologists show in the South-western tribes, there are presently fewer Indians in Arizona's four southern desert counties than there are, for example, Negroes.[30]

Thus, for almost four centuries the Indian played an active role in the colonization of the desert by whites. But in less than forty years these

---

[30] The 1960 *U. S. Census of Population* for Maricopa, Pima, Pinal, and Yuma counties recorded 38,578 Negroes and 23,005 Indians.

people have become no more than passive onlookers at activities over which they have little or no control. In another forty years, Indians may not exist as a clearly identifiable minority, which perhaps explains the keen interest of contemporary anthropologists. For example, among the Papago and Pima there has been a continuing exodus of workers from the reservation. Men find increasing employment as laborers in the fields and cities near the reservations. Their women follow them, working largely as domestics. In Tucson and other cities their occupations, Catholicism, race, and knowledge of Spanish bring them into contact with the larger Mexican minority which is absorbing them as it has absorbed so many other indigenous groups. Thus, the concept of racial conflict along a wide desert frontier so important until recently to the understanding of the desert's social geography must now and in the future be superseded by other considerations. Both the United States and Mexico have finally and effectively occupied the desert which they so rashly partitioned over one hundred years ago.

The growth of cities has brought about in the desert an unparalleled reorientation. Phoenix has become the central city in a desert conurbation with an estimated population of almost 900,000.[31] The other cities, such as Tucson, Mexicali, and Hermosillo, though smaller, have growth rates which place them among those of the highest rank in their respective countries.[32] Nevertheless, between the two countries there are certain differences in the nature of urbanization which throw considerable light on the generally accepted terms of urban and rural.

Throughout much of the United States "urban" and "rural" have lost virtually all meaning. Even what could appear to be a basic methodological difference between agriculture and other productive enterprise has faded during recent years. Winter vegetable gardening provides an example of an agricultural activity which has become an integral part of an organized system of food production, processing, and distribution. The market gardener is completely dependent upon a complex economy and has little of the independence and isolation usually attributable to the agriculturalist. The Salt River or Imperial Valley lettuce grower, though separated by thousands of miles from the urban areas which form his chief market, is more closely associated with an urban economy than with anything which could be called rural. His chief concerns are credit, labor relations, the growers' association, packaging, freight rates, advertising, marketing innovations, and so on.

---

[31] *Arizona Statistical Review, 1965,* p. 10.

[32] Between 1950 and 1960 Phoenix and Tucson ranked first and second in population growth among all American cities over 50,000.

Weather, the traditional concern of the agriculturalist, is thought of in entirely different terms within the desert. The climatic conditions in the Rio Grande Valley of Texas or the Central Valley of California, as they affect a national market, are of at least commensurate importance with those prevailing locally. Irrigation removed at least one of the agricultural imponderables, namely drought, while fast, refrigerated freight trains have brought the Sonoran Desert closer to the eastern markets. This freedom from traditional agricultural concerns has, on the other hand, made the irrigation farmer no more than a cog in a highly organized and capitalized wheel, which includes the dams and canals that deliver water, the banks that provide credit, migrant labor, the farm implement, fertilizer, insecticide and herbicide suppliers, the public utilities which provide natural gas, electricity, and telephones, the railways and trucking companies, and so on, *ad infinitum*. These largely urban agencies provide for the material and social well-being of the Arizona or Imperial Valley farmer, destroying the isolation of an earlier rural frontier.

The Salt River Valley farmer finds that sprawling nonagricultural communities have sprung up on what was formerly irrigated farmland and that the "rural" population is a very small minority of the total population. His fields are obscured among the homes, factories, shopping centers and drive-in theaters which were erected to serve the urban population but serve him as well. He shops at the same supermarket, sends his children to the same school, and eats at the same drive-in restaurant as his suburban neighbor. Needless to say, his house has electricity, a telephone, and the other amenities of modern urban living.

His farm employs the field-factory methods which are a radical departure from the more familiar agricultural pattern of less highly capitalized areas. His use of machinery commonly includes complex picking and packaging devices as well as airplanes; while his dependence upon hired labor welds his farm into the overall economic structure.

The legal concept stating that water rights adhere to the land has resulted in a curious competition of space within the limited but already established oasis. Urban land uses, though they demand less water than irrigated agriculture, nevertheless require on the average such large quantities that the safest method to insure a plentiful supply is to occupy land which was previously devoted to irrigated farming. A complex pattern of urban and agricultural land use has developed across the Salt River Valley's irrigated land. Built-up areas stretch in ribbons along the principal roads, widening at some of the older settlements or new developments, joining to surround orange groves and fields of cotton. Many of these older settlements which at one time had the form and functions of a town have been destroyed as such. These "towns" have become no more than minor nuclei in the amorphous urban sprawl which has engulfed town and country alike. Many have had housing developments of much larger size grafted on to them, presenting all the possibilities of Jonah being able to swallow the whale. Gigantic shopping centers with acres of sterile parking lots have lured away the customers from the now-empty shops that line the traffic-choked streets of the old towns. The old nucleus serves only the conurbation and no longer the town itself. The farmer finds that his material and social well-being is being served by the same metropolitan institutions and not by the town. He may live closer to the courthouse, bank, or shopping center than his urban neighbor. The relations of time and space which created the former contrast between farm and town have changed under the onslaught of technical innovation. The automobile and superhighway, electricity, television, air conditioning, and time payments have destroyed a rural pattern of life. The towns no longer execute their former economic functions but the old terms linger on. "Town" and "country," "urban" and "rural," even "agriculture" are increasingly more difficult to define. Economically they have little meaning.

South of the international boundary the economic implications of urbanization are quite different from those in the United States. The greatest apparent contrast between the two countries rests in the continuing backwardness of the rural areas which has been largely erased in the American sector of the desert. It is true that modern agricultural techniques are employed in the irrigated "colonias" along the coast but there yet remain many thousands of people living within subsistence economies in the back country of eastern Sonora and Sinaloa. The economic contrast between these isolated farmers, ranchers, and *gambucinos,* and the residents of the expanding towns along the coastal highway is, in most respects, greater than the contrast between cities on either side of the border.

Whereas a virtual union has been achieved between town and country within the irrigated desert north of the border, the dynamic growth of modern towns in Mexico has widened an economic breach characteristic of underdeveloped countries. Much of the rapid growth of such towns as Hermosillo, Mexicali, Ciudad Obregón, and Los Mochis is due to the absence of economic opportunity in the isolated rural hinterland. These backward districts with their high birth rates and falling death rates provide an increasing stream of immigrants to the larger cities. A very real and measurable rural overpopulation, as well as disguised agricultural unemployment, drives these people into the cities — often with only the slightest hope of obtaining employment. There

Contrasting desert land use — citrus groves versus power plants. It's not that simple, but in a desert, water consumption as it relates to productivity must be given primary consideration over historical accidents and vested interests. Agriculture has given way only grudgingly.

they congregate on the edge of a town in the tin-can-and-tarpaper slums that are to be seen from one end of the underdeveloped world to the other. In reality the mushrooming cities have little to offer the immigrant economically, and act only as centers of reception for the dispossessed back-country campesinos. The rapid growth of urban population reflects a "spilling" which is in itself the result of economic maladjustment in the rural areas. The industries and commerce which have precipitated the real economic expansion underlying the growth of these cities do not have local origins. Instead they are more generally "enclaves" of foreign enterprise whose products are devoted to international markets. Even when these industries utilize the food and fibers produced on the irrigated lands of the coast, the association is only between these mechanized agricultural "colonias" and the major city. The rural back-country does not enter this productive relationship except to supply bodies; thus its economy stands as a trans-frontier relic. The frontier in this case is the gaping cleavage between the urban- and market-oriented coast and the isolated backcountry with its low agricultural productivity, rural underemployment, and static socio-economic structure. It provides little more than its surplus population to the coastal economy.

It appears that no matter how fast urban industries may grow, there is always a surplus of unemployed willing to congregate in the cities with no more than a remote hope of finding employment. By returning to the fields they could only forfeit that hope. So the slums which ring Mexicali and other Mexican desert cities will remain, constituting an escape from the hopelessly underdeveloped backcountry but not necessarily an escape from extreme poverty.

In contrast, the growing desert economy of Arizona and California has cities which act as centers of attraction for a potentially migrant population that is either already employed elsewhere and enjoying a very high standard of living or retired and affluent. Not that Phoenix and Tucson are free from slums or unemployment, for they are not, but the migrant unemployed contribute very little to the population growth of these cities. More precisely, the migrant unemployed lacking industrial skills are an extremely small contributor to the growth of Southwestern desert cities. The skilled worker may be unemployed for a short time on his arrival in the area but usually finds employment quite soon. More often he has a job promised to him before his arrival. As a last alternative, he has the resources with which to move on.

The urban slums which do exist are usually the products of age and neglect. The not always adequate housing of the past has deteriorated, leaving, as it has in all American cities, an area of blight, usually quite close to the center of the city. Unlike Latin American cities there are no newly constructed packing-crate-and-tarpaper slums ringing the cities and absorbing the displaced rural population. There is poverty among local agricultural workers but there is also continuing need for them on the land. Seasonal unemployment in agriculture is better than total unemployment in urban slums. The agricultural poor of the American Southwest remain in the countryside and in the majority do not migrate to the urban areas. From this it is apparent that the widely contrasting development of the growing desert cities is dependent in large measure on the differing characteristics of their immigrant populations.

A LOOK AHEAD

In the development of the most critical of all desert resources — water — past considerations based upon the orthodox development of surface and subsurface supplies within the watersheds of desert streams must be discarded. The future expansion of agriculture in the desert using the methods of the past will produce only diminishing returns. More likely there will be an actual contraction of total acreage under irrigation as present (and in all likelihood) methods continue to lower water tables drastically. After the great advances made by irrigation in both countries in the years following 1945, there is little possibility for continued growth in acreage through the utilization of ever-more water. Of the five desert states, only one remains in the period of dynamic adolescent growth in the utilization of water resources. California areas that rely heavily on Colorado River sources find that even their present allocation of water is jeopardized through court action. Arizona, though it looks hopefully toward the Colorado, must realize that its surface water is fully utilized at present and its underground reservoirs are being depleted at a startling rate. Both Baja California and Sonora have made almost full use of readily available surface water while water tables are at present being depressed rapidly throughout the areas of heavy pumping. Only coastal Sinaloa has not yet fully appropriated either its available surface or subsurface water.

The only possible conclusion is that agricultural productivity can increase or remain stable only (1) through the more efficient utilization and conservation of existing water supplies which will in all likelihood decline with falling water tables; (2) through the introduction of new and revolutionary methods of procuring water for the region; or (3) through increasing productivity on fewer irrigated areas. More than likely all three methods will be employed. Some success has been achieved in increasing the runoff from desert watersheds, although any comprehensive plan would in part affect adversely the tourist industry of the mountain regions. Improving the methods of distribution by sealing the bottom of irrigation canals and reservoirs is only one of a number of possible methods whereby losses through evaporation and percolation are being lessened. In this way surface water may perhaps supplement pumping as the latter once supplemented surface supplies. At best, these methods will probably be able to do no more than stabilize the total irrigated acreage at its present high level. Another alternative might be the transferral of agricultural activities from one area to another, such as from the middle Gila and Salt River valleys to Yuma where the cost and water loss of the Central Arizona Project as proposed could be in large measure eliminated.

The introduction of revolutionary methods of obtaining water from new sources presents each year more sanguine possibilities. Major breakthroughs may be made in hydraulic engineering, in the utilization of sewage effluents, or in nuclear energy. The desalting of seawater—using either nuclear or solar energy — could, in combination with large investments, make water available from the sea. The latter is a distinct possibility since large areas of the already developed Sonoran Desert are actually below sea level or only slightly above and adjacent to unlimited sources of salt water. It is presently under serious consideration with several studies under way.

A much less romantic prospect does present itself to the desert by increasing productivity on land presently irrigated — or even possibly on a diminished number of acres. This would be no more than a continuation of the evolutionary change which has increased agricultural productivity in years past. Insecticides, herbicides, fertilizers, better seed, improved rotations, new crops, and better marketing practices will perhaps be able to stabilize or improve real agricultural productivity even if fewer acres of irrigated land are available. There may possibly be revolutionary changes in desert agriculture (such as hydroponic cultivation of crops), but the term evolution best describes the continuing change that has so greatly improved the real product of each irrigated area through the years leading to the present. There is no reason to believe that this will not continue to take place.

However, the greatest opportunity to improve the real productivity of the desert without recourse to increasing water resources may be found in the replacement of agriculture by manufacturing and other urban enterprises. The Phoenix example demonstrates that an urban alternate use of land requires a somewhat smaller quantity of water per acre than what is needed for irrigable agriculture. This means that if agriculture were completely replaced on the already existing irrigated acreage around Phoenix, total water consumption would presumably fall — assuming conditions similar to those of recent years in the Salt River Valley. This in turn might allow for some outward expansion of the irrigated districts even if water supplies were curtailed.

Even those concentrations of population which are not surrounded by large irrigated districts should consider the consequences of utilizing scarce water for irrigation. A case in point is Tucson, a city of one quarter million people in the Santa Cruz Valley, depending upon underground sources for its entire water supply. The Santa Cruz basin has "an average annual recharge of perhaps 50,000 to 70,000 acre-feet. Domestic, industrial and mining uses consume 50,000 acre-feet annually, which is a substantial portion, and perhaps all of the annual recharge. [Nearby] a small area of irrigated agricultural land, about 14,000 acres, uses on the average an additional 42,600 acre-feet of water annually."[33] Agriculture in the Tucson area employs less than 1,500 out of a 90,000-man labor force. Thus, less than 2 percent of Tucson's employment utilizes almost half of the water consumed. Under these circumstances, agriculture can only be considered a very wasteful consumer of precious ground water. But for this small amount of irrigated land the Santa Cruz water table might be stabilized without recourse to endogenous supplies.

Under any circumstances, it appears that in the United States at least there is a potential saving to be made in water consumption while at the same time multiplying the real product of the desert economy. This of course presupposes that industry in the desert remains "dry" and that national and regional policy supports the substitution of manufacturing and other enterprises for agriculture. Throughout this volume it has been noted that irrigated agriculture expropriates well over 90 percent of the small proportion of water (approximately 10 percent) made available from meager rainfall. Secondly, the economic productivity of irrigated crops per acre-foot of water is insignificantly small in relation to industrial and commercial uses. Finally — at the present time, at least — there is certainly no need for expanded irrigated acreage while crop "surpluses" are controlled elsewhere. Near Phoenix, Palm Springs, Yuma, and Tucson, the value of irrigated land is established upon the prospect of future urban developments and not upon any "intrinsic" value. Elsewhere, irrigated land value is based upon government crop allotments. It is now impossible to determine the real value of irrigated land, yet huge investments are proposed to restore, preserve, or extend it.

---

[33] Andrew W. Wilson, "Urbanization of the Arid Lands," *Arizona Review,* Vol. 10, No. 3 (March, 1961), p. 8.

All of the irrigated farmland in Maricopa and Pinal counties could be purchased on the open market for less money than the amount proposed to be spent for the importation of water from the Colorado!

The situation in Mexico is different in that its level of industrial development precludes any meaningful speculation along this line although in some limited areas such as Hermosillo and Mexicali, this replacement is already taking place. It is apparent, then, that the development of water resources has reached a point in its history similar to that reached in the development of human resources. Easily exploited supplies of water which created the desert's economy no longer exist anymore than the racial forces and conflicts that created the desert's population. The dam builder and well driller who more than anyone else shaped the desert's human landscape are passing from the picture as surely as the missionary and frontiersman passed before them. To understand their passing is as important as the understanding of their coming and their contribution.

Man is inextricably tied to the resources of his creation. In this work, emphasis has sometimes been placed on the resource and sometimes on its creator, but it is the hope of the writer that the relation between the two has not been lost sight of. The first white men who entered the desert brought firearms, horses, cattle and smallpox with them, and created a new environment from these innovations, some of which we choose to call resources and others not. Disease worked in favor of Colonial Spain on the northwestern frontier as surely as the herds of cattle which for the first time made a great resource out of the immense tracts of upland desert. In time, some of the "resources" became a liability to the frontiers of New Spain, particularly in the hands of the Apache. And yet later, the Spaniard passed entirely from the desert but not until a new race had replaced him. The Mexican of today, who for the first time is firmly in control of the southern desert, is biologically the descendent of the centuries-old conflict and union of white and Indian. He is the mestizo, end-product, fully capable, in Northern Mexico at least, of absorbing what little is left of pure white and Indian stock.

To the north of the border, a changing set of circumstances is likely to mold in the years ahead an altered social geography. In the United States what has been termed an "affluent society" has found in the climate of the American and California deserts a new "frontier" of amenities. An already mobile population has discovered that its increasing wealth can purchase a warm climate as well as worldly goods. It is not coincidental that the regions with the fastest-growing population during recent years are to be found in California, Florida, Arizona, and the nearby desert states; all exhibit greater sunshine, warmth, and less violent climatic changes than the northern and central states which still contain the great majority of America's population. Few nations can afford this luxury, and America through its continental size and diversity of resource can probably among all nations most easily integrate within its national economy the intangible assets possessed by an area such as the Sonoran Desert.

Even the scarcity of water in all likelihood presents no insurmountable control on future growth. The problem will remain and probably become more acute, but a society which has consciously dealt with drought for generations has an advantage denied to others who have seemingly infinite confidence in their water resources, despite the fact that they are in this age as limited as those of the desert itself.

APPENDIX A

Mean Rainfall for Summer Six Months (May-October), Winter Six Months (November-April), and Annual Total. Due to the generally short duration of Mexican records, mean totals were carried to only one decimal point.

SINALOA

	Elevation (ft.)	Length of Record (yrs.)	Average Summer Rainfall (in.)	Average Winter Rainfall (in.)	Average Annual Rainfall (in.)
Ahome	50	10	9.4	3.6	13.0
Culiacán	200	31	21.4	3.5	25.0
El Fuerte		24	19.6	3.7	23.0
Guamuchil	150	28	18.3	2.9	21.2
Huites		10	22.4	5.3	32.8
Jaina		10	31.8	6.5	38.4
Mocorito	200	15	24.6	5.2	29.8
Naranjo	150	22	17.2	2.8	20.0
Sinaloa		26	29.7	3.4	33.1
Topolobampo	20	16	5.9	1.7	7.6

SONORA

	Elevation (ft.)	Length of Record (yrs.)	Average Summer Rainfall (in.)	Average Winter Rainfall (in.)	Average Annual Rainfall (in.)
Alamos	1300	16	20.6	4.3	24.9
Altar	1300	26	7.3	2.7	10
Angostura	3150	13	10.8	3.8	14.7
Arivechi	1850	8	16.5	4.5	20.8
Atil	1200	23	9.5	3.7	13.2
Baviacora		7	8.3	4.4	12.7
Bavispe	3700	9	11.6	4.3	15.8
Caborca	950	3	5.1	2.1	7.2
Chiculi	2150	7	11.2	2.1	13.3
Ciudad Obregón	150	23	9.8	1.8	11.6
El Oregano	950	11	10.8	1.6	12.4
El Riito		3	1.2	.5	1.7
Etchojoa	150	13	7.6	2.2	9.8
Fronteras	3700	10	9.5	3.7	13.1
Guaymas	20	31	7.7	1.9	9.5
Hermosillo	700	25	8.1	1.4	9.5
La Dura	400	18	17.3	4.9	22.2
Libertad	20	7	1.7	2.1	3.8
Magdalena	2550	16	15.3	1.4	16.6
Mazatán		6	15.9	3.6	19.4
Moctezuma	2000	9	12.0	3.3	15.3
Mulatos	5100	9	21.0	4.6	25.6
Nacozari	2800	10	14.0	5.4	19.4
Navojoa	150	28	13	2.9	15.7
Nogales	3700	27	11.5	6.1	17.6
Nuri	1450	7	19.3	4.7	24.0
Opodepe		7	14.2	3.4	17.6

APPENDIX A (Continued)

	Elevation (ft.)	Length of Record (yrs.)	Average Summer Rainfall (in.)	Average Winter Rainfall (in.)	Average Annual Rainfall (in.)
Oviachic	200	3	7.9	1.1	9.0
Puerto Peñasco	40	4	1.3	1.1	2.4
Quiriego		23	21.5	3.1	24.6
Sahuaripa	1500	8	9.6	3.2	12.8
San Bernardo		10	17.3	4.6	21.9
San Javier	2150	8	18.8	10.1	28.7
San Luis	100	21	1.1	1.2	2.3
Santa Ana		29	9.6	3.4	13.1
Santa Teresa	1950	11	8.3	3.2	11.5
Sauqui	1200	9	16.1	3.1	19.2
Tecori	300	11	13.4	2.4	15.8
Tesia		2	11.9	1.0	13.0
Tonichi	600	6	17.9	4.8	22.7
Tres Hermanos		10	17.8	3.4	21.3
Trinidad		6	39.1	21.3	60.4
Ures	1400	23	15.1	4.5	19.6
Yecora	5400	8	30.9	10.1	41.0
ARIZONA					
Ajo	1800	20	4.64	4.14	8.78
Benson	3500	51	7.47	3.60	11.07
Bowie	3750	—	5.54	4.29	9.83
Casa Grande	1400	45	3.81	6.01	8.82
Childs	2650	17	8.10	8.83	16.93
Douglas	4000	38	9.10	3.91	13.01
Florence	1500	30	4.16	5.72	9.88
Gila Bend	700	40	2.59	3.41	6.00
Globe	3400	32	8.25	7.65	15.90
Miami	3600	20	9.54	10.27	19.81
Mohawk	550	20	1.96	2.33	4.29
Oracle	4500	36	9.13	10.60	19.73
Parker	350	39	1.98	3.19	5.17
Phoenix	1100	38	3.43	4.37	7.80
Pinacate Plateau	9900	7	3.25	2.36	5.61
Prescott	5400	66	9.93	10.64	20.57
Salome	1800	25	3.79	4.43	8.22
Tinajas Altas	1050	9	2.31	2.75	5.06
Tombstone	4500	37	10.35	4.49	14.84
Tucson	2400	57	6.37	4.92	11.29
Wickenburg	2100	35	4.30	5.32	9.62
Yuma	150	53	1.35	2.13	3.48
CALIFORNIA					
Amos		32	1.50	1.33	2.83
Blythe	270	29	1.35	2.76	4.11

APPENDIX A (Continued)

	Elevation (ft.)	Length of Record (yrs.)	Average Summer Rainfall (in.)	Average Winter Rainfall (in.)	Average Annual Rainfall (in.)
Brawley	−119	28	0.72	1.71	2.43
Indio	−20	60	0.95	2.33	3.28
Needles	470	46	2.07	2.66	4.73
Palm Springs		33	0.93	4.67	5.60
BAJA CALIFORNIA					
Mexicali		21	1.34	1.84	3.18

Source: See Note 2, Ch. 9.

APPENDIX B

Mean January and July Temperatures and Absolute High and Low Temperatures ever recorded for Sonoran Desert Stations

SINALOA

	January Mean	Absolute Low	July Mean	Absolute Maximum
Ahome	63	34	87	116
Culiacán	66	37	85	110
El Fuerte	63	34	90	116
Guamuchil	64	34	87	114
Huites	66	34	87	127
Jaina	63	30	86	120
Mazatlán	66	53	84	93
Mocorito		34	86	111
San Blas	63	28	88	124

SONORA

	January Mean	Absolute Low	July Mean	Absolute Maximum
Alamos	59	32	82	113
Altar	56	19	88	122
Arivechi	54	12	86	115
Bavispe	51	17	85	113
Caborca	51	19	90	117
Ciudad Obregón	65	30	93	120
Chiculi	61	31	90	117
Fronteras	45	7	82	111
Guaymas	63	37	87	117
Hermosillo	63	34	91	122
Imuris	54	21	85	113
La Dura	60	32	86	117
Mazatán	50	28	87	111
Moctezuma	54	18	89	122

APPENDIX B (Continued)

	January Mean	Absolute Low	July Mean	Absolute Maximum
Nacozari	51	14	81	111
Navojoa	64	32	90	133
Nuri	59	19	86	115
Opodepe	56	28	87	115
Puerto Peñasco	49	17	84	106
Quiriego	63	28	90	122
Sahuaripa	60	28	88	122
San Javier	56	32	82	109
San Luis	54	20	93	136
Santa Ana	54	19	87	125
Suaqui	58	26	87	118
Ures	59	19	85	118
Yecora	43	2	67	102
ARIZONA				
Ajo	52	17	90	115
Benson	46	5	81	113
Bowie	46	8	83	116
Casa Grande	50	17	90	122
Childs	45	2	84	117
Douglas	45	7	80	111
Florence	51	11	90	118
Gila Bend	53	11	93	123
Globe	44	10	82	110
Miami	44	13	83	110
Parker	50	9	92	127
Phoenix	51	17	92	118
Prescott	35	−21	72	115
Salome	48	15	88	118
Tombstone	47	9	79	110
Tucson	50	6	86	113
Wickenburg	46	10	86	117
Yuma	55	22	91	123
CALIFORNIA				
Amos	54	21	93	130
Blythe	50	5	91	122
Brawley	52	19	91	121
Indio	54	13	92	125
Needles	51	18	93	125
Palm Springs	55	18	90	122
BAJA CALIFORNIA				
Mexicali	53	21	89	117

Source: See Note 2, Ch. 9.

APPENDIX C

Total Mean Annual Flow of Major Rivers of the Sonoran Desert and Their Tributaries

	Annual Mean River Flow in Acre-Feet		Annual Mean River Flow in Acre-Feet
Colorado (Lee's Ferry)	16,270,000	Yaqui (Tecori)	1,960,000
Bill Williams	75,000	Bavispe	352,000
Verde (above Bartlett Dam)	351,000	Papigochic	479,000
Salt (above Roosevelt Dam)	650,000	Mayo (Tres Hermanos)	727,000
Upper Gila (Kelvin)	444,000	Fuerte (Huites)	4,190,000
Altar	18,000	Sinaloa (Jaina)	1,230,000
Sonora (El Oregano)	80,000	Mocorito (Guamuchil)	102,000
		Culiacán (S.P. Bridge)	2,610,000

Source: See Note 2, Ch. 9.

APPENDIX D

Watershed Productivity. Mean and Annual Yield of entire watersheds measured in inches at the station recording the average highest streamflow

	Yield		Yield
Colorado	3.0	Yaqui	1.4
Bill Williams	.3	Bavispe	.9
Verde	1.4	Papigochic	3.0
Salt	2.8	Mayo	3.2
Upper Gila	.6	Fuerte	4.9
Altar	.4	Sinaloa	7.1
Sonora	.3	Mocorito	2.5
		Culiacan	7.5

APPENDIX E

Monthly Percentage of Total Flow for Major Sonoran Rivers

	Jan.	Feb.	Mar.	Apr.	May	June
Colorado (Gd. Canyon)	3.1	3.6	5.6	9.9	22.0	24.7
Salt (Chrysotile)	6.5	9.6	18.6	22.5	10.8	3.9
Gila (Safford)	8.8	12.8	16.4	10.7	5.0	2.1
Sonora (El Oregano)	3.3	4.5	.7	.5	.2	.3
Yaqui (Tecori)	6.5	6.4	4.0	1.6	1.2	2.1
Fuerte (San Blas)	10.6	6.3	2.9	1.0	.4	2.1

APPENDIX E (Continued)

	July	Aug.	Sept.	Oct.	Nov.	Dec.
Colorado						
(Gd. Canyon)	10.4	5.0	3.6	4.6	4.0	3.3
Salt						
(Chrysotile)	3.5	5.5	6.4	4.5	3.7	4.5
Gila						
(Safford)	5.0	11.2	10.0	6.0	5.1	6.9
Sonora						
(El Oregano)	28.2	46.2	9.7	4.6	.8	1.0
Yaqui						
(Tecori)	14.8	31.7	16.3	8.7	3.1	3.6
Fuerte						
(San Blas)	17.8	27.2	16.0	6.3	1.8	7.6

APPENDIX F

Principal Crops Grown in the Individual Irrigated Districts of the Sonoran Desert*

COACHELLA VALLEY

Alfalfa	37,000	Sweet corn	5,000
Cotton	22,000	Corn	5,000
Barley	17,000	Oats	5,000
Potatoes	11,000	Carrots	3,000
Sorghum	7,000	Wheat	2,000
Lettuce	6,000	Onion	1,000
Cantaloupe	6,000	Tomatoes	1,000
Watermelon	5,000	Other winter vegetables	2,000

IMPERIAL VALLEY

Alfalfa	130,000	Tomatoes	4,000
Barley	83,000	Corn	3,000
Cotton	50,000	Wheat	3,000
Sugar beet	39,000	Tree crops	2,000
Alfalfa seed	32,000	Oats	2,000
Lettuce	31,000	Cabbage	2,000
Sorghum	15,000	Asparagus	2,000
Cantaloupe	6,000	Clover	1,000
Watermelon	6,000	Other winter vegetables	1,000
Carrots	6,000		

*Crops which have a total acreage of less than 1,000 acres are not included. Areas devoted to pasture are also not included. Crops which are harvested more than once a year on the same land are included for each harvest. Thus in the case of lettuce, 6,000 acres may be grown on 3,000 acres since two harvests are possible each year. Only one crop, alfalfa, is not handled in this manner, for 37,000 acres may actually amount to 370,000 acres harvested each year should there be ten cuttings.

APPENDIX F (Continued)

PALO VERDE VALLEY
(Blythe)

Alfalfa	28,000	Watermelon	2,000
Cotton	18,000	Corn	2,000
Barley	8,000	Sorghum (milo)	2,000
Lettuce	6,000	Alfalfa seed	1,000
Cantaloupe	3,000	Other vegetables	1,000

YUMA DISTRICT

Alfalfa	46,000	Barley	12,000
Cotton	37,000	Alfalfa seed	9,000
Wheat	22,000	Corn	2,000
Sorghum	17,000	Watermelon	1,000
Cantaloupe	15,000	Potatoes	1,000
Tree crops	13,000	Other winter vegetables	3,000
Lettuce	13,000		

SALT RIVER PROJECT AND OTHER
MARICOPA COUNTY DISTRICTS

Cotton	133,000	Alfalfa seed	5,000
Alfalfa	78,000	Corn	5,000
Barley	73,000	Potatoes	3,000
Sorghum	44,000	Watermelon	3,000
Lettuce	29,000	Cantaloupe	2,000
Wheat	23,000	Carrots	2,000
Tree crops	13,000	Other winter vegetables	5,000

CASA GRANDE VALLEY AND OTHER
PINAL COUNTY DISTRICTS

Cotton	129,000	Cantaloupe	2,000
Barley	34,000	Potatoes	1,000
Wheat	23,000	Alfalfa	1,000
Sorghum	21,000	Winter vegetables	2,000
Alfalfa	18,000		

SANTA CRUZ VALLEY AND OTHER
PIMA AND SANTA CRUZ COUNTY DISTRICTS

Cotton	27,000	Alfalfa	3,000
Sorghum	12,000	Corn	1,000
Barley	8,000		

UPPER GILA (SAFFORD-DUNCAN) VALLEY

Cotton	18,000	Barley	5,000
Alfalfa	5,000	Sorghum	4,000

COCHISE COUNTY

Sorghum	39,000	Lettuce	3,000
Cotton	17,000	Wheat	2,000
Alfalfa	5,000	Corn	2,000

APPENDIX F (Continued)

MEXICALI DISTRICT

Cotton	290,000	Chiles	3,000
Wheat	82,000	Tomatoes	1,000
Barley	57,000	Various	8,000
Alfalfa	20,000		

STATE OF SONORA

Wheat	568,000	Milo	13,000
Cotton	273,000	Sesame	13,000
Corn	83,000	Alfalfa	10,000
Frijoles	23,000	Rice	9,000
Flaxseed	22,000	Garbanzos	4,000
Soy beans	20,000	Tomatoes	3,000
Barley	18,000	Safflower	1,000

FUERTE-GUASAVE

Wheat	215,000	Garbanzos	15,000
Cotton	170,000	Sesame	10,000
Sugar	40,000	Vegetables	8,000
Rice	24,000	Tomatoes	4,000
Frijoles	20,000	Milo	1,000
Alfalfa	20,000	Flaxseed	1,000
Corn	16,000	Various	3,000

CULIACÁN DISTRICT

Sugar	46,000	Corn (summer)	3,000
Rice	43,000	Cantaloupe	3,000
Tomatoes	19,000	Watermelon	3,000
Cotton	17,000	Milo	2,000
Sesame	16,000	Chiles	1,000
Wheat	10,000	Flaxseed	1,000
Frijoles	9,000	Alfalfa	1,000
Corn (winter)	6,000	Bananas	500
Garbanzos	4,000		

APPENDIX G

U. S. Foreign Trade Through the Arizona Customs District

Year	Imports $	Exports $	Total $
1950	24,390,000	21,935,000	46,325,000
1951	32,050,000	40,515,000	72,565,000
1952	35,791,000	41,500,000	77,291,000
1953	42,393,000	43,017,000	85,409,000
1954	24,468,000	43,371,000	67,839,000
1955	27,600,000	54,700,000	82,300,000
1956	31,300,000	51,600,000	82,900,000
1957	31,500,000	46,400,000	77,900,000

APPENDIX G (Continued)

Year	Imports	Exports	Total
	$	$	$
1958	47,600,000	43,400,000	91,000,000
1959	57,500,000	32,100,000	89,600,000
1960	59,500,000	34,500,000	94,000,000
1961	59,200,000	34,700,000	93,900,000
1962	74,400,000	36,000,000	110,400,000
1963	75,500,000	39,900,000	115,400,000
1964	78,000,000	44,100,000	122,100,000
1965	77,600,000	41,200,000	118,800,000

U. S. Imports for Consumption from Mexico through Arizona, 1965

Commodity Class	Value
Animal and Vegetable Products	$74,000,097
Wood, Paper, and Printed Matter	477,249
Textile Fibers and Textile Products	147,430
Chemicals and Related Products	3,170
Nonmetallic Minerals and Products	848,649
Metals and Metal Products	431,041
Specified, Miscellaneous and Nonenumerated Products	96,748
Special Classification Provisions	574,245
Imports Under Temporary Legislation	34,215
Total	$76,612,844

Source of data: U. S. Department of Commerce.

U. S. Exports to Mexico through Arizona, 1965

Commodity Class	Value
Food and Live Animals	$ 3,010,938
Beverages and Tobacco	18,756
Crude Materials, Inedible, Except Fuel	2,648,325
Mineral Fuels, Lubricants, and Related	2,375,828
Oils and Fats, Animal and Vegetable	16,805
Chemicals	2,183,739
Manufactured Goods Classified by Material	3,772,132
Machinery and Transportation Equipment	25,763,144
Miscellaneous Manufactured Articles	1,474,532
Unclassified Items	63,812
TOTAL	$41,328,011

Source: Estimates by Division of Economic & Business Research, The University of Arizona, based on reports of the U. S. Department of Commerce.

BIBLIOGRAPHY

ACOSTA, ROBERTO. *Historia de Los Alamos.* Memorias de la Academia Mexicana de la Historia. México, D.F., 1951.

ALEXANDERSSON, GUNNAR. *The Industrial Structure of American Cities.* Lincoln, Stockholm, 1956.

ALMADA, FRANCISCO R. *Diccionario de Historia, Geografía y Biografía Sonorenses.* Chihuahua, 1952.

ARIZONA DEPT. OF MINERAL RESOURCES. *Twenty-First Annual Report.* Phoenix, 1960.

_____. EMPLOYMENT SECURITY COMMISSION. *Farm Labor Report, 1963.* Phoenix, 1963.

Arizona Agriculture. University of Arizona Agricultural Experiment Station, Tucson. Published annually.

ARIZONA DEVELOPMENT BOARD. *Amazing Arizona: Cotton.* Phoenix, 1958.

_____. *Amazing Arizona: Electronics.* Phoenix, n.d.

_____. *Amazing Arizona: Natural Resources.* Phoenix, n.d.

_____. *Amazing Arizona: Recent Migration.* Phoenix, 1959.

_____. *Arizona Directory of Manufacturers, 1960.* Phoenix, 1960.

_____. *Nogales and Santa Cruz County.* Phoenix [1960].

ARIZONA HIGHWAY COMMISSION. *Arizona Highways.* Phoenix, issued monthly.

"Arizona Hitches its Future to Ideas and Industry," *Business Week,* June 23, 1956.

Arizona, the Grand Canyon State: A State Guide. Compiled by workers of the Writers' Program. Revised by Joseph Miller. New York, 1956.

BANCROFT, HUBERT HOWE. *History of the North Mexican States and Texas.* 2 vols. San Francisco, 1884–89.

BANDELIER, A. F. *Final Report of Investigations Among the Indians of the Southwestern United States Carried on Mainly in the Years from 1880 to 1885.* Papers of the Archaeological Institute of America, American Series No. 4. Cambridge, Mass., 1892.

BANNON, JOHN FRANCIS. *The Mission Frontier in Sonora, 1620–1687.* New York, 1955.

BARBOUR, GEORGE B. "Boulder Dam and Its Geographical Setting," *Geographical Journal,* Vol. 86 (1935), pp. 498-504.

BARROWS, HARLAN H. "Roosevelt Dam and the Salt River Valley," *The Journal of Geography,* Vol. 11 (1913), pp. 283-91.

BARSALOU, FRANK, AND OTHERS. *Yuma: Its Economic Growth and Land Use Potentials.* Menlo Park, Calif.: Stanford Research Institute, 1956.

BARTLETT, JOHN R. *Personal Narrative.* . . . 2 vols. New York, 1854.

BAUER, P. T. AND B. S. YAMEY. *The Economics of Under-developed Countries.* Chicago, 1957.

BEALS, RALPH L. *The Aboriginal Culture of the Cahita Indians.* Ibero-Americana: 19. Berkeley, 1943.

_____. "Aboriginal Survivals In Mayo Culture," *American Anthropologist,* Vol. 34 (1932), pp. 28-39.

[405]

BEALS, RALPH L. *The Comparative Ethnology of Northern Mexico Before 1750.* Ibero-Americana: 2. Berkeley, 1932.

————. *The Contemporary Culture of the Cahita Indians.* Bureau of American Ethnology Bull. 142. Washington, D.C., 1945.

BELL, P. L. AND H. B. MACKENZIE, *Mexican West Coast and Lower California: A Commercial and Industrial Survey.* U. S. Dept. of Commerce, Washington, D.C., 1923.

BELL, WILLIS H. AND EDWARD F. CASTETTER. "The Aboriginal Utilization of the Tall Cacti in the American Southwest." *Ethnobiological Studies in the American Southwest,* Vol. 5, No. 1 (1937).

BENSON, LYMAN D. *The Cacti of Arizona.* Tucson, 1950.

BIEBER, RALPH P. "The Southwestern Trails to California in 1849," *Mississippi Valley Historical Review,* Vol. 12 (1925), pp. 342-76.

BLACKMAR, FRANK W. *Spanish Institutions of the Southwest.* Baltimore, 1891.

BLAKE, DEAN. "Sonora Storms," *Monthly Weather Review,* Vol. 51 (1923), pp. 585-88.

BLASQUEZ, LOUIS. *Informe preliminar de la Hidrología subterranea de las cuencas de los Ríos de la Concepción y de Sonoyta distrito de Altar, Sonora.* México, D.F., 1926.

BOJORQUEZ, JUAN DE DIOS. "Descripción de Sonora," *Boletín Sociedad Mexicana de Geografía y Estadística,* Tomo 61 (1946), p. 11.

BOLTON, HERBERT E. *Coronado: Knight of Pueblos and Plains.* New York, 1949.

————. *The Evolution of Society in Sinaloa and Sonora, Mexico.* Berkeley, 1939.

————. "The Mission as a Frontier Institution in the Spanish-American Colonies," *American Historical Review,* Vol. 23 (1917), pp. 42-61.

————. *An Outpost of Empire.* Vol. 1 of *Anza's California Expeditions.* 5 vols. Berkeley, 1930.

————. *Rim of Christendom: A Biography of Eusebio Francisco Kino, Pacific Coast Pioneer.* New York, 1936.

————. *Spanish Exploration in the Southwest: 1542–1706.* New York, 1916.

————. "The West Coast Corridor," *American Philosophical Society Proceedings,* Vol. 91 (1947), pp. 426-29.

————. *Wider Horizons of American History.* New York, 1939.

BRANDES, RAYMOND S. *Frontier Military Posts of Arizona.* Globe, Ariz., 1960.

BROWN, HARRISON. "Life in the Americas During the Next Century," *The Annals of the American Academy of Political and Social Science,* Vol. 316 (1958), pp. 11-17.

BROWN, ROBERT M. "The Utilization of the Colorado River," *Geographical Review,* Vol. 17 (1927), pp. 453-66.

BRYAN, KIRK. *Erosion and Sedimentation in the Papago Country, Arizona.* U. S. Geological Survey Bull. No. 730. Washington, D.C., 1922.

————. *The Papago Country, Arizona: A Geographic, Geologic, and Hydrologic Reconnaissance with a Guide to Desert Watering Places.* U. S. Geological Survey Water Supply Paper 499. Washington, D.C., 1925.

BRYSON, REID A. *The Annual March of Precipitation in Arizona, New Mexico, and Northwestern Mexico.* University of Arizona Inst. of Atmospheric Physics Tech. Report No. 6. Tucson, 1957.

————, AND WILLIAM P. LOWRY. "Synoptic Climatology of the Arizona Summer Precipitation Singularity," *Bulletin of the American Meteorological Society,* Vol. 36 (1955), pp. 329-39.

BUELNA, EUSTAQUIO. *Apuntes para la Historia de Sinaloa.* México, D.F., 1924.

CALIFORNIA STATE ECONOMIC DEVELOPMENT AGENCY. *California Statistical Abstract.* Sacramento, Calif., 1964.

CARREÑO, ALBERTO M. *La Diplomacia Extraordinaria entre México y Estados Unidos, 1789–1947.* 2 vols., México, D.F., 1951.

CARTER, GEORGE F. *Plant Geography and Culture History in the American Southwest.* Viking Fund Publications in Anthropology No. 5. New York, 1945.

CASTETTER, EDWARD F. AND WILLIS H. BELL. *Pima and Papago Indian Agriculture.* Albuquerque, 1942.

————. *Yuman Indian Agriculture: Primitive Subsistence on the Lower Colorado and Gila Rivers.* Albuquerque, 1951.

————. AND RUTH M. UNDERHILL. "The Ethnobiology of the Papago Indians," *Ethnobiological Studies of the American Southwest,* Vol. 4, No. 3 (1935).

CASTRO, JOSUE DE. *The Geography of Hunger.* Boston, 1952.

CHAMBERLIN, WILLIAM H. "From Lewisburg (Pa.) to California in 1849; Diary of William H. Chamberlin, I," *New Mexico Historical Review,* Vol. XX, Nos. 1-4 (Jan., April, July, and Oct., 1945).

CHAPMAN, CHARLES E. *A History of California: The Spanish Period.* New York, 1923.

CHASE, J. SMEATON. *California Desert Trails.* New York, 1919.

CHITTENDEN, HIRAM M. *The American Fur Trade of the Far West.* 2 vols. New York, 1935.

CLARK, COLIN. *The Conditions of Economic Progress.* London, 1940.

CLINE, HOWARD F. *The United States and Mexico.* Cambridge, Mass., 1953.

COMBINED MEXICAN WORKING PARTY, THE JOHNS HOPKINS UNIVERSITY. *The Economic Development of Mexico.* Baltimore, 1953.

Compilation of Records of Surface Waters of the United States through September, 1950: Part 9, Colorado River Basin. U. S. Geological Survey Water Supply Paper 1313. Washington, D.C., 1954.

CONKLING, ROSCOE P. AND MARGARET B. *The Butterfield Overland Mail, 1857–69.* 2 vols. Glendale, Calif., 1947.

CONNER, DANIEL ELLIS. *Joseph Reddeford Walker and the Arizona Adventure.* Norman, Okla., 1956.

COOK, CLINTON A. "Mexico Grows More Cotton and Wheat with Expanded Irrigation," *Foreign Agriculture,* Vol. 19 (1955).

————. "Winter Vegetables in Mexico," *Foreign Agriculture Circular.* Washington, D.C., July 28, 1960.

COOK, SHERBURNE F. *The Extent and Significance of Disease Among the Indians of Baja California, 1697–1773.* Ibero-Americana: 12. Berkeley, 1937.

————. *Population Trends among the California Mission Indians.* Ibero-Americana: 17. Berkeley, 1940.

COOKE, PHILIP ST. GEORGE. *Journal of the March of the Mormon Battalion.* 29th Cong., 2d Sess. Washington, D.C., 1846-47.

COOPERRIDER, C. K. AND GLENTON G. SYKES. *The Relationship of Streamflow to Precipitation on the Salt River Watershed above Roosevelt Dam.* University of Arizona Agricultural Experiment Station Technical Bull. No. 76. Tucson, 1938.

CORKER, CHARLES E. "The Issues in Arizona v. California: California's View," in *Resources Development: Frontiers for Research.* Franklin S. Pollack, ed. Western Resources Conference, 1959. Boulder, Colo., 1960.

COUES, ELLIOT. *On the Trail of a Spanish Pioneer: The Diary and Itinerary of Francisco Garces in his Travels through Sonora, Arizona and California.* 2 vols. New York, 1900.

COVARRUBIAS, ALBERTO. *Datos Agrícolas de Sonora.* Hermosillo, Son., 1952.

CROSS, JACK L., ELIZABETH SHAW, AND KATHLEEN SCHEIFELE (eds.). *Arizona: Its People and Resources.* Tucson, 1960.

CUMMINGS, BYRON. *First Inhabitants of Arizona and the Southwest.* Tucson, 1953.

DAVIS, ARTHUR P. "The New Inland Sea," *National Geographic Magazine,* Vol. 18 (1907), pp. 37-49.

DEASY, GEORGE F. AND PETER GERHARD. "Settlements in Baja California, 1768–1930," *Geographical Review,* Vol. 34 (1944), pp. 574-86.

DECORME, GERARDO. *La Obra de los Jesuitos en México en la Epoca Colonial: 1572–1717.* 2 v. México, D.F., 1941.

DICE, LEE R. "The Sonoran Biotic Province," *Ecology,* Vol. 20 (1939), pp. 118-29.

DOZIER, CRAIG L. "Mexico's Transformed Northwest: The Yaqui, Mayo, and Fuerte Examples," *Geographical Review,* Oct. 1963.

DULLES, JOHN W. F. *Yesterday in Mexico: A Chronicle of the Revolution, 1919–1936.* Austin, Texas, 1960.

DUMKE, GLENN S. "Douglas: Border Town," *Pacific Historical Review,* Vol. 17 (1948), pp. 283-98.

DUNBIER, ROGER, PHILIP G. HUDSON, AND OTHERS. *The Economy of Arizona.* Phoenix, 1964.

DUNNE, PETER M. *Andrés Pérez de Ribas: Pioneer Black Robe of the West Coast, Administrator, Historian.* New York, 1951.

————. *Pioneer Black Robes on the West Coast.* Berkeley, 1940.

DUNNING, CHARLES H. *Rock to Riches: The Story of Arizona Mines and Mining.* Phoenix, 1959.

ECKHART, GEORGE B. "A Guide to the History of the Missions of Sonora," *Arizona and the West,* Vol. 2, No. 2 (1960), pp. 165-83.

EMORY, WILLIAM H. *Notes of a Military Reconnoissance from Fort Leavenworth, in Missouri, to San Diego, in California, . . .* 30th Cong., 1st Sess., House Exec. Doc. 41. Washington, D.C., 1848.

ENGELHARDT, ZEPHYRIN. *The Franciscans in Arizona.* Harbor Springs, Mich., 1899.

ERASMUS, CHARLES J. "The Economic Life of a Mayo Village." Unpublished M.A. thesis, University of California. Berkeley, 1948.

EVANS, (GEORGE) W. B. *Mexican Gold Trail (1849).* San Marino, Calif., 1945.

EWING, RUSSELL C. "The Pima Uprising of 1751: A Study of Spanish Indian Relations on the Frontier of New Spain," in *Greater America: Essays in Honor of Herbert Eugene Bolton,* pp. 259-94. Berkeley, 1945.

FAGES, PEDRO. *The Colorado River Campaign, 1781–1782: Diary of Pedro Fages.* Berkeley, California, 1913.

FARISH, THOMAS EDWIN. *History of Arizona.* 4 vols. Phoenix, 1915-16.

FENNEMAN, NEVIN M. *Physiography of Western United States.* New York, 1931.

FONT, PEDRO. *Complete Diary.* Berkeley, 1933.

FORBES, JACK D. *Apache, Navaho and Spaniard.* Norman, Okla., 1960.

FRANKEL, SALLY H. *The Economic Impact on Under-Developed Societies: Essays on International Investment and Social Change.* Cambridge, Mass., 1953.

FRYER, D. W. "World Income and Types of Economies: The Pattern of World Economic Development," *Economic Geography,* Vol. 34 (1958), pp. 283-303.

GARBER, PAUL N. *The Gadsden Treaty,* Philadelphia, 1923.

GARCES, FRANCISCO. *See* Coues, Elliot.

GARLOCK, LORENE A. "Cotton in the Economy of Mexico," *Economic Geography,* Vol. 20 (1944), pp. 70-77.

GENTRY, HOWARD SCOTT. *Rio Mayo Plants: A Study of the Flora and Vegetation of the Valley of the Rio Mayo, Sonora.* Carnegie Institute Pub. No. 527. Washington, D.C., 1942.

GILBERT, E. W. *The Exploration of Western America, 1800–1850.* Cambridge, Mass., 1933.

GLENDINNING, GORDON. "Desert Contrasts Illustrated by the Coachella Valley," *Geographical Review,* Vol. 39 (1949), pp. 221-28.

GRANGER, BYRD H., ed. *Will C. Barnes' Arizona Place Names.* Rev. ed. Tucson, 1960.

GREEN, CHRISTINE R. *Arizona Statewide Rainfall.* University of Arizona Inst. of Atmospheric Physics Tech. Report No. 7. Tucson, 1959.

GRISWOLD, J. F. *Salt River Project.* Phoenix, 1956.

HACKENBERG, ROBERT A. "Economic Alternatives for Native People in Arid Lands," *Arid Lands Colloquia,* Vol. 1, pp. 46-57. Tucson, 1961.

HALLENBECK, CLEVE. *Alvar Nuñez Cabeza de Vaca: The Journey and Route of the First European to Cross the Continent of North America.* Glendale, Calif., 1940.

HALPENNY, L. C. AND OTHERS. *Ground Water in the Gila River Basin and Adjacent Areas, Arizona: A Summary.* U. S. Geological Survey Water Supply Paper 1283. Washington, D.C., 1952.

HAMMOND, GEORGE P. "Pimería Alta after Kino's Time," *New Mexico Historical Review,* Vol. 4 (1929), pp. 220-38.

————, ed..*The Treaty of Guadalupe Hidalgo.* Berkeley, 1949.

HARDY, OSGOOD. "El Ferrocarril Sud Pacifico," *Pacific Historical Review,* Vol. 20 (1951), pp. 261-70.

HARSHBERGER, J. W. *Phytogeographical Survey of North America.* Vol. 8 of *Die Vegetation der Erde,* ed. by A. Engler and O. Drude, Leipzig, 1911.

HASKETT, BERT. "Early History of the Cattle Industry in Arizona," *Arizona Historical Review,* Vol. 6, No. 4 (1935), pp. 3-42.

HASTINGS, JAMES R. "Vegetation Changes and Arroyo Cutting in Southeastern Arizona During the Past Century," *Journal of the Arizona Academy of Science,* Vol. 1, No. 2 (1959).

HENRY, A. J. "Rainfall in Relation to Altitude," *Monthly Weather Review,* Vol. 47 (1919), pp. 33-41.

HEWES, LESLIE. "Huepac: An Agricultural Village of Sonora, Mexico," *Economic Geography,* Vol. 11 (1935), pp. 284-92.

HIGGINS, BENJAMIN H. *Economic Development: Principles, Problems and Policies.* New York, 1959.

HINTON, RICHARD J. *The Handbook of Arizona, 1877.* Tucson, 1954.

HODGE, FREDERICK W. *Spanish Explorers in the Southern United States, 1528–1543.* New York, 1907.

HOFFMEISTER, HAROLD A. "Alkali Problem of Western United States," *Economic Geography,* Vol. 23 (1947), pp. 1-9.

HOLDEN, W. C. AND OTHERS. "Studies of the Yaqui Indians of Sonora, Mexico," Texas Technological College *Bulletin,* Vol. 12, No. 1 (1936).

HOLLON, W. EUGENE. *The Southwest: Old and New.* New York, 1961.

HOLMES, J. G. "Soil Survey of the Yuma Area, Arizona, California," *Field Operations,* Bureau of Soils. Washington, D.C., 1902.

HOOVER, J. W. "The Indian Country of Southern Arizona," *Geographical Review,* Vol. 19 (1929), pp. 38-60.

HORNADAY, WILLIAM T. *Camp Fires On Desert and Lava.* New York, 1908.

HRDLICKA, ALES. *Notes on the Indians of Sonora, Mexico.* Lancaster, Pa., 1904.

HUMPHREY, ROBERT R. *Arizona Range Grasses, Their Description, Forage Value and Management.* University of Arizona Agricultural Experiment Station Bull. No. 298. Tucson, 1958.

————. *Arizona Range Resources.* Various counties. University of Arizona Agricultural Experiment Station. Tucson, various dates.

————. *The Desert Grassland.* University of Arizona Agricultural Experiment Station Bull. No. 299. Tucson, 1958.

————. "A Detailed Study of Desert Rainfall," *Ecology,* Vol. 14 (1933), pp. 31-34.

"Hungry Workers, Ripe Crops and the Nonexistent Mexican Border," *The Reporter,* April 13, 1954.

IBAÑEZ, RAUL AND OTHERS. *Panorama Económico de Sinaloa y sus Datos Estadísticos.* Instituto de Investigaciones Económicas del Estado de Sinaloa. Culiacán, Sin., 1958.

Industrial Development, December, 1957.

IVES, RONALD L. "Climate of the Sonoran Desert," *Annals of the Association of American Geographers,* Vol. 39 (1949), pp. 143-87.

————. "The Origin of the Sonoita Townsite, Sonora, Mexico," *American Antiquity* (1941), pp. 20-28.

————. "Puerto Peñasco, Sonora," *Journal of Geography,* Vol. 50 (1951), pp. 239-61.

————. "The Sonoran Census of 1730," *Records of the American Catholic Historical Society of Philadelphia,* Vol. 59, No. 4 (1948).

————. "The Sonoran Railroad Project," *Journal of Geography,* Vol. 48 (1949), pp. 197-206.

————. "The Sonoyta Oasis," *Journal of Geography,* Vol. 49 (1950), pp. 1-12.

JAEGER, E. C. *The North American Deserts.* Stanford, Calif., 1957.

JAMES, GEORGE WHARTON. *Reclaiming the Arid West.* New York, 1917.

————. *Wonders of the Colorado Desert.* 2 vols. Boston, 1906.

JOHNSON, HARRY P. "Diego Martinez de Hurdaide." Unpublished Ph.D. thesis, University of California, Berkeley, 1935.

JOHNSON, JEAN B. *The Opata: An Inland Tribe of Sonora.* University of New Mexico Publications in Anthropology No. 6. Albuquerque, 1929.

JONES, L. RODWELL. "Notes on the Geographical Factors which Controlled the Spanish Advance into Northern Mexico and Southern California," *The Scottish Geographical Magazine,* Vol. 39 (1923), pp. 159-71.

JOSEPH, ALICE, ROSAMUND SPICER, AND JANE CHESKY. *The Desert People: A Study of the Papago Indians.* Chicago, 1949.

JURWITZ, LOUIS R. "Arizona's Two Season Rainfall Pattern," *Weatherwise,* Vol. 6 (1953), pp. 96-99.

KELINSORGE, PAUL L. *The Boulder Canyon Project: Historical and Economic Aspects.* Stanford, Calif., 1941.

KENNAN, GEORGE. *The Salton Sea.* New York, 1917.

KERNS, WILLIAM H., FRANK J. KELLY, AND D. H. MULLEN. "The Mineral Industry of Arizona," *Minerals Yearbook.* Bureau of Mines, Washington, D.C., 1959.

KHALAF, JASSIM M. *The Water Resources of the Lower Colorado River Basin.* University of Chicago Research Paper No. 22. Chicago, 1951.

KINNEY, CLESSON S. *A Treatise on the Law of Irrigation.* San Francisco, 1912.

KINO, EUSEBIO F. *Kino's Historical Memoir of Pimería Alta.* Herbert E. Bolton, trans. Berkeley, 1948.

KNIFFEN, FRED B. "The Primitive Cultural Landscape of the Colorado Delta," *Lower California Studies, III; University of California Publications in Geography.* Berkeley, 1931.

KROEBER, A. L. *Cultural and Natural Areas of Native North America.* Berkeley, 1939.

————. *Uto-Aztecan Languages of Mexico.* Ibero-Americana: 8. Berkeley, 1934.

LANG, WALTER B. *First Overland Mail, The Butterfield Trail.* San Franciso, 1940.

LEE, W. T. *Underground Waters of the Salt River Valley, Arizona.* U. S. Geological Survey Water Supply Paper No. 136. Washington, D.C., 1905.

LEWIS, WILLIAM A. *The Theory of Economic Growth.* London, 1955.

LIVINGSTON, BURTON E. *Relation of Desert Plants to Soil Moisture and to Evaporation.* Carnegie Institute Pub. No. 50. Washington, D.C. 1906.

————, AND FORREST SHREVE. *The Distribution of Vegetation in the United States as Related to the Climatic Conditions.* Washington, D.C., 1922.

LOCKWOOD, FRANK C. "The Gadsden Treaty," *Arizona Quarterly,* Vol. 2, No. 2 (1946), pp. 5-16.

LUMHOLTZ, CARL L. *New Trails in Mexico.* New York, 1912.

LYDOLPH, PAUL E. "A Comparative Analysis of the Dry Western Littorals," *Annals of the Association of American Geographers,* Vol. 47 (1957), pp. 213-30.

MACDOUGAL, DANIEL T. *Botanical Features of North American Deserts.* Carnegie Institute Publication No. 99. Washington, D.C., 1908.

————. "A Decade of the Salton Sea," *Geographical Review,* Vol. 3 (1917), pp. 457-73.

————. "The Delta of the Rio Colorado," *Bulletin of the American Geographical Society,* Vol. 39 (1907), pp. 705-29.

————. "North American Deserts," *The Geographical Journal,* Vol. 39 (1912), pp. 105-20.

————."The Salton Sea," *American Journal of Science,* Vol. 39 (1915), pp. 231-50.

MANJE, JUAN MATEO. *Luz de Tierra Incógnita: Unknown Arizona and Sonora, 1693–1721.* Harry J. Karns, trans. Tucson, 1954.

MANN, DEAN E. *The Politics of Water in Arizona.* Tucson, 1963.

MARKS, JOHN BRADY. "Vegetation and Soil Relations in the Lower Colorado Desert," *Ecology,* Vol. 31 (1950), pp. 176-93.

MARTINEZ, PABLO L. *A History of Lower California.* Trans. by Ethel D. Turner. México, D.F., 1960.

MATTISON, RAY H. "Early Spanish and Mexican Settlements in Arizona," *New Mexico Historical Review,* Vol. 21, No. 4 (1946), pp. 285-86.

MCBRIDE, GEORGE MCCUTCHEN. *The Land Systems of Mexico.* New York, 1923.

MCCLENEGHAN, THOMAS J. AND PHILIP G. OLSON. *Douglas, Arizona: An Economic Report.* University of Arizona Bureau of Business Research, Special Study No. 13. Tucson, 1957.

MCCULLAGH, FRANCIS. *Red Mexico.* London, 1928.

MCDONALD, JAMES E. "It Rained Everywhere but Here! The Thunderstorm Encirclement Illusion," *Weatherwise,* Vol. 12, (1959), pp. 158-74.

————. *Variability of Precipitation in an Arid Region: A Survey of Characteristics for Arizona.* University of Arizona Institute of Atmospheric Physics Tech. Report No. 1. Tucson, 1956.

McGEE, W. J. "Sheetflood Erosion," *Bulletin of the Geographical Society of America,* Vol. 8 (1897).

McWHIRTER, N. *The Guinness Book of Records.* 1961 ed. London, 1961.

MECHAM, J. LLOYD. *Francisco de Ibarra and Nueva Vizcaya.* Durham, N.C., 1927.

MEIGS, PEVERIL. "Water Problems in the United States," *Geographical Review,* Vol. 42 (1952), pp. 346-66.

MENDENHALL, W. C. *Ground Waters of the Indio Region.* U. S. Geological Survey Water Supply Paper 225. Washington, D.C., 1909.

METROPOLITAN WATER DISTRICT OF CALIFORNIA. *History and First Annual Report.* Los Angeles, 1939.

MEXICO. BANCO NACIONAL DEL CREDITO EJIDAL S.A. *La Sistema de Producción Colectiva en los Ejidos del Valle del Yaqui, Sonora, México.* México, D.F., 1945.

MEXICO. COMISION NACIONAL DE IRRIGACION. "Informe final sobre el estudio económica del desarollo del riego propuesto por el uso del Río Mayo en el Estado de Sonora," *Boletín de Diciembre 1926.*

————. *Irrigación en México.* Various issues.

MEXICO. SECRETARIA DE ECONOMIA, DIRECCION GENERAL DE ESTADISTICA. *Tercer Censo Agrícola, Ganadero y Ejidal.* México, D.F., 1957.

MEXICO. SECRETARIA DE RECURSOS HIDRAULICOS. *Datos de la Región Noroeste.* Boletín No. 10. México, D.F., 1952.

MILES, CARLOTA. *Almada of Alamos: The Diary of Don Bartolomé.* Tucson, 1962.

MILLER, JOSEPH. *Arizona: The Last Frontier.* New York, 1956.

MOORE, HAL R. "The Salt River Project," *Arizona Highways,* Vol. 37, No. 4.

MOSK, SANFORD A. *Economic Problems in Sonora in the Late Eighteenth Century.* Glendale, Calif., 1939.

MYRDAL, GUNNAR. *Rich Lands and Poor: The Road to World Prosperity.* Rev. ed. New York, 1957. (A revision of Myrdal's earlier *Economic Theory and Under-Developed Regions.*)

NICHOL, A. A. *The Natural Vegetation of Arizona.* Arizona Agricultural Experiment Station Tech. Bulletin No. 68. Tucson, 1943 (revised as No. 127, 1952).

NURSKE, RAGNAR. *Problems of Capital Formation in Underdeveloped Countries.* New York, 1953.

OROZCO Y BERRA, MANUEL. *Geografía de las Lenguas.* Mexico, 1860.

OWEN, ALBERT K. *Interesting Data Concerning the Harbor of Topolobampo and the State of Sinaloa.* Washington, D.C., 1883.

PATTIE, JAMES OHIO. *Pattie's Personal Narrative.* . . . Cleveland, 1905. (Vol. 18 of *Early Western Travels,* ed. by Reuben G. Thwaites.)

PFEIFER, GOTTFRIED. "Sinaloa und Sonora Beitrage zur Landeskunde und Kultur geographie des nordwestlichen Mexico," *Mitt. Geog. Gesell.,* Vol. 46 (Hamburg, 1939), pp. 289-460.

"Potentialidad de la Región Costera de los Estados de Sonora y Sinaloa," *Irrigación in México,* Vol. 23 (1942), pp. 89-103.

POWELL, JOHN W. *Exploration of the Colorado River of the West and its Tributaries Explored in 1869, 1870, 1871, and 1872.* Abridgement by University of Chicago Press. Chicago, 1957.

————. "Report of the Director," Bureau of American Ethnology, *Annual Report* 14, Part 1, 1892-93.

QUINN, CHARLES RUSSELL. *Christmas Journey into the Desert.* Downey, Calif., 1959.

QUIRK, ROBERT E. *The Mexican Revolution, 1914–15.* Bloomington, Ind., 1960.

REED, T. R. "The North American High Level Anti-Cyclone," *Monthly Weather Review,* Vol. 61 (1933), pp. 321-25.

ROBERTSON, THOMAS A. *A Southwestern Utopia.* Los Angeles, 1947.

RODRIGUEZ ADAME, JULIAN. *El Algodón, Conferencia Sustentada en la Universidad de Sonora.* Hermosillo, Méx., 1956.

ROMER, MARGARET. "A History of Calexico," *Southern California Historical Society Quarterly,* 1922.

ROSS, CLYDE P. *The Lower Gila Region, Arizona: A Geographic, Geologic and Hydrologic Reconnaissance with a Guide to Desert Watering Places.* U. S. Geological Survey Water Resource Paper 498. Washington, D.C., 1923.

Rudo Ensayo, by an Unknown Jesuit Padre, 1763. Tucson, 1951.

RUSSELL, FRANK. "The Pima Indians," *Annual Report,* Bureau of American Ethnology, Vol. 26. Washington, D.C., 1908.

SAUER, CARL O. *The Aboriginal Population of Northwestern Mexico.* Ibero-Americana: 10. Berkeley, 1935.

————. *Agricultural Origins and Dispersals.* New York, 1952.

————. *Basin and Range Forms in the Chiricahua Area.* Berkeley, 1930.

————. *The Distribution of Aboriginal Tribes and Languages in Northwestern Mexico.* Ibero-Americana: 5. Berkeley, 1934.

————. "The Personality of Mexico," *Geographic Review,* Vol. 31 (1941), pp. 353-64.

————. *Road to Cibola.* Berkeley, 1932.

———— AND DONALD BRAND. *Aztatlan: Prehistoric Frontier on the Pacific Coast.* Ibero-Americana: 1. Berkeley, 1931.

————, AND ————. *Prehistoric Settlements of Sonora.* Berkeley, 1931.

SCHAEFER, URSULA. "Pimeria Alta, 1711-1767." Unpublished Ph.D. thesis, University of California, Berkeley, 1944.

SEDELMAYR, JACOBO. *Jacobo Sedelmayr: Missionary, Frontiersman, Explorer in Arizona and Sonora.* Peter M. Dunne, trans. Tucson, 1955.

SHAW, EARL B. "Mexico's Foot and Mouth Disease Problem," *Economic Geography,* Vol. 25, No. 1 (1949), pp. 1-12.

SHIELS, W. E. *Gonzalo de Tapia.* New York, 1934.

SHREVE, FORREST. "Establishment and Behavior of the Palo Verde," *Plant World,* Vol. 14 (1911).

————. "Rainfall Run-off and Soil Moisture under Desert Conditions," *Annals of the Association of American Geographers,* Vol. 24 (1934), pp. 131-56.

————. *Vegetation of the Sonoran Desert.* Carnegie Institution Publication No. 591. Washington, D.C., 1951.

SIMPSON, EYLER N. *The Ejido: Mexico's Way Out.* Chapel Hill, N. Carolina, 1937.

SMITH, H. V. *The Climate of Arizona.* University of Arizona Agricultural Experiment Station Bull. No. 279. Tucson, 1956.

SONORA, ESTADO DE. Consejo de Planeación Económica y Social. *Memoria Sesión Plenaria de Abril 20 de 1958.* Hermosillo, Son., 1958.

————. *Sonora en Cifras.* Hermosillo, Son. Published annually from 1956–1961.

————. *Proyecto de Programa de Gobierno del Estado de Sonora.* Hermosillo, Son., 1957.

SPICER, EDWARD H. *Cycles of Conquest: The Impact of Spain, Mexico, and the United States on the Indians of the Southwest, 1533–1960.* Tucson, 1962.

————. "European Expansion and the Enclavement of Southwestern Indians," *Arizona and the West,* Vol. 1, No. 2 (1959).

————. *Potam, a Yaqui Village in Sonora.* American Anthropological Association, Memoir 77, 1954.

STANISLAWSKI, DAN. "Early Spanish Town Planning in the New World," *The Geographical Review,* Vol. 37 (1947), pp. 94-105.

Summary of Records of Surface Waters at Stations on Tributaries in Lower Colorado River Basin, 1888–1938. U. S. Geological Survey Water Supply Paper 1049. Washington, D.C., 1947.

SUMMERHAYES, MARTHA. *Vanished Arizona.* 4th ed. Ray Brandes, ed. Tucson, 1960.

"Sunny Sonora, Mexico," *Sunset,* Jan. 1961.

Surface Water Supply of the United States, 1959: Part 9, Colorado River Basin. U. S. Geological Survey Water Supply Paper 1633. Washington, D.C., 1961.

SUTHERLAND, MASON. "Sonora is Jumping," *National Geographic Magazine,* Vol. 107 (1955), pp. 215-46.

SWEENEY, THOMAS W. *Journal.* Los Angeles, 1956.

SYKES, GODFREY. "The Camino del Diablo with Notes on a Journey in 1925," *Geographical Review,* Vol. 17 (1927), pp. 62-74.

————. *The Colorado Delta.* American Geographical Society Spec. Pub. No. 19. New York, 1937.

————. "The Isles of California," *Bulletin, American Geographical Society,* Vol. 47 (1915), pp. 745-61.

————. "Rainfall Investigations in Arizona and Sonora by Means of Long Period Rain Gauges," *Geographical Review,* Vol. 21 (1931), pp. 229-33.

SYME, RONALD. *Colonial Elites: Rome, Spain, and the Americas.* London, 1958.

TANNENBAUM, FRANK. *The Mexican Agrarian Revolution.* New York, 1929.

————. *Mexico: The Struggle for Peace and Bread.* New York, 1950.

TAX, SOL. *Heritage of Conquest: The Ethnology of Middle America.* Glencoe, Ill., 1952.

Ten Rivers in America's Future. U. S. President's Water Resources Policy Commission. Washington, D.C., 1950.

THOMAS, CYRUS AND JOHN R. SWANTON. *Indian Languages of Mexico and Central America.* Bureau of American Ethnology Bull. No. 44. Washington, D.C., 1911.

TIMM, CHARLES A. *The International Boundary Commission, United States and Mexico.* Austin, Texas, 1941.

"Tossed Salad," *Newsweek,* Feb. 20, 1961.

TOYNBEE, ARNOLD. *A Study of History.* 8 vols. London, 1954.

TREUTLEIN, THEODORE E. "The Economic Regime of the Jesuit Missions in Eighteenth Century Sonora," *Pacific Historical Review,* Vol. 8 (1939), pp. 289-300.

———— (trans. and ed.). *Sonora: A Description of the Province by Ignaz Pfefferkorn.* (Coronado Cuarto Centennial Publications, Vol. 12.) Albuquerque: University of New Mexico Press, 1949.

TUCK, FRANK J. *Stories of Arizona Copper Mines: The Big Low-grades and the Bonanzas.* Phoenix: Arizona Department of Mineral Resources, 1957.

TURNAGE, W. V. AND T. D. MALLERY. *An Analysis of Rainfall in the Sonoran Desert and Adjacent Territory.* Carnegie Institute Publication No. 529. Washington, D.C., 1941.

TURNER, SAMUEL F. *Available Water for Urban Development in the Phoenix Area.* Phoenix, 1959.

ULLMAN, EDWARD L. "Amenities as a Factor of Regional Growth," *Geographical Review,* Vol. 445 (1954), pp. 119-32.

U. S. BUREAU OF THE CENSUS. *Census of Business, 1962.* Washington, D.C., 1962.

U. S. BUREAU OF MINES. *Mineral Production in Arizona in 1960.* Washington, D.C., 1960.

————. *Minerals Yearbook.* Washington, D.C., 1960.

U. S. BUREAU OF RECLAMATION. *Coachella Division, All-American Canal System.* Boulder City, Nevada, 1950.

————. *The Colorado River: A Comprehensive Report on the Development of Water Resources of the Colorado River.* Washington, D.C., 1946.

————. *Future Needs for Reclamation in the Western United States.* Committee Print No. 14 for the Senate Select Committee on National Water Resources, 86th Cong., 2d Sess. Washington, D.C., 1960.

————. *Reclamation on the Lower Colorado River.* Washington, D.C., 1959.

————. *Reclamation Project Data.* Washington, D.C., 1961.

U. S. DEPT. OF AGRICULTURE. *Climate and Man: Yearbook of Agriculture, 1941.* Washington, D.C., 1941.

————. *U. S. Census of Agriculture, 1959.* Vol. 1. Washington, D.C., 1959.

U. S. House of Representatives. *The Central Arizona Project.* Hearings, 82d Cong., 1st Sess., Washington, D.C., 1951.

U. S. Senate. *Report of the United States and Mexican Boundary Survey.* Senate Exec. Report No. 345, 32d Cong., 1st Sess., Vol. 2. Washington, D.C., 1852.

Valley National Bank. *Arizona Progress.* Phoenix, published monthly.

————. *Arizona Statistical Review.* Phoenix, published annually.

Vasquez, Raul E. *Geografía del Estado de Sonora.* México, D.F., 1955.

"Violence in the Oasis," *Time,* Feb. 17, 1961.

Wagoner, Junior J. *History of the Cattle Industry in Southern Arizona, 1540–1940.* University of Arizona Social Science Bull. No. 20. Tucson, 1952.

Waibel, Leo. "Die Inselbergerlandschaft von Arizona und Sonora," *Zeitschrift der Gesellschaft fur Erdkunde zu Berlin,* sonderband zur 1928.

Webb, Walter Prescott. *The Great Frontier.* Boston, 1952.

————. *The Great Plains.* New York, 1931.

Weigert, Hans W. *Principles of Political Geography.* New York, 1957.

Western Resources Conference. *Western Resources Handbook, 1956.* Boulder, Colo.

Whetten, Nathan. *Rural Mexico.* Chicago, 1949.

Whipple, Amiel W. *Report of Expedition from San Diego to the Colorado, 1849.* 31st Con., 2d Sess., Senate Exec. Doc. 19. Washington, D.C., 1851.

White, C. Langdon. "Whither South America: Population and Natural Resources," *The Journal of Geography,* Vol. 60 (1961), pp. 103-12.

"Why the Big Boom in the Desert States," *U. S. News and World Report,* Oct. 11, 1957, p. 80.

Williamson, R. S., W. P. Blake, and others. *Pacific Railway Survey Reports.* Washington, D.C., 1853-56.

Wilson, Andrew W. "Urbanization of the Arid Lands," *Arizona Review of Business and Public Administration,* Vol. 10, No. 3 (1961).

Wilson, Eldred D. *Arizona Gold Placers and Placering.* 4th ed., rev. Arizona Bureau of Mines Bulletin No. 135. Tucson, 1933.

————. "New Mountains in the Yuma Desert, Arizona," *Geographical Review,* Vol. 21 (1931), pp. 221-28.

Winther, Oscar O. *The Transportation Frontier, Trans-Mississippi West, 1865–90.* New York, 1964.

Wissler, Clark. *The American Indians.* New York, 1922.

Wylie, Kathryn. "Mexico's Agrarian Reform," *Foreign Agriculture* (Feb. 14, 1961).

Wyllys, Rufus K. *Henry A. Crabb: A Tragedy of the Sonoran Frontier.* Berkeley, 1940.

————. "The Historical Geography of Arizona," *Pacific Historical Review,* Vol. 21 (1952), pp. 121-28.

————. "Padre Luis Velarde's Relacion of Pimeria Alta, 1716," *New Mexico Historical Review,* Vol. 6 (1931), pp. 111-57.

Index